RADICAL ORTHODOXY

'Despite all the media claims about the imminent demise of mainstream Christianity . . . a collection such as this displays an intellectual power, a learning and conceptual imagination, that few if any other groups could achieve.'

Fergus Kerr, *University of Edinburgh*

'If theology offers a continuing reflection on the implications which the practice of faith holds for probing the reaches of the human condition, then it will constantly be utilizing philosophical strategies in its quest for such understanding. That makes philosophy a "handmaid of faith," yet rather than reduce its stature, offers ways of extending its tentative explorations. The contributors to this volume provide just such explorations to tease us well beyond "philosophy of religion" to fresh theological horizons.'

David B. Burrell CSC, *Hesburgh Professor of Philosophy and Theology, University of Notre Dame*

Radical Orthodoxy returns theology to the centre of contemporary critical debate. The contributors develop a drastic critique of secular assumptions in order both to recover and develop the most authentic Christian thought of the past. Arguing that it is no longer acceptable to accommodate theology to prevailing wisdom and fashion, they reject both humanism and postmodernism, in favour of a theological construal of the radically indeterminable.

The endeavours of *Radical Orthodoxy* are characterised by four crucial claims:

- secular modernity is the creation of a perverse theology;
- the opposition of reason to revelation is a modern corruption;
- all thought which brackets out God is ultimately nihilistic;
- the material and temporal realms of bodies, sex, art and sociality, which modernity claims to value, can truly be upheld only by acknowledgement of their participation in the transcendent.

Radical Orthodoxy is a remarkable collection of papers that aims to reclaim the world by situating its concerns and activities within a theological framework.

This is essential reading for anyone eager to understand religion, theology, and philosophy in a completely new light.

John Milbank is Reader in Philosophical Theology at Cambridge University and Fellow of Peterhouse. His previous publications include *Theology and Social Theory*, and *The Word Made Strange*. **Catherine Pickstock** is a Fellow of Emmanuel College, Cambridge. Her previous publications include *After Writing: On the Liturgical Consummation of Philosophy*. **Graham Ward** is Dean of Peterhouse, Cambridge. His previous publications include *Barth, Derrida, and the Language of Theology* and *Theology and Contemporary Critical Theory*.

RADICAL ORTHODOXY

A new theology

Edited by John Milbank,
Catherine Pickstock and Graham Ward

London and New York

First published 1999
by Routledge
2 Park Square, Milton Park, Abingdon, Oxon, OX14 4RN

Simultaneously published in the USA and Canada
by Routledge
270 Madison Ave, New York, NY 10016

Reprinted 1999

Transferred to Digital Printing 2006

Routledge is an imprint of the Taylor & Francis Group

© 1999 Selection and editorial matter, John Milbank, Catherine Pickstock
and Graham Ward; individual chapters, the contributors

Typeset in Baskerville by
M Rules

British Library Cataloguing in Publication Data
A catalogue record for this book is available from the British Library

Library of Congress Cataloguing in Publication Data
A catalogue record for this book has been requested.

ISBN 0–415–19698–1 (hbk)
ISBN 0–415–19699–X (pbk)

For X has the pow'r of three and therefore he is God.
(Christopher Smart, *Jubilate Agno*)

CONTENTS

CONTENTS

CONTRIBUTORS

Frederick Christian Bauerschmidt is Assistant Professor at Loyola University, Baltimore, where he teaches theology. His essays have appeared in several journals including *Modern Theology* and *New Blackfriars*.

Phillip Blond is at Peterhouse, Cambridge, where he is completing his PhD in Theology in the Faculty of Divinity at the University of Cambridge. He has published articles on phenomenology, aesthetics and theology. He is the editor of *Post-Secular Philosophy* (Routledge, 1997).

William T. Cavanaugh is Assistant Professor of Theology at the University of St Thomas, St Paul, Minnesota. He is the author of various articles and reviews, and *Torture and Eucharist: Theology, Politics, and the Body of Christ* (Blackwell, 1998).

Conor Cunningham is at St Edmund's College, Cambridge, where he is completing his PhD in Theology in the Faculty of Divinity at the University of Cambridge.

Michael Hanby is at Girton College, Cambridge, where he is completing his PhD in Theology in the Faculty of Divinity at the University of Cambridge.

Laurence Paul Hemming is at Peterhouse, Cambridge, where he is completing his PhD in Theology in the Faculty of Divinity at the University of Cambridge. His articles have appeared in several journals including *New Blackfriars*, *The Thomist* and *Literature and Theology*.

Gerard Loughlin teaches Christian theology, ethics and philosophy of religion at the University of Newcastle upon Tyne. Besides contributing to a number of leading journals, including *Modern Theology* and *New Blackfriars*, he is the author of *Telling God's Story: Bible, Church, and Narrative Theology* (CUP, 1995).

John Milbank is Reader in Philosophical Theology at Cambridge University and a Fellow of Peterhouse. He is the author of *The Religious Dimension in the Thought of Giambattista Vico* (Edwin Mellen, 1991), *Theology and Social Theory: Beyond Secular Reason* (Blackwell, 1990) and *The Word Made Strange: Theology Language Culture* (Blackwell, 1997).

CONTRIBUTORS

John Montag is a member of the Society of Jesus studying at St Edmund's College, Cambridge, where he is completing his PhD in Theology in the Faculty of Divinity at the University of Cambridge.

David Moss is Director of Studies at St Stephen's House, Oxford, where he teaches theology. He is the author of several articles which have appeared in *Modern Theology* and *New Blackfriars,* and the co-author of *Balthasar at the End of Modernity* (T & T Clark, 1998).

Catherine Pickstock is a Fellow of Emmanuel College, Cambridge where she teaches philosophical theology. She is the author of *After Writing: On the Liturgical Consummation of Philosophy* (Blackwell, 1997).

Graham Ward is Dean of Peterhouse, Cambridge, where he teaches theology, philosophy and literary analysis. He is the author of *Barth, Derrida and the Language of Theology* (CUP, 1995) and *Theology and Contemporary Critical Theory* (Macmillan, 1996), as well as editor of *The Postmodern God* (Blackwell, 1997). He is the senior editor of *Literature and Theology* (OUP).

ACKNOWLEDGEMENTS

Seven of the contributors to this volume are Anglicans, all of a High Church persuasion; five contributors are Roman Catholics. Eight of the twelve are British; four of them are American. Three teach theology in the Cambridge University Divinity Faculty; five are graduate theological students in the same faculty; of the others, two were educated in theology at Cambridge and two are Americans who owe much to Cambridge influences. It is, therefore, very much a Cambridge collection, and other contemporary Cambridge figures who have influenced the volume and would sympathise with much, but often not all of it, should be mentioned: Donald Mackinnon, Rowan Williams, Nicholas Lash, David Ford, Janet Soskice, Tim Jenkins, Lewis Ayres. We should also like to mention the influence, from outside of Cambridge, of Stanley Hauerwas, David Burrell, Michael Buckley, Walter Ong and Gillian Rose.

We feel that our positive invocations of Plato, Augustine, Anselm and Aquinas have resonances with the Cambridge past. And we hope that what we have written is not foreign to the spirit of Ralph Cudworth and Christopher Smart.

INTRODUCTION

Suspending the material:
the turn of radical orthodoxy

John Milbank, Graham Ward and Catherine Pickstock

For several centuries now, secularism has been defining and constructing the world. It is a world in which the theological is either discredited or turned into a harmless leisure-time activity of private commitment. And yet in its early manifestations secular modernity exhibited anxiety concerning its own lack of ultimate ground – the scepticism of Descartes, the cynicism of Hobbes, the circularities of Spinoza all testify to this. And today the logic of secularism is imploding. Speaking with a microphoned and digitally simulated voice, it proclaims – uneasily, or else increasingly unashamedly – its own lack of values and lack of meaning. In its cyberspaces and theme-parks it promotes a materialism which is soulless, aggressive, nonchalant and nihilistic.

The present collection of essays attempts to reclaim the world by situating its concerns and activities within a theological framework. Not simply returning in nostalgia to the premodern, it visits sites in which secularism has invested heavily – aesthetics, politics, sex, the body, personhood, visibility, space – and resituates them from a Christian standpoint; that is, in terms of the Trinity, Christology, the Church and the Eucharist. What emerges is a contemporary theological project made possible by the self-conscious superficiality of today's secularism. For this new project regards the nihilistic drift of postmodernism (which nonetheless has roots in the outset of modernity) as a supreme opportunity. It does not, like liberal theology, transcendentalist theology and even certain styles of neo-orthodoxy, seek in the face of this drift to shore up universal accounts of immanent human value (humanism) nor defences of supposedly objective reason. But nor does it indulge, like so many, in the pretence of a baptism of nihilism in the name of a misconstrued 'negative theology'. Instead, in the face of the secular demise of truth, it seeks to reconfigure theological truth. The latter may indeed hover close to nihilism, since it, also, refuses a reduction of the indeterminate. Yet what finally distances it from nihilism is its proposal of the rational possibility, and the faithfully perceived actuality, of an indeterminacy that is not impersonal chaos but infinite interpersonal harmonious order, in which time participates.

This new theological approach may be placed under the rubric 'radical ortho-doxy'. In what sense *orthodox* and in what sense *radical?* Orthodox in the most straightforward sense of commitment to credal Christianity and the exemplarity of its patristic matrix. But orthodox also in the more specific sense of re-affirming a richer and more coherent Christianity which was gradually lost sight of after the late Middle Ages. In this way the designation 'orthodox' here transcends confessional boundaries, since both Protestant biblicism and post-tridentine Catholic positivist authoritarianism are seen as aberrant results of theological dis-tortions already dominant even before the early modern period. Much of this perspective is in profound continuity with the French *nouvelle théologie* which par-tially undergirded the reforms of Vatican II, but where radical orthodoxy wishes to reach further is in recovering and extending a fully Christianised ontology and practical philosophy consonant with authentic Christian doctrine. The conse-quences of modern theological decadence for philosophy and the wider culture were never fully considered by the *nouvelle théologie* (and indeed it sometimes uncrit-ically embraced various modes of secular knowledge) and while this certainly was considered by Thomistic currents in the wake of Gilson and Maritain, the exclu-sively Thomist perspective is not seen by radical orthodoxy as necessarily decisive. At the same time radical orthodoxy, while sharing a great deal with Barthian neo-orthodoxy, departs from this theology also, in a somewhat similar fashion: by refusing all 'mediations' through other spheres of knowledge and culture, Barthianism tended to assume a positive autonomy for theology, which rendered philosophical concerns a matter of indifference. Yet this itself was to remain cap-tive to a modern – even liberal – duality of reason and revelation, and ran the risk of allowing worldly knowledge an unquestioned validity within its own sphere. By comparison with this, radical orthodoxy is 'more mediating, but less accommo-dating' – since, while it assumes that theology must speak *also* of something else, it seeks always to recognise a theological *difference* in such speaking. But just as important as a contrast in substance, here, is a general contrast of approach and style: where Barthianism can tend to the ploddingly exegetical, radical orthodoxy mingles exegesis, cultural reflection and philosophy in a complex but coherently executed *collage*.

And just how is it *radical?* Radical, first of all, in the sense of a return to patris-tic and medieval roots, and especially to the Augustinian vision of all knowledge as divine illumination – a notion which transcends the modern bastard dualisms of faith and reason, grace and nature. Radical, second, in the sense of seeking to deploy this recovered vision systematically to criticise modern society, culture, pol-itics, art, science and philosophy with an unprecedented boldness. But radical in yet a third sense of realising that via such engagements we *do* have also to rethink the tradition. The fact of its late medieval collapse, the fact that such a collapse was *pos-sible*, can sometimes point to even earlier weaknesses. Equally, since the Enlightenment was in effect a critique of decadent early modern Christianity, it *is* sometimes possible to learn from it, though in the end the Enlightenment itself

2

massively repeated the decadence. Fourth, the great Christian critics of the
Enlightenment – Christopher Smart, Hamann, Jacobi, Kierkegaard, Péguy,
Chesterton and others – in different ways saw that what secularity had most ruined
and actually denied were the very things it apparently celebrated: embodied life,
self-expression, sexuality, aesthetic experience, human political community. Their
contention, taken up in this volume, was that only transcendence, which 'suspends' these things in the sense of interrupting them, 'suspends' them also in the
other sense of upholding their relative worth over–against the void. Such radical-
ism indeed refuses the secular, but at the same time it does 're-envision' a
Christianity which *never* sufficiently valued the mediating participatory sphere
which alone can lead us to God. This is not at all to deny that the *worst* Christian
puritanism – acts of disciplinary confinement, categorisation of banished human
categories (homosexuals, lepers) – and the worst otherworldly piety upholding a
centralised tyrannising politics were the result of late medieval theological deviation. However, once one has realised, following the great English literary visionaries
William Shakespeare and Thomas Nashe that sexual puritanism, political discipli-
narianism and abuse of the poor are the result of a *refusal* of true Christianity (see
Lear and *Measure for Measure*), one is led to articulate a more incarnate, more participatory, more aesthetic, more erotic, more socialised, even 'more Platonic'
Christianity.

The central theological framework of radical orthodoxy is 'participation' as
developed by Plato and reworked by Christianity, because any alternative configuration perforce reserves a territory independent of God. The latter can lead only
to nihilism (though in different guises). Participation, however, refuses any reserve
of created territory, while allowing finite things their own integrity. Underpinning
the present essays, therefore, is the idea that every discipline must be framed by a
theological perspective; otherwise these disciplines will define a zone apart from
God, grounded literally in nothing. Although it might seem that to treat of diverse
worldly phenomena such as language, knowledge, the body, aesthetic experience,
political community, friendship, etc., apart from God is to safeguard their worldliness, in fact, to the contrary, it is to make even this worldliness dissolve. This
happens in two directions. First, without an appeal to eternal stability, one has to
define a purely immanent security. Whereas the former allows temporality, the contingency of language and the fecundity of bodies to retain their ultimacy in the
finite sphere, the latter abolishes these phenomena in favour of an immanent static
schema or *mathesis*. Curiously, perhaps, it is immanence that is dualistic and tends
to remove the mysterious diversity of matter in assuming that appearances do not
exceed themselves. Second, since the schema or *mathesis* is only transcendental, and
grounded in nothing, one has to assume either ontologically or pragmatically (i.e.
it might as well be the case for all practical purposes) that this essential structure is
only an illusion thrown up by the void, even if, as for Derrida *et al.*, the essential
structure is itself the moment of a delusory and contradictory concealment of the
void. One can go even further to say that the void itself as a static given assumed
by knowledge is the *mathesis* par excellence. In this way, the two different paths to

dissolution of finite integrity – modernist epistemological humanism and post-modern ontological nihilism – merge into one (a dismal promenade).

By contrast, the theological perspective of participation actually saves the appearances by exceeding them. It recognises that materialism and spiritualism are false alternatives, since if there is only finite matter there is not even that, and that for phenomena really to be there they must be more than there. Hence, by appealing to an eternal source for bodies, their art, language, sexual and political union, one is not ethereally taking leave of their density. On the contrary, one is insisting that behind this density resides an even greater density – beyond all contrasts of density and lightness (as beyond all contrasts of definition and limitlessness). This is to say that all there is *only* is because it is more than it is.

This perspective should in many ways be seen as undercutting some of the contrasts between theological liberals and conservatives. The former tend to validate what they see as the modern embrace of our finitude – as language, and as erotic and aesthetically delighting bodies, and so forth. Conservatives, however, seem still to embrace a sort of nominal ethereal distancing from these realities and a disdain for them. Radical orthodoxy, by contrast, sees the historic root of the celebration of these things in participatory philosophy and incarnational theology, even if it can acknowledge that premodern tradition never took this celebration far enough. The modern apparent embrace of the finite it regards as, on inspection, illusory, since in order to stop the finite vanishing modernity must construe it as a spatial edifice bound by clear laws, rules and lattices. If, on the other hand, following the postmodern options, it embraces the flux of things, this is an empty flux both concealing and revealing an ultimate void. Hence, modernity has oscillated between puritanism (sexual or otherwise) and an entirely perverse eroticism which is in love with death and therefore wills the death also of the erotic, and does not preserve the erotic as far as an eternal consummation. In a bizarre way, it seems that modernity does not really want what it thinks it wants; but, on the other hand, in order to have what it thinks it wants, it would have to recover the theological. Thereby, of course, it would discover also that that which it desires is quite other than it has supposed.

Thus the following essays seek to re-envisage particular cultural spheres from a theological perspective which they all regard as the only non-nihilistic perspective, and the only perspective able to uphold even finite reality. The first four essays move broadly from a concern with issues of knowledge through questions of ethical and political practice to questions of aesthetic envisioning.

In the first essay, John Milbank suggests that the writings of Hamann and Jacobi in the late eighteenth century are of special significance for radical orthodoxy, because they undertake a theological critique of philosophy itself which recognises and refuses the specifically modern dualism of reason and revelation. Their conception of reason as achieving truth only when it gives creative expression to its recognition of God as visible in the world is, he further suggests, more critically viable than Kant's confinement of theoretical reason within 'limits'. In the latter case, the epistemological project assumes an earlier philosophical shift which it does not question: namely that it is possible to speak with certainty and clarity of merely finite, circumscribed being without raising the question of its relation to Being as such. In so far as Kant remained haunted by this question of ontological depth 'behind' finite phenomena, then, for Hamann and Jacobi, he was bound to recognise that what could be known with certainty need not have anything to do with the ultimately real. For Jacobi this was the basis of what he called Kant's 'nihilism': ontologically speaking we must treat reality 'in itself' as nothing. By contrast, Milbank argues, Hamann and Jacobi's insistence on knowledge only 'by faith', whereby we allow that the visible affords some clue to the invisible, alone prevents nihilism, and at the same time ensures that sensory desire is neither denied nor hypostasised, but instead treated as a site of divine presence (Hamann) and a path of possible purification (Jacobi).

If Milbank's essay suggests that, for radical orthodoxy all real knowledge involves some revelation of the infinite in the finite, John Montag's essay suggests in complementary fashion that revelation should not be set over–against reason, but is, on the contrary, an intensification of human understanding. He shows how, for Aquinas, revelation was essentially a matter of special illumination of the intellect, in which the imaginative interpretation of external signs, the recognition of these signs as revelatory and the inner transformation of the soul were all one single, indivisible occurrence. However, modern theology has, by and large, not followed this authentically Thomist account of revelation. It has instead assumed the account provided in the late sixteenth–early seventeenth century by the Jesuit theologian and philosopher Francisco Suárez. In Suárez the integrity of Aquinas's account is undone: now one can recognise the positive fact of revealed truth, before assenting to it, and the movement of assent requires both a divine motion and an independent disclosure in external images. And no longer does revelation disclose God himself; instead it concerns pieces of information which God has decided to impart. All these developments assume, according to Montag, the loss in the late Middle Ages of the metaphysical framework of participation, and the concomitant loss of an intrinsic link between sign and thing signified. As a result, the content and the authorisation of revelation are prised apart, and both aspects are thought of as isolated occurrences grounded in the Will rather than a necessity intrinsic to the real. Revelation is now something positive in addition to reason, precisely because a rational metaphysics, claiming to comprehend being without primary reference to God, frames all discourse, including the theological. Ironically, revealed truth becomes something ineffably arbitrary, precisely because this is the only way it can be construed by an already intrinsically godless reason.

Thus we can see from Montag's conclusion that what is apparently most 'pious' in modern times (for both Catholicism and Protestantism) is precisely that which is most in league with, and indeed helps to ground, the secular. For while it is the case that the 'epistemological' era, which assumes that the true is that which is fully graspable by human reason, derives from an earlier prising away of ontology from theology in the wake of Duns Scotus, this prising apart was itself governed by ironically 'pious' motives: it arose because God was now regarded as a supreme,

5

untrammelled individual Will rather than that *esse ipsum* in which mere existences come to share. Hence while Scotus and Ockham, like Aquinas, were still interested mainly in human knowledge in so far as it reflected and afforded clues to divine knowledge, in the case of the former two thinkers the 'pious' conjecture that God might so dispose things that what *appears* to humans has no connection to the truly real itself opens the space for the emergence of the modern 'epistemological' focus. Without formally surrendering the circumstances in which they were nearly always doing theology and *not* philosophy (deploying philosophical texts only for the assistance their partial truths could offer to theology), the later medieval theologians nonetheless managed to construct the theological preconditions for the modern autonomy of philosophy and secular practice.

While the resulting dualism of reason and revelation is charted by Montag, then what Milbank's opening essay argues for is the later implicit recognition and undoing of this paradoxical theological construction of an autonomous secular reason, operating only 'within limits', by the radical pietist thinkers – Hamann, Jacobi and others. Moreover, he suggests that this undoing runs like a secret subterranean stream through much of the thought of the last two centuries, since many of its key themes – the linguisticality of reason, the ontological difference, the priority of existence over essence, the priority of dialogue, the sensuality of all human thought – were articulated first by the radical pietists.

The essays which follow take up several of these key themes, and show that frequently modern secular thought seeks to articulate something with only semi-coherence, since it fails to see that a fully coherent articulation requires the theological. First of all, Conor Cunningham examines 'the linguistic turn' with reference to the early and late works of Wittgenstein. Whereas Wittgenstein is normally seen as the supreme inventor of a post-metaphysical style of philosophy, Cunningham shows that he still works in a post-Kantian space which ignores the kind of metacritical considerations concerning the relation of philosophy to theology averred by Milbank and Montag. For while Wittgenstein refuses any general outlook on the ultimately real, he still assumes, as Cunningham argues, that such a 'metaphysics' would be what only a philosophy would deliver. He does not entertain the view that an ontology of this kind is something that could be articulated by a discourse concerned not only with reason but with the inherited assumptions of a specific way of life, and with certain disclosing 'attitudes' such as those of a higher desire, or of faith, hope and charity. Indeed, as Cunningham insists, Wittgenstein abjures the theological, because he defines the 'truly' religious as ritual practice without articulation – though this must be to insinuate (in a fashion that Wittgenstein purportedly abhors) that *actual* religious traditions have badly misunderstood themselves.

Moreover, as Cunningham points out, Wittgenstein retains a shadow-image of philosophy as metaphysics, since he still thinks pure reason can attain to a certain 'finality' – namely, that it can establish limits as to what language can and cannot achieve. For the *Tractatus* this was undertaken on the basis of reduction to pure atomic units of reference; for the *Philosophical Investigations*, on the basis of an appeal to certain sheerly given 'language games' or else 'forms of life'. These can be iso-lated as 'given', as transcendentally presupposed, only if there is a difference between what is 'said' within these forms and what the structure of these forms merely 'shows' about human inhabitation of the world. The latter, for Wittgenstein, can only be 'described' but not 'explained'; just as Kant's categories are of knowledge, not of being. And yet, Cunningham argues, if showing is to be distinguished here from saying, and if description is to be objective, there must be a privileged metalanguage – 'philosophy' – in which this description is carried out. But will not the terms of such language have to presuppose some general account of the relation of language to the real, some sort of 'explanation' after all, just as Kant's confining of himself to epistemology still required him to make problematic pronouncements concerning the relation of phenomena to noumena? And it is in relation to this metalanguage that Wittgenstein's position hovers uneasily between some sort of naturalistic vitalism or pragmatism, on the one hand, and a kind of *ad hoc* culturally relative transcendentalism, on the other. The first option is somewhat 'realist', the second somewhat 'idealist', and yet, according to Cunningham, it is exactly this realist–idealist alternative which Wittgenstein wishes to escape. In Cunningham's analysis realism must contradictorily begin with an 'idea' of what constitutes the real, while idealism must assert the prime 'reality' of thought, although only on the basis of the unattainability of a real beyond thought, which it still, by default, privileges.

Hence what is really assumed here is the perfect immanent circle of mutual con-firmation of object-graspable-by-subject and subject-able-to-command-object. For both idealism and realism, this circle is gnoseologically complete and self-sufficient within its own limits. Yet this amounts to a denial that the world can be truly known only in its participation in the eternally transcendent. So both 'idealism' and 'realism' are methodologically atheistic and operate within the post-Scotist space of pure ontology, which is theologically questionable.

For Cunningham, therefore, Wittgenstein's desire to break out of both idealism and realism – the circle of pure ontology which is also the realm of epistemol-ogy – might be construed as a will to restore the primacy of the theological. However, the persistent belief in the 'finality' of philosophy, plus the fact that pur-ported pure description of forms of life must be a mode of transcendental 'explanation' after all, ensures that the idealist–realist oscillation returns, albeit in a significantly undecidable form. But the claim to establish a metalanguage which reveals where language transgresses its own possibilities – 'goes on holiday' – inevitably amounts, for Cunningham, to the view that nothing essentially new can arrive in the world. And in that case Wittgenstein has just repeated the tendency of metaphysics to suppress time, language and matter. If time discloses nothing radically new, then the contingencies of *parole* cannot refigure what is Wittgenstein's (albeit muddier) equivalent of Saussure's *langue*, and therefore lan-guages in their specificities and historically contingent diversities are subordinate to a universal grammar which must really condition all language from a supra-linguistic site. Meanwhile, the loss of the possibility of significant surprise betokens also a lack of depth in the material: matter is reduced to what we must always inevitably make of it. By contrast (as say with Hamann) only a theological discourse which selects *specific paths* through language as uniquely significant, and which would claim only 'to describe' language in preferential, 'biased' terms, themselves linked to a specific grammatical vision, could really claim to fulfil the linguistic turn without lapse into either idealism or realism. For here the *constraint* upon language which is the condition for the possibility of its being true (of 'adequation' in some sense) lies in the transcendent and is mediated to language only through linguistic response – which involves always the inseparable fusion of given matter and our envisaging of what might be made of this matter. Since language is, in the end, referred for its truth to an ineffable 'beyond', it need not now be referred to any extralinguistic, immanent, given reality, whether real or ideal, if it is to be constrained and truthful.

Thus, for Cunningham, there are two ways of regarding Wittgenstein's project: either, after all, it is just another post-Kantian philosophy, or else it requires a specifically theological articulation for its completion.

If Wittgenstein is here located as a kind of theologian *manqué*, then Lawrence Hemming positions Heidegger in a somewhat similar fashion. Here also one finds an identification and a refusal of the self-confirming circle of a finitude supposedly constituted without reference to the infinite. According to Hemming, the loss, after Scotus, of the idea that existence coincides with 'being created' eventually ushers in the notion of being-as-an-object which exists primarily for a knowing or commanding subject. He argues that for Heidegger this subordination, via objectivity, of being to a human contemplative grasp (definable in terms of its forming the basis for technical manipulation) was the ground of modern 'nihilism'. This nihilism, however, was encouraged initially by an ontotheological overlay, because there remained a need to account for the existence of the object which was nonetheless *defined* by its graspability for the knowing subject. Given this demand and this definition it was inevitable that an individual 'I' would be projected onto the eternal. Thus once again we have an instance of a suppression of temporality linked to a hypostasisation of an immanent given: for the divine 'I' is formed entirely in the image of my given finite 'I' which in turn is defined by its capacity to image (and so control) an equally given object. Here the apparent modesty of empirical obeisance before the object and the confinement of the 'I' to its present state (another false piety, first perfected by Descartes) disguise a will to technocratic power and a creation of God after our own replete image. By contrast, Hemming suggests, it is exactly when we seek the arrival of our truer selves in the future, through the 'poetic' endeavour to transform and release the material into its fullest significance, that we really 'wait upon God' in prayer. This alone allows us to receive God as the forever new, and guarantees his ontological plenitude without confining him to the category of the ontic given.

By questioning the reduction of Being to object, Heidegger opens up once again the ontological difference between Being and beings already known to Aquinas, whereby there can be no co-incidence between *what* a thing is and *that* it is. For both Aquinas and Heidegger this interval ('real distinction' of essence and existence in Aquinas) constitutes that 'depth' in beings which forbids any once and for all definition of their reality. This interval exists only as participation in the fullness of Being, yet its *ratio* to Being constitutes the thing in such a way that we could never *survey* this ratio without impossibly comparing the thing to itself (to that 'innermost' self which nonetheless exceeds the thing). We cannot, for this reason, ever fully know what a thing discloses, what is possible for it, or what it may yet come to be.

Hence, Hemming suggests, Heidegger restores a sense of 'disclosure', or of 'revelation', as germane to all thinking. Being 'shines out' in beings, and this is apparent, not to inert technological contemplation, but to active expressive shaping which seeks 'to speak' Being. In this way, we can see how Heidegger points to a new closure of the modern gulf between reason and revelation and reiterates much of the perspective of the radical pietists. However, one may add to Hemming's analysis here that much in Heidegger remains ambivalent, for all the positive talk of disclosure: the very desire to avoid a 'nihilist' characterisation of Being as Will tends to give rise to the idea of Being as an impersonal nothingness exhausted by its manifestations in beings who nonetheless can never coincide with it. If Being is thus manifest only in its concealment, then the ontological difference itself can appear only as disguise and opposition. *Nothing* after all is revealed. And yet, as Hemming rightly argues, there remains in Heidegger a will beyond nihilism, and a correct recognition that nihilism is our real historical situation. Heidegger's talk of a positive disclosure of Being in beings can, as Hemming argues, be allowed to stand, if we go on to see that it is fully articulated only with reference to a plenitudinous transcendent God giving us to be, and re-making us through all our co-creative endeavours which themselves manifest in part the divine production in the *logos* (which is infinite 'future-directed' art, and not technical production on the basis of a pre-contemplated plan).

The next group of essays is concerned primarily with human practice. If Milbank and Montag's essays are concerned to reconnect knowledge with divine disclosure, then Michael Hanby's seeks to rethink willing in indissociable connection with divine grace. He insists that for Augustine there is no notion of will entirely in command of its own choice, but that for this Latin Church Father the will is free only when it is intentionally directed towards its true *telos*: a *telos* which constantly re-arrives as the gift of grace. In consequence, any dualism of divine activity over human passivity is alien to Augustine, and likewise the most radically interior depth of a human being – his 'true self' – is precisely that which is most radically 'exteriorised', or turned away from itself towards God and created others. It is indeed *only* this exterior 'distance' which engenders that new sense of inner profundity so striking in Augustine's writings. And just for this reason it is false to ascribe to Augustine a later individualism or concern with the lonely self or self-positing will equal in its indeterminacy to the infinity of God (the position of Descartes). To the contrary, Augustine recovers his true self only at the point where he also recovers a true vision of the cosmos, and both visions are themselves made possible by the Church's mediation of the restoration of the true human image, and thereby the cosmos, in the incarnation of God in Christ. Hanby indicates that if 'philosophical' interest in the will in Augustine is indissociable from his 'theological' interest in grace, then we have also to understand how his Christological and sacramental notions are revised ontological categories. For example, the famous *aporias* of time in Augustine are resolved practically and Christologically only when, having concluded that time makes no sense because it can be comprehended only by that infinity which it reflects, Augustine further concludes that this infinite comprehension is nonetheless reflected in time through Christ's restoration of time's true numerical rhythm. Although we cannot comprehend the transition from past to future via the present, we can, for Augustine, as Catherine Pickstock argues in the last essay in this volume, nonetheless hear and repeat the truth of this passage in the ecclesial praise of the Father offered through the Son in the Spirit.

Since Augustine discovers for the first time the radical *temporality* of the human soul, his Christological resolution of the riddle of time applies to the self also. Only through ecclesial inclusion is the free expressiveness of the individual consummated. However, as Hanby argues, if Augustine refuses a later notion of the will, independent of truth, he refuses by the same token a later notion of truth as independent of desire. Augustine could not yet be either an idealist or a realist in the modern sense, since, as Hanby says, he had no notion of knowledge as 'representation' or as 'the mirror of nature'. Instead, in a Platonic and biblical lineage, he thought of human knowledge as a recapitulatory recovery of a lost link to the infinite, a lost state of original human integrity. Indeed his constant and almost obsessive concern with the Platonic '*aporia* of learning' – how can I seek for knowledge of something if I do not already know it; yet how can I know something without having come to know it – shows that Augustine (like Plato himself) already refused (in their antique versions) all metaphysical foundationalisms which fantasise either empirical givens which precede our knowledge of them or else *a priori* modes of knowledge somehow given in advance of our actually knowing anything. It is for just this reason that the Platonic doctrine of recollection springs – contrary to almost all usual assumptions – from an entirely *anti*-'metaphysical' imperative, as it attempts not to fantasise any 'given' and yet not to surrender our intuitive sense that we can 'be in the truth'. The radically orthodox perspective recognises a certain surprising kinship between Platonic recollection, the linguistic turn and the temporalisation of being. For the eternal forms 'recalled' are *not* pre-given like transcendental categories: instead we are constantly and perplexedly 'reminded' of the forms by radically new encounters with the material world. The forms paradoxically turn us towards the body and towards the future.

In Augustine, as in Plato, the *aporia* of learning is resolved through appeal to forms, now 'ideas' in the mind of God. However, for Augustine the ideas are much more emphatically mediated by the psychic inhabitation of time: for us the recovery of the infinite is the recovery of true time. This means that both the re-

10

memorising of the past and also a correct anticipation of the future are directed towards God. The latter 'anticipation' involves desire, and while, as Hanby stresses, will in Augustine is only desire lured by its true object (known through judgement), it is also the case, as he equally stresses, that judgement requires the right attitude, a knowing of something through an intimation of its true orientation to the infinite. Thus if 'divine ideas' are part of Augustine's resolution of the *aporia* of learning, 'desire' is an equally important part (as it was for Plato also): for if the forms/ideas are not *a priori* givens, then there remains the problem of how we would ever begin to re-invoke them. Here, in Augustine, 'will' or 'desire' indicates that aspect of our being (indeed of all created beings) which somehow already has something and yet does not have it. In this way 'will' names not, as for Pelagius or later in Western tradition, *a faculty*, but simply that problematic site where inner is also outer, active is also passive, present is also past and future, and knowing is also loving. And what justifies such a remaining with the problematic (which otherwise would betoken a purely philosophic scepticism) is precisely the incomprehensible faith in the world as created out of nothing: that is to say, as 'other' from God and yet constituted only out of God. But if 'will' names this incomprehensibility of creation in relation to God – its baffling 'surplus' to God which still fully returns to God – Augustine thinks that this strange cancelled surplus has a ground in God himself. God as Holy Spirit is himself will, or that desire beyond judgement which alone fulfils judgement. Somehow, the conundrum of creation is 'resolved' in God's ecstatic self-grounding.

Hence, as Hanby intimates, this vision of creation is indeed a vision of the value of the unique and individual with its own free desiring, yet is equally a vision of the sustaining of these things 'in truth', rather than as a rupture of truth – a vision therefore of the harmony and co-ordination of individuals through their participation in God.

Hanby's essay juxtaposes Augustine's account of selfhood to modern Western accounts of the individual. David Moss's essay, which follows, critically aligns Anselm's account of friendship with postmodern celebrations of otherness, or 'alterity'. He expands Hanby's demonstration of the interweaving of interiority with exteriorisation in Augustine by emphasising that *theoria* in pre-Christian tradition and in the Patristic legacy was rooted in *amicitia*, and therefore was never originally that lonely gaze of an isolated subject upon the object which it later became. Moss suggests that the experience of friendship might be the true pre-reflective horizon for human thinking, rather than, for example, the Heideggerean experience of anxiety. This suggestion would seem to have much in common with Emmanuel Levinas's thesis about the preontological priority of the ethical demand upon us of 'the other'. However, Anselm's 'friendship', as Moss shows, does not make a virtue of anonymity as essential to the category of 'the other', but insists on real, concrete, explicit affiliation and bonding. This refraction of our open and infinite responsibility through the specificity of neighbours and established affinities is surely truer to finitude, temporality and corporeality than the hidden hubris of an infinite responsibility exercised by a form of voluntarist decree towards all others in their mere generalised otherness. (One can note here that even a thinker like Balthasar, supposedly sympathetic to the Middle Ages, makes the mistake of claiming that many human spheres – the familial, economic, technical, political – cannot be entirely suffused by love, because he thinks of love in too post-Kantian a fashion as the fulfilment of a universal pure ideal by a solitary individual.) As creatures, we have to cleave to a specific path to the infinite, or else we will substitute for the infinite our own fantasised universal. For this reason we need not, like Levinas, be suspicious of all 'imaging' of the other, by which alone the other can be a specific other. Such suspicion still assumes that all imaging occurs within the transcendentalist space of our grasp of phenomena that are 'for us' only, and seeks to preserve the integrity of the other only as the vacant unknowability of the noumenal. It disallows entirely that a depth of Being might 'shine through' beings, and that a certain kind of imaging might of itself prevent domination through the gaze.

Such a non-appropriative imaging is involved for Anselm in friendship, as Moss describes it. We are bonded to the friend in his specific density, and yet this specificity which we cherish is none other than the friend's gaze upon us, his giving himself away towards me. Therefore the image we recognise is from the outset gift, and we would betray its gift character if we sought to hang on to it and not to return it, with difference. For the freely offered gaze of friendship (unlike that of one-way 'charity' – *caritas* falsified and misunderstood by modernity and postmodernity) seeks – that is to say, hopes for and cannot demand – the gaze back, in return. And it is this initial seeking, if respected, which ensures that my receiving of the image-as-gaze (gaze-as-image) can be neither domineering nor appropriative. As Moss says, what is exchanged is exchange – and yet this exchange assumes always a specific shape. Characters are formed conjointly through friendship, and in this way desire assumes a form and divine ideas are recollected. Friendship, therefore, starts to *know*, in a manner of knowing that we have largely forgotten. And indeed, as Moss suggests, the knowing of God is itself the re-establishment of friendship between heaven and earth, commenced at the incarnation. Further: to re-establish friendship with God is to enter into the infinite trinitarian realisation of friendship.

The next three essays seek to make more concrete visions of selfhood and friendship by speaking of sexuality, bodies and politics.

Following Balthasar, Gerard Loughlin's essay on 'erotics' rightly eschews as unbiblical any duality of *agape* and *eros*; without the latter, how can love be for *this* specific person and so be love at all? And how can love unite, to others and to God? Loughlin follows Balthasar also in seeking to connect not just *eros* in general, but sexual difference itself with some ground in the trinitarian differentiation within God. However, he identifies and resists a persisting element of male superiority in Balthasar's work, showing how this links with some liking for an 'excess' of the Father, as origin, over the generation of the Son, which does not do full justice to the doctrine of substantive relation and suggests a certain secondary and supposedly 'female' passivity. In addition, Loughlin insists that we can see divinely grounded 'difference' within the homosexual, because the difference between the sexes, although it is the supremely important sign of divine difference, does not exhaust valid and theologically significant difference. Following George Bataille, Loughlin sees a link between the transformatively parodic character of finite reality (everything exists always as a copy) and the erotic, which works by invitation, fusion and reproduction. However, Loughlin contends that if this indeterminate and open-ended 'parody' that is the sexual is to have significance and depth, it must be a participatory echo of God's infinite agapeic and erotic love. Likewise, if the 'dispossession' intrinsic to the erotic is to be a losing of oneself to find oneself, and not a masochistic self-surrender to death, it must be a letting go of the finite and apparently autonomous to discover once again one's true divine origin.

Indeterminacy and the letting go of the finite is central also to Graham Ward's essay 'Bodies'. In effect, Ward extends Augustine's reading of created reality as perforce, in its createdness, aporetic and indeterminate. He does this with reference to the body of Christ, the Christian paradigm for all bodies, and, therefore, with respect to Christology and ecclesiology. Whereas, for the Fichtean, Hegelian and Nietzschean traditions, these circumstances of creation are viewed always ultimately as signs of the 'nullity' of the apparently present world (or as marks of a lesser contingent reality that has yet to be finally 'sublated'), for Augustine they are signs of the nullity of things apart from their sharing in the divine gift – a sharing which is specific and yet unlimited. Examining particular sites for the displacement of the body of Jesus Christ in the New Testament – the transfiguration, the last supper, the crucifixion, the resurrection and the ascension – Ward points out that 'body' is conceived as something dynamic and non-circumscribable. The physical body is always imbricated with the social and civic body, the ecclesial and sacramental body, and the textual bodies (of witness and testimony) which produce and promote this imbrication. As such, the body of Jesus Christ performs a mission which exceeds local appearances. His body is both actual and metaphorical: actually male, but metaphorically both male and female. It is both individual and historically particular, and collective and historically extended through time. It is both a receptacle for food and food itself. And yet, through the representation of all these metamorphoses, through the displacements and extensions of this body, a consistency is nevertheless evident, as all is gathered into Christ, is made possible (and all the stronger) *by way* of the transformations, and not in spite of them.

Thus Ward's analysis further helps us to see that if the radically indeterminate and aporetic is 'read' (against the postmodern) as a sign of participation in the fullness of truth (which is in-finite *rather than* totalising) then one is uniquely able to value both the open-ended *and* the clearly preferential and specific. The aporetic, as such, becomes the means of grace: constitutive of the dynamic of salvation operating through Christ within the Church towards creation. We should not, theologically, necessarily refuse a singular or unusual preference (of a sexual kind, for example), for diversity and the power-to-transform have theological significance, and yet this does not preclude the need to judge the specific instance. One can accept, in certain cases to be discerned, the new, the strange and the transformed. But that judgement or acceptance is continually involved in a process of discrimination, which recognises that by the many concrete ways (though not all ways) lies the one path. It is a path which, in being rightly judged, is rightly desired and rightly preferred.

Ward ends his essay by pointing out how the body of Jesus Christ becomes the Church as the erotic and eucharistic community. William Cavanaugh's essay takes up the examination of the body real, ecclesial and political. And just as for Milbank and Montag theology pre-invented secular reason, and for Hanby it pre-invented secular will, so for Cavanaugh it pre-invented the secular 'state'. The latter is, indeed, for Cavanaugh's 'Christian anarchism', nothing but a rather crude parody of the body of Christ. It commenced, once more, with the late medieval loss of a sense of participation – this time in objective divine justice – and the emergence of the view that the infinitely free God hands over to human beings a certain sphere in which by right they can make decisions. Justice starts in consequence to mean merely that which is formally validated according to certain procedures and certain entitlements. And this perspective grounds both absolutism and liberalism. To begin with it was not, indeed, a sheerly secular perspective, but a new construal of Christ's body: this was now something primarily spatially present rather than repeated in time, whose integrity consisted no longer in the analogical blending of parts, but rather derived from forceful imposition by the rightfully ruling possessor at the centre (whether acting in the name of Papal or royal divine right, or else that of unmediated scriptural authority).

At first the new 'sovereign state' – often imitating Papal absolutism – sought to be the body of Christ thus reconstrued. And it tried to establish the unity of this body in a new way: by alienating all the 'public' dimensions of the Church to the secular arm. The so-called 'wars of religion' were to do with this struggle to establish the modern state (often they were conflicts primarily between the nobility or gentry at the peripheries and the monarchy at the centre) and to achieve this new sort of politico-religious settlement. They were *not* therefore conflicts about essentially religious belief which later came to necessitate the creation of the neutral secular state. All our 'quality' press now assumes that religion is a prime (often *the* prime) source of violence, and the modern state and market the great bringer of peace. Cavanaugh shows this assumption to be without historical warrant: it was rather the struggle for an already semi-secularised state before and then alongside the emergence of religious divisions (and it can be argued that the new notion of the state forced these to a new degree of schism or even, to a large degree, shaped and created them) which engendered an unprecedented degree of violence. Moreover, for Cavanaugh, this violence is secretly sustained to this day: in the state's monopoly of power at the centre, its frequent suppression of the public aspects of religion, and its authorisation of distributions of wealth and power first established by coercion.

For this reason the state's claim 'to make peace' is rather dubious. And in any case it offers only the uneasy peace of tolerance of boundaries, within which we are free to disagree as violently as we like. There is no aim here for substantive harmony, and even its more modest aim is a fiction, since boundaries are established only by victory and remain forever in dispute. If individuals do co-dwell peacefully under this regime, they do so only indirectly by virtue of their common submission to a sovereign centre (even if this is increasingly the global state/market centre) with which they all have sovereign dealings. By contrast, the body of Christ, for Cavanaugh, is the enterprise grounded in, and seeking further true consensus through, multiple real affinities. Here the body is itself the outcome of endless local negotiations: Christ the head is in every part, and each local church is, in itself, the whole Catholic Communion. And whereas voluntarist or secular justice is based upon the private appropriation of property, theological justice is grounded in assimilation to that body of Christ which one imbibes. For the body of Christ is at once a given actuality, and yet an arriving idea; where the eucharistic body of Christ does not produce the fruits of Christian practice, it holds over the ecclesial body of Christ the sway of negative judgement.

The final three essays in the volume are concerned with the contemplation and production of the beautiful. And, given the assent of all the contributors to the intraconvertibility of the transcendentals, this means that these final essays repeat with difference what has already been said – but with a difference that is essential if we are really to see what has already been said.

Frederick Bauerschmidt discusses Hans Urs von Balthasar's proposal to put the aesthetic at the centre of theology. For Balthasar this is intended to overcome the post-Renaissance split between 'rational' natural religion and 'revealed' positive religion, continuously criticised through this volume. Furthermore, Balthasar's theology refuses any post-Romantic attempt to ground religion in supposedly indefeasible structures of subjectivity. The point about aesthetic experience is that it is at once objectively disclosing and yet disclosive only for subjective feeling. For a vision which insists (against the Kantian legacy) on the objectivity of the beautiful, the intense feelings of compulsion and longing aroused by the beautiful correspond to a depth in beautiful things which is the prompting of Being itself at the surface of the various beautiful forms. For Balthasar, this showing of a source in and through a surface can be taken as a finite vestige of the Trinity, while he adds that the cross refigures our sense of the beautiful by displaying beauty through and despite the ugliness of dereliction. Here Bauerschmidt notes some kinship between Balthasar's Christological beauty and Jean-François Lyotard's postmodern sublime which is an inner-worldly rapture occurring in the shattering of previous norms of form and order. However, the Balthasarian 'sublime', unlike Lyotard's, remains *also* beautiful in that the de-figuring here is indeed re-figuring: the divine glory shines through the fragments, re-gathering them and re-integrating them as the promise of a restored future.

If, as Bauerschmidt claims, the experience of the aesthetic involves the integration of the objective with the subjective, and yet, as the other contributions show, this integration is rendered impossible for modern and postmodern epistemological assumptions, then what is disclosed in modern art? Phillip Blond's answer is that the latter tends to strive after either the purely subjective or the purely objective. However, in what is taken by modernity to be the *restricted* realm of art, this division nonetheless occurs within the sphere of 'the subjective' in the broadest sense, and in a fashion that involves a reversal. For 'the purely subjective' here means, not Romantic feeling, but the attempt to capture the original phenomenon of sensation prior to reflection, as with the Impressionists. And 'the purely objective' here means the rigorous display of ideal forms, often supported by a false gnostic Platonism which regrets the mediations of the body.

In either case there is, curiously, a denial of the active moment of art. For in the first case it is not seen that reflective interpretation has always already occurred; in the second artistry fades before a shamanic conveying of the impersonal and invisible. And yet it is equally true that, along with the active, a passivity before the *embodied* real also is lost: if the artist *must* interpret, then this is in response to the promptings of phenomena which are somehow perceived to be in excess of the phenomenal. Realism is in fact guaranteed by the necessity of one's intellectual as well as sensory seizure of the world: as with Balthasar, so again here, the 'surplus' of idealising thought over sensation in the perception of the beautiful corresponds to the depth 'in' the surface of things which is surplus to that surface. And this reminds us of the insight of Hamann and Jacobi earlier described by Milbank: only the vision of the world as created sustains as in any way 'comprehensible' the thought that there might be a 'depth' to things, lurking in and yet beyond the surface – a depth reinforcing or supplementary to the surface, and yet not denying it, after the fashion of deconstruction.

For Blond, therefore, a pure subjectivity 'loses the object'; but, thereby also, any subjectivity as we know it becomes unthinkable. Likewise a pure objectivity 'loses the subject', since the artist, with his specific contingent life, and specific contingent means, must here fade towards that ideality he strives to convey. And yet these means are the entire resources of art, and cannot fade, not even through minimalism (which is really just an especially cunning deployment of the means), and so to seek to restrict their role is simply to lose art, and so also the artist as subject of art. Thus the real tendency of pure abstraction is towards post-artistic nihilism (often now aspired to more simplistically by an art of shock or atrocity), and the real tendency of pure phenomenalism is the same: in the latter case, both because this is a will towards an impossible original experience, and because the phenomena are denied their anchorage in the real.

Blond's prime target, however, is not modern art as such – for he points to examples of abstraction which appear to presuppose just the kind of realism for which he is arguing. It is rather modern secular accounts of art. These, he suggests (for the kinds of reason already seen by Hamann and Jacobi), lack the resources to account for depth on the surface, or the simultaneity of active and passive in the work of the artist (the 'middle-voiced' aspect). At this point, Blond invokes the Bible, and suggests that therein the presence of the invisible in the visible is the essence of divine disclosure and of human response to God. Thus he reads Christ's saving work as the restoring of the world's true visibility, as well as the restoring of a true activity (or, one might say, the restoring of a true response which is also creatively appropriative and a true activity which is also responsive). Since the depth of things is, for Blond, a divine depth, then it follows for him also that this depth is most adequately invoked within the finite by human beings: thus nature is both there *before* us and in excess of us, and yet there *for* us, to be consummated by us.

The final essay in the volume, Catherine Pickstock's 'Music', fuses aesthetic with cosmological concerns. In Bauerschmidt's account of Balthasar it is mentioned that the latter regards his 'aesthetic' path as an alternative *either* to modern 'subjectivism' *or* to the 'cosmological' approach of pre-modernity. However, this scheme leaves the aesthetic poised uneasily between a revelatory positivism, on the one hand, or a generalised category of the aesthetic, on the other – a category which, if it is not to be 'cosmological', must be transcendentalist or phenomenological (and therefore *still* subjectivist). Here one has an example of the philosophical ambivalence of the *nouvelle théologie* legacy. One can note that, while Balthasar resists the Renaissance natural–positive religion split, he fails to see that the notion of a 'cosmological' approach might be, in part, a projection backwards from this split. This is to say that while, indeed, pre-modernity assumed a sacralised cosmos, it did not think of this as 'a given fact', on the model of a scientific fact, since such a notion of 'objectivity' is only the concomitant of modern subjectivism. On the contrary, as Balthasar himself mostly insists, the sacrality of the cosmos was registered only for an aesthetic vision which was active–passive and intuited the invisible in the visible. But, since the vision of the beautiful under the promptings of a good desire alone revealed the true, it did indeed display the ontological and the cosmic in the fullest senses (although it can be noted here in partial defence of Balthasar that early modern writers, like the Cambridge Platonist Ralph Cudworth, who sought *to restore* a sacral cosmology, seem even more to have foregrounded its aesthetic presentation; as if, indeed, the centrality of beauty shines more clearly in retrospect). Why then speak of the 'cosmic' as something surpassed, when to do so would seem to compromise the intraconvertibility of the transcendentals?

The answer may be twofold: first, Balthasar sometimes assumes too simply that old cosmologies are outdated, and that modern science reveals, truly, a desacralised world. He is, however, by no means consistent here, for while he questionably assents to the specifically modern separation of philosophy (and so of science) from theology and seems to disallow a significantly theological invasion of 'other domains' of knowledge, he nonetheless laments the handing over of all 'worldly being' to such knowledge, in a way that would demand that his aesthetic assume a 'cosmic' dimension. It is to this latter demand that radical orthodoxy prefers to respond. For to accept, theologically, that science can provide an ontology of nature is to fail to see that science operates entirely within the disjunctions of (epistemological) object over (teleologically indeterminate) subject, disjunctions which for a true theology result only from a decadent late medieval perspective or else from secular assumptions. For theology, therefore, the ontological scope of science is very limited, even as regards nature: with the Church Fathers (*and* many scientists, in a lineage from Francis Bacon), it confines scientific disclosure to the revealing of the technical transformability of the world, thereby allowing it to be potentially subservient to *charity* (again, this was the original vision of Bacon).

The second possible reason for Balthasar's confusion concerns his limited mode of embracing modernity. What he identifies as demonic in the modern is the Promethean, or the over-emphasis on human construction. By contrast, the empirical passivity of science can be pietised: even its disclosure of a godless world can be seen to prepare the way for a purer focus on the gospel (yet here Balthasar the Goethean is schizophrenic, for he *adores* sacralised cosmologies!). However, to condemn the Promethean is only to half-locate the villain, for such Prometheanism *requires* a given fixed matrix of objective facts and objective laws, or *a priori* rules, which then permit its predictable manipulations. To be technologically active, it must first be utterly passive in the face of objects to which it is in no sense teleologically related (this is why Descartes embraced a *mathesis* in apparently 'pious' *rejection* of a Renaissance stress on human creativity). By contrast, where objects are taken, as by previous tradition, to be teleologically directed to our knowing of them, the moment of activity is inherent to knowledge from the outset, and cannot be even notionally divided from the passive moment, in Kantian fashion.

Hence by implicitly embracing the 'passivity' of science, Balthasar is evading the fact that this is to embrace the counterpart of the Promethean. But in doing so he also evades taking a clear stance about certain other aspects of intellectual modernity – the recognitions of the primacy of language, of the historical and cultural character of humanity, of the way the bodily and erotic necessarily shape so much of our thought. Balthasar oscillates between embracing these things and finding in them traces of 'the Promethean'. By contrast, for radical orthodoxy, a handing over of the cosmic to modern science is far more obviously Promethean, whereas language, historicity, embodiedness and sexuality are seen much more positively: not only as compatible with orthodoxy, but as confirming it (though only at the point where they themselves become fully manifest without distortion).

It is in this context that one should view Pickstock's attempt to present as still believable Augustine's blending of the aesthetic and the cosmic in *De Musica*. How can we speak, without blasphemy, of a 'desacralised cosmos', unless one means merely the cosmos as perceived by fallen humanity? Hence one should take seriously Greek and Christian teaching concerning the 'harmonies' of the physical world. As Pickstock argues, the vision of 'cosmos' is in fact specifically Western, because Eastern thought is fixated upon a vision of purification of the self from nature. Thus Indian music reflecting this vision is paradigmatically wind music, the sigh of released selfhood. In the West, by contrast, where there is a much stronger thought of sacred *logos* informing nature, music is paradigmatically stringed, although the music of the pipe is also integrated. For here music is a structured flow, in a manner which denies priority either to spatial harmony or to temporal melody. Polyphony, Pickstock argues, was the eventual expression of this balance, but it required also an integration of the role of the structuring pause to become possible as a mode of musical practice. Significantly, this role of the pause was anticipated by Augustine, who understood it in terms of the ordering of all music, including the cosmic, by that very nullity out of which God creates. Augustine, according to Pickstock, relayed and perfected the Pythagorean vision by understanding the non-prioritised and non-groundable interplay between harmony and melody, space and time, as possible only within the scope of creation out of nothing. For here no immanent spatial fixity guarantees order, and yet we are not thereby left with *disorder*.

In later Western musical theory, Pickstock traces the breakdown of this balance: Rameau's naturalistic *mathesis* which locates the essence of music in harmonic simultaneity is opposed by Rousseau and, later, by Wagner's neo-oriental vision which celebrates pure melody. (From this perspective one can see the potential truth of Hermann Hesse's prophecy in *The Glass-Bead Game* that the early music revival would prove to be of deep metaphysical significance.) Once music is viewed in this way it becomes impossible to link it any more with the real: for the first case is like the 'subjective' art of the Impressionists – one seeks merely an empiricist science of predictable mechanical production of sensations – while the second case is equally subjective, but seeks to convey the pure ineffability of emotions unconstrained by one's specific cosmic position, from which perspective alone, according to Augustine, one could hope to partake in music.

Beyond this integration of the aesthetic and the cosmological, Pickstock's essay rounds off the collection by linking both thematics also to the gnoseological, the psychological and the political. For Augustine, to think is not passively to receive, even for a moment, as it was for Aristotle: instead it is 'active reception' by the soul of those harmonic 'intellectual' relations which it recognises in the cosmos by way of its own body's participation in the cosmos – that body which like a little cosmos the soul itself harmoniously organises. Music, in this perspective, becomes the type of all knowing and not an exception, for in Music we hear measurable ratios, and yet we select these according to a subjectively felt emotional 'atunement'. However, once again Pickstock argues (and we can see the parallels to the cases of visual art discussed by Blond), an earlier integration is later dissolved: the subjective emotions of music cease to denote a disclosure of the real. Meanwhile, the objectively mathematical side of music also migrates to the subjective side: the post-Ives preference for a pseudo-Platonic pure music without performance is the musical equivalent of pure abstraction.

Finally, there is the politics of music. If music is only, as it is for modernity, an aesthetic and not a cosmological matter, then at some point harmony is only phenomenal: it is not *real*. And a belief in some sort of vestigial Wagnerian subjective 'reality' will soon fade: instead we will arrive, as we indeed have, at the postmodern politics of noise: accepted music must be deciphered as simply the noisiest noise, that which has drowned out all others. Thus its innate logic will consist not in sounding, but in silencing: all music becomes the sacrificial rejection of unwanted music, and the only alternative music is that which 'mourns' the older music, irrevocably vanished.

Against such a vision, as Pickstock argues, it is now clear that one cannot seek to reinstate the humanist concert-hall of escapist private emotion: this will be rightly decoded as mere sonorous enforcement. Instead, if it is to be thought possible that there is music, and if it is thought possible, in consequence, that there can be human political harmony, then we have to hear the cosmic music, as restored to us in the dissonance of the cross, like the Christological restoration of vision (Blond) in the scattered fragments (Bauerschmidt). Then there can be again a cosmos, a psyche, a polis. . . .

1

KNOWLEDGE

The theological critique of philosophy in Hamann and Jacobi

John Milbank

Modern theology on the whole accepts that philosophy has its own legitimacy, its own autonomy, apart from faith. Philosophy articulates categories of being in general, or else of what it is to know in general, but speaks only obscurely, if at all, of God. Theology reserves to itself the knowledge of God as a loving creator who has also redeemed the human race. But various currents of 'liberal theology' seek to articulate this knowledge in terms of philosophically derived categories of being and knowing, the legitimacy of which liberal theology has forfeited the right to adjudicate. In the case, by contrast, of various currents of neo-orthodoxy, an attempt is made to articulate this knowledge in terms of categories proper to theology itself: usually this means granting a methodological priority to the full revelation of God in Christ, with all its narrative specificity, over the seemingly more general and abstract acknowledgement of God as creator. And yet what often remains unclear here is the degree to which these theological categories are permitted to disturb a philosophical account of what it is to be, to know and to act, without reference to God. In the case of Karl Barth, a broad acceptance of a post-Kantian understanding of philosophy is turned to neo-orthodox advantage, in that he can insist that natural reason discloses nothing of God and yet that this opens the way to a renewed and, indeed, now more radical recognition that only God discloses God in the contingency of events as acknowledged not by reason but by faith.

But, here one might ask, does not this leave behind a certain liberal residue, a certain humanistic deposit? For it seems that natural reason *can* recognise certain features of the created order – whether ontological or epistemological – in their pure finitude, without reference to any ratio of finite and infinite, as well as certain features of the *fallen* created order, which it nonetheless fails to decipher *as* fallen. Moreover, this liberal deposit arguably looms large, like an enormous slag-heap, undermining the intent of neo-orthodoxy, and obscuring its gaze upon the transcendent. For if philosophy determines what it is to be and to know, then will it not pre-determine how we know even Christ to be, unless we allow that the structure of this event re-organises also our ordinary sense of what is and what we can know, in such a way that the autonomy of philosophy is violated. The danger here is, as is well exemplified in Barth, that if we fail to redefine being and knowledge theologically, theological difference, the radical otherness of God, will never be *expressible* in any way without idolatrously reducing it to our finite human categories. Hence Barth is confined to a Christomonism, in which Christocentricity reduces to a focus on an enormous black hole, so radically other that it cannot be at all pictured or conceptualised as the new characteristic *practice* of the Church under the guidance of the Holy Spirit. And, worse still, Barth's continued and heterodox reduction of Christ's personal, and expressively imaging, character to a mere conveyance of the Paternal will betrays the fact that he projects God as the supreme instance of what a post-Kantian philosophy, as Fichte correctly realised, must logically understand human existence to be: namely, a willed positing of reality without other constraining grounds of necessity. Therefore, while the Barthian claim is that post-Kantian philosophy liberates theology to be theological, the inner truth of his theology is that by allowing legitimacy to a methodologically atheist philosophy, he finishes by construing God on the model, ironically, of man without God.[1]

We are left, then, with a double question: has there really been in this century, at least within Protestantism, *any* post-liberal theology? And would not such a theology have to challenge, at least in some sense, the autonomy of philosophy, and articulate a *theological* account of what it is to be and to know in general? But these two questions can immediately merge with an historical observation: in his account of the history of eighteenth- and nineteenth-century Protestant theology, Barth so set things up that an era of treacherously humanistic theology was brought to an end only with his own endeavours. In doing so he either ignored or travestied the work of a group of thinkers, whom one can inadequately dub 'radical pietists', at the end of the eighteenth century: the most important of these were Johann Georg Hamann, Franz Heinrich Jacobi, Thomas Wizenmann, and, in a certain way, Johann Gottfried Herder.[2] These thinkers *did* produce a theological critique of philosophy construed as the autonomy of reason, but in Barth's work, as in those of later commentators, this central characteristic of their work is passed over, watered down, or else seen as an illegitimate confusion of faith with reason which betrays the pure word of God. But the result of these evasions and misconstruals is that we are left with a seriously impoverished account of the genesis of much of modern thought itself. Until recently, we have failed to see that it was the radical pietist assault on philosophy which forced Kantianism to be so quickly abandoned, and both provoked and made in turn to collapse in quick succession the defences of critical reason by Fichte, Hegel and Schelling, culminating in an astonishing re-assertion of the radical pietist vision by Søren Kierkegaard. Moreover, even their idealist opponents, from Kant onwards, were forced by the pietists to find a way of *including* Christian faith as knowledge within their accounts of reason itself, from Kant's 'rational faith', through Hegel's crucified *logos* to Schelling's 'philosophy of revelation'. Hence in all this long history of ideas theology remained central, and

22

not at all merely reactive in relation to philosophy; on the contrary, it is to the essentially theological contributions of the radical pietists that one can trace many of the most potent themes of modern philosophy: for example, the priority of existence over thought; the primacy of language; the 'ecstatic' character of time; the historicity of reason; the dialogical principle; the suspension of the ethical; and the ontological difference. Is it not eccentric, in the face of this consideration, to make Schleiermacher pivotal for the history of modern theology? One does so, I would suggest, only because one has already assumed a liberal sundering of philosophy from theology, and because it was Schleiermacher who first defined, for modern times, a discrete theological domain and method. Yet from another perspective one might rather argue that Schleiermacher produced a diluted and compromised version of the themes of radical piety, one which was insufficiently critical of both Romanticism and rationalism. It is not that I am suggesting, like Balthasar, that Hamann *might* have been, instead of Schleiermacher, the pivotal figure for the nineteenth century, or that Hamann and Jacobi are neglected because they sadly had little influence. Rather, I suggest that their influence was tremendous: subterranean and concealed perhaps, yet still objectively traceable.[3]

So far, then, I have implied one perspective under which we might today view Hamann and Jacobi. They are the source not of neo-orthodoxy, but of a more genuinely anti-liberal *radical* orthodoxy, which does not hesitate to argue even with philosophy itself and which, just *because* it is more mediating, is also less accommodating than the theology of Barth (or even of Bonhoeffer). And as such ancestors, they were not entirely without heirs, and a legacy, although today we need to re-assemble its fragments. There is also, however, a second historical perspective in which we need to view both Hamann and Jacobi, this time looking backwards rather than forwards. There is absolutely no doubt as to the Lutheran character of both these thinkers: what they articulate is a kind of theory of 'knowledge by faith alone' to complement the notion of 'justification by faith alone'.[4] However, it is a mistake to view them only within Lutheran and German horizons: they are European thinkers – first of all geographically, since they are as much indebted to English, Anglo-Irish, Scottish, French and Italian as to German thought; and, second, historically – because we cannot understand them simply as renewing and re-expressing Luther's vision. Indeed this would be to belittle them, and to fail to realise that they were even greater conservative revolutionaries than Luther himself.

The very phrase I have already used, 'knowledge by faith alone', indicates this. For Luther entertained no such project: on the contrary, he broadly accepted the framework of late medieval nominalist philosophy. Now this philosophy was itself the legatee of the greatest of all disruptions carried out in the history of European thought, namely that of Duns Scotus, who *for the first time* established a radical separation of philosophy from theology by declaring that it was possible to consider being in abstraction from the question of whether one is considering created or creating being. Eventually this generated the notion of an ontology and an xepistemology unconstrained by, and transcendentally prior to, theology itself. In the late Middle Ages and in early modernity, philosophy became essentially the pursuit of such an ontology and epistemology, and the Reformation did nothing to disturb this situation.[5] Indeed, the Reformation was itself pre-determined by it, in that once philosophy has arrogated to itself the knowledge of Being as such, theology starts to become a regional, ontic, positive science, grounded either upon certain revealed facts or upon certain grace-given inner dispositions or again upon external present authority (the Counter-Reformation model). The very notion of a reason–revelation duality, far from being an authentic Christian legacy, itself results only from the rise of a questionably secular mode of knowledge. By contrast, in the Church Fathers or the early scholastics, both faith and reason are included within the more generic framework of participation in the mind of God: to reason truly one must be already illumined by God, while revelation itself is but a higher measure of such illumination, conjoined intrinsically and inseparably with a created event which symbolically discloses that transcendent reality, to which all created events to a lesser degree also point.[6]

Viewed from this perspective, it is easy to see how Jacobi and Hamann, *unlike* Luther, tacitly called into question the entire post-Scotist legacy. It was possible for them to do so, in part because the much more *scholastic* character of German eighteenth-century philosophy, compared with philosophy in France or England, carried with it, as it were somewhat more clearly on view, the hidden scholastic founding assumptions of all modern philosophy: in particular, the transcendent univocity of being as manifest in the clearly knowable *object* and the priority of possibility over actuality (I shall elucidate this shortly).[7] In two ways the legacy was questioned by Jacobi and Hamann: first, they insisted that no finite thing can be known, *not even to any degree*, outside its ratio to the infinite; hence they denied the validity of the enterprises of ontology or epistemology as pure philosophical endeavours, or *else* argued that if they were valid their conclusions would be *nihilistic* – and indeed it was Jacobi who first thematised the notion of nihilism.[8] Second, and correspondingly, they argued (and more especially Hamann here) that if the truth of nature lies in its supernatural ordination, then reason is true only to the degree that it seeks or prophesies the theoretical *and* practical acknowledgement of this ordination which, thanks to the fall, is made possible again only through divine incarnation.[9] Hence there can be *no* reason/revelation duality: true reason anticipates revelation, while revelation simply is *of* true reason which must ceaselessly arrive, as an event, such that what Christ shows supremely is the world as really world, as creation (this point has been well re-asserted recently by Phillip Blond).[10]

We can now link up these two historical perspectives on Hamann and Jacobi: one forwards and one backwards. It turns out that their apparent merging of reason and faith, and apparent fusion of nature and grace, are not suspicious traces of enlightenment, but rather the signs that they were the real conservative revolutionaries, more so than Barth in the one direction, or Luther in the other. This is not at all to deny that they *did* learn something positive from the generosity of enlightened universalism which prevents them from advocating any sort of simple return to the past, but nonetheless they refracted this universalism in a wholly traditional and Christian fashion. In fact we can now replace Hamann and Jacobi the neglected Lutherans with Hamann and Jacobi the supremely mediating figures: between lost tradition and postmodernity, between English and German thought, and finally between Protestantism and Catholicism.

It should be clear, from what I have already said, that it is not at all accidental that Jacobi and Hamann helped to foment the nineteenth-century Catholic revival in Germany: for what they did was to open the way to recover an earlier Catholicism more authentic than *either* Protestantism or Tridentine Roman Catholicism.[11] On the other hand, here again they did more than simply 'recover': their very Lutheran insistence on the priority of faith and language points to a position that allows even less autonomy to a universal reason than that permitted by the Church Fathers, and moreover installs a wholly unprecedented sense of the final inescapability of picture, musical rhythm and linguistic narrative in all thought. Only this new sense, one can conjecture, will really prevent Scotist deviations in the future – since the latter assume one can derive the real from the logically abstracted – and after Hamann especially, it can be recognised that we are only Christian men and women as a certain kind of *animal*, a certain *Lebensart*[12] (which seems to foreshadow Wittgenstein's *Lebensform*) whose behaviour is ultimately inscrutable.

But how can I possibly substantiate these large claims for Hamann and Jacobi's significance? And, in particular, how could they possibly have challenged philosophy as such, that is to say the possibility of pure disinterested rational inquiry as such? One key here is Hamann's deployment, after Francis Bacon, of the figure of Pontius Pilate, in 'Aesthetica in Nuce'.[13] Pilate represents enlightenment, since he both rules and inquires after truth. 'What is truth?' he asks, as if to ask 'What is enlightenment?' But, notoriously, he only jests, and will not stay for an answer. If he had stayed, of course, he would actually have *seen* the truth, enthroned before him as a suffering body. Therefore, Hamann suggests, in turning his back, Pilate has separated the inquiry after truth from sensory vision. Moreover he has not simply turned his back on sensation and the body. His gesture of handwashing implies either that he is about to eat a meal or that he has carried out a death sentence. The former, for Hamann, is the figure of a basely sensual relation to reality: we consume it, altogether end it, for our pleasure. The second, however, is a figure for a purely rational relation to the world: it, too, *ends* the real (though without ingesting the corpse) because it abstracts from it, or takes from it only what is absolutely clearly graspable: but this of course must remove all its qualities, its objective existence, and even its real spatiality, since this dissolves into space-less points and lines. The rational gaze on space evaporates the real into phantoms, whereas to hold on to each reality we must regard it as an unfathomable 'revelation'.

Equally, a rational gaze which seeks the objectively true, must seek the stable, and therefore that which can be 'held still' in a present instance. But since, argues Hamann in his 'Fliegende Brief', the present moment is also a measureless point, here too the rational gaze on time must lose hold of the real.[14] Reason, pure philosophic reason, like modern science, has, he claims, a totally non-realist impulse, which leaves commonsense perception altogether behind. It turns out by contrast – and here Hamann like Jacobi is indebted to both Hume and Reid – that a kind of 'faith' is involved in everyday life when we recognise the real.[15] This does *not at all* mean for Hamann, or for Jacobi, that since we know only what we think, or our own inner sensations, we need faith to believe in an external world or our own noumenal reality. On the contrary, both thinkers (especially Jacobi) believe, after Reid, that we see directly the real world, *not* mirrored sensations from which we 'infer' the real, and both also believe that our ontological identity lies only in our characteristic patterns of repeated external action.[16] The question is rather – are these primary appearances themselves disclosive of the real, or do they float upon a void to which they afford no clue? If we assume the latter, then the only solid reality in things will be what we can *logically* grasp as instantiating repeated *laws*, and the commonsense reality of things will then evaporate in the manner already indicated. As Jacobi argued in relation to Spinoza, if pure reason can accept as real only the identically repeated according to logically necessitated laws, then a fated chain without meaning must float above an abyss identified by the fundamental law of identity: $a = a$. This abyss is the underlying real, and yet it is nothing; the only 'something' is the phenomenal fated flux, yet as only phenomenal this is *also* nothing.

In this fashion, Jacobi was able to argue that the Spinozistic absolute, being not *in addition* to its phenomenal modes of expression, was a void, and that Spinozism was really nihilism.[17] Moreover, by claiming that Leibniz and Wolff equally identified the real with the logically necessitated, Jacobi was also able to claim that all Germanic rationalism could take a consistent form only as an immanentist nihilism on the Spinozistic pattern.[18] Finally and supremely, he was able to show that Kant's critical turn left unperturbed the requirement that the real be only recognised before a court of irresistible rational necessity (even if this now admitted the synthetic *a priori*) and with the same basic upshot: the Spinozistic void re-appears as the things-in-themselves which are epistemologically nothing, and therefore beyond Kant (as Fichte soon agreed with Jacobi) might as well *be* nothing. And again, what we truly know are only appearances – so, in effect, once more: nothing.[19]

These steps of the argument are spelled out by Jacobi rather than Hamann; indeed Hamann denied that he was prepared to affirm that Spinozism must lead to nihilism.[20] And yet here, as elsewhere, there is a certain strange peevishness about Hamann's response to Jacobi, which disguises the fact that he nearly always concurs with the latter. Hence in the present case, Hamann claims precisely that philosophical abstraction makes real appearances vanish, and that without God, created things can only be perceived as *nothing* since they are, indeed, in themselves nothing.[21] His short cryptic statements to this effect seem to require an elucidation along the lines of Jacobi's argumentation. And it is, in fact, this line of reasoning, despite Hamann's accusation that Jacobi was too otherworldly, which alone secures the central Hamannian insight that worship of God and celebration of corporeality and sensual beauty absolutely require each other. For the point here for

26

Hamann is that we have a sense of the corporeal *depth* of things only because we take the surface of things as signs disclosing or promising such a depth. This primordial and spontaneous human attitude has, Hamann claims, a 'religious' dimension in that it takes appearances as disclosing the real, as *declaring* or 'revealing' something to us, such that the natural unseen depth of things goes, as it were, 'all the way back' – the solidity of things derives from an eternal permanence.[22] Otherwise, as we have seen, if we take things as *only* finite, their solidity paradoxically vanishes. Equally, certain apparently real properties of things, like colours, being not fully comprehensible by reason, will tend to vanish also. Hence there is a spontaneous trust involved in perception that is indeed like a kind of faith, even an implicit faith in God. And by comparison with this perspective, the Kantian view that we perceive only within a supposed legal constitution of the finite is a false modesty that must turn dialectically into Promethean *hubris*: since, if the finite does not convey some inkling of the infinite, it might as well be a finitude our subjectivity has somehow constructed and the infinite might as well be the trans-subjective abyss our subjectivity emerges from and again negatively projects – as Fichte, Hegel and Schelling all in the last analysis concluded.[23]

Now it might well seem that what we have here in the radical pietist account of knowledge as faith is a kind of appeal to natural religion by a natural theology. And in a sense this is true: Hamann and Jacobi were children of the Enlightenment. And yet the logic of this argument about natural faith is very much that it requires faith in the God who creates *ex nihilo* and sustains all in being, rather than a remote, designing deity. Furthermore, for Hamann at least (though Jacobi sometimes echoes this) we can never have an abstract faith in God as author of nature, sustaining the reality of things, without *reading* these things in their specific, revealed and always *historical* contingency as the primary divine language. Here again it is a question of invisible depth as *alone* securing the reality of the apparent. Hamann persistently claims, in 'Aesthetica in Nuce' and elsewhere, that we only *see* things when they *speak* to us, or that we cannot have sight if we are deaf.[24] What exactly can this mean? Hamann explicates his position with the biblical phrase, 'one day tells another, and night makes known to the other'.[25] What he seems to mean is that we *never* grasp a thing in isolation, but only as articulated with something else, and yet that in such articulation there is a necessary 'taking together', or reading of the conjunction over and above what merely appears: for example a tree does not *appear* to me as one tree, rather I *construe* this. Yet if such reading or construing is taken as non-arbitrary this means that what is invisible in the tree 'speaks' to me as one tree, just as day must 'speak' to day if they are to form an organised series of categorised periods. It is for this reason that Hamann always links the 'depth' in things with the depth in the human subject which images the creative power of God (especially in 'Aesthetica in Nuce'). Day may speak to day, and night to night, but I know this only if I creatively express it, and make the sign 'day' a non-identically repeatable expression. Following Berkeley, Hamann understands universal concepts as having a non-abstractive *validity* in this necessary use of signs to decipher the analogically continuous aspects of reality.[26] This shows clearly that he was not, like Luther, a nominalist, but rather, like Jacobi (and Berkeley), a subtle sort of realist, and is further evidence that his critique of abstraction belongs to a Jacobi-style assault upon the nihilism of philosophy, rather than a somewhat tame empiricist critique of universals.[27]

The idea that the natural human response to the world in faith is a reading of the world as a language emanating from a mysterious source directs faith, as I have said, already in a somewhat contingent, historical direction, especially when the necessary mediation by culturally specific human language is allowed for. But Hamann's reflections upon time take us further down the path of revealed specificity. Here, if the parable for truth in space was the case of Pontius Pilate, the parable for truth in time is the story of the three wise men.[28] These magi, according to Hamann, lived prophetically, by faith, which is to say that they retained in their memory certain images which they judged appealing – the legend of a star and a birth – and projected these into the future according to their desires. Since, as we have seen, for Hamann the present moment is never punctually present, objective vision is always interfered with by selective memory and prompting desire.[29] To know, Hamann repeatedly suggests, is to select and desire, and even chains of reasonings, beyond the case of mere tautology, are only aesthetically preferred patterns.[30] Thus, for Hamann, the philosopher and the natural scientist who take their knowledges for the final truth are merely men with a highly stringent, puritanical sense of taste. But not so the real wise men – they set off, on a pure whim, on a lure, irresponsibly into the unknown. In doing so they abandoned their own legal king for a rumoured monarch, precipitated the massacre of innocent babies in a foreign land and forced the baby messiah they sought to flee to Egypt. The story, claims Hamann, shows the uselessness of good intentions, as also of *all assumptions*, upon which reason nonetheless relies – for the magi sought a king, but found a baby. But despite their apparent failures to do good or know the truth, the wise men are nonetheless justified by faith because, unlike Pilate, they have lived *solely* to see the truth, and thereby have become a part of the story of this truth and its sign.

The lesson here, for Hamann, is that God alone is good, alone true, alone being, and as there is nothing extra alongside God, the best we can do is *wait* to discover our identity which is 'hidden with Christ in God'. But this waiting is also a journey: since, after the fall, we no longer persist in our identity in God, we must set off on an eschatological pilgrimage in which we hope to see God's restoration in person of the human form. After the fall, there is nothing we can do or know for ourselves that is either good or true, beyond this journeying in expectancy. However, though we cannot guarantee either our intentions or observations, it is enough to discern and desire in trust and hope that we will then participate in some fragmentary way in the divine design. There is, one should note, no Lutheran duality of faith and works involved here: rather, Hamann plays up the more radical 'antinomian' side of Luther when he suggests that faith itself is a new kind of doing good, and he affirms this by making love, in a Catholic fashion, as vital for salvation as is faith.[31] This story, in effect, is Hamann's attack on 'the beautiful soul': like Hegel afterwards, he seems to place the 'political', in the sense of a risky acting for the human future, above a personal attempt to 'be moral'; unlike Hegel, however (as Oswald Bayer rightly points out), he does not seek to secure this action in trust in an objective universal knowledge, any more than in a reliable intuition. Instead he secures it in a recollection (*Wiedererinnerung*) of the divine word which (unlike the Enlightenment's reason) was never perfectly present to us in the first place, and therefore must be ceaselessly heard and expressed in action ever anew.[32]

[margin handwriting: Grounds for morality]

One should note here also that it is precisely this 'political' dimension which integrates 'the spirit of observation' with the 'spirit of prophecy' – for although the present moment is never simply 'there', neither is Hamann content (like post-structuralism) to dissolve time into a pure formless flux. The point of life is rather to set up, in hope, certain contingent structures of truth and justice – to set up Jerusalem not Babylon, and no Lutheran duality of law and gospel is invoked here – informed by our entire feeling-imbued and also hermeneutically discursive response to the world and present only in so far as they are taken to reflect eternity, since eternity alone can truly be present at all.[33] Here one can see most acutely how Hamann and Jacobi's 'realism' involves no *mimesis* of an external real but rather (and in this instance Jacobi like Herder echoes Spinoza) the expressive registering of the other according to our own creative modality. We *correspond* to the other only in so far as our expressions approximate to the entire expression of the thing by the mind of God, which is the thing's actual existence over against nothing. This is *not at all* like the constructivism of German idealism, which oscillates between or combines a pure voluntarism and a pre-determination of the will by logic, since it still assumes an empty subject over against a given alien object in the Cartesian mode. Instead, for the radical pietists (Herder as well as Jacobi and Hamann) creative expression is the answer of a specific, positioned subject to an object which itself mediates a personal address, and it is governed neither by will nor by logic, but by faith which seeks simultaneously to utter an adequate song of praise to the divine and to construct a more adequate humanity. We are to act, with the whole person, which is to say 'religiously', *rather* than simply to know – which is always to deny, to negate – or than simply to feel, which would be to dissolve into 'the night' of poetic Romanticism or pagan fatalism which for Hamann is dialectically identical with its seeming opposite, philosophical abstraction.[34]

Thus where poetry was primitively linked to the 'kyriological', speaking in mimetic pictures, and philosophy is linked to an equally *purely spatial* script of algebraic abstraction (a *mathesis*), prophecy, politics and history are linked to the 'hieroglyphic', or to cryptic symbols which must be deciphered by memory and desire. In deciphering these symbols we must, thinks Hamann, as humans in a fallen world, submit always to a *philologia crucis*, to the cross of the anguished, fearful and uncertain, though not thereby merely arbitrary, act of literary judgement.[35]

In this fashion, Hamann's notion of natural faith and naturally 'prophetic' habitation of the earth turns imperceptibly towards Christology. And yet the latter secretly has priority all along, for a simple reason: in a fallen world, humans do *not* generally have a clear awareness that the world is God's speaking it out of a void; this is normally prevented by the double departure of Pontius Pilate – of the body towards sensuality, and of the mind towards disembodiment. From neither the body gone astray nor the mind gone astray can any truth emerge *except* as an obscure prophetic seeking for re-integration into a *genuinely* erotic body for which desire would not consume, and knowing would remain a desiring. This genuinely erotic body is fully restored only in Christ, who offers it to his bride, the Church, or to all Christian souls, who through this union do again receive the world as divine appearance and divine speaking.[36] Hence Hamann can declare that only the God–man resolves the (nihilistic) contradictions of philosophy, since philosophy, of its own resources, must engage in Pilate's double dismissal: of reality either into phenomenal consumed nothingness, or else into abstractly crucified intellectual nothingness.[37] This, for Hamann, also corresponds to Kant's arbitrary sundering of linguistic expression into supposed sensory intuition without conceptuality on the one hand and a conceptual structure supposedly free of intuitive presence on the other.[38] Thus in Pilate, precisely, we see what human rule and reason is: the slaying, through indifference and impatience of the God–man or the human future.

The above considerations suggest that any neo-orthodox accusation that Hamann 'naturalises' faith would miss the point of his radical questioning of dubious modern distinctions. But at the same time we should resist, also, Balthasar's 'Catholic' accusation that Hamann fails to respect the specificities of our natural existence.[39] I doubt whether this suggestion is true to the Greek Fathers, Augustine or even Aquinas, since if for them, as Balthasar, following de Lubac, recognises, nature was finally defined by its orientation to the supernatural, then this leaves nothing in nature which the light of faith might not re-interpret and indeed no true nature which has *not* been transfigured by grace. Thus Aquinas says that *all* the conclusions of philosophy are open to deepening and transformation by theology (ST I. q.1. a1, a5). And even if Hamann's Lutheranism renders him more radical than ancient tradition, he is still not necessarily wrong. After all, his conclusions are informed by a correct sense, unavailable to the ancient tradition, of the sheer natural and cultural contingency of all our reasonings. This suggests, indeed, that our only solid anthropological resource may now be Christological; that is to say that we can construe some faint human integrity only from the point where we glimpse an absolute integrity. Thus Hamann, in an astonishing fashion, denies, against Herder, all the usual claims to the effect that we have some *attribute* distinguishing us from the animals. All supposed differences in kind *cannot* really be distinguished *in* kind, he says, from differences in degree: we are simply a more various, more imitating, more multi-voiced, more open-ended sort of animal.[40] Our language derives from no special faculty (since what would we know of this outside external linguistic practice?) and is just our peculiar mode of animal behaviour, given with us, expressed by us, but *not* invented by us. This would seem to leave us but a higher gorilla, an unruly, *nihilistic*, aggressive animal, were it not for Hamann's remarkable

Christological overlay. The relation of spiritual depth to bodily surface in us, he suggests, is like that of the hypostatic union of God and Man in Christ, construed in terms of the Lutheran *communicatio idiomatum*.[41] Just as with Christ, we *see* only his human nature, and his divine nature is manifested in the unique narrative pattern of his life which has the integrity of the *divine* person and *logos*, so also all we *see* in human beings are animals, but it is the beauty of their unique form of life, their strange 'political' blending of solitude and sociality which displays, in human personhood, a human nature.[42] Hence it is only our faint anticipation and then echo of a divine redeemed humanity, intelligently erotic, erotically intelligent, which *at all* distinguishes us as more than animal, more than *nihilistic*. But for philosophy, Hamann allows that there is no longer any stable identifiable human essence. Therefore Balthasar is wrong to think that any natural integrity of humanity has here been violated by an over-hasty anticipation of grace. On the contrary, it is surely true that the idea of 'soul' makes sense only as the echo in the creation of a creative source, and that the idea of soul/body unity only makes sense as the anticipated achievement of a right dwelling with other creatures: a right aesthetic judging and desiring of them *as* creatures under God.

If there *is* a fault in Hamann, then it might be that he tends to *replace* altogether a sense of an analogical ascent to God, or of a continuously deepened participation in divine eternity, with the notion of God's kenotic adaptation to us – in creation as well as in redemption. This allows for the incarnation and rightly deploys it as *a cipher*, but it does not allow for the equally New Testament notion that God became man in order to incorporate us into the Trinity – to make us indeed more heavenly and more spiritual, if not, thereby, less corporeal. This theme need not be in opposition to the looking for God in the future, but Hamann tends to displace a heavenly with a temporal eschatology. Yet here Hamann and Jacobi balance each other out: for while Jacobi embraces Hamann's Christology only fleetingly, Hamann lacks Jacobi's sense of a mystical ascent to unity with God.[43] As I have hinted, Hamann's attitude to Jacobi is strange and problematical, since he time and again accuses him either inaccurately or else of positions he himself embraces: thus, for example, Jacobi's category of intuitive feeling (*Empfindsamkeit*: the essential component of 'faith') does *not*, as Hamann alleges, exclude discursivity any more than it does for Hamann himself; nor, as Hamann implies, does Jacobi's idea of Platonic mental vision of eternal realities exclude a necessary mediation via physical seeing.[44] And, similarly, Hamann's claim that Jacobi is a mere fideist who denigrates reason is strange, for *both* men, and indeed Herder also, *redefine* reason as faith, and Hamann asserts that philosophy by itself does purely *negative* work in showing that it can in its own terms only conclude to contradiction and nothingness (it is in this way, as he says, like the law in Luther's theology). This assertion precisely parallels Jacobi's description of a Spinozistic or else Fichtean nihilism as the true philosophy if, and only if, one decides to remain in reason without faith.[45] Or again, Hamann's accusation that Jacobi hypostasises the word 'Being' ignores the fact that he construes it as the given created dimension of existence that reason can never catch up with, or check its reflections against, so that reflections, which we cannot avoid, remain the gestures of faith. And, indeed, Hamann himself argues that 'Being' for the Greeks was originally the fact of existence itself, beyond the philosophical dialectical determination of 'is' or 'is not'.[46] For Hamann, this original sense of Being as ontological and not ontic is continued and fulfilled by the theological diagnosis of 'is not' as *lack* – rather than as error construed as a kind of 'real absence' or 'real nothing', as dialectics on its own must suggest. And like Jacobi, once again, Hamann points out in his metacritique that once, in modern philosophy, God is bracketed out, we cannot escape merely subjective appearances, such that the real is reduced to the logically *possible*, and the primary subject of philosophy becomes not *ens* but *aliquid* (*etwas*) – something which might equally well be or not be.[47] For without God, *nothing* becomes as real and actual as actuality itself. This is the *irrational* conclusion which reason *must* reach. By contrast, only the transgression of reason by faith establishes common-sense reason which requires the priority of the actual. On this point, as on their fideistic realism, Hamann and Jacobi are agreed.

And herein lies the heart of their significance for today. Because they point theology to a radical orthodoxy they also show how theology can outwit nihilism. *Not* by seeking to reinstate reason, as many opponents of postmodernity would argue. This is absurd, because nihilism is *not* scepticism, nor relativism. No, as Hamann and Jacobi understood, the rational Enlightenment *already* in effect taught nihilism. For nihilism is the purest objectivity, since it is possible objectively to conclude that there is only nothing. Indeed, as Catherine Pickstock has argued, only nothing fulfils the conditions for a perfectly inert, controllable and present object.[48] What the radical pietists realised was that to be human means, primarily, that we must reckon with an immense depth behind things. There are only two possible attitudes to this depth: for the first, like Kant, we distinguish what is clear from what is hidden: but then the depth is an abyss, and what appears, as only apparent, will equally induce vertigo. This is why critical philosophy, the attitude of pure reason itself, is also the stance of nihilism. The twist added by postmodernism is simply that appearances themselves cannot be made clearly present, but are in ceaseless flux. The second possibility is that we trust the depth, and appearance as the gift of depth, and history as the restoration of the loss of this depth in Christ. By comparison with *this reason* – Christianity – we can see easily the secret identity of all impersonal religions which celebrate fate or the void with the nihilism of modernity. Hence it is indeed for radical orthodoxy an either/or: philosophy (Western or Eastern) as a purely autonomous discipline, or theology: Herod or the magi, Pilate or the God–man.[49]

Notes

1 See Karl Barth, *Protestant Theology in the Nineteenth Century*, trans. Brian Cozens *et al.* (London: SCM, 1972), p. 308: 'Philosophy, however, is in itself a strict study covering a vast field, and it is not for the theologian to conduct himself as if he were in a position to propound a philosophy, as if this were some subsidiary part of his office and to pull a philosopher's work to pieces, especially if that philosopher happens to be Kant.' See

also p. 339 where Barth sees Kant as preparing the way for a pure 'biblical theology'. It is perfectly true, however, that, as I say in the main text, Barth is in the end 'unclear' about the reach of theology: at times he can indeed sound 'radically orthodox' – especially when he insists that the real, concrete world is the world assumed by Christic enhypostasisation (yet even this affirmation runs into the problem that God can only assume, *incognito*, finite forms already confined by a supposedly known possible 'reach' of human intuition) . Nevertheless, his statements at the outset of *Church Dogmatics* that there *might be* a 'Philosophia Christiana', and that theology is only a 'stop-gap' in default of other disciplines ceasing to be 'pagan' and 'secular', are misleading. They have to be set in the context of his *thoroughly Baroque* (Gerhardt is invoked) account of theology itself as a positive science which measures the Church's 'talk of God' against 'the being of the Church' which is Jesus Christ. As such a science, theology is simply 'alongside' other sciences, and has its 'own object', whereas they have other objects. And, indeed, since the exegetical check on the Church's talk of God is in some sense objectively measurable, theology, in the strict sense as reflexive science, is itself 'secular' (and so, presumably, properly teachable in secular universities). Were the other sciences to cease being 'pagan' and 'secular' (in some sense), so rendering theology redundant, this, for Barth, would merely mean that they also, in terms of their own methods and (supposedly) inviolable spheres, as 'philosophy, history, sociology, psychology and pedagogics', would themselves carry out the testing of the Church's speech against God's revelation in Christ. From Barth's already quoted later remark regarding Kant, one can assume that this examination *cannot* really call into question their own construal of their objects and methods. Indeed, the opposite is the case; these objects and methods must be presumed to predetermine any inquiry they would carry out concerning the Church's authenticity. And given that, as Barth (rightly) says, theology is a sort of emergency measure with no special method of its own, presumably theology for Barth *is only* the *ad hoc* deployment of other positive sciences (especially historical sciences) to test the Church against exegesis (albeit with a *faith* that the Bible conveys the Word of God). But in that case theology is distinguished only by the specificity of its empirical object, and the question of whether this object can *call in question* the methods and supposed 'objects' of other sciences cannot really arise; theology remains liberal. It is significant that Barth does not seem to question the inherent secularity of sociology and psychology *as such*. It appears that they are purely 'secular' or 'pagan' only in not applying their approach to the Christological object: this application would, indeed (if they approached Christ in faith), help to tell us more about the most essential things concerning man – he is created, fallen, redeemed – yet this for Barth, it seems to follow, would leave intact and inviolable the limited and less important things one can know about man under the rubric of 'historical object' and so forth. What is lacking here is an older understanding of Christ as restoring to us participation in the mind of God: thus Christ *himself* as *theologic* (*logos*), not the 'object' of theology. Theology is *not* positive knowledge of an object, but finite intimation of infinite understanding. (Barth grasps, indeed, that God is not an object, yet only in a post-Kantian manner which confines God in himself to a formally known and uncharacterisable source; inversely, when God is shown, *it is* in the realm of objects which are in no sense transparent to Being as Being, the ground of the objective.) Hence, indeed, as Barth says, ideally theology is no special science, but the perspective to which all disciplines are orientated. However, since this is an all-inclusive (but not fully graspable) perspective, not just one perspective among many, other disciplines, especially philosophy, would become theological when they were *utterly transfigured*, when the infinite transformed their sense of their finite objects and methods, and in ever unpredictable ways. They would not become theological through applying their perspectives to Christ-as-object: here Barth reveals himself as thoroughly late-scholastic, thoroughly positivist, thoroughly muscle-bound by the constricting 'professional' norms of theology faculties. See Karl Barth, *Church Dogmatics*, vol. I, trans. G.W. Bromley (Edinburgh: T. & T. Clark,

1975), pp. 3–11. See also Bruce McCormack, *Karl Barth's Dialectically Realist Theology* (Oxford: Clarendon Press, 1995), pp. 207, 216–19, 221–23, 245–46, 280, 466.

2 Karl Barth, *Protestant Theology*, pp. 266–341, especially p. 338 where he misunderstands Herder's account of experience and faith as merely empiricist and p. 339 where he over-looks Herder's deployment of Hamann's meta-critique and asserts that Herder's redefining of faith as reason was 'bound to be exposed to a possibly lethal counterblast from the other side, in a sphere where pure rationalism was simply master'. Barth truly assumed that there *was* such a sphere. See also p. 482.

3 Hans Urs von Balthasar, *The Glory of the Lord: Theological Aesthetics*, vol. III, trans. Andrew Louth *et al.* (Edinburgh: T. & T. Clark, 1986) pp. 239–78. See also: Andrew Bowie, *Schelling and Modern Philosophy* (London: Routledge, 1993); *From Romanticism to Critical Theory* (London: Routledge, 1997), pp. 28–53; George di Giovanni, 'Introduction: the Unfinished Philosophy of Friedrich Heinrich Jacobi', in *The Main Philosophical Writings*, trans. G. di Giovanni (Montreal: McGill–Queen's, 1994), pp. 3–169; 'The First Twenty Years of Critique: the Spinoza connection', in *The Cambridge Companion to Kant*, ed. Paul Guyer (Cambridge: CUP, 1992), pp. 417–49; Frederich C. Beiser, *The Fate of Reason* (Cambridge, MA: Harvard, 1987); Klaus Hammacher (ed.), *Friedrich Heinrich Jacobi: Philosoph und Literat der Goethezeit* (Frankfurt-am-Main: Vittorio Klostermann, 1987), essays by M. Brüggen and Gerhard Höhn; Dieter Heinrich, *Der Grund im Bewusstsein: Untersuchungen zu Hölderlins Denken* (1794–5) (Munich: Klett-Cotta, 1992), pp. 17–185; Michael Allen Gillespie, *Nihilism Before Nietzsche* (Durham, NC, Duke: 1995).

4 On Hamann as Lutheran, see Oswald Bayer, *Zeitgenosse im Widerspruch; Johann Georg Hamann als Radikaler Aufklärer* (Munich: Piper, 1988); *Liebliches Wort: Reformation und Neuzeit im Konflikt* (Tübingen: J.C.B Mohr, 1992), pp. 105–51; *Schöpfung als Anrede* (Tübingen: J.C.B. Mohr, 1986), pp. 9–33. For the most crucial radical pietist account of 'knowledge by faith alone', see F.H. Jacobi, *David Hume on Faith, or Idealism and Realism, A Dialogue* (1787), in Giovanni, *The Main Philosophical Writings*, pp. 253–339, from the German *David Hume über den Glauben: oder Idealismus und Realismus, Ein Gespräch* (Breslau: Gottlieb Lowe, 1787).

5 See Jean-François Courtine, *Suarez et le Problème de la Métaphysique* (Paris: PUF, 1990); Eric Alliez, *Capital Times*, trans. Georges Van den Abbeele (Minneapolis: Minnesota UP, 1996), pp. 141–241; Michel de Certeau, *The Mystic Fable*, vol. I, trans. Steven Rendall (Berkeley, CA: University of California Press, 1984).

6 See Avery Dulles, *The Assurance of Things Hoped For: A Theology of Christian Faith* (New York: Oxford University Press, 1994); René Latourelle, *Theology of Revelation* (New York: Fordham UP, 1967).

7 See Alliez, *Capital Times*, pp. 141–241 and Lewis White Beck, *Early German Philosophy* (Bristol: Thoemmes, 1996), pp. 160–306.

8 Jacobi, *Jacobi to Fichte* in *The Main Philosophical Writings*, pp. 498–536, especially p. 519; from the German *Jacobi an Fichte* (Hamburg: Perthes, 1799).

9 J.G. Hamann, 'A Flying Letter to Nobody Whom Everybody Knows', in Ronald Gregor Smith, *J.G. Hamann: A Study in Christian Existence* (London: Collins), pp. 234–36; 'Fliegende Brief', in *Johann Georg Hamann, Sämtliche Werke*, ed. Josef Nadler, vol. III, pp. 348–409; referred to as Nadler, hereafter.

10 See Phillip Blond, 'Theology and Perception', in *Modern Theology* (forthcoming); for reason and event in Hamann, see 'Socratic Memorabilia', in Dickson, p. 383 (see note 12); 'Socratische Denkwurdigkeiten', in Nadler, II, p. 69: 'every and each idea can be seen as a special and entire birth in itself'.

11 See Alexander Dru, *The Church in the Nineteenth Century: Germany 1800–1918* (London: Burns & Oates, 1963), pp. 27–86.

12 J.G. Hamann, 'Philologische Einfalle und Zweifel', in Nadler, III , p. 37. Gwen Griffith Dickson indeed translates *lebensart* as 'form of life': Gwen Griffith Dickson, trans. 'Philological Ideas and Doubts', in her *Johann Georg Hamann's Relational Metacriticism* (Berlin: Walter de Gruyter, 1995), p. 477.

13 J.G. Hamann, 'Aesthetica in Nuce', trans. G.G. Dickson in Dickson, p. 420; Nadler, II, p. 206.
14 J.G. Hamann, 'A Flying Letter', in Ronald Gregor Smith, p. 234; Nadler, III, pp. 382–84.
15 See Hamann, 'Philological Ideas and Doubts', Dickson, pp. 479–80; Nadler, III, p. 40; 'Socratic Memorabilia', Dickson, p. 387; 'our own Being and the existence of all things outside us must be believed and can be made out no other way', p. 391 (Nadler, II, p. 73); see Dickson, p. 392 (Nadler, II, p. 74); 'Aesthetica in Nuce', Dickson, p. 420: 'Your lying murderous philosophy has cleared nature out of the way'; 'All colours of the *fairest* world pale; as soon as its light, the *first-born* of creation, is quenched' (Nadler, II, p. 206). Hamann goes on to say that, when the real is lost through sensuality, 'Every creature will become alternately your sacrificial offering and your idol.' That is to say, sensuality *like* rationalism establishes an immanentism which oscillates between over-valuing and undervaluing creatures; but since in the end every idol may be replaced by a new one, the real logic of immanentism is continual sacrifice to the void: nihilism as the consummation of a pagan sacrificial order. For Jacobi, see J.H. Jacobi, *David Hume on Faith*, especially p. 266.
16 *David Hume on Faith*, pp. 265–66 (*David Hume über den Glauben*, pp. 24–28), and see di Giovanni's note 20 on p. 608; p. 297 and note to Jacobi's footnote 22 on p. 640; *Concerning the Doctrine of Spinoza* (1785), p. 240: here 'life style' dictates 'thought style', and see p. 231; *Ueber die Lehre des Spinoza* (Breslau: Gottlob Löwe, 1785), pp. 186–89, 163–65; also *Concerning the Doctrine of Spinoza* (1789), p. 370 (*Ueber die Lehre des Spinoza*, 1789, pp. 402–4). (The 1785 and 1789 datings represent the first and second versions of the work on Spinoza.)
17 *Concerning the Doctrine of Spinoza* (1785), p. 190: 'But as far as the one infinite substance of Spinoza is concerned, it has no determinate existence on its own outside the individual things' (*Ueber die Lehre*, 1785, p. 21).
18 *Concerning the Doctrine of Spinoza* (1785), p. 191 (*Ueber die Lehre*, 1785, pp. 22–24), and in general.
19 *David Hume on Faith*, pp. 284 ff. (*David Hume über den Glauben*, pp. 84 ff.); *David Hume on Faith* ('Preface', 1815), pp. 543–56; *Friedrich Heinrich Jacobi's Werke*, ed. J.F. Köppen and C.J.F. Roth 1815, vol. II, pp. 16–45.
20 See Hamann's letters to Jacobi: 23 January 1785, 27 April 1787, in *Briefwechsel*, Funfter Band, R.G. Smith, pp. 255–56; *Briefwechsel*, Siebster Band.
21 'Socratic Memorabilia', Dickson, p. 392 (Nadler II, p. 74); 'Konxompax' Nadler, III, p. 224; 'Fragments', in R.G. Smith 163; Bayer, *Schöpfung als Anrede*, p. 30.
22 'Aesthetica in Nuce', Dickson pp. 409–31 (Nadler, II, pp. 195–217), especially pp. 418 (Nadler, II, p. 204) and 420 (Nadler, II, p. 206); Letter to Jacobi 1 December 1784, R.G. Smith, p. 250, *Briefwechsel*, Funfter Band: "Original Being is Truth, Communicated Being is Grace'.
23 See Gillespie, *Nihilism Before Nietzsche*.
24 'Aesthetica in Nuce', Dickson, p. 412 (Nadler, II, p. 198).
25 *Ibid.*
26 J.G. Hamann, 'Metacritique of the Purism of Reason', Dickson, p. 519; 'Metakritik über den Purismus der Vernunft', p. 283; 'Aesthetica in Nuce', Dickson, p. 418 (Nadler, II, p. 204).
27 See J.H. Jacobi, *David Hume on Faith* ('Preface', 1815), di Giovanni, pp. 538–90; *Jacobi's Werke*, vol. II, pp. 4–123, where he sets out most fully his Platonism. For a denial of Berkeley's supposed nominalism, see John Milbank, 'The linguistic turn as a theological turn', in *The Word Made Strange: Theology, Language, Culture* (Oxford: Blackwell, 1997), pp. 84–123.
28 J.G. Hamann, 'The Wise Men from the East in Bethlehem', R.G. Smith, pp. 190–93; 'Die Magi aus Morgenlande zu Bethlehem', Nadler, II, pp. 139–41.

29 'Flying Letter', R.G. Smith, pp. 234–36 (Nadler, III, pp. 382–84).
30 'Socratic Memorabilia', Dickson, pp. 392 (Nadler, II, p. 74): 'The connection and agreement of concepts is precisely the same in a demonstration as the relation and sympathy of numbers and lines, sounds and colours are in a musical composition and painting.'
31 On Luther in this respect, see John Milbank, 'Can Morality be Christian?', in *The Word Made Strange*, pp. 219–33.
32 Oswald Bayer, *Leibliches Wort*, pp. 123 and 125–48.
33 'Flying Letter', R.G. Smith, p. 234 (Nadler, III, p. 382): 'Philosophical genius expresses its power by striving, by means of abstraction, to make the present absent, unclothing real objects and making them naked concepts and merely thinkable attributes, pure appearances and phenomena. Poetic genius expresses its power by transfiguring, by means of fiction, the visions of the absent past and future into present representations. Criticism and Politics resist usurpation by both powers, and try to preserve a balance by means of the same positive forces and means of observation and prophecy.' See also von Balthasar, p. 271.
34 'Aesthetica in Nuce', Dickson, p. 420 (Nadler, II, p. 206). Here Hamann associates the poet with night and polytheism (many stars) in contrast to the 'daylight' of Christianity's 'single truth': the true enlightenment of faith. Yet at the same time the original poetic language is described as *kyriological*, alluding in part to *kyriôs*, and it is said that 'The poet at the beginning of days is *the same* as the thief at the end of days' – alluding to the eschatological coming of Christ as a thief in the night. The point is that, though for now we must live in the conjecturally prophetic and projectively political associated with the cryptically 'hieroglyphic', in the end the fully pictorial ('poetic') will return, but the one God will prove far more vivid than the many. For Jacobi's *positive* use of Spinoza, see *Concerning the Doctrine of Spinoza* in both 1785 and 1789 versions. For Herder, see *God: Some Conversations* (1787), trans. F.H. Burkhardt (New York : Veritas 1940).
35 J.G. Hamann, 'Kreuzzüge des Philologen', Nadler, II, pp. 113–246.
36 Balthasar, pp. 255, 257–62 (see note 3 above).
37 'Konxompax', Nadler, III, p. 222.
38 'Metacritique of the Purism of Reason', Dickson, pp. 519–25 (Nadler, III, pp. 283–89).
39 Balthasar, pp. 276–77.
40 J.G. Hamann, 'Herderschriften', Dickson, pp. 445–505 (Nadler, III, pp. 15, 17–19, 20–23, 27–33, 37–53), especially 'Philological Ideas and Doubts', Dickson, p. 477 (Nadler, III, p. 37).
41 'Philological Ideas and Doubts', Dickson, p. 479 (Nadler, III, p. 39): 'The *analogy* of the animal economy is the only *ladder* to the *anagogical* knowledge of the spiritual economy'; Dickson, p. 480 (Nadler, III, p. 40): Philosophers who try to separate soul and body are 'heretics of psychology', 'Arians' who 'try to give an account of the soul from a *single positive power* or *entelechy*'; 'The Last Will and Testament of the Knight of the Rose-Cross on the Divine and Human Origin of Language', Dickson, p. 463; 'Die Ritter von Rosencreuz lezte Willensmennung', Nadler, III, p. 27: 'The *communicatio* of divine and human *idiomatum* is a fundamental law and the principle key of all our knowledge and the entire visible economy.'
42 'Philological Ideas and Doubts', Dickson, p. 477 (Nadler, III, p. 37).
43 'Aesthetica in Nuce', Dickson, p. 418 (Nadler, II, p. 204): God's *kenosis* in creation is 'A miracle of such infinite silence, that makes God as nothing', 'Golgotha and Scheblimini', R.G. Smith, p. 225; 'Golgotha und Scheblimini', Nadler, III, pp. 303–4: 'Because I too know of no eternal truths save those which are unceasingly temporal, I do not need to mount into the cabinet of the divine understanding nor into the sanctuary of the divine will . . .'; see J.H. Jacobi, *Concerning the Doctrine of Spinoza* (1785), p. 231 (*Ueber die Lehre*, 1785, pp. 164–66), citing Hamann's 'Golgotha und Scheblimini' (Nadler, III, p. 313) and *David Hume on Faith* ('Preface', 1815), for Jacobi's account of analogical

ascent. Although Hamann speaks much of analogy this means mostly 'horizontal', inner worldly analogy between finite things on the model of eighteenth-century English writers like Young and Butler; Balthasar goes wrong in assuming this is to do with something akin to the *analogia entis*.

44 See Jacobi and *David Hume on Faith* ('Preface', 1815) and Hamann's letters to Jacobi of 27 April 1787 and 29 April 1787, R.G. Smith, pp. 255–57; *Briefwechsel*, Siebster Band.

45 Hamann, 'Socratic Memorabilia', Dickson, p. 392 (Nadler, II, p. 74); Balthasar, p. 268; Jacobi, *Concerning the Doctrine of Spinoza*, and *Jacobi to Fichte*, in de Giovanni (ed.), *The Main Philosophical Writings* (see note 4 above).

46 Hamann to Jacobi, 1 December 1784, R.G. Smith, p. 250; *Briefwechsel*, Funfter Band; J.H. Jacobi, *Concerning the Doctrine of Spinoza* (1785), p. 231 (*Ueber die Lehre*, pp. 163–64). It should be mentioned here that both di Giovanni and Beiser, like many others, accept the notion of a Hamann–Jacobi rift, though the former acknowledges Hamann's 'peevish' tone. Yet Jacobi saw no rift, and Hamann's claim that his own position is quite different does not bear examination.

47 'Metacritique of the Purism of Reason', Dickson, pp. 519–20 (Nadler, III, pp. 283–84): Hamann alleges that for the 'subjective conditions' of transcendental philosophy, 'All, Something and Nothing can be taken as the object, source or kind of knowledge.'

48 Catherine Pickstock, *After Writing: On the Liturgical Consummation of Philosophy* (Oxford: Blackwell, 1997) Chapter 3.

49 I do not, however, imply here any exact analogue between my attitude to philosophy here and that taken towards 'social science' in my *Theology and Social Theory: Beyond Secular Reason* (Oxford: Blackwell, 1990). In the latter work, social science was refused because its very *objects* were deemed fictional: e.g. in the case of sociology its 'society' was deciphered as an illusory, ahistorical, transcendental *a priori*. Here, however, the 'object' of Philosophy – being – is not denied; rather it is argued, after Jacobi, that a philosophical treatment of being on its own, or the search simply to know being by reason, will reach aporetic and nihilistic conclusions. Yet reason *cannot* ground the attempted purely rational disclosure of being, and rationally the disclosure by faith remains possible. Theology *can* evaluate philosophy: moreover this allows one to surpass the aporetic, as hinted above. Therefore theology saves reason and *fulfils* and *preserves* philosophy, whereas philosophy left to itself, brings itself, as Heidegger saw, to its own end.

2

REVELATION

The false legacy of Suárez

John Montag SJ

Introduction

One of the great difficulties of all-knowing modernity (including postmodernism and the other reactionary '-isms' into which it tends to fragment itself) is its blindness to its own blindnesses. Recent critical historical analysis[1] has at least pointed out how these very blindnesses have structured the modern way of looking at the past. This limited way of looking involves all disciplines, so that, like any other discipline, much modern theology suffers the same kinds of faulty vision about its past. One remarkable insensibility has to do with the modern notion of revelation. Specifically, certain trends in modern theology fail to come to terms with the origin of the notion of revelation from within modernity itself and its metaphysical framework, rather than from patristic or medieval notions. Given that so many Christian theologians, both Catholic and Protestant, regard revelation as the most fundamental category, this lacuna takes on particular significance for any account of theology within modernity.

One contemporary apologist for versions of this modern notion of revelation, Avery Dulles, has recognized that 'the biblical authors and theologians prior to the sixteenth century rarely used the term "revelation" in the modern sense as a technical concept to designate whatever is needed to make something a matter of divine faith.'[2] Instead, he confirms that the term *revelatio*, when used by these 'older authors,' has a differently restricted sense, 'usually understood as an extraordinary psychic occurrence in which hidden things are suddenly made known through mental phenomena such as visions and auditions' – what today is considered 'special' or 'private revelation,'[3] or perhaps something of what Thomas Aquinas and other medieval theologians thought of as prophetic inspiration. Dulles goes on to acknowledge that

> if we today say that the events together with their interpretation are revelation, that is because we are drawing on certain modern conceptions of revelation, which must first be justified. For a systematic treatment, therefore, it seems best to begin with contemporary theology. In the light of a

systematic conception of revelation the biblical scholar or the church historian can then find elements of a theology of revelation in the Bible and in the ancient and medieval theologians.[4]

Dulles properly places his fundamental theology before the project of dogmatics and apologetics. He wishes to provide possible foundations to dogma, but through a properly theological discipline.[5] Yet even this pre-dogmatic, pre-apologetic, foundation begins and ends in a Baroque problematic, as will be shown. Indeed, despite his pre-apologetic positioning, Dulles's effort is to some degree dictated by the objections of F. Gerald Downing,[6] who argues against the coherence of any modern notion of revelation. Without having to defend all of Downing's arguments, one can admit that his emphasis on the historical variation and the inconsistency of use of the term 'revelation' points up many difficulties in trying to offer a *prima facie* account of the notion.

Hence, Dulles chooses his method of approach from within his specific tradition of contemporary theology as a way to anchor an account of the disparate notions of revelation into a nuanced and broadly coherent overview. Systematic theology as he conceives it, however, may neglect to attend to the different historical situations in which such systems take form; it then remains blind to the formative shifts of meaning and especially the discontinuities and incommensurabilities involved in such shifts. Even where such an overview rehearses historical differences, it remains ahistorical in its approach. Dulles's method of reading the systematic conception of revelation back into history may help to understand the ideas and attitudes of the past *in terms of contemporary ideas*, but it also may actively obscure precisely how these contemporary ideas find true and critical rivals in these former ways of understanding. Whatever systematic theology may be, it has a task other than the laying bare of the 'archaeology of ideas,' without which the mere translation of ideas into one's own conceptual idiom masks their gaps and discontinuities through accommodation. By ignoring the egg-shells of earlier notions which cling to the contemporary conception, such reading-back cannot offer an accurate sense of the development of a given understanding, nor its directedness within a living tradition.[7]

In any case, accounts of the modern concept of revelation do not lack for such rehearsals of historical difference.[8] However, most discussions during at least the first half of this century (and even later) have focused less often on late sixteenth- and early seventeenth-century scholastic theology,[9] looking to either the periods of development of doctrine in the apostolic, patristic and early medieval centuries, to the early sixteenth century and the Reformation, or finally to the period of apologetics during the late seventeenth and eighteenth centuries.[10] The neglect of this period may be due to two prejudices. Primarily, some scholars give a general impression of unproblematic continuity between medieval scholastic thought and late or Baroque scholasticism, which may suggest a lack of development. In addition, some regard such late-scholastic thought as already too decadent or obsolete to be worthy of careful consideration. A brief glance at the times, however, and especially at the thought of Francisco Suárez SJ[11] may show that such presumptions are unwarranted.

Surprisingly, studies of early modern thought often neglect Suárez, except in passing. Works on modern philosophy and political thought make more room for him, but most often he is relegated to studies on late medieval thought, which normally place him squarely within the late-scholastic revival of Thomism in Spain.[12] Admittedly, the authors of such works often recognize Renaissance philosophy and theology as well, noting the transitional character of the period. Nevertheless, they tend also to emphasize that Spain's medieval character outlasted that of the rest of Europe, surviving until its *siglo de oro* in the sixteenth century. Spain never truly had a 'renaissance' like much of the rest of Europe, and was left relatively unscathed by the humanist rejection of scholasticism. Hence, a direct connection passes between St Thomas and his Paris-educated Dominican successors teaching at Salamanca in the early and mid-sixteenth century – Melchior Cano, Francisco de Vitoria, Domingo de Soto, Francisco de Toledo and others who had such a powerful influence on Suárez and Thomism in general. Suárez thus takes his place as the last medieval.

The story, however, is not so simple. Between thirteenth-century Paris and seventeenth-century Coimbra lies a vast intellectual and cultural bottomland,[13] marked off by an often-rehearsed gamut of horrendous plagues, famines and wars; fundamental shifts in kinship and social roles; the rise of nations, vernaculars and new political institutions; immeasurably influential 'discoveries,' such as the Americas, the Copernican universe, and the printing press; and the spread of nominalism, the Great Schism, and the Reformation, to mention only the most salient landmarks. Apparent continuity with the style and content of discussions from the Middle Ages often misleads into superficial identifications. And after all, 'decadent' though the Baroque Spanish scholasticism may have been – especially in comparison to the thirteenth-century scholasticism of the University of Paris – its influence was nonetheless profound, not only on Catholic philosophy and theology, but on the development of modernity in general.[14]

Many standard accounts of revelation from the first half of the twentieth century typically follow the same view of history, recognizing a general continuity and even a close identity between the use of the term *revelatio* (or *apokalupsis*) from the biblical through the medieval periods and on into early modernity. Suddenly with the reform movements of the sixteenth century, and especially with the rise of rationalism in the seventeenth, the modern notion is seemingly born Athena-like from out of the arcane scholastic elucidations.[15] Any heterogeneity of thought that may have existed between the deaths of Thomas Aquinas and Cajetan is of little consequence in such accounts. The problem usually traces to the difficulty outlined above: a simplistic conflation of all the theology and philosophy between *c.* 1150 and 1550 (or 1650 and later, for Roman Catholicism) into a simple category called 'scholasticism,' of which the most important and influential part is 'Thomism.' There were, however, many scholasticisms, and even a great variety of Thomisms, not all of which Thomas himself would likely have embraced.

Early modern theology faculties often established diverse chairs in an attempt to domesticate the different scholasticisms that had grown up around the religious families active in the university (mainly Franciscans and Dominicans) and the more secularized nominalists, each of which taught constellations of rival doctrines.[16] No doubt, as this kind of multiplicity lost its dialectical vitality, it became a sign of the very decadence in scholasticism to which the humanists such as Erasmus objected so strongly. But this multivalent scholasticism itself, and especially the culmination of the sixteenth-century revival of Thomism at Salamanca in the work of Suárez, already carried within it the seeds of modernity. 'Suárez,' Alasdair MacIntyre comments, 'both in his preoccupations and in his methods, was already a distinctively modern thinker, perhaps more authentically than Descartes the founder of modern philosophy.'[17]

Nonetheless, given this sort of habitual conflation of scholasticisms, we seem readily able to give a uniform account of the use of the notion of *revelatio* in the *Summa theologiae* in terms of its use in the commentaries on the *Summa* of the sixteenth-century professors at Salamanca. This uniform account has, until fairly recently (and despite much properly revisionist investigation[18]), been unproblematically called 'Thomist,' along with the apologetic dogmatic theology that came later. Leaving Thomas aside, Thomists (and many others), beginning in the seventeenth century, wrote countless treatises on the subject of revelation. Within the organization of modern Catholic dogmatic theology (at least until the second Vatican Council[19]), treatises *De revelatione sive vera religione* usually came first, both structurally and in order of importance, and were almost exclusively apologetic, serving primarily 'to vindicate the validity of dogma and its function of providing the premises for systematic rational theology.'[20] Most theologians today agree that the apologetic nature of these treatises, and indeed their very formulation, owe virtually everything to the deist polemics of the seventeenth and eighteenth centuries. Having got past that misunderstanding, it might seem that we have no need to account for the use of the term *revelatio* until then; such a usage no longer matters, since we have generally given up the apologetic orientation to dogmatics and the bind it engendered for theology. This attitude, of course, disregards the organic character of the legacy of dogmatic theology. We do better to take the Wittgensteinian principle that 'the way out is the way in' – we can escape the binds in which we find ourselves only by retracing and understanding the shifts and formations which led us into them. Insofar as 'revelation' remains attached to the vestiges of the apologetic dogmatics by which it was conceived, we may neglect the extent to which we are still bound by such a problematic approach when we discuss it in other ways, unless we uncover (and abandon) its historical roots.

Thus we can see how modernity circumscribes 'revelation.' Within Dulles's overview of the various 'models,' the only shift worth recognizing in the historical development of the notion of revelation seems to be the one separating the objectivist theory of propositional revelation developed by 'Thomists' and other scholastics (especially Suárezians) from the other accounts which have tried subsequently to address the shortcomings of this scholastic 'standard theory.' We are thus bound to see modern theology's notions of revelation not in terms of any constant which may be discerned throughout the history of belief, but rather in terms actually born from within modernity itself. We need to take advantage of the space opened up between Thomas and the Thomists in order the better to place the kinds of shift involved in the rise of this modern notion of revelation. In understanding how later scholasticism (and especially Suárez) is more modern than truly Thomist, we gain a better understanding of how the late-scholastic notion of revelation formulated modern rather than medieval preoccupations and presuppositions, and indeed of how Thomas's theology may rival modern accounts. But, first, those medieval preoccupations and presuppositions need clarification, especially from Thomas's representative perspective.

Thomas Aquinas and revelation

Despite the breadth and depth of his ambitious efforts, Thomas Aquinas did not write about everything. But the mortal limitations of time, intellect, awareness, and enthusiasm did not alone determine the range of his topics; some were simply not worth writing about. For example, neither Thomas nor any of his disciples ever wrote a treatise *De homine*.[21] One might insist, of course, that his entire body of work bears that title, because every page of it deals in some way with the theoretical understanding or the practical guidance of men and women. Certainly no résumé of his works could accomplish anything more – indeed, it could only diminish his overall accomplishment – were it collected under such a topic. Nor, for similar reasons, did Aquinas or any other medieval writer bother to write a treatise *De revelatione*.[22] Nothing properly discrete and delimited would have offered itself as material for such a treatment, any more than would material 'concerning humankind' allow itself to be so practically and necessarily circumscribed. Nevertheless, the title *De revelatione* may, perhaps, apply as broadly to Aquinas's work as would *De homine*, since some idea of divine revelation certainly animates much of his writings.

Does Thomas have a concept of revelation? He certainly talks about *revelatio*, especially in his treatises on prophecy.[23] However, despite the thoroughness and detail with which he discusses *revelatio* in relation to prophecy, and despite the attention given to these specific treatises in discussions of Thomas's 'concept of revelation,'[24] the primary context for understanding his use of the term *revelatio* is his treatment of *sacra doctrina* in the first *quaestio* of his *Summa theologiae*. The opening article indicates the place of revelation in his scheme:

> [H]uman well-being has the need for schooling in what God has revealed,
> in addition to the philosophical researches pursued by human reasoning.
> Above all, because humankind is destined by God for an end that sur-
> passes the grasp of reason; according to Isaiah 64:4, *Eye hath not seen, O
> God, without thee what thou hast prepared for them that love thee.* Now an end must
> be recognized by humankind, who then ought to order their intentions

and actions for it. Hence the necessity for the well-being of humanity that divine truths surpassing reason should be signified to them through divine revelation.[25]

Thomas quotes Augustine with approval: the *scientia* he calls *sacra doctrina* is 'anything that breeds, feeds, defends, and strengthens the saving faith which leads to true happiness.'[26] The point of *sacra doctrina* is to strengthen faith, and so it is that *scientia* about revealed things shares in this end.[27] But in recognizing 'revelation,' Thomas is not interested in an investigation of a limited realm (or range of realms) of experience or knowledge in the way an Aristotelian *episteme* concerns a single kind of subject (for example, arithmetic treats numbers; biology treats living things). 'Revelation' is not such a subject matter, as we see when Thomas takes such pains to show that the relation of God and creature is not one of opposed subject matters.[28] Rather, any thing whatever which is 'reveal-able' comes under the heading of 'revelation' because of the interest it engages rather than because of the kind of thing it is.[29] One of the problems Downing tried to confront[30] – the use of the term 'revelation' without a clear sense of its referent – arises in part because of this kind of failure to attend to grammar. For Thomas, the grammar of the incomprehensible God controls the meaning of the term 'revelation'; God is not revealed or 'uncovered' the way things in the world are revealed or uncovered, and yet we take our understanding of the term in relation to God from our applications of it regarding things in the world.

Thus we see that, for Thomas, revelation has to do primarily with one's perspective on things in light of one's final end. It is not a supplementary packet of information about 'facts' which are around the bend, as it were, from rational comprehension or physical observation – but which nonetheless factor into our ultimate happiness. Revelation is received as a gift; but it does not help to imagine a 'revelation' prior to the reception, as if already set aside by God before his giving it and our taking it in. In the very first article of his *quaestio* on *sacra doctrina*, Thomas discusses the objection that humanity, in fact, has no access to *sacra doctrina*, because it doesn't really exist as such; the *scientia divina* of Aristotle's *Metaphysics* is broad enough to include whatever can be known or learned. Thomas claims otherwise: *sacra doctrina* is a different *scientia*, and a necessary one; it looks to the same matter of other *scientiae*, but *differently*. Thomas here writes of *cognoscibilia* to refer to things known under the light of natural reason[31] (the objects of Aristotelian *episteme* of one kind or another, whether divine or physical). Later, in the third article (where he discusses whether this *sacra doctrina* is a single *scientia* or *episteme* in the Aristotelian sense), he writes of *revelabilia* in a parallel context to denote those very same things as considered under another, divine, light.[32] The *scientia* is singular, because it has a single formal object: namely, the source of everything. 'One's final end' remains a mystery, but the light of that mystery dawns over the whole of creation. It does not fall from the sky as a new matter for consideration; nor does it shine merely as a torchlight in the hollows and interstices of 'knowledge according to natural reason.'

For Aquinas, the 'revelation' is fundamental to the rationality:

We should not forget that, in St Thomas's view, the whole business of the employment and application of reason to articles of faith and revealed data, its whole effort at rational clarification or 'manifestatio' of the content of revelation by means of logical method and philosophy, is essentially a concession to our mental feebleness; it is not on account of deficiency in the divine teaching itself.[33]

This notion of 'applied reason' as a 'concession to our feebleness' itself may strike a modern sensibility as strange; we brandish our 'scientific method' with finesse and confident ease. Thomas, however, is not concerned here with our power to penetrate the secrets of the physical world. He has in mind the difficulty of a bat, looking not merely at the daylight world around him, but directly at the sun. The specific methods of a circumscribed enquiry may allow one the luxury of a sense of mastery, but nothing circumscribes God and the enquiry of faith; we are inevitably out of our depth in any effort to embrace or comprehend it.

Indeed, to settle for philosophy, in Thomas's way of thinking (and that of medieval theology in general), was to fall decisively shy of the mark; philosophy and its 'theology' were, in relation to the theology relevant for *sacra doctrina*, as carpentry and bricklaying are to architecture. The bricklayer who -- finding the architect constantly resorting to his services -- regards his science as on a par with architecture, is sorely abused; he misunderstands the principles of what he is about. Moreover, the one who opts to call himself a 'philosopher' in such an enquiry is like a technician who chooses to use inadequate (if not faulty) or even irrelevant apparatus or resources in an investigation for which much better methods and resources are available -- infrared light, for example, where daylight cannot suffice.[34] The coherence and rationality of the account of reality offered by a Latin Averroist, for example, remains blind to more important truths which point to meanings and realities beyond the realm of Aristotelian physics. *Sacra doctrina* argues from authority rather than from demonstrative proof, 'in that the principles of its teachings are held from revelation, and thus it must accept the authority of those to whom [the thing] has been revealed.'[35] In other words, what is revealed and subsequently understood is simply not available to any other *scientia*.

So much for the relation of *revelatio* and *sacra doctrina*. What has Thomas Aquinas to say about revelation as a subjective phenomenon? We can sort this out only in terms of his treatment of various other issues. However, not only does Thomas fail to expound a general dogmatic concept of revelation, but the disparate topics under which he does discuss *revelatio* -- mostly prophecy, rapture, and angelic mediation -- seem rather strange and irrelevant to a modern sensibility. Moreover, his discussion may well strike the modern mind as confused, focusing as it often does on 'nature' and what is 'natural' or 'supernatural' in medieval rather than modern ways.

Thus, before drawing out of Thomas some account of his notion of a subjective experience of *revelatio*, it may be useful to consider briefly Thomas's notions of 'nature,' 'natural,' and 'supernatural,' and how they differ from modern usage.

Natura, for Thomas and for the medieval world generally, translates the Greek *physis,* which has to do with the world that precipitates and dissolves; that heats up, cools down and moves around, struggling for its precarious balance of earth, air, fire and water; full of things that live, give birth and die. The natural world is the physical world, but this identity tells the modern person very little, since the meaning of 'physical' has shifted as well. A *natura* denotes the kind of thing a thing is, from its origin or birth – in a world full of such kinds of things. Each thing is what it is and does what it does because of its *natura:* in its beginning is its end; in its end is its beginning. Thomas, in addition, places bounds on nature in terms of creation: all *naturae* are ordered into a single hierarchical whole. Unlike Aristotle, who did not attempt to account for the origin of 'natures' themselves, Thomas recognizes the origin of all origins in the free giving of the Creator. Thus all beginning and ending, all birthing and dying, have their fundamental origin and end in God's act of giving.

In contrast, for the modern mind, 'nature' (whether created or not) tends to denote the manipulable material at our disposal.[36] Despite the contemporary remorseful crusades against the most egregious of such manipulations (especially the ecological ones) among the wealthy of the world, the modern world still tends to understand 'nature' strictly in terms of its manipulability and intractability. Its antonym is 'artifice'; what is 'natural' is opposed to the 'artificial,' and both stand in opposition not to the divine creator, but to the human maker.[37]

In a world of natural kinds, one thinks in terms of what runs counter to nature: the way things deviate from their end and fail to become that at which they aim *ex natura.* Depending on the situation, a great diversity of events may be either 'natural' or 'unnatural' – the death of an elderly man versus that of an infant, for example. Of course, even an infant's death may be 'natural'; the term here denotes a relation, or formal aspect, not a characteristic. Accordingly, whatever is 'supernatural' takes its significance as such in relations within the world of natural kinds. Within Thomas's conception of creation-as-gifted, the 'supernatural' refers to gifts which are beyond the nature of fallen humanity, and thus to 'the human being whom one finds behaving generously, justly, truthfully. (And, of course, it is only *God* to whom the term "supernatural" could *never* be applied: who graces God? Who elevates the nature of divinity?)'[38] In the broadest and most basic sense, any aspect of a thing which is not concerned merely with its natural kind in the world of hierarchically related natural kinds is 'supernatural.'[39] So, too, what is 'supernatural' may also be either 'unnatural' or in conformity with the 'natural.' On the other hand, in terms of the radical givenness of creation, existence itself is giftedness. Hence, in Thomas's understanding, an ambiguity always remains, for natural humanity undeniably has a 'supernatural' beginning and end. In some sense then, any supernatural event directed toward God in the natural lives of men and women is ultimately a 'natural' one. In any case, the notions 'natural' and 'supernatural' are, by and large, adverbial or adjectival in Thomas's thought. The substantive opposition between 'the natural' and 'the supernatural' is unknown to him or his contemporaries.

The problem for the modern thinker arises in two ways: first, in the lack of appreciation for the relation between God and creation as one of radical giftedness, in which no autonomous stance before God is possible; and, second, in the confusion between nature as inert matter and nature as a proper kind. One thus tends to think of the 'supernatural' as 'unnatural' in the material sense: as some *thing*, opposed to and apart from the self-enclosed manipulable world of matter in which one lives. 'Supernature' denotes a super-matter on top of the matter accessible to us; it is imposed on us by God, added to our 'pure nature.'[40] Either that, or it is the world of the 'paranormal,' of spooks and seances. But within the perspective of created natural kinds in a world of constant becoming which is directed to God *ex natura*, a 'supernatural' direction and finality indicate the openness of a nature to becoming what is not only beyond the realm of its own origin and end, but beyond the whole of *all* origins and ends. Thomas takes up this discussion in the *prima secundae* of his *Summa*, where human freedom frames his treatment of virtue, sin, and grace.

Where Thomas writes at greatest length and in most detail about *revelatio*, he in fact writes about *prophetia*, the biblical phenomenon of prophecy, which he considers 'a certain sort of knowledge mixed with clouds and darkness.'[41] Despite a close conceptual connection, the difference between *revelatio* and *prophetia* should not be neglected. Thomas is not interested here in identifying a kind of revealed object by which then to characterize prophecy; he is interested simply in accounting for what happens in the Bible, and his account is given to observation rather than to theory or system. Whatever the prophet knows by some 'revelation,' it is not clear and distinct; nor is it easily governed by rationalist modes of thinking. It is a *passio* to be undergone, not a *habitus* to be used.[42] Thomas calls it *intuitus, visio, instinctus, inspiratio*; its normal vehicle is not the straightforward conceptual or propositional expression, but image, fantasy, dream, imagination.[43] Prophetic inspiration is completely independent of good morals or personal sanctity.[44] Prophecy requires, rather, that excellence of imagination belonging to the poet. For Thomas, prophecy is not clairvoyance or prediction *per se*; indeed, the prophet need not tell anything at all to be a prophet.[45] *Usus* of the *denuntiatio* is secondary and distinct from the perception, involving an opposite kind of process: whereas the reception of inspiration is wholly passive on the part of the prophet, completely undetermined by his own powers and beyond his control, the 'employment' or 'proclamation' of what is received accords with the prophet's own powers of speech and imagination, his character and desire.[46] Thomas clearly points out that prophecy is not merely a kind of direct speech involving the reception of propositions and their mere repetition, but a kind of consciousness or knowledge.[47] Prophets see what is remote to others; that it be temporal 'foreknowledge' is not the primary concern. Nor does this suggest that the prophetic field of vision differs from that of ordinary vision, but rather that the prophet perceives 'beyond' ordinary perception within that same field.

Hence revelation relates to prophecy in terms of a *recognition* of something *given*. 'Revelation' clearly enough means 'uncovering,' but this is not to say that some veil is removed from God; whatever happens in relation to God with its effects in the world happens to the creature rather than to God.[48] Revelation is the 'very perception itself of divine things, by which prophecy is brought about; and by this very perception the veil of darkness and ignorance is taken away.'[49] The clouds part; the prophet can see what was unseen. God is not uncovered; nor is the 'distance' one of God's presence, but rather of cognition: our absence (consciously, spiritually) from God and the beatific vision. Prophecy involves the imperfect image of the beatific vision,[50] what is otherwise, in any case, 'far removed' from our minds.

Thomas's varied use of the term *revelatio* quite naturally makes it difficult to trace any full notion of 'revelation,' because so many disparate phenomena count for consideration.[51] We cannot look for a single, all-embracing, *a priori* theory of the 'mode' of revelation.[52] How God reveals follows no one pattern, no method which theology is at pains to elucidate. Nor does *sacra doctrina* merely collect and describe 'revelations.' As I have already noted, theology assigns causes and purposes in consideration of the things revealed themselves, and classifies them on the basis of the knowledge obtained – in short, it brings the sheer diversity of things revealed into some unity without prejudice or loss to that diversity and richness. Its method is primarily inductive, but it uses any method toward knowledge, all to the end of clarifying what is contained in *sacra doctrina*. Thus, we seriously misread Thomas if we find here a 'theory of knowledge of God.' Nor does Thomas describe an 'invasive' God, reconfiguring nature according to some single, established, prior scheme which theology sets out to detect, but rather prophecy (and subsequently, 'revelation') brought about in conformity with nature itself,[53] through its causes, processes and characteristics.[54] Nevertheless, Thomas provides a consistent formal notion of revelation as a kind of illumination, a power of seeing.

More may be said about this positive character of Thomas's *revelatio*. He gives two clear principles, relating revelation to knowledge: illumination and judgement.[55] 'The act of revealing is an act of enlightenment, and the gift of divine light is the formal characteristic of prophetic revelation';[56] and yet, prophetic revelation-as-knowledge is first of all a matter of judgement ('quia iudicium est completivum cognitionis'), for which the light is given. In any case, these two principles must not be separated; that is, judgement itself becomes part of the illuminated power of vision. Knowing depends on more than the gaze that sees in the revealing light.

Aquinas makes this unity clear in his discussion of Daniel's prophecy concerning the writing on Belshazzar's wall. As Thomas Hughson points out,[57] the prophet does not receive a divinely formulated proposition and then make an act of divinely enlightened assent to the proposition; rather, apprehension and affirmation are one and the same act of judgement. Interpretation here involves no preliminary decoding of meaning and subsequent recognition of divine authority and ultimate reasoned assent. This 'division of acts' comes necessarily into the picture only with a later metaphysics, one which conflates all being into a unity susceptible to decoding. The Scotist and later nominalist *universitas* of univocal being offers no ground on which to judge without a preliminary separating-out of 'intelligibility' and 'authority'; intelligibilities – concepts of a kind with divinity itself, first discriminated from illusion by the natural light of 'reason' – only then become 'illuminated' for affirmation as if under the discriminating torchlight of divine will. But Thomas Aquinas did not suffer this contortion. For Thomas, the divine light dawns over the whole intellect of the prophet, in the two aspects of seeing and judgement, enabling him to see as such the mysterious, supernatural *truth*.

What does the seer see, beyond what is 'natural' to her vision? We have already noticed that for Thomas, 'supernatural' and 'natural' are not opposed as characteristics of separate subject matters. Nor does prophetic revelation necessarily depend upon the infusion of new species into the imagination. Thomas assumes that prophecy is not merely supernatural, but natural as well: some visions are naturally explained.[58] 'Natural prophecy' – a natural vision of what is ordinarily remote to men and women – depends on the powers of the imagination interacting with the merely physical forces of the world as well as the intelligent and willful spiritual powers of creation. With such a distinction, we recognize again that for Thomas the scheme does not depend on a division or gap between the natural and supernatural. These he differentiates, but principally in order to show that for prophecy the supernatural always acts *in accord with the natural*.[59] 'Grace builds on nature' is his well-known *leitmotif*. Thomas speaks of 'supernatural revelation' only from within the context of what is generally understood as 'natural revelation': for example, the visions and 'readings' of sages and magi as many societies have recognized them. For divine revelation, the imagination is again the vehicle of vision,[60] but the remoteness from what is perceived is merely relative; whatever event or reality – distant or future – is ultimately humanly knowable, from within the world, as it were. As he reiterates, time and again, the 'things observed' by the prophet are not themselves 'supernatural': 'for bodily sight to be supernatural new bodily species must always be formed. But this is not needed for the sight of imagination or understanding to be supernatural.'[61] God, however, remains absolutely 'remote,' unknown until the beatific vision itself, known only in created effects. Our 'remoteness' from God (which is not to say his remoteness from us) is absolute, until we share that final vision.[62]

Victor White has pointed out the central role of the agency of angels in Thomas's account of prophecy and revelation,[63] in part at least because angels have such a role in biblical accounts[64]: the law was promulgated to Moses and the people by angels, and was not the effect of immediate divine agency.[65] Although his treatment might appear to be dictated merely by the scriptural texts, Thomas's account of angelic mediation may help again in understanding more clearly the place of 'natural' and 'supernatural' in his thought. First, for Thomas, 'angel' names not a substance, but a *function of service*.[66] Thus does he maintain that each is its own species. An angel is a 'job-doing,' as it were, not a thing doing a job. Although Thomas identifies angels with immaterial intelligences, he considers them as such in terms of the tasks and functions fulfilled: here namely, the service of the human end, the *salus* of humanity, through faith. In addition, the role of angels indicates the 'natural' hierarchical scheme of revelation. Angels communicate more than what is received in 'natural prophecy,' but no direct perception of

God; they are the means of enlightenment in the human mind of God's purposes and designs for creation. Whereas God alone imparts faith directly, angels set forth what is to be believed (as well as what is to be done about it).[67] But angels, as created beings, are limited in the resources available: they must work through the senses with natural experience. They cannot penetrate the mind directly to form images, or impose themselves in any other direct way. Such a presence of angels is, of course, a perfectly 'natural' thing for St Thomas, as much a part of the normal order as the motions of 'spirits and humours' in the body. Angels simply help give, as it were, more of the proper light by which to judge. Here Thomas conforms his own understanding to the neo-Platonic hierarchical account of pseudo-Dionysius and other more contemporary mystical writers.[68]

In a world of such seamless hierarchical continuities – where spiritual powers can mediate the will of the creator (and their own wills, for good or ill); where the created order of nature includes relations beyond the merely mechanical laws of causality, which have to do with ends and purposes going beyond the purely natural and created – 'prophecy' and 'revelation' make sense only as a matter of judging things, not so much in terms of the 'supernatural' versus the 'natural,' but in terms of a different locus altogether: that of *symbol*, understood within a neo-Platonic context of communication and participation. Avery Dulles singles out four aspects of symbolic communication which parallel the use of the term 'revelation' for Thomas. These are the participatory, transformative, motivational and supradiscursive properties of symbols, which invariably point beyond whatever is disclosed, toward mystery.[69] Revelation finds its true place as *generative* of grace and the re-creation of the believing community when that community construes its account of things with a proper eye to its end beyond creation, allowing creation to manifest symbolically what exceeds its grasp.[70]

When these hierarchical continuities and divine dynamics internal to creation no longer determine our mode of understanding the world, such terms as 'revelation,' 'nature,' and 'supernatural' necessarily take on new uses and meanings.[71] The greatest confusions may surround these terms, and even the notion of 'world' itself. For Thomas, the seamlessness of the world of hierarchical continuities is not that of the later scholastic philosopher–theologian, who, as I mentioned earlier, seeks to mould, circumscribe and then to grasp a (conceptual) *universitas* of Being, an *inclusio* of God and creation. Rather, his is a 'catholicity' – a 'world shot through' (*katá hólos*) with its own giftedness, an open wholeness tending toward that end (given in its beginning) which is beyond itself, in the One who gives.[72]

Suárez and modern revelation

As noted earlier, only in the sixteenth century, with Martin Luther and others, did 'revelation' become technically restricted in a new way, at least partly in response to the challenge (and opportunity) of vernacular translation.[73] Luther began to differentiate the word *Offenbarung* from words such as *Eröffnung* and *Mitteilung* ('opening, disclosure,' 'communication') in his scriptural translations, giving the former its clear supremacy of usage. 'Offen,' 'eroffenung,' 'eroffenen,' and 'offen werden' gave way consistently to forms such as 'offenbarung,' 'offenbaren,' and 'offengebaret werden.'[74] Apparently, the word *revelatio* had already undergone a considerable restriction in meaning by the time of Luther's translations. Whereas for Thomas the symbolic, dynamic nature of the apprehension of divine truths implied an intimacy and union with God in the very perception of that truth, by the sixteenth century a radical break had been introduced into that relation. Language became disenfranchised from its participatory role, as we shall see further on, and was reduced to pointing out objects. For Luther, such a preference for *Offenbarung* emphasized the same novelty and otherness suggested by 'Eröffneten' without the strong tone of objectivity and literal 'unveiling' he inevitably heard in the Latin and Greek words *revelatio* and *apokalupsis*. Rather, by *Offenbarung* Luther meant to express and reappropriate the direct, naked, personal self-giving of God (as opposed to the hierophantic or 'sacred' and inscrutable manifestation of theophany), in conformity with the connotations of the word's Old High German root: 'baring oneself.'[75] With this emphasis on the unmediated (i.e., immediate) self-manifestation of God, Luther tried to recover what he thought was missing from the (no longer truly Thomist) scholastic theology of his day, but which had actually only been eclipsed by a new construal of language's function.

Such a construal was perfectly understandable, given the nominalist scholasticism prevalent at the time – which Luther had imbibed, and against which he instinctively struggled at times.[76] Nominalism, and its attendant voluntarism, at least preserved the transcendent otherness of 'what has been made apparent,' but did so by emphasizing an absolutely inscrutable divine will, and by consequently restricting the meaning of *revelatio* to 'the exposure of a hidden reality,' an objective 'unveiling' of a *thing*, as it were, rather than the richer and broader multiplicity of meanings available to patristic and early medieval thinkers in their symbolic, polysemous, Latin-unified world. Luther recognized the inadequacy of this nominalist restriction, and with the term *Offenbarung* tried to reinvent – or at least reinvoke – the lush kind of *communicatio/participatio* between God and creation allowed by the pre-Scotist hierarchy of being. The real difficulty, however, was not merely the proper restriction of meaning or use, but the rupture inherent in the new notion of meaning. Luther sought to translate Scripture accurately, but as situated within a philosophical 'realism' of linguistic 'representation,' as Michel de Certeau describes it – a realism which

> postulated a divorce between words and things. The traces of Ockhamism are apparent. Also, whereas in medieval ontology all treatment of language was in itself an experiment or a manipulation of the real, language would henceforth stand face to face with what 'manifested itself' in it: it was separate from that real that it intended, depicted, and was confronted with. The experiment, in the modern sense of the word, was born with the deontologizing of language, to which the birth of a linguistics also corresponds. In Bacon and many others, the experiment

stood opposite language as that which guaranteed and verified the latter. This split between a deictic language (it shows and/or organizes) and a referential experimentation (it escapes and/or guarantees) structures modern science. . . .[77]

We might extend de Certeau's conclusion only slightly to suggest that this split tends to structure all modern accounts of knowledge. But the split characterizes not just modernity, but late-medieval thought as well. It was not Francis Bacon, or even Ockham, but Duns Scotus who, merely a generation after Thomas Aquinas, first deontologized language by construing being as that univocal *universitas*, the whole inclusive of God and creation.[78] Without any distinction in being between the infinite God and finite creation, created beings have nothing by which to gain their bearings in relation to God. The invention of a conceptual relation to the 'map of being' on which they plot both God and all else provides an *ad hoc* solution. The significance of this consequence of univocity became apparent only in the subsequent bifurcation made possible by the rise of modern science: the 'model' (i.e., the 'map of being,' the object or referent of deictic language) was set apart from 'reality itself' (the referent of experimentation-as-guarantor). With this division, the patristic and medieval accounts of participation became completely incoherent. Such a trajectory seems inexorable in the philosophical theology of the fourteenth and fifteenth centuries.

Furthermore, given such univocity and the divorce Certeau sketches, language cannot but mask reality. As a result of shifts in language and reappropriations over time, speech becomes radically vulnerable to its provisionality and the need for its own constant re-establishment, either in 'experimentation' or in God's absolute power. But if language must find its guarantor in God *as opposed to* experience – the secure 'manipulation of the real' from within the created order – a new and frightening question arises: the problem of illusion. Thus Luther was harrowed by the problem of securing knowledge of his salvation, just as Descartes was vexed by the question of establishing any certain knowledge at all. Their potential mastery of the created order from within had allowed men and women to cope with the illusions of the senses, but God, in his infinite (and yet univocal) hiddenness, offers no such purchase. Such potential illusion is absolute, requiring an absolute guarantor of authenticity. The divorce between words and things, coupled with the conflation of God and things, introduces a fundamental irrationality into what had been an ordered and intelligible realm of relations, an abyss between intelligibility and human intelligence.

Meanwhile, new practices and situations have allowed continuities of usage and expression which mask, with their own accommodating innovation, the very shifts upon which the new practices and continuities may depend. Olaf Pedersen provides the illustrative example of the metaphor of the sun as 'king of the universe': in the Middle Ages, the sun was understood to circle the earth in the midst of the planets, influencing their motions. The image of the king was a suitable metaphor to describe its role in the heavens. But Copernicus – having intuited that the sun remained stationary as the planets circled around it – also called the sun 'king of the universe' without any apparent confusion. The metaphor lived on, because the notions of kingship and the universe had changed as well: the medieval king touring his kingdom on horseback amid unruly barons became the Renaissance ruler at the head of a centralized regime, at rest in the capital.[79] Hence a continuity in usage (the metaphor of kingship) masked a shift in cosmology (the understanding of the relative situation of the sun, and of an infinite universe) because of a further shift in practice (the role of the king). So, too, a continuity in usage (the term 'revelation') masked a shift in theology (the understanding of the relation of God and creation) because of further shifts in practice (the divorce between words and things, and an exchange of a hierarchy of being for a univocal Scotist metaphysics). Such was the difficult situation of theology inherited by Francisco Suárez.

A quick study of their backgrounds shows a series of striking similarities between Thomas and Suárez. Both studied at independent imperial universities, Thomas at Naples and Suárez at Salamanca; both entered very young yet rapidly growing and vibrant religious orders at the beginning of their careers; both studied theology after major reforms in the curriculum, when the foundational texts had only recently been established – Lombard's *Sentences* in Thomas's case, and Thomas's *Summa* in Suárez's case; each lived in a period of intense interaction with and focus on distant or alien cultures from Europe: Islam in the thirteenth century, and America in the sixteenth; and the works of both were received immediately into a subsequent climate of profound insecurity and skepticism.

Although Suárez and Thomas Aquinas shared a further most important similarity – their common desire for educational reform, which motivated their writing – they hardly shared a vision of where to begin. Thomas considered the state of education in his day, or at least of instruction in *sacra doctrina*, rather poor. Instruction was pointless and confusing, following practices which made little sense or were insensitive to the need at hand, or which were generally beyond the capacity or skill of the students.[80] As he expressed it in the prologue to the *Summa*, 'the point of our intention in this work is to hand on the truths which pertain to Christian religion in a way appropriate for the training of beginners.'[81] With regard to 'Christian religion,' Thomas had in mind not a vague modern notion of what qualifies as either 'Christian' or 'religion,' but rather something generally much more defined by a community's daily practice and ritual, or as one commentator specifies: 'life in a religious community under the vows of poverty, chastity, and obedience.'[82] That is, he had in mind a formation within a rich and intricate way of life, one long-tested as a path to an envisioned end in life (and beyond), and one not necessarily the focus of concern within the University of Paris. By 'training' (*eruditionem*), Thomas meant something much more basic and practical than the higher level 'instruction' in theory.[83] He had in mind, rather, the kinds of operation that led to a *habitus* (Aristotle's *hexis*). His *Summa* was not intended as a textbook for complete 'beginners,' but rather as the groundwork for those charged with such training within a living tradition.[84] The foremost 'beginners' were those learning the *techne* of a religious life. In order for *doctrina* to become *disciplina*, one must have more than a body of knowledge. *Disciplina* requires guidance in the practice of inquiry, in order that one might learn how learning is done properly, with a view to its end. The *Summa* instructs teachers to be such guides, consolidating the range of knowledge (insofar as possible) in light of the relation of the created order to God, the ultimate end of all.

Suárez found a comparable chaos in the instruction of his day, and he sought to redress the confusion much as Thomas had done, by reorganizing it. But Suárez went about it in an entirely different way. Rather than direct his reorganization directly according to formation in the life of faith as Thomas did, he set as his foundation the life of reason, separating philosophy and theology as he had learned to do from Duns Scotus.[85] In an age becoming obsessed with method, Suárez wished to find the right approach first. In so doing he rearranged the metaphysical corpus handed down from Aristotle, excising anything confusing or repetitious and systematizing the arguments:

> And for having always believed that the greater part of the effectiveness for understanding problems and for deepening the understanding of them is rooted in the opportune method of investigation and judgement – which only with difficulty and hardly even then could I follow, were I (according to the custom of the commentators) to treat all the questions occasionally and randomly, as they come up according to the text of the Philosopher – I thus judged it would be more useful and effective, keeping an order of teaching, to investigate and place before the eyes of the reader all the things that can be studied or missed with reference to the total object of this wisdom.[86]

This systematic revision – the very first of such approaches to metaphysics – is important, because metaphysics further serves as the proper foundation of theology for Suárez.

> As it is impossible for one to become a good theologian without having first been established on the solid foundations of metaphysics, thus I always believed it important, Christian reader, to offer you previously this work [the *Metaphysical Disputations*] which – diligently expounded – I place now in your hands. . . . Each day . . . I saw with more clarity how divine and supernatural Theology require and demand what is human and natural, to the point that I did not hesitate to interrupt for a time the work begun [i.e., his commentaries on Thomas] in order to grant – or better, to restore – to metaphysical doctrine the place that belonged to it.[87]

Whereas Aquinas sees 'theology which pertains to holy teaching' founded on principles separate from philosophy, but able to use philosophy to sort out the difficulties of discourse (for what else is there to use?), Suárez sees theology itself as standing on the structure provided by philosophy, specifically an ontologically univocal metaphysics. In order to speak well about God, one must begin with the clear foundation provided not by *sacra doctrina*, but the metaphysical structure of Being, which rises up to meet what is revealed.

Although the approach of each was determined by the specific place and time – the genre of university lectures, formation within religious orders, foundations for preaching – nonetheless, Suárez's efforts were determined by printing and publishing in a way Thomas's were not. The dissemination of books and the consequent pressures from an international readership motivated Suárez to publish an enormous and widely distributed *oeuvre* during his last years, while only rarely leaving Coimbra. Moreover, his situation encouraged the style of thought generative of a truly systematic theology, and of the *manualia* and *cursus philosophiae et theologiae* which followed. In his own lifetime and after (thanks to certain events and influences, such as the Condemnation at Paris in 1277 and the Franciscan animosity towards his works), Thomas's writings never held the stature Suárez's works did during his (except in the estimation of a few important bishops and popes over the centuries); the *Summa* reflected merely one (admittedly masterful) approach among many within Thomas's highly contentious and often polarized university milieu.

This is not to say Suárez was without rivals, both within his order and without, especially during his lifetime. But none of the medievals had the advantages offered by early modern Europe in gaining and consolidating an audience. The number of Jesuit universities, and the virtual explosion of higher education across Europe in the early modern period significantly characterizes Suárez's world.[88] Of the 140 or so established institutions with at least a *de jure* claim to university status existing in Europe for some time between the early thirteenth century and the end of Suárez's lifetime, only 14 or so had existed before Thomas Aquinas died. Another 46 such institutions at least were established in Europe before the end of the eighteenth century, during the heyday of readership for Suárez's works – a large proportion of them Jesuit.[89] From the time of the establishment of the Society of Jesus in 1540 until their suppression in 1773, the Jesuits founded or ran 44 universities, founded 20 *gymnasia academica* (mostly in Germany and Central Europe), and established an additional 26 university theology faculties (mostly in France and Germany[90]), all of which would have eventually employed Suárez's works in their well-defined and uniform *Ratio studiorum*. Indeed, such was the popularity of Suárez's metaphysics that most Protestant universities taught it as well. Moreover, these numbers fail to include the lesser colleges, numbering more than 300,[91] scattered around Europe, or the new universities in America under the influence or auspices of the Jesuits. The printing press, coupled with the rapid growth in numbers of institutions of higher learning, allowed a propagation of Suárez's ideas with a decidedly modern character: a wide and rapid dissemination which effectively buried competing genres less suited to the new lecture environment of the universities.

On faith

Volume XII of Suárez's *Opera* includes his treatise *De fide, spe, et caritate*,[92] considered – at least superficially – a commentary on Thomas's *Summa*, IIa-IIae, qq. 1–46. Whereas Thomas devotes 16 *quaestiones* to the topic of faith, 6 to hope and 24 to charity, Suárez attends to the theological virtues differently: 24 *disputationes* covering nearly 600 double-column pages deal with faith, compared to a mere 2 disputations on hope, and 13 on charity, together covering another 240 pages of text. 'Faith' is his overwhelming concern, and primarily within this treatise he discusses revelation. For Suárez however, faith is no longer a virtue in the sense Thomas had regarded it. Building as he does on the basis of his discussion in IIa-IIae, on the ultimate end of humanity and the moral nature of the human person on the journey toward that end, Thomas expounds a clear, nuanced, and thoroughly comprehensive vision of the human being as free and responsible, in relation to God's free giving of grace. He describes all human activity fundamentally in terms of virtues, following Aristotle, and then further traces all virtues back to the seven cardinal virtues. The discussion in IIa-IIae centers around these seven, and the species to which their vices correspond.[93] 'Virtue' here has the clear sense of a 'habit,' or category by which to understand characteristic human activity directed toward its final end or beatitude; together these virtues constitute the structure by which we recognize the shape of human identity. Faith (along with hope and charity) is a specific virtue informing that identity insofar as its end is directed to God.

For Suárez, faith relates to the believability and knowability of an object. He begins his own discussion of the formal object of faith[94] not with Thomas, but with a consideration of two distinctions taken from Cajetan and Capreolus: the formal object *in esse rei* and *in esse cognoscibilis*. The former apparently corresponds to the material object (or *obiectum quod*) described by Thomas; the latter to his formal object (the *obiectum quo*).[95] Of Capreolus's 'concomitant principle' (*ratio concomitans*), Suárez explains it is nothing more than 'the denomination of the material object by the formal, which in the present matter is the *principle of credibility*.'[96] Suárez further characterizes these distinctions in terms of *Deus ipse revelans* and *eius revelatio*: 'God revealing himself' as material, and 'the revelation of him' as formal. Most significant is the 'third principle,' which Suárez recognizes not as a further distinction of the two other accounts of the object of faith, but as a distinction in the mind. With a 'principle of the worthiness of belief,' Capreolus (and Suárez with him) accepts a break between intelligibility and assent, which attends to the problem of illusion mentioned above. Words need something more to guarantee their object now; the formal object and the material object can no longer meet in the judgement, because words have become rigidly restricted to representations. We cannot be sure of what is said, except by the light of reason; if what is said truly reveals what is beyond reason, we must have proofs other than reason to discern such truth from illusion. Hence, Suárez allows the distinction *revelans* and *revelatio* since, as he says, revelation is God's action *ad extra*. The revealing God confirms his revelation (the things proposed for belief) through the infused light of faith. For Thomas, things revealed led to faith, but for Suárez, faith confirms what is revealed. This construal introduces a new grammar, in which 'revelation' becomes something totally extrinsic to the economy of nature, and which brings with it many of the misunderstandings discussed earlier.

Suárez then begins his discussion of the formal object of faith by arguing against the position that one must believe or assent to only what has persuaded, and been understood by, human reason.[97] Thomas takes a different approach, noting that the object of faith, as 'what is to be believed,' seems too diverse to be the apprehension of some singular identity.[98] How could God then be its object? He explains that every apprehension has two aspects: that which is apprehended materially, and that through which it is apprehended – its 'formal relation' (*formalis ratio obiecti*). We know, for example, an infinite diversity of conclusions from the study of geometry; these are the 'matter known.' But *how* we know them is through one and the same demonstrative or 'formal' account. The demonstration 'mediates' the knowledge. Or, to use another image, light mediates an infinite range of color.[99] In the same way, the 'matter known' by faith is infinitely diverse, but it is known (assented to) through what is revealed, which is itself the divine first Truth. Thus the image of revelation as *light* is most appropriate here, in order to distinguish material and formal objects. But we must be careful not to identify the 'matter known' with God who, as the 'object of faith,' is the object of trust, not of 'light.' Our assent in faith (the 'middle between knowledge and opinion'[100]) is thus 'mediated' through the middle term of revelation, just as knowledge of geometric truth is mediated through the middle term of demonstration. Anything having to do with faith has to do with God, and what God reveals – just as anything having to do with color involves light as its formal object, and anything having to do with medicine, health.[101] Thomas clearly does not think of mediation here in terms of intermediaries, of 'go-betweens' to bridge a supernatural or epistemological gap. Form simply mediates intelligibility in that a thing is grasped according to how it is given, as well as according to the way of the one who grasps.[102] A habit of faith inclines one to grasp what the light of faith reveals, just as a habit of prudence or temperance inclines one toward what is appropriate to those virtues.[103]

Suárez sums up the account he attributes to Thomas, Cajetan, Capreolus, Duns Scotus, Bellarmine, 'et alii Scholastici': God as revealing or testifying to things to be believed through faith (*res credendas per fidem*) is the formal object of faith.[104] 'This is the clear opinion of St Thomas,' says Suárez, 'for one may speak of theology; thence by necessity one is led likewise to faith, because one receives the propositions of faith, as immediately revealed. . . . Thomas says that the first Truth is the formal object of faith, because nothing is believed unless revealed by it.'[105] He concludes: 'This account convinces, because God does not move to belief unless mediated through his witness; for how should we believe him, unless he speak to us? Thus he is not the formal object of faith, unless testifying and revealing.'[106]

Both Thomas and Suárez cite Romans 10:17: 'So faith comes from what is heard, and what is heard comes through the word of Christ.'[107] Thomas intends by this citation to distinguish faith from knowing by associating knowledge with seeing, and faith with hearing.[108] He distinguishes the words that signify from the things themselves about which one has faith; the ability to talk about the belief clearly is not the same as seeing what is believed. Suárez uses Paul's maxim to emphasize not the difference between seeing and hearing, knowing and believing, but rather the difference between mediated and unmediated faith or revelation. The sufficient, and ordinary, way of proposing and conceiving the faith is through mediators or intermediaries: the Apostles, sent by Christ to preach, and the Church in turn, which preserves and teaches the apostolic faith. We hear the Word of Christ through the mediation of physical words, for what else could hearing mean if not through preaching?[109]

But Thomas understood this 'mediation of revelation' differently than did Suárez. We have seen that Thomas never had cause to reify the mediation into words or propositions through which God hands over 'things to be believed.' Nor does Thomas separate the moment of belief or assent from some prior moment of apprehension. We have seen, too, that for Thomas, revelation takes place in the judgement and understanding, as part of the assent of faith. Revelation does not occur 'on its own,' as if it were a thing apart, before becoming part of human thought and experience. But, for Thomas, what God reveals has precisely that quality which Luther sought to recover in his translation – that is, the intimate self-manifestation, the word which pours from the heart, and which animates faith.

Thomas emphasizes that with respect to the conferral of species, but not to the conferral of light, 'human teaching can be likened to prophetic revelation, for a man shows his pupil certain realities through speech signs, but he cannot illuminate interiorly as God does.'[110] By this he restricts the direct infusion of images or perceptions in the imagination to the power of God alone, since only God can in this sense create. But such infusion is exceptional with regard to revelation; it is certainly not necessary, as we have seen. On the other hand, there is no question in Thomas's account of God's necessary aid in perceiving the 'things revealed,' since these are not other than that perception brought about by God as the formal object of faith. In this way revelation leads to faith. Suárez interprets the action of grace by making a stronger distinction between object and illumination:

> Scripture sometimes calls revelation inspiration and the infusion of interior light which efficaciously gives rise to faith. It is thus that Christ tells Peter (Mt. 16): *Flesh and blood have not revealed to you, but my Father*, and (Mt. 11): *No one knows the Son except the Father, nor does anyone know the Father except the Son, and anyone to whom the Son willed to reveal Him*. This revelation takes place, not only on the part of the object, but also on the part of the power and, as a result, includes the proposition of the object as well as the inspiration and help to believe.[111]

In this way, Suárez can underscore the propositional character of revelation, in order to isolate a conceptual, rational object apart from the judgement of faith itself. This proposition of faith becomes the sufficient object of revelation, strictly speaking.[112] Suárez thus defines revelation not in terms of the power of judgement and perception, as Thomas tends to do, but rather in terms of the object to which faith assents.

Theology of revelation has apparently come a long way since Suárez, covering a good deal of ground throughout modernity. It passes through the period of attempts at the invention of a 'universal language' during the seventeenth century, in which revelation was first opposed explicitly and schematically to the natural world by the likes of John Wilkins and the members of the Royal Society. It continues on through the apologetic defense of God's role in the world through revelation, against the deist mechanism of the universe, and then through the invention and development of dogmatic theology as an independent realm of study, based on the corpus of 'revealed truths.' Finally it reaches the twentieth century, with its various fundamentalisms about 'reason and revelation.' However, none of these efforts to clarify the nature of revelation and the rest of theology have gotten behind the explication given by Suárez at the beginning of the modern period, for they all have shared the same presuppositions with which Suárez framed his discussion – presuppositions widely divergent from those of Thomas and many other medieval theologians. Revelation became the 'technical concept to designate whatever is needed to make something a matter of divine faith,' as Dulles puts it,[113] because of the dire need for an object rather than a relation in the realm of faith. Suárez's metaphysics of 'real entities' reflected a new world in which the grasp of the mind was made to reach between God and creation, supplanting the reach of God himself as the communicator of intelligibility. God authorized assent to his truths, his supernatural 'real entities,' through the infusion of faith – but for Suárez (or perhaps more especially his disciples), the truths become the important thing for the way they conform to and authorize his rational system, in the face of the threat of illusion and skepticism. Faith is necessary to understanding, as Augustine had said, but in this account, such faith is of a perverse order. Setting aright Suárez's account would involve a reversal of 'the divorce between words and things' as well as a reversal of the order of assent and revelation.

Notes

1 I mention (by way of example) only: Stephen Toulmin, *Cosmopolis: The Hidden Agenda of Modernity* (Chicago: University of Chicago Press, 1990); three works by Alasdair MacIntyre: *After Virtue* (Notre Dame IN: University of Notre Dame Press, 1984); *Whose Justice? Which Rationality?* (London: Duckworth, 1988); *Three Rival Versions of Moral Enquiry* (London: Duckworth, 1990); and Michael Polanyi, *Personal Knowledge: Towards a Post-Critical Philosophy* (Chicago: University of Chicago Press, 1958, 1962).

2 Avery Dulles SJ, *Models of Revelation* (Maryknoll NY: Orbis, 1983, 1992), p. 19.

3 *Ibid.*

4 *Ibid.*, p. 20.

5 *Ibid.*, p. 15.

6   F. Gerald Downing, *Has Christianity a Revelation?* (London: SCM Press, 1964); cf. also his
    'Revelation, Disagreement and Obscurity,' *Religious Studies* 21 (1985), pp. 219–230. Cf.
    Dulles's discussion in *Models*, pp. 8–14; 276–278.
7   Cf. MacIntyre, *Versions*, pp. 116–122. I am aware that Dulles himself approaches the-
    ology from within an historical faith tradition (cf. *Models*, p. 14), although he does not
    emphasize this.
8   Cf. Hugh D. MacDonald, *Ideas of Revelation: An Historical Study AD 1700 to AD 1860*
    (London: Macmillan & Co, 1959), pp. 51–55; also Downing, *Has Christianity A
    Revelation?*; René Latourelle SJ, *Theology of Revelation* (Staten Island NY: Alba House; St
    Paul, 1966); Gabriel Daly, 'Revelation in the Theology of the Roman Catholic
    Church,' in Paul Avis, ed., *Divine Revelation* (London: Darton, Longman & Todd,
    1997), pp. 23–44; and Dulles, *op. cit.*
9   Brief discussions may be found in Latourelle, *Theology of Revelation*, pp. 181–191, and
    Peter Eicher, *Offenbarung: Prinzip neuzeitlicher Theologie* (München: Kösel-Verlag, 1977),
    pp. 80–86.
10 Cf., for example, Downing, *Has Christianity a Revelation?* and MacDonald, *Ideas of
    Revelation.*
11 Suárez (1548–1617), born at Grenada to a wealthy and influential family, studied
    canon law at Salamanca before entering the Society of Jesus at the age of 16.
    Unpromising at first, he excelled in the study of both philosophy and theology and
    began a university career while still in his formation as a Jesuit. After stints at
    Salamanca, Alcalá, Rome and other centers of learning, he spent the last twenty
    years of his life as professor at Coimbra. He did not publish until his forty-second year,
    but the (incomplete) 1854 Vivès edition of his works runs to twenty-eight large vol-
    umes. The standard biography is Raoul de Scorraille SJ, *François Suarez de la Compagnie
    de Jésus, d'après ses lettres, ses autres écrits inédits et un grand nombre de documents nouveaux*, 2 vols.
    (Paris: P. Lethielleux, 1912). Several more brief biographical discussions are cited
    below.
12 Cf., for example, Norman Kretzmann, Anthony Kenny, and Jan Pinborg, eds., *The
    Cambridge History of Later Medieval Philosophy* (Cambridge: The University Press, 1982),
    and Frederick Copleston SJ, *A History of Philosophy*, 9 vols; vol. 3: *Late Medieval and
    Renaissance Philosophy* (New York: Doubleday, 1953, 1993). There are, however, signif-
    icant exceptions; cf. Jean-François Courtine, *Suarez et le système de la métaphysique* (Paris:
    Presses Universitaires de France, 1990), which deals with Suárez largely in light of his
    influence on modern philosophy. Cf. the more nuanced discussions in Jorge J. E.
    Gracia, 'Francisco Suárez: the Man in History,' *American Catholic Philosophical Quarterly*
    65:3 (1991), pp. 259–266, and 'Francisco Suárez (1548–1617),' in Jorge J.E. Gracia,
    ed. *Individuation in Scholasticism: The Later Middle Ages and the Counter-Reformation,
    1150–1650* (Albany NY: State University of New York Press, 1994), pp. 475–510.
13 For a classic account, cf. Johan Huizinga, *The Autumn of the Middle Ages*, trans. Rodney
    J. Payton and Ulrich Mammizsch (Chicago: University of Chicago Press, 1996). For
    an excellent account of 'the axioms which went without explaining,' cf. John Bossy,
    Christianity in the West 1400–1700 (Oxford: Oxford University Press, 1985).
14 Cf. for example, accounts of scholastic influence on Descartes, Leibniz and Wolff in
    Courtine, *Suarez*; and José Ferrater Mora, 'Suárez and Modern Philosophy,' *Journal of
    the History of Ideas* 14 (1953), pp. 528–543.
15 For an example of how inadequate such a survey may be, cf. Daly, *op. cit.* (see note 8).
16 This practice began at Alcalá in 1508, and spread quickly to other universities; cf.
    Melquiades Andrés, *La Teología Española en el Siglo XVI*, vol. II (Madrid: Biblioteca de
    Autores Cristianos, 1977), pp. 77–78.
17 MacIntyre, *Versions*, p. 73.
18 The work of scholars of Thomas Aquinas, such as Gilson, Chenu, Weisheipl,
    Lonergan, MacInerny and many others, has revealed how Cajetan and other late

scholastics misrepresented Thomas. Cf. John A. Trentman, 'Scholasticism in the Seventeenth Century,' in *Cambridge History*, pp. 818–837.

19 Cf., for example, Josepho Aldalma SJ *et al.*, *Sacrae Theologiae Summa*, 4 vols. (Madrid: La Editorial Católica [Biblioteca Autores Cristianos], 1961).

20 Cf. Victor White OP, 'St Thomas's Conception of Revelation,' *Dominican Studies* 1: 1 (1947), p. 5; his emphasis (not important).

21 Victor White OP, *God and the Unconscious* (London: Harvill Press, 1952), pp. 82–83.

22 René Latourelle SJ, *Theology of Revelation* (Staten Island NY: Alba House; St Paul, 1966), p. 155: 'A special investigation into the nature and properties of Christian revelation is not among the preoccupations of Scholasticism in the thirteenth century, nor in the theological frameworks sketched out before their time.'

23 *De veritate*, q. 12 and *Summa theologiae* (hereafter ST) II-II, qq. 171–174.

24 Cf., for example, Thomas Hughson SJ, 'Dulles and Aquinas on Revelation,' *The Thomist* 52 (1988), pp. 445–471; and White, 'Revelation,' pp. 3–34, and *God and the Unconscious*.

25 ST I. 1. 1. (All translations are mine unless otherwise noted.)

26 Augustine, *De trinitate*, XIV, 3: 'Huic scientiae attribuitur illud tantummodo quo fides saluberrima gignitur, nutritur, defenditur, roboratur.' Quoted in ST I. 1. 2 sc.; English translation from Augustine, *The Trinity*, trans. Edmund Hill OP (Brooklyn NY: New City Press, 1991), p. 371.

27 Cf. Eleonore Stump, 'Revelation and Biblical Exegesis: Augustine, Aquinas and Swinburne,' in Alan G. Padgett, ed., *Reason and the Christian Religion: Essays in Honour of Richard Swinburne* (Oxford: Oxford University Press, 1994), p. 171.

28 Cf. ST I. 1. 3 obj. 1; ad 1.

29 ST I. 1. 3.

30 Cf. Downing, *Revelation?* and 'Disagreement,' note 6 above.

31 ST I. 1. 1. ad 2.

32 Cf. notes 27 and 29.

33 White, 'Revelation,' p. 9. Cf. ST I. 1. 5 ad 2: 'non est propter defectum vel insufficientiam eius, sed propter defectum intellectus nostri, qui ex his quae per naturalem rationem . . . cognoscuntur, facilius manducitur in his quae sunt supra rationem' (also, cf. *In Boeth. de trin.*, II. 2. 3).

34 But even here, 'light' as a 'resource' or even 'method' is only a metaphor for revelation, not the characterization of some substance. This grammatical point must be kept in mind with regard to any usage of *revelatio* in Thomas's thought.

35 ST I. 1. 8 ad 2.

36 Amos Funkenstein elucidated how this shift came about in his *Theology and the Scientific Imagination: From the Middle Ages to the Seventeenth Century* (Princeton NJ: Princeton University Press, 1986), pp. 23–72.

37 One might mention another contemporary alternative: the deification of the goddess *Natura*, in the way of many of the ancients.

38 Nicholas Lash, *The Beginning and the End of 'Religion'* (Cambridge: The University Press, 1996), p. 168.

39 Cf. E. L. Mascall, *Nature and Supernature* (Darton, Longman & Todd, 1976), pp. 39–65.

40 This account was de Lubac's target in Henri de Lubac SJ, *The Mystery of the Supernatural*, trans. Rosemary Sheed (London: Geoffrey Chapman, 1967).

41 *De veritate* 12. 12: 'quaedam cognitio obumbrata et obscuritati admixta'; cf. White, 'Revelation,' p. 7.

42 *De veritate* 12. 1; ST I-II. 171. 2; *De veritate* 12. 3 ad 19: 'magis aguntur quam agunt.'

43 *De veritate* 7. 8; ST I-II. 173. 2.

44 *De veritate* 12. 5; ST II-II. 172. 4.

45 White, 'Revelation,' p. 13.

46 *Ibid.*, pp. 13–14.

47 ST II-II. 171. 1.
48 Cf. ST I. 13. 7 (esp. ad 1); 43, 3 ad 2 etc.; cf. White, 'Revelation,' p. 15.
49 ST II-II. 171. 1 ad 4.
50 Cf. *De veritate* 12. 6; ST II-II. 174. 4; cf. White, 'Revelation,' p. 15.
51 Latourelle, *Revelation*, p. 159.
52 White, 'Revelation,' pp. 10–11.
53 ST I. 1. 8 ad 2.
54 White, 'Revelation,' pp. 12–13.
55 Cf. *De veritate* 12. 7; ST II-II. 173. 2.
56 Hughson, *op. cit.* (note 24), p. 450, n. 26.
57 Cf. Daniel 5; ST II-II. 173. 2; Hughson, *op. cit.*, pp. 452–453.
58 Cf. *ibid.*, 173. 2.
59 White, 'Revelation,' pp. 15–16.
60 Cf. *De veritate* 12. 7; cf. White, 'Revelation,' p. 20.
61 *De veritate* 12. 7.
62 White, 'Revelation,' p. 20.
63 *Ibid.*, pp. 21–24.
64 Cf. Acts 7:38, 53; Galatians 3:19.
65 ST I-II. 98. 3 ad 2.
66 *In Matt.* 15. 1: 'Angelus est nomen officii tantum et non substantia'; cited in White, 'Revelation,' p. 22.
67 ST I. 111. 1 ad 1.
68 Cf. White, 'Revelation,' p. 24.
69 Dulles, *Models*, pp. 136–139.
70 ST I. 1. 9 ad 1: 'Dicendum quod poeta utitur metaphoris propter repraesentationem; repraesentatio enim naturaliter homini delectabilis est. Sed sacra doctrina utitur metaphoris propter necessitatem et utilitatem, ut dictum est' – which is to say, towards the end of human 'weal' (*salus*), beyond what lies within the realm of nature; cf. ST I. 1. 1: 'Finem autem oportet esse praecognitum hominibus, qui suas intentiones et actiones debent ordinare in finem. Unde necessarium fuit homini ad salutem quod ei nota fierent quaedam per revelationem divinam, quae rationem humanam excedunt.' See also the account of 'symbolic mediation' in Dulles, *Models of Revelation*, pp. 131–154. On the generative role of revelation, see especially Rowan Williams, 'Trinity and Revelation,' *Modern Theology* 2:3 (1986), pp. 197–212.
71 Cf. Williams, 'Trinity and Revelation,' p. 197: 'Theology, in short, is perennially liable to be seduced by the prospect of bypassing the question of how it *learns* its own language.'
72 Cf. John Milbank, 'History of the One God,' *Heythrop Journal* 38 (1997), pp. 371–400.
73 On the importance of new 'linguistic spaces' and vernacular translations in general during the sixteenth century, see Michel de Certeau SJ, *The Mystic Fable*, trans. Michael B. Smith, vol. 1: *The Sixteenth and Seventeenth Centuries* (Chicago: University of Chicago Press, 1992), pp. 114–124.
74 M. Vereno, 'Offenbarung: I. Religionsgeschichtlich,' in *Lexikon für Theologie und Kirche*, 7ᵗᵉ Band (Freiburg im Breisgau: Herder, 1962), col. 1104.
75 *Ibid.*
76 Graham White, *Luther as Nominalist: A Study of the Logical Methods used in Martin Luther's Disputations in Light of their Medieval Background* (Helsinki: Luther-Agricola-Society, 1994).
77 de Certeau, *Mystic Fable*, p. 123.
78 Cf. Eric Alliez, *Capital Times: Tales from the Conquest of Time*, trans. Georges Van Den Abbeele (Minneapolis MN: University of Minnesota Press, 1996), pp. 197–228.
79 Cf. Olaf Pedersen, *The Book of Nature* (Vatican City: The Vatican Observatory, 1992), pp. 3–4.
80 ST I, prologus.

81 *Ibid.*
82 Mark D. Jordan, 'Introduction' in Thomas Aquinas, *On Faith: Summa Theologiae, Part 2–2, Questions 1–16*, trans. Mark D. Jordan (Notre Dame IN, and London: University of Notre Dame Press, 1990), pp. 3–4.
83 Cf. Victor White, 'Holy Teaching: the Idea of Theology According to Thomas Aquinas' (paper presented at the Aquinas Society of London, 1958), p. 4.
84 John I. Jenkins CSC, *Knowledge and Faith in Thomas Aquinas* (Cambridge: The University Press, 1997), pp. 78–90.
85 John Duns Scotus, *Tractatus de primo principio* 1.2: 'Adiuva me, Domine, inquirentem ad quantam cognitionem de vero esse, quod tu es, possit pertingere nostra ratio naturalis ab ente, quod de te praedicasti, inchoando.'
86 Francisco Suárez SJ, *Disputaciones Metafísicas*, trans. Sergio Rábade Romeo, Salvador Caballero Sánchez, and Antonio Puigcerver Zanón, vol. 1 (Madrid: Editorial Gredos, 1960), 'Ratio et discursus totius operis: ad lectorem,' p. 18.
87 *Ibid.*, p. 17.
88 Cf., for example, Willem Frijhoff, 'Patterns,' in Hilde de Ridder Symoens, ed., *A History of the University in Europe*, 4 vols; vol. II: *Universities in Early Modern Europe* (1500–1800) (Cambridge: The University Press, 1996), chapter 2 (pp. 43–110).
89 *Ibid.*, p. 81–89.
90 *Ibid.*, p. 104.
91 Carlos Noreña, 'Suárez and the Jesuits,' *American Catholic Philosophical Quarterly* vol. 65: 3 (1991), pp. 267–286.
92 Originally published posthumously, in 1621, but based on the lectures at Coimbra of 1614–15. Cf. G. A. Lousteau-Heguy and Salvador M. Lozada, *El Pensamiento Político Hispanoamericano*, 21 vols; vol. 1: *Selección de* Defensio fidei *y otras obras*, trans. Luciano Pereña (Buenos Aires: Ediciones Depalma, 1966), p. vi.
93 Cf. ST II-II, prologues.
94 *De fide* III. intro.
95 Cf. ST II-II. 1. 1.
96 *De fide* III. intro.
97 *De fide* III. 1. 1.
98 ST II-II. 1. 1.
99 ST II-II. 1. 3.
100 ST II-II. 1. 2 sc.
101 ST II-II. 1. 1.
102 ST II-II. 1. 2.
103 ST II-II. 1. 4 ad 3.
104 *De fide* III. 2. 3. A clear indication that Suárez shares in modernity (and at least some of its blindnesses) is his frequent invocation of a long list of names with whom he associates a specific opinion, thereby subordinating to his modern method a narrowly conflated medieval dialectic; cf. his *Disputationes metaphysicae*, I. 1. 26, where he anachronistically attributes his definition of the adequate object of metaphysics as 'ens inquantum ens reale' to Thomas and others. In any case, this habit is largely suited to textbooks for lectures (a modern phenomenon dependent upon printing), rather than true disputation in the medieval style.
105 Cf. ST II-II. 1. 1, where Thomas actually writes 'si consideremus formalem rationem obiecti, nihil est aliud quam veritas prima: non enim fides de qua loquimur assentit alicui nisi quod est a Deo revelatum; unde ipsi veritati divinae fides innititur tanquam medio.' Cf. below.
106 *De fide* III. 2. 3: 'Dicendum vero est Deum, ut revelantem, seu testificantem res credendas per fidem, esse objectum formale fidei. Haec est aperta sententia D. Thomae, dicto art. 3; nam licet loquatur de Theologia, necessario inde infertur idem de fide, quia revelatio divina non spectat ad Theologiam immediate sed mediante fide, quia

accipit propositiones fidei, ut immediate revelatas, et illis utitur tanquam principiis; hic etiam, art. 1, ait D. Thomas primam veritatem esse obiectum formale fidei, quia nihil creditur nisi ut revelantum ab ipsa . . . Ratio etiam hoc convincit, quia Deus non movet ad crededum nisi mediante testimonio suo; quomodo enim ei crederemus, nisi nobis loqueretur? Ergo non est obiectum formale fidei, nisi ut testificans et revelans.'

107 'Ergo fides ex auditu, auditus autem per verbum Christi.'
108 ST II-II. 1. 4 ad 4 (and obj. 4). Note that 'knowledge as seeing' reminds us of his use of Isaiah 64:4 ('eye hath not seen. . .') in ST I. 1. 1, concerning a knowledge of our end which surpasses the grasp of our reason, through what God reveals.
109 *De fide* IV. 1. 2, cited in Latourelle, *Revelation*, p. 189.
110 ST II-II. 173. 2.
111 Suárez, *De trinitate*, L. I. 12, cited in Latourelle, *op. cit.*, pp. 184, 189–190.
112 *Ibid.*, p. 184.
113 Cf. note 2.

3

LANGUAGE

Wittgenstein after theology

Conor Cunningham

This essay attempts to examine the work of Ludwig Wittgenstein from a theological point of view. In doing so, a reading is offered that challenges the 'establishment' view of Wittgenstein: namely, that his work is so original that it resists criticisms levelled at philosophy of a more typical kind. The essay argues that philosophy employs three types of what can be termed 'explanation'. The first is that form of explanation which appeals to a reality; the second is that which appeals to an ideality; and, third, there is explanation that collapses ideality into reality and reality into an ideality. It will be suggested that Wittgenstein comes within the ambit of the third form of explanation. Thus one can include his work within a more general critique of philosophical discourse developed from a theological point of view. For at a certain methodological level a 'philosopher' who is said to be beyond philosophy continues identically to repeat the founding moment of philosophical discourse, especially in its more metaphysical guise.

This essay defines *philosophical* metaphysics as the positing of a reality other than God. Furthermore any philosophy which treats itself as other than metaphysical is said to exemplify the establishment of a metaphysics by default. Such a philosophy that is otherwise than metaphysical renders itself intelligible only by way of a whole host of metaphysical presuppositions, and in particular the view that existence does not require explanation. Hence Being is treated as a given as opposed to a gift.

It is further argued that if metaphysics (the science of Being) is to be metaphysical it must disassociate itself from philosophy and continually demand theological discourse on the question of Being. Metaphysics must escape philosophy because the latter's forms of explanation will violate each question supposedly asked. It must also demand theological discourse on the question of Being because only theology, which appeals to transcendence, can offer a form of explanation that will escape the aporias of philosophical explanation. Metaphysics resides only between this refusal and this demand.

Such an upshot would enable metaphysics to be metaphysical, and philosophy to be philosophica, *viz:* purely descriptive. To be so philosophy would have to reposition itself with regard to theology, deferring to the latter's mode of discourse, yet in doing so opening up a space for its own articulation. Only in this way will there ever be metaphysics and philosophy proper. Wittgenstein does not accomplish this, and so his work remains open to the critique offered here, even though in many ways he came close to doing so.

Wittgenstein's early and late philosophy(?)

My fundamental ideas came to me very early in life.[1]

Wittgenstein's way of thinking about language shows a considerable degree of continuity.[2]

Wittgenstein's philosophy is usually divided up into two quite different philosophies. Each of these is circumscribed by its own *summa*, namely the *Tractatus Logico-Philosophicus* and the *Philosophical Investigations*. Only the former was published during Wittgenstein's lifetime; in fact it was the only substantial piece of work published by Wittgenstein during his lifetime. All later work is published under the effort and guidance of various entrusted editors. The problem with this is that it may well be that editorial influence has contributed towards establishing the prevalent view that there are actually two philosophies. For example the *Philosophical Investigations* was published by Blackwell within two years of Wittgenstein's death, while other, earlier, material appeared only later. But by that time the polarisation of the *Tractatus* and the *Philosophical Investigations* was firmly in place. Yet the question of difference between the early and the late Wittgenstein cannot simply be dismissed by this approach, for there is too much textual evidence which makes explicit Wittgenstein's determination to see a fundamental difference between his earlier tractarian work and his later significant revision of his philosophical methodology. An example of this is to be found, tellingly, in the Introduction to the *Philosophical Investigations* (Blackwell edition) where Wittgenstein says: 'I have been forced to recognise grave mistakes in what I wrote in that first book.' In a letter to Schlick, Wittgenstein writes, with reference to the *Tractatus*: 'I am today in disagreement with very, very many of the formulations of the book.'[3] Even though Wittgenstein clearly articulates what he perceives as a radical, almost Copernican, shift in his work, it is argued in the present essay that it may well be possible to read this change as less than it is normally thought to be. (It may be that the change is demanded by the earlier tractarian work and so in some sense is continuous with it.) Whatever our conclusion we must not, as Koethe warns, read 'the rhetoric of disavowal complacently'.[4]

The *Tractatus* is considered a classic of Western philosophy. In a sense it can be seen as representing both the zenith and the nadir of certain philosophies. It was taken up by the logical positivists as representative of their work, but this could be done by reading the text selectively.[5] The *Tractatus* embodies the philosophical desire to explain the world, to be able to break it down into analysable parts, whether non-composite simple objects, elementary propositions (*elementarsatz*), or logical structures. This impulse is akin to that of the logical positivists. But within that very movement lies the demise of that impulse, at least in terms of significance. For the *Tractatus* confers on philosophy the capability to analyse the world 'completely' in terms of philosophical explanation, and yet this explanatory competence is also debased. This type of explanation loses its worth because fundamental to the *Tractatus* is a relocation of 'significance'. Significance lies no longer in the ability to explain the world logically – that which can be said – but rather in what is 'transcendental', *viz*: ethics and aesthetics. The *Tractatus* stipulates that what is transcendental cannot be spoken of, but can only be shown (*zeigen*); this dichotomy will be dealt with below. The *Tractatus'* manifesto of logical positivism therefore appears to threaten both the relevance and the competence of philosophy as a whole: 'A proposition can express nothing that is higher' (T 6.42*) The irony is that this competence is threatened by itself, because the *Tractatus* as itself a supreme example of philosophical competence declares both that philosophy is fully competent in terms of philosophical explanation, and yet that this explanation is not particularly significant. Philosophy remains philosophically competent, but its remit has been altered: that which is most significant no longer falls within its ambit. In this way the *Tractatus* is a precursor to the *Philosophical Investigations*, because that text also redefines philosophy's remit, restricting it to a purely descriptive role. The *Tractatus* may well be collapsing philosophy through over-explanation, in a sense finishing philosophy by way of an analytical overkill.[6] As Coffa says, 'he joined the enemy camp in order to display its failure from within'.[7]

The *Tractatus* is set out in brief pronouncements, spanning only seventy-four pages. It carefully elaborates a schema akin to that of the logical positivists (or atomists). The world is said to be made up of simple objects which are the basis of all analysis, as it is the presence of these simple objects that is thought to prevent indeterminacy. Without these objects, 'it would be impossible to frame any picture of the world (true or false)' (T 2.0212). The *Tractatus* appears to display an adherence to the ancient belief that there are simple elements. These simple elements prevent an infinite regress in terms of propositional knowledge: if these elements do not exist a proposition would be unable to establish a determinate meaning – 'The requirement that simple things be possible is the requirement that sense be definite' (T 3.23). If there were only composite phenomena, then any proposition would be open to further analysis, and so on *ad infinitum*. Without these objects there would be 'the threat of reference failure', leading to 'meaning failure'.[8] Any meaning arrived at could take place only by way of convention. This type of arbitrariness is anathema to a great deal of philosophy, because it renders Philosophy as an enterprise redundant. For Philosophy is then unable analytically to explain reality, and even the concept of reality could be challenged. So philosophical stances such as Russell's logical

---

* Abbreviations are used for Wittgenstein's published works throughout the text of this essay. A key to the abbreviations is given at the end, following the Notes.

atomism and that articulated in Wittgenstein's *Tractatus* sought to establish the necessary existence of these simple elements (or the 'ultimate furniture of the world', to use a famous phrase of Bertrand Russell).

The 'tractarian' schema begins with the simple objects, which configure to create 'states of affairs' (*Sachverhalt*). A possible configuration is a possible 'state of affairs', an actual configuration is an actual 'state of affairs'. 'Each thing is, as it were, in a space of possible "states of affairs"' (T 2.013). The possibilities available to each thing are fixed. This is the form of the object (T 2.0141), and the *Tractatus* holds that the world as a whole has a form, that is a fixed number of possible states of affairs: 'The existence and non-existence of states of affairs is reality' (T 2.06). 'The sum total of reality is the world' (T 2.063). It was this belief that would enable philosophy to give a complete analysis of the world in terms of propositions: 'A proposition is a picture of reality' (T 4.01). If a proposition has sense, it pictures a possible state of affairs. Whether that state of affairs is true or false depends upon empirical verification. There are two types of proposition: elementary propositions, and non-elementary propositions. The former is its own truth function, *viz*, it does not rely upon another proposition for its veracity, and the latter, non-elementary proposition is composed of elementary propositions. Elementary propositions are themselves composed of names, and these are simple signs that refer to simple objects, which they represent (T 3.22). So we have configurations of objects giving rise to states of affairs, and a configuration of simple signs which represents that state of affairs. This is the structure of what is called the 'picture theory'. Language (or thought) depicts reality by representing it in terms of propositions which are models of reality (T 2.12). The pictures deputise for the situations they represent, reproducing their form.

The picture theory, as said, relies upon simple objects – otherwise its idea of determinate representation is brought into crisis. However, Wittgenstein's later philosophy relativises simple objects, reducing them to a purely regulative and conventional role; the point being that what is counted as simple and what is counted as composite are arbitrary in terms of logic. It is dependent, instead, on cultural convention. This disables philosophical explanation of the type deemed necessary by philosophical schools such as the logical positivists. But already the *Tractatus* is in some sense disempowering philosophy, because that which is most significant lies in the realm of that which can only be shown. The tractarian schema adumbrated above inhibits the realm of 'saying': 'What belongs to the essence of the world cannot be expressed in language' (PR 54). All that is most important is to be 'found' in the realm of what can only be shown (*zeigen*), and 'what can be shown cannot be said' (T 4.1212). Philosophical explanation was already severely constrained.

The *Philosophical Investigations* (PI) is drastically different from the *Tractatus*. Its idiom is less formal and more aphoristic,[9] and is usually viewed as radically altering Western analytical philosophy, ushering in the 'linguistic turn'. This work does not offer a picture theory of language as the *Tractatus* is said to have done. Most commentators doubt whether the *Philosophical Investigations* actually offers a theory, but it is said to establish a new type of philosophy, sometimes called 'ordinary language philosophy'.

It is difficult to give a synopsis of the *Philosophical Investigations*. The usual suggestion is that in this text Wittgenstein refutes the picture theory of language and also metaphysical explanation.[10] He does this in a number of ways, but it is sufficient here to mention that, with regard to the picture theory, Wittgenstein problematises the idea of simple objects. The *Philosophical Investigations* criticises the belief that the distinction between simple and composite objects is absolute (see paragraphs 47–49). Instead, an object can be both simple and composite according to its performance of different conventionally determined roles. The premiss of the *Tractatus*, that sense needs to be determinate to be sense (hence the dependence on the existence of simple objects), is abandoned to the degree that the determination needed for sense is rather more *ad hoc*, stemming not from simple objects but from language games with their specific grammars. Meaning and sense are generated in and by linguistic practices and life-forms (*lebensforme*). Because of this partial constructivism, the picture theory becomes unintelligible.

The *Philosophical Investigations* also examines various metaphysical problems, and, rather than trying to resolve any of them, it dissolves them through an examination of the language used to generate them. These philosophical problems arise 'when language goes on holiday' (PI 116), when there is 'a false and idealised picture of the use of language' (PG 211). By means of linguistic clarification the problems and their respective questions disappear (PI 133). This move disables what Wittgenstein calls 'explanation'. Explanation is the endeavour to speak from a meta-position, which would in a sense reside outside language (and correspond to the requirement of pre-linguistic meaning). Instead, philosophy is able only to describe what is occurring: 'philosophy may in no way interfere with the actual use of language; it can in the end only describe it' (PI 124). Wittgenstein recommends a kind of therapy to relieve us from metaphysical bewitchment, by both dissolving the metaphysical questions and precluding the need for these misleading and, in a sense, nonsensical (*unsinnig*) questions to arise in the first place. He thereby gives philosophy 'peace, so that it is no longer tormented' (PI 133). This enables the philosopher to 'stop' philosophising (*ibid.*).

It is often thought that the *Tractatus*, because of its metaphysical overtones, both in its talk about what is mystical (T 6.44; 6.45; 6.522) and in its 'explanatory' idiom, is exactly that type of philosophy that the later Wittgenstein is trying to dissolve. This essay will now challenge this reading on two fronts. First, it will be argued that both the *Tractatus* and the *Philosophical Investigations* can be interpreted as having a number of overlapping concerns which bring the two works closer together; second, the popular understanding of the later philosophy as non-metaphysical will be questioned.[11]

One should perhaps, therefore, follow Koethe, who does not 'believe that we can neatly divide [Wittgenstein's] work into earlier, middle and later periods'.[12] Can we in fact interpret the later philosophy as a corollary of the earlier? As mentioned above, Wittgenstein from the outset debased the value of philosophical explanation by way of explanation. Thus the *Tractatus* develops an elaborate explanatory schema, but at the end of the text Wittgenstein says, 'my propositions serve as elucidations in the following way: anyone who understands me eventually recognises them as nonsensical' (T 6.54). Now 'elucidation' remains the concern of the later works, and its 'self-obliterating' aspect persists in that through the process of elucidation problems disappear, as they are found to be nonsensical. Because they are nonsensical, the acts of elucidation undermining them are only the destruction of houses made from cards (PI 118). Thus when the *Philosophical Investigations* deflates the value of philosophical explanation, it can be seen as tractarian in 'spirit'. As Koethe says, in Wittgenstein's 'very last writings, we can still hear clear echoes of the *Tractatus*'.[13]

Wittgenstein perhaps had to move beyond, and even undermine, the *Tractatus* in order, ironically, to remain tractarian. After writing the *Tractatus* Wittgenstein thought that philosophy as such was finished. But the vulnerability of the *Tractatus* to misinterpretation, especially by the logical positivists who, as we have seen, misrepresented it, forced Wittgenstein to continue his project of finishing philosophy. He had to clarify what he was doing.

There are, of course, undeniably identifiable differences between the two periods, some of which have already been pointed out. Norman Malcolm in his book *Nothing is Hidden* lists in the Preface fifteen tractarian positions rejected by the later Wittgenstein.[14] Koethe writes 'The later work dispenses with the whole imposed conceptual framework of objects, propositions, facts, logical form and so on'.[15] But this difference can be read as continuous with the *Tractatus* if the *Tractatus* demands this difference, even though it will obviously not have demanded any particular manifestation of any subsequent difference.[16] It could be argued that Wittgenstein himself rejects this type of historically interpretative approach:

> I might say: if the place I want to get to could only be reached by way of a ladder, I would give up trying to get there. For the place I really have to get to is a place I must already be at now. Anything that I might reach by climbing a ladder does not interest me.
>
> (CV, p. 7e)

But this disowning of the ladder can come only from its prior use. The ladder is therefore to be seen as the explanatory format for the tractarian propositions: it is this that must be discarded, and yet this alone gives rise to the idea of 'elucidation'.[17]

A particular area of continuity between the early and later philosophy is the dichotomy, showing/saying. 'A certain broad principle runs throughout his work, both early and late: language's semantic aspects, what a word means, what a sentence says, what its truth conditions are – are shown, or manifested by its use', according to Koethe.[18] As already mentioned this is an explicitly tractarian doctrine: 'what can be shown cannot be said' (T 4.1212). And this doctrine is not only operational in the later works, but actually underpins them.[19] As Stern says: 'Both the early and the late Wittgenstein are driven to the Heraclitian conclusion that the nature of language can only be shown';[20] although, in the *Investigations* 'showing' has a wider purview, since tractarian explanation has been abandoned and the meaning of all sayings must now be ultimately referred to a 'showing', just like the meaning of the ethical and the aesthetic for the *Tractatus*.

This continuity-with-difference is evident in a number of ways. The first concerns the switch just mentioned in the later work from description to explanation. In the *Philosophical Investigations* Wittgenstein insists that philosophy is not allowed to interfere with that which occurs; it may only describe (PI 124). The process of description appears to be linked to the doctrine of showing. Because one is unable to explain (*viz*: to say what the essence of language for each utterance is), linguistic philosophy's role must, instead, be one of description. Wittgenstein says of philosophers: 'we now demonstrate our method by examples' (PI 133). The reason for this is that there is in language no one articulable essence. Language games 'have no one thing in common' (PI 65), and that which gives language its sense is the diversity of linguistic practices. It would be futile to attempt to say where the 'centre' of language is located:

> What holds the ship to the wharf is a rope and the rope consists of fibres. But it does not get its strength from any fibre which runs through it from one end to the other, but the fact that there is a vast number of fibres overlapping.
>
> (BB, p. 87)

If philosophy is to make sense of what is occurring it must describe that which is occurring. Any attempt to explain would be to rely upon the realm of that which can be said, which would be to veer off into the nonsensical and somewhat irrelevant, for what can be said with genuine meaning falls only within the parameters of language games, specific and diverse linguistic practices. Explanations violate this transcendental limit and so they stray from the realm of *sinnlos* or that of the *unsinnig* (the former is related to the shown, the latter to the said). But even description threatens to fall into this realm, and so in *On Certainty* Wittgenstein says: 'am I not getting closer and closer to saying that in the end logic cannot be described. You must look at the praxis of language, then you will see it' (OC 501). The 'structure' is that which shows itself, not that which is said (*viz*: explained). This showing (*zeigen*) is also translatable as 'coming out'; and that which 'comes out' is in a sense the *sinnlos*.

Another similarity between the *Tractatus* and the later philosophy, especially the *Philosophical Investigations*, is that they both state that everything is foreseeable. This claim is usually associated with the *Tractatus*. There Wittgenstein notes that 'A new possibility cannot be discovered later.' Furthermore 'There cannot be a proposition whose form could not have been foreseen' (T 2.0123; T 4.5). In the *Tractatus* Wittgenstein had attempted to furnish philosophy with a 'complete analysis' (PG 211). This appears to become what is later called 'complete clarity' (PI 133). In the

Philosophical Investigations Wittgenstein insists that 'everything lies open to view' (126), or indeed that 'nothing is hidden' (435). It seems that post-*Tractatus* the idea of something which was unforeseeable was still an operational anathema. A statement which is post-*Tractatus* but still pre-*Philosophical Investigations* sums it up:

> The wrong conception to which I want to object in this connection is the fallacy that we cannot yet see, that we can discover something wholly new. That is a mistake. The truth of the matter is that we have already got everything and we have got it actually present, we need not wait for anything. We make our moves in the realm of the grammar of our ordinary language and this grammar is already there. Thus we have already got everything and need not wait for the future.
>
> (WVC, pp. 182–183)

So it seems that both the *Tractatus* and the later Wittgenstein argue for the presence of foreseeability. But in *On Certainty*, Wittgenstein says that a language game is 'unforeseeable'(OC 559).[21] However it is only unforeseeable in terms of explanation, not in terms of what is shown or of description. What 'comes out' is that which could possibly emerge: it is all that could be, hence there is no room for explanation.

Just as we relate 'complete analysis' to 'complete clarity', and saying–showing to explanation–description, it may also be possible to link other tractarian terms to later developments, so as to strengthen the argument for some degree of analytical, or methodological, continuity. A candidate for comparison would be the tractarian 'simple object', which the *Philosophical Investigations* found to be a conventional, and regulative, *ad hoc* 'phenomenon'. The simple object is a central tenet of the tractarian schema. The later philosophy found it nonsensical, but this is, as already mentioned, a demand of the *Tractatus* itself since discovery of a simple object reduces to the mere tautology 'such is the case if such is the case'. The *Tractatus* too has an equivalent at a methodological level for language games (and their respective grammars). The 'simple objects' of the *Tractatus* become the 'simple complexities' of the language game. In the *Philosophical Investigations* (130) Wittgenstein refers to language games as 'clear and simple' Language games, therefore, occupy the same analytical space once occupied by simple objects. Both simple objects and language hold the position of that which is 'the primary thing' (PI 656). Language games *regulate* the philosophical discourse as did the assumption of simple objects, allowing for 'determinate' sense. As Koethe says:

> The idea of language as a family of overlapping language games or semiautonomous patterns of linguistic activity is in its own way as much a conceptualization of language as the idea of language as ultimately constituted by linguistic names arranged in pictorial or logical form.[22]

Another candidate for association is the tractarian notion of form. Can this be equated with what Wittgenstein refers to in the *Philosophical Investigations* as 'life form'? Life form is that which enables the language game, as it is the life form that acts as a ground: 'This is not agreement in opinions but in life form' (PI 241).[23] This may seem more convincing when we consider that Wittgenstein refers to 'the human language game' (OC 554), 'our language game' (OC 558), and 'the whole language game' (BB, p. 108). In the *Tractatus* form is defined as 'the possibility of structure' (T 2.033), while in the *Philosophical Investigations* Wittgenstein declares that 'the common behaviour of mankind is the system of reference by means of which we interpret an unknown language' (PI 206). The form of life, therefore, performs at a conceptual level the same task as the idea of form in the *Tractatus*.

It remains the case that the later Wittgenstein was not explaining signification, but only describing it. Yet the argument for radical discontinuity (perhaps espoused by Wittgenstein himself) assumes that there is indeed a strict difference between non-metaphysical description and metaphysical explanation. It is this dualism which must now be called into question.

Description *v.* explanation: a question only of battle cry?[24]

Under the influence of Hertz,[25] Wittgenstein came to hold the position that the resolution of problems does not require new information or definitions. Instead of this, one is to dissolve problems by a clearer understanding of existing information.[26] This type of approach can be seen in Wittgenstein's advocacy of description, as opposed to explanation. Description endeavours to clarify that which is already occurring. By descriptive elucidation one can gain an *'Übersicht'* (PI 122). Wittgenstein states that a philosophical problem takes the form of 'I don't know my way about' (PI 123). Description helps one escape from the philosophical problem by showing 'the fly the way out of the fly-bottle' (PI 309).

Philosophical description develops terms such as 'language game' and 'life form' in the hope of clarifying what is taking place, and to expel 'illusions' that may give rise to pseudo-problematics. The word 'illusion' is meant to suggest that philosophical problems are the result of an ungrammatical application of language, an application that attempts to reside outside 'ordinary use'. These grammatical illusions lead to philosophical explanations which take themselves to be without language, as opposed to descriptions which are (supposed to be) within language: 'Our illness is to want to explain' (RF, p. 333). The reason why it is an illness is because 'every explanation is a hypothesis' (RFGB, p. 30), and a hypothesis attempts to move beyond the particular, for it is part of our 'craving for generality' (BB, p. 18). It is this craving which Wittgenstein wishes to dissolve through therapeutic description, insisting that 'we may not advance any kind of theory. There must not be anything hypothetical in our considerations. We must do away with all explanation and description alone must take its place' (PI 109).[27]

By advocating description Wittgenstein is supposedly avoiding any philosophical metaphysics, because his philosophy refuses to offer any mode of hypothesis. But because of this Wittgenstein is obliged to refuse philosophy the right to posit an objective reality, since it must not speak from a place 'before' description (in terms of both a pre-linguistic something waiting 'in front' and that which description must, conceptually, follow). A reality would provide a 'place', logically speaking, outside language, even though the concept is developed from within language: 'The great difficulty here is not to represent the matter as if there was something one couldn't do. As if there were really an object from which I derive its description, but I were unable to show it to anyone' (PI 734).

The problem with this advocacy of pure description is that Wittgenstein does not abide by it, and perhaps could not have done so (a one-sided diet, see PI 593). Are we perhaps ironically held captive by the picture of Wittgenstinian philosophy as purely descriptive? (See PI 115.) 'It is an exaggeration to regard the methodology of the *Philosophical Investigations* as purely descriptive, free of anything that might be thought of as philosophical theorizing', as Koethe puts it.[28]

The difference between description and explanation may well be one only of 'battle cry' (see RPP II, p. 339). Description may well become re-description, *viz*: definitive. If description was found to be 'definitional', then it would indeed be a type of explanation. For Wittgenstein could legitimise this re-description only by way of an explanation or by the positing of a reality which explains why this re-description is more accurate. These two options will obviously not be found appealing, but there may be no other choice than 'description of description' *ad infinitum*.

The idea of grammar is used by Wittgenstein as an example of the permitted 'explanation' (re-description). 'Grammar' enables a sort of legitimation which is apparently descriptive and not explanatory, because grammar offers itself as the inherent structure that makes description possible, a type of reality without having to posit a reality. But grammar itself may be able to perform this task only if it 'solidifies', becoming somewhat metaphysical. Description is discursively enabled by grammar, but one must have been able first to describe grammar to enable that very description. But at this stage it seems that grammar becomes in some sense *a priori*, providing the conditions or possibility for description, and in doing so it provides the grounds for a kind of explanation.

At points description is legitimised for Wittgenstein by the presence of certain general facts of nature, or even, as already mentioned, as a human language game.[29] But then he seems to immediately withdraw this positing of a reality,[30] and instead views phenomena as the result of language games, life forms, practices, linguistic use, etc.[31]

But what guarantees that these categories are purely descriptive, and not explanatory or metaphysical? To obtain such a guarantee, Wittgenstein must 'describe description'. This task is only in fact carried out to the extent that Wittgenstein is continually talking about description without actually describing anything in particular.

Description appears to achieve an *Übersicht*, as it seems to be able to inform us about what is occurring, devising the concepts to describe what it is describing. If this were not the case then the concepts used in any description would after all be first-order empirical statements, re-interpretations of what really exists. Thus philosophic description is explanatory, as it either itself espouses a reality, or else offers *a priori* categories. And to be sure that it is the latter, one requires, as has been said, a 'description of description'. Yet when one looks for this one finds it missing. In the *Wittgenstein Dictionary*,[32] one can see that there is no entry on 'description'. Koethe points out that Wittgenstein constantly critiques philosophy by drawing attention to 'the absence of the posited mechanism',[33] yet if no description of description can be provided the remark seems to rebound upon itself. This absence is understandable because a guarantee of the purely meta-status of description, i.e. its adhering to *a priori* norms of objective description, would itself involve an 'explanation' in general of the process of knowing reality, just as much as a re-description of the real world would involve an explanation of being.

Despite these evident difficulties Wittgenstein claims to dissolve the 'use' of explanation, declaring it to be a confusion synonymous with philosophical 'metaphysics'. But what goes unnoticed here is that Wittgenstein is still assuming that only philosophy can provide metaphysics in the sense of an overall ontology, whereas in both Platonism and Christianity, metaphysics as ontology in a sense escapes philosophy, if the latter is taken as the realm of pure reason, since they speak of a *theoria* beyond reason, either a higher desire (*eros*) or faith. But Wittgenstein makes the further claim that philosophy is *unable* to provide metaphysical explanation. So one is left in a quandary: only philosophy can be metaphysical, but philosophy has outlawed metaphysical explanation, such that there cannot be any 'metaphysics'. It is this assumption that only philosophy can be metaphysical which explains why Wittgenstein can assume that he is offering a final re-description without offering a 'description of description'. For even though Wittgenstein refuses metaphysical explanation, its shadow persists in the assumption that philosophy can provide an ultimate meta-description. And what Wittgenstein has failed to see is that the ultimate undergirding of the philosophical command of ontology (i.e. of philosophical metaphysics) is not the giving of final explanations, but the claim that any sort of final verdict lies in the power of reason. It is on this basis that a purely descriptive philosophy must erect grammar into an *a priori*. Yet thereby it remains the guardian of 'philosophical metaphysics', not of grammar! Wittgenstein says 'problems arise when language goes on holiday' (PI 38), but Wittgenstinian philosophy does make language go on holiday if it takes philosophy as able to provide any sort of final description – even a description which merely traces supposed bounds which prevent metaphysical explanation. One cannot then obviously completely agree with Wittgenstein's understanding of his own work: 'Its advantage is that if you believe, say, Spinoza or Kant, this interferes with what you believe in religion; but if you believe me, nothing of the sort'.[34]

Wittgenstein's neo-Kantian grammar?

> Wittgenstein's 'critique of language' (T 4.0031) is a radicalization of
> Kant's critique of reason.
>
> (Kerr, *Theology after Wittgenstein*, p. 37)

Wittgenstein uses a collection of concepts in a manner parallel to Kant's use of the categories of the transcendental analytic: 'Like Kant, Wittgenstein presents his readers with a set of basic concepts that are supposedly constituents of every experiential judgment.'[35] It is the role of these concepts, along with other factors, that may legitimize this essay's contention that Wittgenstein is to some degree neo-Kantian (not in the technical late nineteenth-century sense, but in the sense of still working within a Kantian space).[36] As Stern puts it,

> the idea of shared social activity does not simply supply a model for thinking about language, it is also part of an account Wittgenstein seems to offer of how language and thought are possible. Of course the attribution of such a constructive view to him will be resisted by many philosophers.[37]

Towards the end of the *Philosophical Investigations* Wittgenstein says: 'What has to be accepted, the given, is – *so one could say* – forms of life' (226e, emphasis added). Forms of life are a given;[38] it is these that one requires in order to be able to say anything; without them intelligibility is impossible: they are the possibility of intelligibility. Is this why Wittgenstein says in the above 'so one could say'? This comes even more to the fore when he says 'to imagine a language means to imagine a form of life' (*ibid.* 19). Language then as a 'form of life' acts as the precondition for intelligibility and, more importantly, it becomes the precondition for 'experience', at least in terms of meaning ('Grammar is not the expression of what is the case but of what is possible' (CV123, p. 10)). Wittgenstein declares that 'the great problem round which everything that I write turns is: Is there an order in the world *a priori* and if so what does it consist in?'.[39]

Coffa suggests that 'Wittgenstein transposed Kant's Copernican turn to the field of semantics . . . what we witness circa 1930 is a Copernican turn that, like Kant's, bears the closest connection to the *a priori*; but its topic is meaning rather than experience'.[40] Yet we must bear in mind that for Wittgenstein the idea of pre-linguistic experience would have seemed wrong-headed.

Wittgenstein's 'use' of language becomes analytically more reductive as he begins to introduce 'descriptive' concepts, for example language games (PI 7). It is sometimes supposed that, because the concept of a language game repels any notion of an identifiable essence for linguistic categories, introducing instead the notion of family resemblance, it cannot operate as a metaphysical term. But if Wittgenstein does make language games a precondition for 'experience' (in terms of meaning), then 'language game' may well be a metaphysical term. This can be seen in his aforementioned talk about the 'human language game' and 'our language game'.[41] The operational *a priori* nature of the concept of a language game comes further to the fore when Wittgenstein refers to 'the framework on which the working of our language is based (for example in giving descriptions)', or declares that 'the common behaviour of mankind is the system of reference by means of which we interpret'; meanwhile radical human concurrence 'is agreement not in opinion but in form of life' (PI 240; 206; 241).

Wittgenstein articulates this *a priori* centrality of language by systematically 'describing' its workings. Our linguistic experience is governed by grammatical 'structures' operated through 'foundational' rules: 'The rules of grammar distinguish sense from nonsense and if I use the forbidden combinations I talk nonsense' (WLDL, p. 47). Norman Malcolm recalls Wittgenstein saying that 'the meaning of any single word in a language is "defined", "constituted", "determined" or "fixed" . . . by the grammatical rules'.[42] Grammar enables signification, intelligibility, and does so by regulatively demarcating sense from nonsense in whatever guise.[43] 'Without these rules the word as yet has no meaning, and if we change the rules, it now has another meaning (or none) and in that case we may just as well change the word'(PG, p. 184). In *Investigations* he writes: 'So does it depend wholly on our Grammar what will be called (logically) possible and what is not, i.e. what that grammar permits? But surely that is arbitrary, is it arbitrary?' (PI 521). Wittgenstein stipulates that grammar is 'akin both to what is arbitrary and what is non-arbitrary' (Z 358). The reason for approaching grammar in this way is that when 'one is tempted to justify rules of grammar by sentences like "but there really are four primary colours"', then 'saying that rules of grammar are arbitrary is directed against the possibility of this justification' (Z 331). Wittgenstein is here obviously endeavouring to prevent a naive 'metaphysical' realism, which would come 'before' description. The problem with this, however, is that, at a formal level, grammar itself may still come 'before' description in that it enables description. The very fact that grammar is in some sense autonomous gives weight to the aprioricity of grammar. If grammar constitutes sense then this constitution is arbitrary, since the benchmark is the grammar itself. It is in this sense that one cannot speak senselessly: 'What if I offer senseless combinations of words?' (PI 512) The answer would be that 'we continue to move in the system of language'.[44] And the very fact that Wittgenstein stipulates that grammar is also non-arbitrary illustrates the *a priori* formalism of the term: 'If we could justify a rule, it could be violated.'[45] It is the transcendental nature of rules that renders justification unintelligible.

The procedure of 'following a rule' develops the logic of grammar: 'A change of rules is a change of meaning' (PG 111). There is a way of grasping a rule which is not an interpretation, but which is exhibited in what we call 'obeying the rule' and 'going against it in certain actual cases' (PI 201). To obey a rule is beyond interpretation because this rule-following is somewhat structural[46]: 'To think one is obeying a rule is not to obey a rule' (PI 202). If one were so aware, then one would be able to stand outside those rules. To do so would be to inhabit a place 'before' description, *viz*: one would be before language. So one can see that both rules and grammar, along with the 'form of life' and the 'primary' language games (PI 656), perform similar roles to those of the categories deduced by Kant. Stern comments that Wittgenstein 'remained Kantian in the sense that he thought of philosophy as validating human knowledge, by clarifying the rules to which it conforms'.[47] It becomes more obvious when one remembers that the *a priori* is relocated in meaning rather than in experience: 'Wittgenstein would want to insist that all *a priori* truth is truth in virtue of meaning'.[48]

Wittgenstein might well have come along and said to Kant 'don't look in here for the object (the necessary connection) that Hume looked for out there'; instead it is to be looked for in the semantic realm. In this sense Wittgenstein relativises any description of that which enables experience, and it is this semantic relativisation that enables Wittgenstein to appear non-metaphysical. Also there is a valid argument to the effect that Wittgenstein de-transcendentalises his 'categories' by invoking terms such as use, because the actuality of usage disturbs any rigid explanatory classification. What Wittgenstein does in his later work is to provide what could be called an '*ad hoc* transcendentalism'. Whatever categories may be assumed, everyday practice continually relativises them, and so in a sense it is this 'usage' which becomes the *a priori*: 'Every sentence is in order as it is' (PI 19). If a sentence makes sense as it is, then its existence is its own declared application of aprioricity. Thus Wittgenstein asks: 'Am I not getting closer and closer to saying that in the end logic cannot be described? You must look at the praxis of language, then you will *see* it' (OC 501; my italics). And it is why he says also that 'meaning is a physiognomy' (PI 568).

There appear therefore to be two competing moments in Wittgenstein's later work. The first is that of the positing of certain constitutive 'categories' or concepts; the second is that of indeterminate actuality which de-differentiates that which preconditions. This actuality causes the veridicality of any posited 'categories' to be placed constantly in question, veracity residing only ever in what is shown (*zeigen*), that which 'comes out'. For this reason it is better to think of Wittgenstein as advocating an '*ad hoc* transcendentalism'.[49]

Idealistic realism and realistic idealism

The fact that Wittgenstein's transcendentalism is of an *ad hoc* variety would suggest that his 'idealism' also contains a 'realist' component. It is presumed by some that Wittgenstein is a constructivist or a linguistic idealist[50]: 'If there is such a thing as idealism about rules, about the necessity of doing *this* if you are to be in conformity with *this* rule, then here Wittgenstein was a linguistic-idealist', says Anscombe.[51] Those who argue that Wittgenstein is an idealist do so on the back of certain textual evidence. Wittgenstein is keen to argue for the fundamental contribution that linguistic practice makes to the formation of everyday concepts. This contribution can at times come across as advocating an out-and-out idealism: 'The great difficulty here is not to represent the matter as if there were something one couldn't do.

As if there were really an object' (PI 374). 'No object' suggests idealism, and the suspicion is reinforced when Wittgenstein declares: 'One is tempted to justify rules of grammar by sentences like, "but there really are four primary colours". And saying that the rules of grammar are arbitrary is directed against the possibility of this justification' (Z 331). With regard to colour Wittgenstein says that knowledge of the colour red is dependent upon language (PI 381), and that even the concept of pain is language-dependent (*ibid.* 384). It appears that the reality we inhabit is an idealist one, constructed by and from language. Wittgenstein states that 'the connection between "language and reality" is made by definitions of words and those belong to grammar, so that language remains self-contained and autonomous' (PG, p. 97).

However, Wittgenstein's work does give weight also to a realist reading, at least a qualified realism.[52] For example, he states categorically that language is not our invention: 'Did we invent human speech? No more than we invented walking on two legs' (RPP vol. 2, p. 435). But, more importantly, as mentioned in the previous section, he does advocate the existence of very general laws of nature[53] (PI 56e), some sort of an operational naturalism. As Newton Garver says: 'Wittgenstein's naturalism is the key to the relation of grammar to metaphysics in his later philosophy'.[54] It is this naturalism that is utilised so as to escape explanations, but it will in the end be an explanation itself – a 'form of naturalism which assumes that forms of life, world views, and language games are ultimately constrained by the nature of the world'.[55] This naturalism enables Wittgenstein to avoid certain problems: as Glock says, 'Wittgenstein never comes to explore the rational limitations to relativism because he increasingly stressed the naturalistic limitations.'[56] It is this naturalism which seeks to defuse the possibility of his work being read as transcendental, as it problematises ideality by making its processes more bodily.

'From the very outset "realism", "idealism" etc. are names which belong to "metaphysics". That is, they indicate that their adherents believe they can say something specific about the essence of the world' (PR 55). One can see that for this reason Wittgenstein will not be happy with either philosophical category. This may well suggest that he subscribes to a continuous dialectical interplay between language and what could be termed a 'reality'. But Wittgenstein lessens the difficulties facing such a position by rendering language more bodily, and reality more linguistic. Language is conceived by Wittgenstein as bodily: it does not have a 'soul' (see PR for a discussion of this), or at least its soul is its body, this body being one of actual practices. And such practices are inextricably intertwined with that which is, so in one sense they are non-linguistic. 'For Wittgenstein it is our bodiliness that founds our being able, in principle, to learn any natural language on earth',[57] according to Fergus Kerr, who states also that Wittgenstein's 'later writing is so dialectical that he cannot be read as plumping for either realism or anti-realism'.[58] (Kerr is here redefining idealism as anti-realism in line with Dummett.[59]) He reads Wittgenstein as problematising both realism and anti-realism because each 'unwittingly depends on the picture of us as subjects over against objects which it is our principal activity to represent'.[60] It is refusal of the belief that the world is there to be represented rather than inhabited which forces Wittgenstein to reject realism, since we have nothing to represent, but to reject also idealism, since there is no one to do the representing.

The problem with the philosophical dichotomy of idealism–realism is that 'each is each other'. This means that idealism will be realist and that realism will be based on a form of idealism. The reason for this is that they are both examples of philosophical metaphysics,[61] and they exhibit a common logic. The realists are idealists because the *idea* of reality is that upon which their logic is 'founded'. The idealist is realist because his ideas, language, etc., are the only *reality*. In being driven by the *idea* of a reality the realist posits this reality, or a manifold of noumenal substance, as the thing-in-itself, while the idealist has a more immediate access to the noumenal. The idealist may protest that to say that linguistic appearances are all the reality there is makes no 'metaphysical' claim like that of the realist, who posits an unsynthesised substance awaiting conceptualisation. But appearances are deceptive! Idealism is a reactive logic, as it operates by way of rejection. The idealist (or non-realist) says that realism does not work, and different arguments are offered to justify this conclusion. The problem with this is that at a conceptual level idealism (non-realism) remains complicit with realism, since its logic rests on the word '*because*'. This means that the failure of realism constitutes idealism. The idealist says to the realist: there cannot be a reality because of 'X'. Logically, if one were to remove this problematic, then the idealist and the realist would be discovered to be sharing the same (conceptual) bed. So we see that Wittgenstein is neither a realist nor an idealist, at least as those designations are traditionally understood, although his work contains features of both. This blending of realism and idealism is, as we have seen, tantamount to a full expression of their inevitable collusion. It meshes perfectly with Wittgenstein's *ad hoc* transcendentalism which similarly blends the categorically and the naturally pre-given. In that case also, perhaps, a collusion is expressed: the natural is only expressible as structured, while unavoidable structures simply belong to 'our embodied reality'.

Wittgenstein after theology: the philosophical loss of language, matter and time

It has been argued so far that Wittgenstein's work cannot simply be divided into early and late periods, and that there is indeed a strong measure of continuity. It has been suggested also that Wittgenstein's attempt at a 'purely descriptive philosophy'(BB, p. 18) is somewhat problematic. Furthermore, we have seen how Wittgenstein appears to eschew the categories of idealism and realism while blending apriorism with naturalism, and that this renders it difficult to establish his exact relationship to the Kantian legacy. Now I shall attempt a slightly more precise location of Wittgenstein's approach to philosophy.

Philosophical explanation is correctly attacked by Wittgenstein, as it seems to lead one away from the 'heart of the matter', by forcing actuality out of itself. Explanation does this because it has a 'contemptuous attitude towards the particular case' (BB, pp. 17–18). I will now show that this move is only possible following a 'doubling of existence', that is to say, presupposing that 'existence exists'. This 'doubling' appears to be a fundamental characteristic of philosophical discourse, while theological discourse by contrast, as I will show, believes in existence but does not believe that 'existence exists'. To double existence is to essentialise existence (one has the existence of an essence rather than the essence of an existence). The presence of this presumptuous move is to be discovered in philosophical explanations of the type that Wittgenstein sought to dissolve by way of linguistic 'therapy'.

It is argued here that there are three main types of philosophical explanation, namely realism, idealism and 'descriptive-shows' (or, in the case of Derrida, the economy of *différance*). In contradistinction, theology argues for mediated transcendence (here this takes the form of what is termed 'linguistic materialism'). Each philosophical explanation forces actuality out of itself by insisting that it must inhabit an essentialist realm. Because of this 'loss of actuality', philosophical discourse loses language, matter and time.

Realism and idealism have already been touched upon with regard to Wittgenstein. It was argued that each operated using the same conceptual logic. The argument of each is reactively constituted by the failure of the other. Idealism is as it is 'because' realism does not work and vice versa. Now it would seem that all arguments naturally take this form: one would hope that one would not disagree with another if his or her arguments were correct while one's own were faulty. The problem here, however, lies not in disagreement but in agreement. That is to say that the positions in this case are only apparently opposed to each other. Each is, in fact, the required opposite of the other, such that question or dispute can never actually exist. The realist is in the end an idealist, I have claimed, because his conceptual ratiocinations are governed by the operational *ideal* of a reality. An example of this would be materialism, for which the reality of the material is what is real and lies before us; to make this claim the materialist must have a constitutive *idea* of what the material is, or rather what it means to be material. Since the materialist has a certain *idea* of what materiality entails, materiality is forced out of itself into the ideal realm by this foundational circumscriptive finitude. And conversely, as I showed, the idealist moves by way of the *reality* of its ideals or of the ideal.[62] This is exemplified in transcendentalism, which rests upon the *reality* of its *a priori* categories.

So as each is, in some way, the other, we begin to see their shared conceptions. And one can begin to realise that philosophical questions are really non-questions that always follow their answers (*hysteron–proteron*), for to render their questions intelligible the answers must already have occurred. This is why each of the two opposing explanations appears to require the other. Each pursues what has been there in its question from the beginning, as the beginning. Both seek a place about and from which to speak that they have secretly already assumed 'in the heart'. Yet this place is only the circle constituted by being-in-general represented by knowledge in general. Such a circle is inherently immanentised and establishes the autonomy of philosophy on the assumption that one can speak of a reason capable of representing being as it is in its mere finite presentation without reference to any infinite source.

Thus philosophical questions presume they have their purely philosophical answers because of the presumptuous and questionable 'space' which their asking inhabits. Yet such answers are, as we have seen, always empty because all they can do is repeat the assumption that there is being representable without reference to an infinite donating source. Yet the reality of this being can be only an unwarrantable idea while the idea of this being can be only an assumed reality. Thereby reason on its own becomes unreasonable and appears to require a supplement which cannot come from reason or the ideal. It seems that one needs 'faith', but, in that case, to begin with faith in transcendent donation and escape the immanent circle is just as rational as is the standpoint of philosophy. Indeed, beyond reason, it is more rational.

It is suggested below that Wittgenstein attempts to offer a third option which does not confront some of the difficulties encountered by either realism or idealism; and so he would seem to point beyond the futility of the circle of immanence. But before this is discussed it may be helpful to adumbrate a highly abbreviated history, within which can be seen certain active presumptions that are in constant use. This will lead us to a hopefully better understanding of Wittgenstein's efforts.

Philosophical explanation can be thought of as foolish because it re-enacts the legacy of the fall, adopting its logic for its own. The fall can be thought of as the attempt to find 'a part of the world apart from God', to assume a given object without the support of a transcendent depth to uphold the object's actuality. But it seems that the heritage of modern Western history lends us just this logic. If one recalls the 'dissolution of the medieval outlook',[63] under the force of voluntarist theologies, one can begin to trace this inherited logic in however cursory a manner.

Paris in the thirteenth century was host to a series of theological controversies that resulted in condemnations issued by the then bishop of Paris, Etienne Tempier. Although the condemnations were disparate, the common concern was to correct the licence taken by the faculty of arts in matters affecting theology. From the condemnation of the Averroist doctrine of monopsychism, to issues of naturalism, the mood of the condemnations appears to have been to counteract that which appeared to limit the freedom of God. Implicit in the type of move outlawed was, of course, a feeling of philosophical independence; philosophy was assumed to possess a 'place' from which to speak, a 'place' that any other discipline could not speak of since philosophy was assuming the architectonic right of a discourse about being as such. This is epitomised by the condemned proposition; that no profession is superior to that of philosophy (*quod non est excellentior status quam vacare philosophiae*).[64] But what is relevant here is the effect that this curtailment had. The condemnations seemed to pose God's freedom in a manner that 'the next generation extolled and ultimately deformed'.[65]

This move to protect the freedom of God encouraged a conception of freedom that was in the end voluntarist. As Etienne Gilson put it:

> Pious minded theologians proceeded joyfully to annihilate God's own creation. God is great, and high, and almighty; what better proof could be given of these truths than that nature and man are essentially insignificant, lowly and utterly powerless creatures?[66]

This gave opportunity to the philosopher 'who grants the theologian's success in proving that nature is powerless but [then] emphasizes his failure to prove that there is a God. Hence the logical conclusion that nature is wholly deprived of reality and intelligibility'.[67] This conception of God in voluntarist terms (however slight) marks, one might say, the first moment in an intellectually re-enacted fall. This world without intermediary causes becomes 'emptied', despite the fact that this ontological abandonment is carried out under the misguided aspiration of protecting God's freedom and with it the discipline of theology. The world is emptied of God precisely because it becomes subject to his absolute sway (any ordained powers methodologically deferring to absolute power).[68] For if the world is absolutely contingent and no more, it cannot show God or point to him and is thus effectively independent of him. It becomes possible to treat the world as a given apart from God.

This residue, that which is left, becomes the purely ontic realm. Existence is separated from constitutive purpose, becoming divorced from any notion of a non-arbitrary *telos*. In consequence existence becomes 'doubled', and can now be said to exist purely on its own (although at this point this assertion is thoroughly negative and can be gleaned only by a noted default). Even finite existence exists without any lack or deficiency in being, because to exist is no longer inextricably linked with a teleological structure which would admit degrees of being. As a result one can essentialise existence. Of course the world was still created by God but what 'to be created' meant has changed. It was now taken to mean determined in its nature by absolute power, not as exhibiting the absolute truth by virtue of its very existence. Thus while creation had been rendered abjectly subject, the heart of the mystery, its being, is now allowed unproblematically to be its own possession. Hence in its increasingly autonomous existence it is also deprived of ontological worth. This evacuation, which (through default) presupposes 'existence exists', meant that, for maybe the first time, it was conceivable to think of God as absent from that which is, so rendering the finitely ontic independent from the ontological (in Heideggerian terms).

The advent of the ontic opened a realm that philosophy (and science) could quite happily colonise, a move that often went unresisted because theology believed it had a voluntarist veto. In a second moment this emptiness (an essentialist existence devoid of purpose) became filled. The merely ontic realm, which can be thought of as a deficiency, became filled by its own 'space' in a process here termed *anaplerosis*. The empty ontic realm acquired an absolute immanent space, a form of existence without God, a realm before (or beyond) the sacred. In this way 'atheism' was born. This moment is evidenced most in Descartes' total demystification of matter – which previously had consisted of ineffable ideal points, lines, forces and

82

potentialities – as pure extension. This ensures that the world is no longer empty in the absence of God, but is rather everywhere replete.

The third moment, after the filling of this abandoned place with the space of its own emptiness, is that of 'ontologising'. The ontologically reduced ontic reality is 'ontologised'. Now the finite, without God, occupies the reality of its own space; but this space develops a form of self-value, and it is only a matter of time before it becomes 'the only' space. The theologian can no longer qualitatively protest because quantitative logics now enforce a hegemonic hold on the conceptual framework. If God is God purely because of quantitative omnipotence, then a Nietzschean remains 'holy' in his hubristic rebellion, as it is only a matter of amount which separates creator from the created. God in effect is immanentised because God is only one more ontic entity struggling for 'expression'.

The epitome of this third moment is found in the work of Baruch Spinoza. The ontic realm not only becomes filled, as it does for Descartes, but it quite explicitly becomes the only 'reality'. Its 'space' becomes the only 'space', its substance the only substance. This is truly the war against transcendence as Spinoza attempts to pull off the ultimate philosophical goal: to render immanence 'transcendent', a mock transcendence. The exclusion of transcendence is enabled by a plenitudinal immanence, that of 'substance' which now provides all the resources for ethical and political value as well as the parameters for physical interpretation. There is neither 'rhyme nor reason' for God, and there is certainly nowhere to put him. All that exists does exist, and finite existence itself belongs to the one absolute substance. This is reinforced by Spinoza when he refers to this immanent generative reality as 'God'. The ontic realm has now been filled to its capacity (one can see this as a pre-cursor to capitalism, in the sense that it is the privatisation of the means of production, the immanentisation of *ex nihilo*). On account of their perverted use of the nominalist motto, *entia non sunt multiplicanda praeter necessitatem*, one can see that Henry More was correct to call Descartes *et al.* 'nullibists'. This is truly the corollary of a fallen logic.

The problem with the above is that in this process philosophical explanation may lose language, matter and time since its immanentised self-reference reduces to a suspension over a void. Wittgenstein may well have been aware of some of these problems, which is why he offers a third option beyond either realism or idealism, reciprocally locked as they are in the general problematic of philosophical questions: namely, the inability to speak, as they always follow rather than precede answers. Since an answer is always assumed by a philosophy without faith, both secular realisms and idealisms are transcendentalisms which work within an immanent assumed 'given' for which they cannot further account.

'Transcendental' explanations will always posit or construct a reality to cope with that which occurs (a reality in this sense is a principle of explanation). For if that which occurred was not so explained by this recourse, the possibility of an appeal to a transcendent source would remain. For example, a chair will be explained by an underlying reality, or an undergirding ideality. Both act as a 'reality' (principle of explanation) which explains away that which occurs, by subordinating an event to supposed horizons circumscribing possible modes of occurrence. In doing so that which 'is' is forced out of itself in such a way that it loses actuality, and in a sense one loses matter altogether. The chair will remain only as that which is other than what it is – that is to say, the chair will be absorbed by the explanatory reality. This displacement occurs because that which occurs does so before it does, for it assumes that a known thing contains within itself all the possibilities of that which occurs, or could occur. In this way transcendental explanation is a perfect expression of the view that the merely ontic is self-standing. At the same time the mode of this explanation reveals that such a view suppresses the temporality of things – the non-anticipatable – along with a transcendent background to things.

It follows, in addition, that the language of philosophy undoes that of which it speaks at the very moment it is spoken. A chair, for example, must come before its own actuality in the virtual realm of explanatory realities. So language is lost since it here undoes its own utterance. Equally, questioning is lost since questions cannot in philosophy really precede their answers; this would be to preclude their being asked. Philosophy without theology, therefore, consummated as transcendentalism, evades future time (the captured futurity of transcendental explanations).

It might, however, be objected that to invoke transcendence instead of the transcendental is still to invoke something which precedes that which is to be explained. Does it therefore likewise displace it, resulting in a similar loss of language, matter and time? Transcendence does not, however, effect this type of closure because it does not double existence. The difference is that 'transcendental' realities generate, while transcendence creates, and in this sense its ultimate intimacy includes ultimate distance. Because God is being (*ipsum esse*) that which is only is as it participates in God. If this were in any way compromised, that which is would not have been created and would instead be generated by way of an essentialised existence. As Owens says, commenting on Aquinas: 'Esse . . . is the characteristic effect (*effectus proprius*) of God in creatures. It should therefore be the one effect that in virtue of itself points in the direction of God.'[69] Whereas, then, in transcendental explanation things are left as only themselves, but thereby are displaced from their own temporal, bodily, unpredictable actuality into a rigid ideality, in the case of 'explanation' by transcendence things are seen as rooted in being which more than themselves in themselves as, but thereby they are permitted an open and consistent, yet not fully graspable, teleological horizon.

How can all this be related to Wittgenstein? It seems that he attempted to offer a way around the impasse of philosophical explanation, eschewing both realism and idealism. This takes the form of what this essay calls 'descriptive shows'. Does this escape the general dilemmas of pure philosophy as already outlined, and how can it be related to the invocation of the transcendent instead of the transcendental?

'Those Greeks were superficial out of profundity', said Nietzsche.[70] Wittgenstein attempts to have the real without a substitutive epistemological reality; and so he endeavours in a sense to emulate theology. He goes about this by deliberately collapsing ideality into reality and reality into ideality. And by doing this he seeks to avoid his 'explanations' substituting for that which they explain: by doing this he seeks rather to make explanations 'coincide' with the explained. If this is possible, then Wittgenstein avoids both 'transcendental' explanations and transcendence, doing so by making immanence do what I would maintain only transcendence can do: namely, securing the real without displacing it by known 'reality'.

By de-essentialising philosophy, Wittgenstein tries to dissolve questions which require an ossifying reality. Philosophical problems become a matter of 'I don't know my way about' (PI 123). One cannot transform this into 'I don't know my way about this place of unknowing, I don't know'. Wittgenstein prohibits this essentialist projection that would take one out of the place one inhabits by insisting that philosophy does not need to look in strange lands for answers: all that is needed is already present (this is Wittgenstein's scythe).

Language is rendered bodily by this analysis; which means that ideality is rendered real. It, too, is a phenomenon: 'Language is part of the human organism' (T 4.002). Because of this, knowledge cannot flee the real, because the ideal, the transcendental, is never more than the real, as it is never more than 'bodily'. One can picture this if one thinks of the air inside a balloon. The ideal as the air only is, as it is, inside the balloon. It rises up against the ceiling of the inside, but cannot seek to go beyond this. There is, then, for the ideal no place outside the real, as it is also bodily and is only while embodied. 'I would like to say "what the picture tells us is itself"' (PI 523).

Wittgenstein reduces generative processes to the status of phenomena and refuses to see them as essences lurking behind phenomena. In doing so all mystery is erased. Anything which appears to be a source of mystery is turned 'into a move in one of our language games, and by that it loses everything that is philosophically astonishing' (OC 622). Diamond is correct to say that Wittgenstein is teaching us to look for 'reality' in places we have never looked, namely the real.[71] By letting 'language speak for itself' (PG 63), Wittgenstein teaches us that one does not need a substitutive philosophic 'reality'; his 'descriptive shows' come with that which is, as part of that which is.

And yet is there still a transcendental moment in Wittgenstein's descriptive shows? If language with its games, practices, rules and form of life is not to become just such a moment, the games and so forth must be in a sense removed. The first move is, as said, to render language part of the world. Consequently every prospective candidate for the appellation 'category' is upset by the actuality of use, which appears to allow only for *ad hoc* categories. Wittgenstein's 'descriptive shows' can be read as a species of 'transcendental-vitalism'.[72] This means, as we have seen, that each posited 'category' is undone by its own application. He must have a vitalistic moment so that the 'categories', which form, are likewise dis-informed, so rendering them *ad hoc*. However, the vitalistic moment must in turn be disturbed by the transcendental moment to prevent vital forces from becoming an underlying reality which would be the ground for an explanation. But this 'transcendental-vitalism' produces a 'Heraclitian stasis' (the beast of vitalism, the monstrosity of transcendentalism). Wittgenstein remains twice caught within pure philosophy through this idealist–realist oscillation.

Wittgenstein's descriptive programme effectively initiates a practice of *ontic alchemy* as the essence of that which is 'lies open to view', becoming 'surveyable by rearrangement' (PI 92). The real 'comes out'[73] within that which occurs, as that which occurs. Since this real is either transcendentalist or vitalist, or a mixture of both, it claims that all lies before our eyes, that one already has everything, that one need not wait for the future, that there are no surprises. Thereby it is not only definitive, but rests upon a foundational circumscription.[74] Again language here loses its linguisticity, matter its actuality, time its temporality: *'language giveth and language taketh away'*. Because Wittgenstein's discourse is non-theological, its only point of possible stability is an immanent one. And this means that, within finitude, something fixed is more fundamental than time, matter, language and so forth, from which it is furthermore dualistically separated. All philosophy from Plato onwards, in order to be true, has required a stable reality of which to speak, and where, as with Platonism and Christianity, this being is transcendent and eternal then (paradoxically, it might seem) within finitude, time, matter and language can retain their actuality.

Wittgenstein's comments on religion are few and far between, but those ones recorded give an insight into his 'philosophical metaphysics'. Through conversations recorded by Engelmann one can read that Wittgenstein appeared to advocate what Engelmann was to call a 'wordless religion'.[75] A wordless faith because, 'any doctrine uttered in words is the source of its own misconstruction by worshippers, disciples and supporters';[76] and 'if only you do not try to utter what is unutterable then nothing gets lost. But the unutterable will be unutterably contained in what has been uttered'.[77]

However, this view itself dogmatically postulates the transcendent as the unutterable and inexpressible. Such a transcendent cannot really make a difference to finite reality, and therefore is far removed from the transcendents of active religions, with their myths, allegories and creeds. Furthermore, where time, matter and language have been immanently suppressed, an exit to the entirely ineffable, is the naturally correlative upshot. Thus Wittgenstein is the ally only of a dualistic theology and religion, by the same token as his philosophy in the end suppresses the various grammatical specificities of language. By contrast, only a grounding in a transcendent source which expresses itself in specific language saves the ultimacy of language. Only for theology, not philosophy, is grammar the last word.

Notes

1 Quoted by Fergus Kerr in *Theology After Wittgenstein* (Oxford: Blackwell, 1986), p. 37. It allegedly comes from a conversation recorded by Drury.

2 J. Koethe, *The Continuity of Wittgenstein's Thought* (Ithaca, NY: Cornell University Press, 1996), p. x.

3 20 November 1931. Quoted by J. Coffa in *The Semantic Tradition from Kant to Carnap* (Cambridge: CUP, 1993), p. 220.

4 Koethe *op. cit.* p. 62.

5 Coffa writes (*op. cit.* p. 241): 'when Schlick invited Wittgenstein to meet with his Vienna

Circle colleagues in order to talk about the *Tractatus*, it was like inviting Christ to discuss the Gospels with Voltaire'.

6 This can almost be compared to a Deleuzian stammer, in which one becomes a 'foreigner in one's own language', so as to effect a radical move. See Giles Deleuze and Claire Parnet, *Dialogues* (London: Athlone Press, 1987).

7 Coffa, *op. cit.* p. 142.

8 Robert Fogelin, 'Wittgenstein's Critique of Philosophy', in *The Cambridge Companion to Wittgenstein* (Cambridge: CUP, 1996), p. 41.

9 This aphoristic style was a form of strategy. As Genova says, Wittgenstein 'like Kierkegaard before him had learned the methods of indirection', Judith Genova, *Wittgenstein, A Way of Seeing* (New York: Routledge, 1995), p. 18.

10 This may be true but there are still some fundamental similarities: 'The idea that sentences can only be explained by their places in a system is commonly held to be peculiar to his later philosophy. In fact it is one of the central points of the picture theory.' David Pears, *The False Prison* (Oxford: Clarendon Press, 1987), vol. 1, p. 121, footnote 34.

11 'The fundamental assumption of the *Tractatus* is a metaphysical one, namely, that neutral monism alone provides the means for solving epistemological problems and that this same premise underlies the *Investigations*, so that the two works are fundamentally alike and their differences relatively unimportant.' J. Cook, *Wittgenstein's Metaphysics* (Cambridge: CUP, 1994), p. 9.

12 Koethe, *op. cit.* p. x.

13 *Ibid.*

14 Norman Malcolm, *'Nothing Is Hidden': Wittgenstein's Criticism of His Early Work* (Oxford: Blackwell, 1986); see Preface, p. viii. But see John Cook who lists six similarities between the *Tractatus* and the *Philosophical Investigations*: '(a) philosophy being an a priori discipline . . . can say nothing about the world, since any significant proposition can have a significant negation; (b) philosophical problems must be stated in the formal mode; (c) by answering questions so formulated philosophy can show something about the essence of the world; (d) philosophical problems arise from our misunderstanding the logic of our language; (e) such misunderstandings occur because our language contains grammatical forms ("forms of words") that mislead us as to the essence of the world; and so (f) the job of philosophy is nothing more than the job of clarifying those propositions of ordinary language which, by their grammar, generate philosophical problems.' Cook, *op. cit.* p. 101.

15 Koethe, *op. cit.* p. 45.

16 'The therapeutic or destructive task succeeds only against the background of the constructive one', *ibid.* p. 49.

17 Cora Diamond argues that to read Wittgenstein in this way is 'chickening out': *The Realistic Spirit* (Cambridge, MA: MIT Press, 1996), p. 181. Diamond views Wittgenstein's comments on showing to be 'transitional' (p. 183) as seeming to mean that one cannot stop to consider showing in itself as if it were 'something' that could not be said. To do so is to treat it not as *zeigen* but as a type of *sagen*. Rather, showing is a functional occurrence which is transitional, and its functioning provides no space for some sort of 'apophatic' discourse.

18 Koethe, *op. cit.* p. 1.

19 In the *Tractatus* the grammar of our language was hidden beneath our actual use . . . in the *Investigations* the grammar of our language – like the purloined letter – is hidden in plain view.' G. Bearn, *Waking to Wonder: Wittgenstein's Existential Investigations* (New York: SUNY, 1997), p. 81. Both require 'showing'.

20 D. Stern, *Wittgenstein on Mind and Language* (Oxford: OUP, 1995), p. 19. Koethe, *op. cit.* p. 19 concurs.

21 The Paul and Anscombe edition translates 'unforeseeable' as 'unpredictable'.

22 Koethe, *op. cit.* p. 7.

23 This section is often read as saying 'forms' instead of 'form'. For example: Koethe, *op. cit.* p. 175; Naomi Scheman in *The Cambridge Companion to Wittgenstein*, p. 386 (Scheman also cites as the source PI 242 instead of PI 241).
24 The phrase 'battle cry' comes from RPP II, p. 339.
25 See Introduction to the *Principles of Mechanics* (London: Macmillan, 1989).
26 'We will cease to ask illegitimate questions', *ibid.* pp. 7–8.
27 We are 'wrongly expecting an explanation whereas the solution of the difficulty is a description' (Z 314); 'At some point one has to pass from explanation to description' (OC 189).
28 Koethe, *op. cit.* p. 6.
29 See PI 142, p. 56, p. 230; PR 147 and 47.
30 See BB, p. 1; PI 374; PG p. 97.
31 See PI p. 174.
32 *A Wittgenstein Dictionary*, compiled by Hans-Johann Glock (Oxford: Blackwell, 1996).
33 *Op. cit.* p. 59.
34 Kerr, *op. cit.* p. 32.
35 Stern, *op. cit.* p. 132.
36 'Kant . . . plays a seminal role in Wittgenstein's thinking'; 'Wittgenstein echoes Kant's conception of philosophy precisely' (Genova, *op. cit.* pp. 8 and 105); 'A Kantian spirit' (Diamond, *op. cit.* p. 32); 'Guided by the spirit if not the letter of Kant's constructive method' (Genova *op. cit.* p. 101); 'The philosophical line of descent is from Kant' (David Pears, *op. cit.* vol. 2, p. 289).
37 Koethe, *op. cit.* p. 66.
38 The word 'given' is used here to signify that which is opposed to the gift, *viz:* that which is subsistently present, lacking all indications of donation.
39 *Wittgenstein's Notebooks*, quoted by Coffa, *op. cit.* p. 259.
40 *Ibid.* p. 263.
41 See OC 554, 558; BB, p. 108.
42 *Wittgenstein's Lectures, 1930–32*, p. 252; quoted in Coffa *op. cit.* p. 261.
43 Wittgenstein 'shows us life with definitions that fix meaning, life with formulations of rules that do . . . contain all their applications' (Cora Diamond, *op. cit.* p. 6).
44 But Cora Diamond argues that for Wittgenstein there is no positive notion of nonsense. See *Realistic Spirit*, p. 106.
45 Coffa, *op. cit.* p. 269. See also PR, pp. 53 and 55.
46 'It would be misleading to say that rules are what constitute the mind but something akin to that is true' (Cora Diamond, *op. cit.* p. 5).
47 Stern, *op. cit.* p. 115.
48 Coffa, *op. cit.* p. 266.
49 'Wittgenstein is in just the situation that Kant found himself . . . there are certain things which cannot quite literally be said . . . for Kant these were claims about the noumena, for Wittgenstein they are structural claims' (Graham Priest, *Beyond the Limits of Thought* (Cambridge: CUP, 1995), p. 210).
50 Don Cupitt holds this view; see *Sea of Faith* (BBC, 1984), p. 222.
51 G.E.M. Anscombe, *From Parmenides to Wittgenstein: Collected Philosophical Papers* (Oxford: Blackwell, 1981), vol. 3, pp. 112–33.
52 'I agree that Wittgenstein does not accept what might be called a naive form of classical realism. I maintain only that he does not offer any global arguments for a wholesale rejection of classical realism' (Koethe, *op. cit.* p. 133).
53 'To deny that he intended to depart from what I call the common sense idea that much of what we say is rendered true or false by a reality independent of our saying and also to deny that, whether he intended it or not, his later views embody a critique of this idea' (Koethe, *ibid.* p. 124).
54 Newton Garver, *op. cit.* p. 158.

55 Hans Sluga, *Cambridge Companion to Wittgenstein*, Introduction, p. 22.
56 H. Glock, *op. cit.* p. 127.
57 Fergus Kerr, *op. cit.* p. 109.
58 Fergus Kerr, 'What's Wrong with Realism Anyhow?', in *God and Reality*, ed. C. Crowder (London: Mowbury, 1997), p. 131.
59 See Michael Dummett, *Truth and Other Enigmas* (London: Duckworth, 1978).
60 Kerr, *op. cit.* p. 137.
61 This essay defines 'philosophical metaphysics' as the positing of any reality other than God.
62 As Wittgenstein says, 'Idealism leads to realism if it is strictly thought out', *Notebooks*, p. 85.
63 See G. Leff, *The Dissolution of the Medieval Outlook* (New York: Harper Torchbooks, 1976).
64 See G. Leff, *Heresy in the Later Middle Ages* (Manchester, 1967), 2 vols.
65 David Knowles, *The Evolution of Medieval Thought* (London and New York: Longman, 1962), p. 249.
66 Etienne Gilson, *The Unity of Philosophical Experience* (London: Sheed & Ward, 1938), p. 38.
67 *Ibid.*
68 On the question of absolute and ordained power, see W. Courtenay, *Capacity and Volition* (Bergamo: Pierluigi Lubrina Editore, 1990); M. Pernoud, 'Innovation in Okham's references to the *Potentia Dei*', *Autonianum* 45 (1970), pp. 65–97; 'The theory of the *Potentia Dei* according to Aquinas, Scotus and Okham', *Autonianum* 47 (1972), pp. 69–95; A. Funkenstein, *Theology and the Scientific Imagination from the Middle Ages to the Seventeenth Century* (New Jersey: Princeton University Press, 1986); H. Oberman, *The Harvest of Medieval Theology* (Cambridge MA, 1963).
69 Joseph Owens, *St Thomas Aquinas on the Existence of God* (New York: SUNY Press, 1980. Editor John Catan), p. 285.
70 F. Nietzsche, *Gay Science*, Preface to the second edition [1887] (New York: Vintage, 1974).
71 'Letting us see a reality somewhere else than where we are looking', *ibid.* p. 142.
72 The use of the word 'vitalism' is not strictly traditional *à la* Bergson. What it is meant to signify is a dispossessing actuality that 'comes out, within' every application, that which can only be shown.
73 The phrase 'comes out' or 'coming out' is how the word *zeigen* can also be translated, instead of as 'shows' (see PI 287; 559; 590). This interpretation helps us to see the transcendental vitalism involved in Wittgenstein's work. It also enables us to notice the similarity between Wittgenstein and Derrida. Derrida like Wittgenstein attempts to have the real without a reality through the operation of *differance*: 'Now if differance is . . . what makes possible the presentation of the being-present, it is never presented as such. It is never offered to the present' (*Margins of Philosophy* (Brighton: Harvester Wheatsheaf, 1982), p. 6). Coincidentally Rorty refers to Derrida as a French Wittgenstein, see Rorty's *Derrida: A Critical Reader* (Oxford: Blackwell, 1990). See also Staten's *Wittgenstein and Derrida* (Oxford: Blackwell, 1985).
74 The wrong conception which I want to object to in this connection is the following, that we can hit upon something that today we cannot yet see, that we can discover something wholly new. We have already got everything and need not wait for the future' (WVC, pp. 182–83); 'In grammar you cannot discover anything. There are no surprises' (*ibid.* p. 77); 'The problems are solved, not by giving any new information, but by arranging what we have always known' (PI 109); 'God grant the philosopher insight into what lies in front of everyone's eyes' (CV p. 67).
75 P. Engelmann, *Letters from Ludwig Wittgenstein with a Memoir* (Oxford: Blackwell, 1967), p. 135.
76 *Ibid.* p. 133.
77 *Ibid.* pp. 7, 82–85.

Abbreviations

BB   *The Blue and Brown Books* (Oxford: Blackwell, 1958).

CV   *Culture and Value*, ed. G.H. von Wright in collaboration with Heikki Nyman, trans. Peter Winch (Oxford: Blackwell, 1980).

LC   *Lectures and Conversations on Aesthetics, Psychology and Religious Belief*, ed. C. Barrett (Oxford: Blackwell, 1966).

OC   *On Certainty*, eds. G.E.M. Anscombe and G.H. von Wright, trans. Denis Paul and G.E.M. Anscombe (Oxford: Blackwell, 1969).

PG   *Philosophical Grammar*, ed. R. Rhees, trans. A.J.P. Kenny (Oxford: Blackwell, 1974).

PI   *Philosophical Investigations*, eds. G.E.M. Anscombe and R. Rhees, trans. G.E.M. Anscombe (Oxford: Blackwell, 1953).

PR   *Philosophical Remarks*, ed. R. Rhees, trans. R. Hargreaves and R. White (Oxford: Blackwell, 1975).

RF   *Remarks on the Foundations of Mathematics* (1956).

RFGB   *Remarks on Frazer's* Golden Bough, ed. R. Rhees, trans. A.C. Miles and R. Rhees (Retford: Brynmill, 1979).

RPP   *Remarks on Philosophy and Psychology*, vols I and II. *Vol. I*, ed. G.E.M. Anscombe and G.E. von Wright; trans. G.E.M. Anscombe (Oxford: Blackwell, 1980); *Vol. II*, ed. G.H. von Wright and Heikki Nyman; trans. C.G. Luckhard and M.A.E. Ave (Oxford: Blackwell, 1980).

T   *Tractatus Logico-Philosophicus* (London: Routledge & Kegan Paul, 1961).

WLDL   *Wittgenstein's Lectures: Cambridge, 1930–32*, ed. Desmond Lee (Oxford: Blackwell, 1980).

WVC   *Ludwig Wittgenstein and the Vienna Circle*, ed. Brian McGuiness, trans. J. Schulte and Brian McGuiness (New York: Harper & Row Publishers:, 1970).

Z   *Zettel*, eds. G.E.M. Anscombe and G.H. von Wright, trans. G.E.M. Anscombe (Oxford: Blackwell, 1967).

Note: Where 'p' is given in the text, reference is being made to the page rather than the thought unit in the translations of Wittgenstein's texts.

4

NIHILISM

Heidegger and the grounds of redemption

Laurence Paul Hemming

It has become a commonplace to oppose 'nihilism' to Christian faith. Coupled to this has been the prevailing sense that Christianity is 'losing the battle' with a rip-tide of secularity. The varying shades of theological liberalism of the post-war period, either explicitly or implicitly, have represented a response to this, itself little more than a 'feeling', although backed up by a consensus claiming a basis in sociological fact.[1] Against the influence of 'liberalism' has been a kind of conservatism, sometimes styled as a 'neo-orthodoxy', which has sought through various (often authoritarian) means to roll back the tide in a triumphal assertion of 'Christian truth' – through fundamentalisms of differing hues, biblical, moral or ecclesial. The pressure mounting, particularly in the United States, for a 'millennial' Infallible Statement from the Vatican proclaiming Mary as 'Co-redemptrix' and 'Mediatrix of all Graces' is a good example of this. Concern with 'orthodoxy' appears exemplified by a concern with Mary. Framed correctly, there need be no actual problem with the dogma. (We are, are we not, all called to be co-redeemers, and mediators of grace? What Mary exemplifies, we also are called to be – indeed, as co-redeemers we must first be co-creating.) That this movement is *neo*-orthodox is indicated in that, were they ever proclaimed in the way being sought, the dogmas would have the effect of detaching the working out of the nature of human salvation from Mary's person, which has been her role, above all in the first centuries of the Church's life – as even so cautious a Mariologist as Karl Barth attests.[2] The danger arises of appearing to stand the Mother of God anthropologically over against the common mass of humanity. Quite apart from the potential difficulties for œcumenism, the real motive appears to be the desire, not so much to clarify points of Marian dogma, as for an *infallible* Statement that will settle dispute by edict and so exemplify, not the power of God revealed through Mary, but the power of the Papacy as such.

The explicit view of this essay is that orthodoxy is orthodox because it is in the vanguard of the working out of questions concerning faith and salvation, and never bringing up an angry or reluctant rear. The marks of orthodoxy might be well described as openness, generosity and risk, or what in a different age would easily have been described as self-abandonment.

In this essay I want to ask what nihilism is and how it came about, and to answer this question by showing its relation to the unfolding of scholasticism's concern with *esse* and *ens* as determinations of being, and to Nietzsche's understanding of the death of God. If scholasticism concludes by seeking to speak of being as a way of speaking of God, nihilism, in speaking of the death of God, is also seeking to speak of being – which means to speak of how things are. I want in particular to appeal to Martin Heidegger as one who seeks to understand what it means to speak of being, and thereby to show how his speaking of being speaks of the overcoming of nihilism. I want to raise the question of how we might speak faithfully again of God and being in consequence of Heidegger's work.

This understanding of faith has to do with how truth and time are thought. Faithfulness is so, not because I attempt to bring myself into conformity with a particularly conceived tradition or body of thought – a kind of 'correspondence' of myself to what is true (carried out as an act of will and its repetitions) and which therefore is always looking backwards, into what has gone before as the deciding and so decisive determination of my being-true as being-faithful. This understanding of time immediately raises the unfolding development of tradition as a problem. Rather, I belong to the tradition as something which lies ahead of me and from within which, and so out of which, I am formed. Tradition, the *traditio* or 'handing over', is not simply something which is handed over to me, but rather something over to which I am first delivered, am 'proper to'. In this sense 'I' am constitutive for the tradition as being in an intimate dialogue with it: I am the potential horizon of its being made actual, its realisation. Thought in terms of salvation, my being is the place where, through this conversation, this 'being proper to . . .' God comes to be, which means the 'how' of my being Christian will indicate something about me (from the perspective of my growth and maturity in Christ) and something about God (how God comes to be found in me by others).

From this perspective, faith becomes the conditioning mode of making something real, of bringing it about. What does my faith make real? Faith in God, specifically in the God of Christianity, makes God real within the horizon of my 'I', which is to say faith in God makes me the horizon where God is made real and so expressed. In this sense my time with God is not just something I spend (in church, in prayer and so on) but time I create, as a way of being in the world. Faithfulness – my 'being appropriated' by the Christian tradition – can in this way be understood only as what forms me as a faithful person. Orthodoxy is a possible way, a 'how' of my realisation of God, in this case, of God as revealed in Christ. It is in this sense that (from the perspective of Christianity) I am as *alter Christus*, another Christ.

Implicit in this view is that orthodoxy is partly disclosed in the 'how', the manner, of its disclosure as much as in the 'what' of its content. This 'how' and 'what' are modes of disclosure of being-human. Thought as faith, they order the orthodox person towards her and his fellow beings, and towards God. This ordering can best be understood as piety, for piety is the mode of disclosure of my being together with God. Orthodoxy in this sense ceases to be 'assertion' and is better understood as prayer and, most formally, as sacrament – as relationship to God brought about in the communal speech of the assembly as a mode of being of Christ: a mode of revelation of something not-human (the divine) within something human (me, the assembly). In outline (and it is here no more than a sketch), this is the way in which many of the patristic authors at least thought the relationship between God, the creation and the human person: pluriformity redeemed as unity.

What has this to do with nihilism? For Nietzsche, 'nihilism is a normal state of affairs',[3] which we might paraphrase to mean 'nihilism is the prevailing condition of the end of modernity'. What, then, do we mean by nihilism? For Nietzsche, what brings nihilism to light as the normal state of affairs is the spoken proclamation 'God is dead'. Michael Gillespie has claimed a different provenance for nihilism, tracing its origin to nominalism and questions concerning human freedom.[4] In Gillespie's view it was William of Ockham's rejection of the scholastic reconciliation of theology and philosophy that laid the basis for an understanding of the divine that leads, in fact, to nihilism. Gillespie notes that for Ockham 'omnipotence means the supremacy of God's *potentia absoluta* over his *potentia ordinata* and of theology over philosophy'.[5] For Ockham, God is the only necessary being, and so there is (considered in one way) a fundamental difference between the being of God and the being of created things: creation in this sense is contingent, which means that every creature or created thing is radically dependent for its existence on the will of God. This in turn means that no creature is in any sense dependent on or explained by creation in general, but is explicable only in consequence of the Divine will. Gillespie concludes: 'for Ockham, the idea of divine omnipotence thus means that human beings can never be certain that any of the impressions they have correspond to an actual object'.[6] Ockham's position is in fact the radical assertion of interiority.[7] Gillespie notes that 'Ockham even cites Augustine's claim that the greatest certainty is the certainty that "I know that I am living"'.[8] Put like this, Descartes' *cogito ergo sum* seems but a short step away – indeed (and Gillespie would not be the first to hint towards it) the question remains whether Augustine or Ockham and not only Descartes are the founders of modern subjectivity.

In fact caution needs to be exercised, not least because it is not at all self-evident that 'living' is the same as 'thinking' in the sense that it would have been at all intelligible for Augustine that I might 'live' apart from creation. The radical departure signified by Ockham and brought to fruition by Descartes is that 'to live' is possible apart from world or creation such that world or creation then become objects (or domains of objects) which have to be explained subsequent to my discovery that I live, rather than being the conditioning possibility for any explanation at all. More important still, my 'to live' is the only thing which I might explain apart from God (assuming my radical dependence on his will), which means that even in the face of an omnipotent God, my 'I live' (I think) is the only thing of which I might be certain *irrespective* of the omnipotence of God. The most radical aspect of

Ockham's formulation is that in its denial of the meaning of creation, God comes to be· understood as *a* being apart from any human being, and most particularly, apart from me. Ockham prepares the way for God to become an 'object' of theological investigation. The very separation of the human from the divine in this way (with its concomitant devaluation of creation) actually has the effect of bringing Creator and creature under the same determination, that of 'being'.

This is exactly the position arrived at by Duns Scotus in 'De Metaphysica'.[9] Scotus says [§3]: 'for God is not known to us naturally unless being is univocal to the created and uncreated'. This leads him to conclude [§4]: 'thus it follows that if some being is finite, then some being is infinite . . .'. Finally [§5] we learn that 'being is the subject and God is the end of Metaphysics'. This demonstrates conclusively that the position often erroneously ascribed to Aquinas is in fact held by Duns Scotus – that God is known by way of an enquiry into being (*ens*), and therefore that God as univocal *primum ens* is the same as being (which, for St Thomas, the whole doctrine of analogy was set up to avoid), and therefore that God is understood as *summum ens*, and *ens finis*. It shows also that for Scotus God is not subsumed under being where being is a separate (and so higher) category from God, but that God as highest (infinite) being subsumes all created things as univocally dependent on him. Whereas it can be argued that Dionysius and Aquinas used the language of metaphysics to work out an understanding of God, with Scotus and Ockham the question of the nature of God comes to be worked out solely as a metaphysics. One of the most important thinkers to point to this, at least with respect to Aquinas, is Martin Heidegger. In a 1931 lecture course he describes the doctrine of analogy as a 'formula' which played the role of 'a welcomed means of formulating a religious conviction in philosophical terms'. He adds that by use of this formula '*ens infinitum* and *ens finitum* both [can] be named ens, both be thought in the same concept, "being"'.[10] About the same time he pointed out that 'Thomas and mediæval philosophy . . . are important only to a lesser extent for the development of modern metaphysics . . . direct influence . . . was exercised by one theologian and philosopher . . . the Spanish Jesuit Franz Suarez'.[11]

Aquinas continues to maintain that nothing can be said (known) concerning the essence of God in itself – God (and God's essence) is known only through God's effects (i.e. in creation). This means that insofar as Aquinas is enquiring into God through an enquiry into being, *esse*, being is still understood as creation, or created being. What is Aquinas doing, if he is not undertaking a metaphysics? Aquinas' understanding of being (*esse*) and the being of God are, I would contend, strictly elaborated in virtue of his understanding of salvation. When Aquinas asks 'Whether Essence (*essentia*) and Existence (*esse*) are the same in God?'[12] he replies to the second objection by saying that *esse* can be understood in two ways: either as act of being – '*actus essendi*' – of a thing in creation, or as 'the composition of a proposition effected in the soul (*anima*) . . .'. The existence (*esse*) of God is understood only in this second sense – as a spiritual (ensouled) act.[13] He concludes: 'We know that this proposition which we form about God when we say *God is* is true; and this we know from God's effects.'[14] So the existence (*esse*) of God is only in consequence of

94

an act of mine; an act, we might say, of my speaking to myself. God's existence is realised in mine. The question therefore becomes 'how?' The 'how' of God's existence realised in mine must in general mean the spiritual life, my way of being in Christ, which means: what of Christ is realised in me. To call God *summum ens* is therefore to refer to myself. I am the only *ens* that, strictly, speaking can be referred to here. *Summum* must therefore be *that way in which* I realise God. *Summum* – 'highest' – is a rising up to the heights to know God – to be Godly (*esse divine*): it is a manner of (my) being. I am reminded here of Eckhart's claim that to God's word I must be a *biwort*, an ad-verb.[15] This is not a metaphysical projection; it is where I am to be carried to know God.[16] In contrast, it is certainly debatable that Suárez and Cajetan's reading of Aquinas rendered 'Thomism' as a metaphysics, and that the soteriological force of Aquinas' understanding of *esse*, being, falls away. For Aquinas, being as creation is the place in which God is to be realised and, in so realising, creation is literally divinised and redeemed.

In consequence of nominalism, however, being ceases to mean being-created, which means it ceases in any sense to explain creation except as a formal, logical, dependence.[17] The bringing about of God as *a* being means the bringing about of one who can also be declared to be dead, and it means simultaneously the bringing about of an object who lies beyond, outside, or other than the Subject who knows this.[18]

For Heidegger, the coming to fruition of the elaboration of subjectivity, first in Descartes and finally in Hegel and Nietzsche, was only the playing out of the end of the whole history of metaphysics. For him, 'theology' as Christian philosophy ('a . . . round square and a misunderstanding'[19]) belongs firmly within the realm of metaphysics, hence his elaboration of the term '*onto-theo-logy*' in his 1936 lectures on Schelling.[20] He understood metaphysics to assume that being and God are the same. The word *onto-theo-logy* says no more than this. What does it mean for God and being to be the same? Heidegger says that 'God' as 'being' is the thought of 'beings as a whole' and 'highest being', construed as what gives being to beings, what is most 'being-ful' about them, what lies prior to them (hence its temporality, the temporality of eternity) and so makes it possible for them to be. Heidegger draws the distinction between metaphysics construing being in this way, which is *Seiendheit*, 'being-ness', the being-ness of beings (*die Seienden*) and so remains *a* being rather than *das Sein*, being itself (which is not *a* being). He adds:

> Every philosophy is theology in the original and essential sense that the conceiving (λόγος) of beings as a whole asks about the ground of Being, and this ground becomes named as θεός, God. Indeed, Nietzsche's philosophy, for instance, in which an essential saying states 'God is dead' is in accord with this saying 'Theology'.[21]

The theological question in metaphysics is contrasted to the ontological question, the question of beings 'as such'. Philosophy in the widest sense, then, 'is *ontotheology*. The more originally it is both in one, the more authentically is it philosophy.'[22]

For Heidegger, all that is under consideration either in philosophy or in theology (construed metaphysically) is the nature of beings – either as a whole or in particular. So even when we are treating this topic in relation to God, nothing more is actually said about God than that God is 'beings as a whole'. In other words this is an enquiry determined solely by what we find in the world, and allows for nothing outside it. It *already* is solely factical. Far from Heidegger being the champion of a nihilism that disbars anything beyond the purely phenomenal, the purely factical (in which role he has certainly been portrayed), Heidegger's accusation is that metaphysics is already this facticity and nihilism.

Heidegger's understanding of metaphysics is that 'God' is in consequence of the hidden transcending of being-human. Put more clearly, 'God' as thought in metaphysics is not the God of faith, but a consequence of the way metaphysics thinks transcendence. What has been overlooked in much scholarship concerning Heidegger's discussion of God is that for him the coming about of nihilism historically, and most particularly in the declaration 'God is dead', actually makes it possible to think about the essence of God at all. The spoken declaration 'God is dead' declares dead only the God of metaphysics, not the God of faith. There has been a lingering suspicion that for Heidegger either God is subsumed under the phenomenology of being (the accusation that he is in some sense a modern-day Scotist,[23] or, as Jean-Luc Marion has suggested, that Heidegger's God is an idol[24]) or that for Heidegger being (*das Sein*) is simply a secularised notion of God.

For Heidegger, to think God in terms of being is to impose limit and finitude on God. Heidegger noted in 1931 that 'Meister Eckhart . . . says God "is" not at all because "being" is a finite predicate and absolutely cannot be said of God';[25] and Heidegger understood the temporal analytic of *Dasein* outlined in *Being and Time* to have demonstrated decisively that human existence cannot be accounted for apart from the world. He makes exactly the same point when in Zurich in 1951 he was asked 'Need being and God be posited as identical?' He replies, referring specifically to St Thomas Aquinas: 'God and being is not identical . . . being and God are not identical, and I would never attempt to think the essence of God through being. . . . If I were yet to write a theology – to which I sometimes feel inclined – then the word "being" would not occur in it.'[26] There is no syntactical error here, and the move from '*is*' to '*are*' in the reply is the very movement of Heidegger's thinking through the separation of being and God from their metaphysically posited togetherness.

Heidegger added in the same seminar: 'I believe that being can never be thought as the ground and essence of God'.[27] There is here a deliberate play on the words 'believe' and 'think'. Heidegger begins by saying that faith (*der Glaube*) and the thinking of Being (*das Denken des Seins*) have no need of each other.[28] The next sentences begin 'I think . . .' and 'I believe . . .'. In what follows it becomes clear that *thinking* points us away from determining the essence of God, while *believing* points us towards that place where God appears within the dimension of being ('insofar as God meets with humanity'). Each mode of human being (*Dasein*) determines us differently with regard to God. Thinking, then, points us in one direction with regard to God: thinking yields its own history as a coming to itself in both appropriating and pointing towards the overcoming of metaphysics. Believing points us towards the *experience* of God's revelation: to God as appearing in the realm of being, 'insofar as he meets with humanity'. Thinking cannot determine in advance (which means from out of the content and structure of thinking itself and what is given to thinking to think *of*) the God who will be met, who might appear 'insofar as God does' in the realm of being. The separation of faith and thinking opens up a critique of the necessity of explaining God metaphysically. Thinking opens up a space in which theology, as reflection on faith can clarify and correct its reflection. Above all, this space is not 'founding', which means it does not determine the outcome of *what* is to be thought, only a *how* as a reflection on experience, on a content given from elsewhere than thought itself.

It becomes clear therefore that the project to 'destructure' the metaphysics of subjectivity announced by *Being and Time* has as a consequence a re-thinking of the way the nature of God has been thought. In the light of Heidegger's work, in the proclamation 'God is dead' or 'God does not exist', might the contested meaning be not the word 'God' but the word 'exist', so that what 'God' names is able to be secured in itself apart from existence and only contestable when *brought into* the realm of existence (being)? Might it not just be that Nietzsche's proclamation of the death of God leaves open the question of God's essence? I have already indicated that this 'bringing into the realm of . . .' can be understood to occur within the horizon of 'my own' unfolding existence. If we pursue this enquiry beyond what Heidegger himself was willing to say, could it not also have a trinitarian reference, in the sense that God enters the realm of existence as the second person of the divine Trinity? This is not so problematic when it concerns the person of Jesus, but what about the Old Testament revelation? Here again, we have a hint from the patristic writers (among others) that the revelation of God both in creation and in the Old Testament is through the second person of the divine Trinity.[29]

In Heidegger's difficult but important work *Beiträge zur Philosophie*, dating from 1936–38, there is in the seventh division a section entitled 'Der Letzte Gott', 'The Last God'. This section opens with a chapter called simply 'das Letzte', the last (but also having the sense of 'latest' or 'newest').[30] Here we are told that

> The last God has its most unique singularity, and stands outside each reckoning determination which the titles 'mono-theism', 'pan-theism' and 'atheism' intend. Monotheism and all kinds of theism come about as that Judæo-Christian 'apologetic' which takes for granted the thinking of metaphysics. With the death of God all theisms collapse.[31]

So for Heidegger, all theisms (of which atheism is also a determination – we might note, the determination which historically brought theism to light *as* theism), are determinations of the same thing. What thing? Metaphysics. With Nietzsche's madman's proclamation of the death of God (re-echoed throughout *Also sprach Zarathustra*), metaphysical thinking is seen for the first time as that thinking which speaks of God as a being, an existence, that renders and reckons the 'thing' God as an object, a reckoning reckoned by a Subject. The God who appears not in the realm of being but in the subject–object distinction. Heidegger says:

> The word 'God is dead' is not an atheistic doctrinal principle, but the formula for the basic experience of an event of western history.[32]

The word 'event' here translates *das Ereignis*, the word Nietzsche himself uses in *Die fröhliche Wissenschaft*. This word is also used to describe nihilism itself, for Heidegger says:

> We can say, in turning towards the word itself, that nihilism is an event that means a doctrine, which is a concern with the *nihil*, the Nothing. Considered formally, the Nothing is the negation of something, indeed of every something. *All* 'something' constitutes beings as a whole. The positing of the Nothing is the negation of beings as a whole.[33]

So nihilism is that event (*Ereignis*) which brings before us as a 'basic' or 'grounding' experience that there is 'beings as a whole', the Something in General – God – and it brings us before it in the character of a nihilation. Heidegger presents nihilism as the bringing together of God (understood as 'beings as a whole') with the Nothing. To speak of the death of God is to speak of how beings are now grounded differently, no longer in God, but in the Subject. In other words, creation, 'being' which was understood by nominalism as the radical dependence of all things on the will of God, now becomes (in valuation, in the concern with the Nothing) the radical dependence of all things (for their meaning, their existence) on *me* as Subject. It is here that we might take gentle issue with Michael Gillespie's claim that nihilism has a resonance different from that suggested by Nietzsche. Nietzsche's madman's proclamation 'sums up', speaks of and resonates, as the very history that Gillespie outlines. Nietzsche's brilliant understanding of his 'word' is that the omnipotence of God is supplanted by a claim to omnipotence of the subject – the will to power *as* re-valuating.

At its outset, metaphysics conceives God as the 'ground' of beings as a whole, as what underpins them as their founding possibility. For Heidegger's interpretation of Nietzsche, 'nihilism is the event (*Ereignis*) of the dwindling away of the weight out of all weighty things, the fact of the misplacing of the centre of gravity'.[34] In the death of God the ground becomes groundless and weightless: it floats off. This has the effect of depriving things of their weight. Nihilism is therefore also the experience of the coming about of 'ground' or 'basis' as something other than God, namely subjectivity, figured in the will to power. The 'weightiest' of thoughts, and the hardest (*das größte Schwergewicht*[35]) is the eternal recurrence of the same. What is the eternal recurrence of the same in relation to 'beings as a whole'? The eternal recurrence of the same is the securing of all things as the permanentising of presence, 'being' secured in terms of 'becoming'.

'God' as the 'ground of all things' (Plato) is the *inverse* of this. This understanding of the securing of all things, everything that becomes, is in consequence of what most *is*, God. Becoming is secured in terms of being. Here, therefore, is the explanation why, for Heidegger, Nietzsche's nihilism is a movement that is above all a countermovement (*Gegenbewegung*),[36] and 'inverted Platonism'. This event brings to light the circular movement which is the fulfilment of Western metaphysics. Always in these various ways of understanding 'event' there are two contrary movements taking place from the perspective of a (third) place, a site. For at the same time as the will to power, the eternal return of the same, the death of God and the basic experience and determination of nihilism come about and are seen for what they are *for the first time* in Nietzsche's philosophy, so also is the possibility of the turn out of nihilism, and the promise of something, new, more original and deeper than went before. This moment, this yielding of a site which appears (literally, arrives) to put the 'I' in question, which means appears as the very putting of the 'I' into *that* question which is to be asked, the being-question, *this alone* is *das Ereignis*. This putting of the self into question is also named in *Sein und Zeit* as the 'structural analytic of *Dasein*'. To be in the place of questioning is to 'be' 'there'. *Da-sein*.

Have 'I' never been questionable before? How, for instance, did the 'Subject' first come into view, and is that not a self-questioning? Heidegger remarks that in the coming-about of the Subject the *only thing* that is not put into question is me. 'Descartes . . . begins philosophising with doubt, and it seems everything is put into question. Yet it only seems so. *Dasein*, the I (the ego) never comes into question at all. . . . All that is ever put into question . . . is knowledge, consciousness of things.'[37]

In this way, metaphysics as a history of being comes into view, for the first time, as questionable. This question-worthiness can be understood as asking: 'How did God arrive in philosophy?'[38] If metaphysics takes 'God' as ground, and if the move out of metaphysics shows the ground to be ground-less, then precisely that thinking which brings me before the being-question is the thinking about ground that also shows me how metaphysics came to think 'God' as ground. When 'I' become questionable, the God whom I took as ground prior to questioning is also put into question with me, for the first time. 'God' enters the question not as a *Gottes-frage*, but put into *the* questioning and questionable, the *Seinsfrage*, or being-question. In *Identität und Differenz* Heidegger notes:

> The question about the onto-theo-logical character of metaphysics is sharpened into the question: How did God enter into philosophy, not only in the modern period, but philosophy as such? The question lets itself be answered only after it has been sufficiently unfolded as a question.[39]

How could it be sufficiently unfolded? In the being-question, Heidegger notes that the question comes about as a 'conversation with the whole history of philosophy'. How can this conversation come about? By the interrogation of my study of this history, and by interrogating my having been thought (and this means 'produced') by this history. I 'am', in consequence of how 'am' (being) has been thought (and not thought) in the West, and that means in the whole history of Western philosophy. A further question also unfolds, a *being*-question, not a *God*-question: 'Who now is the God?'

If Michael Gillespie is correct, and nihilism is what comes about in response to the need to establish the self, my 'I' in the face of an omnipotent (and so potentially capricious) God, then nihilism is itself a way of being towards God (as being-apart), and the unfolding of nihilism as a history (specifically, the history of subjectivity) bears within it the trace of this being-with. It also has the structure of a conversation. Recalling how at the beginning of this essay I suggested that faithfulness is a way of being, it now becomes possible to say the same of nihilism. In other words, both nihilism and faithfulness belong to ways of being – being towards (being-with, being-apart-from) other beings and God. If we can name nihilism and Christian faithfulness as standing opposed, then we can also begin to see the way in which we can speak of them as belonging together. This is speaking of them both in a historical unfolding of *something* which has intimately to do with God. To ask this returns us to the question with which we began, which is how we might faithfully speak of God when we also speak of being and nihilism.

There is a prior question here. How can we better understand speaking? Which we might paraphrase to ask 'what is the power of speech?' The question of how speaking and being belong together is one that concerned Heidegger from the beginning, and certainly is a prime motor for the writing of *Being and Time*. Heidegger returns to the dictum of Parmenides τὸ γὰρ αὐτὸ νοεῖν ἐστίν τε καὶ εἶναι right up until the end.[40] Heidegger unfolds the 'speaking (knowing) of being' by investigating the meaning of the Greek term λόγος.

Heidegger understands λόγος as a kind of producing in speaking. In his work on Aristotle he considered Aristotle's dictum from the *Metaphysics*: τὸ ὄν λέγεται πολλαχῶς – 'being is said in many ways'. Heidegger's interpretation of this saying is that to speak of *a* being is to speak of it in the being of its being. To speak of a being brings it to light in a particular way, *as* what it is. This speaking (λόγος) is that speaking-to-oneself that occurs in the laying out and producing of a thing (a being) that selects 'this' way and not 'that' way, hence a deciding-in-producing that includes within itself the other ways of speaking in their concealment, i.e. as the 'unsaid' in any given being, because the same being could be 'said' in different ways. There is always in speaking, then, a deciding, a selecting. Speaking is therefore in itself a dividedness (*Zwiespältigkeit*) and at the same time a finitude, in the sense of the producing–perceiving of a thing in its 'how' as a *this*-thing rather than a *that*-thing and as a finite thing.

Λόγος also belongs to being ensouled (ἔμψυχον), which means it belongs to human being. This means simply that speaking of a being in its being implies that there is one who (here) speaks – even if only to her or himself. So λόγος is not only the 'how' of making a thing (a being) present, but also the 'how' of making a soul present *at the very same time as* the coming about and making present of a thing.

Speaking, then, is in this sense 'comportment' (*Verhältnis*), the 'how' (the mood) of how I and a thing come about, futurally. Heidegger claims this is exactly Aquinas' notion of ensoulment, where the soul is *ens quod natum est convenire cum omne ente*.[41]

In Heidegger's 1931 investigation of λόγος, he simultaneously investigated the term ἀρχή, which we are apt to translate as 'origin', in order to show how the horizon of time is also at work in all this 'coming about'. This has a bearing on how I spoke at the beginning of how 'I' am the horizon of God's coming about in the world in faith. For Heidegger; ἀρχή belongs to λόγος not as its origin (what lies behind and so 'causes') but its end (what I'm trying to get to, what lies ahead of me) – it is then a projection, the striving after the thing in its being-produced, the 'ὀρεκτόν' or 'projection of what is to be produced there, making known of the outward appearance.'[42] How, therefore, did ἀρχή as the projected-towards and so named and known become understood as 'origin' and so later as αἰτία, 'cause'? It is not possible here to do anything more than sketch Heidegger's argument in the briefest terms. The ἀρχή of λόγος is οὐσία, which comes to be named as substance. But οὐσία thought in this way does not mean 'substance' at all, but the here-brought-forward-produced-and-known. What occurs in consequence of 'speaking' (even the 'speaking to myself')? The 'dragged out from what is ahead of me': not 'presence', but 'the presencing', as that which is brought into presence, into being. Heidegger does not make this explicit in 1931, but later shows, with respect to Aristotle's understanding of φύσις, that in the two meanings of οὐσία, 'becoming present' and 'being present', 'being present' takes over and dominates so that 'being present' becomes 'that which always already underlies', later ὑποκείμενον and *substantia* as the under-lying (*sub-stans*), and therefore ground. Thus 'grounding' becomes 'being-caused'. Substance as such then becomes the 'being caused' of all and any given 'being'.[43] All of this is in consequence of *speaking*, as the 'speaking to myself' that knowing is.

Western thinking names the relation to being of beings in a reversal, where the being-present of things takes over and masters their 'how' of becoming-present in λόγος, where the I-speaking that produces disappears in favour of the already-present of any given being in itself. This reversal determines an outcome for human being, and also for God. In this reversal the 'I' that speaks-in-producing disappears in favour of something else, and so loses its determination to λόγος, yet it also retains the trace of its origin, understood no longer as the Greek experience of λόγος, but rather as relation.[44]

How is this? Heidegger never makes this entirely explicit, but it is clear that it was his thinking of God that entirely governed his critique. If 'I' am no longer the being that has and holds myself in λόγος,[45] (setting aside for now Heidegger's question 'in what way does λόγος have me and hold me in itself?'), then I am no longer that being whose being it is to come across and speak of the being of beings in their being, but rather I discover beings as already founded, as already being-present (in a sense as 'already spoken', but with the meaning of this 'already spoken' having been covered up to be thought of as 'origin' and 'being-caused').[46] Put another way, the 'real' is not something I produce in 'speaking', but into which

I enter as already 'there', already other than me, and so from where I am already displaced.

To discover this 'real' as already there conceals the meaning of my existence, *Dasein*, in favour of understanding myself as that one who has to account for the origin of what I find (because I do not participate in originating it), *these* beings in their already *being-present*. Such a thinking retains within it the trace of the being of beings and their being-known, precisely because in being 'already spoken', which means *now* 'originated' and 'caused', a soul is implied – an originator, or even a 'first cause'.

Moreover, I am transformed *from* one who reaches into the future in order to speak (even to myself) of beings and bring them here, now, in their being *into* one who must reach into the past for the origin and primary cause of everything that is, as something extraneous to me.

So if I do not discover myself as that being who brings forth and gives these beings to be discovered in the being of their being (futurally), then (because being is the same as being-known) there must be some other 'I' for whom this has already occurred (previously). Such an 'I' must be that 'I' who precedes every other 'I' and explains the origin of 'I'-being as such, overall. The 'I'-being of the God of metaphysics. This is the basis for Heidegger's claim that knowing is transcending, and that in metaphysics transcending understood in this way disappeared in favour of the already-transcendent, God. God, thought in metaphysics, is therefore the trace of my 'I', its universalisation. Again, for this reason, the God of metaphysics (who is no more than human transcendence, an anthropomorphism) can never be the God of faith.

The God of metaphysics is therefore that being who precedes, founds, universalises and omnitemporalises every possible being and time that my 'I' might ever be. *Ens*, but only as *ens infinitum*. 'God' as given in metaphysics, but nothing other than a projected and transcendent 'I'. Myself, reflected back as wholly other than me.

Nihilism proclaims this 'I' dead, and so open to question. The 'I' that is this reflection becomes questionable in and *as* nihilism. As 'I' become questionable in nihilism, which means as 'I' enter the question, God, as the universal 'I', is no longer 'transcendent' being but 'dead' in favour of something else transcending. Heidegger understands transcendence as a speaking of the being of beings. The speaking of the being of beings means different things in the history of being. Thought by Aristotle and Plato, the speaking of the being of beings means 'the relationship leading from the changeable being to a being in repose. Transcendence, finally . . . is that highest being itself which can then also be called "being".'[47] Transcendence here, therefore, means 'being' (in general) thought as 'God', beings determined out of prior (thus 'causal') being, universality sought in a higher (*meta-*, *über-*, *trans-*) sphere. Here, speaking means transcending into universality, transcendence experienced and thought as the being of beings in metaphysics. This is another way of understanding that, for Heidegger, perceiving and knowing as 'striving-towards', or the 'ὀρεκτόν' described earlier, are all what it means to transcend. In other words, knowing, speaking and transcending are all different ways of understanding the same thing, the human being (*Dasein*) in its being (*das Sein*). It is for this reason that human freedom is 'transcending into nothing'.

If God is dead, *Dasein*, '*Ich-heit*', 'egoity', 'I' find myself as that being which transcends in order to be, and which transcends into nothing, which is the mark of my finitude and the finitude of being. Which means 'I', as questionable, am questioned, and that my being-questioned brings me before myself *as myself* for the first time. Questioning is in this sense no different from transcending, which means that 'knowing' and 'speaking' (even to myself) are re-connected as two aspects of the same thing, my 'I'. All of this is also part of the 'conversation' of *Dasein* with the whole history of philosophy. This is a conversation of the human-being with her and himself, that 'speaking to oneself' which for Heidegger characterises λόγος, or what he elsewhere calls the 'worlding of world'.[48]

When transcendence ceases to mean 'highest being', for Heidegger, and comes to mean the finitude of being as transcending into nothing, then what 'nothing' is comes to be heard for the first time. When 'I' come into the question, I can ask aloud 'who now is God?' This question is above all mine, a question in consequence of my becoming *Dasein*, not as an object, but as self-existing.

What is the force of this critique? What might theology be, in consequence of nihilism understood in this way? In the first instance it becomes possible to rethink the spatiality and temporality of faith, which is to say something which takes place as worlded, 'mooded' and in modes of being-human, as a 'life of faith'. What is at issue here is that this analytic is always 'mine', and it is continuing. It may encompass growth or estrangement, depth or disengagement. It is a way of having 'my' time. In this sense it is the way in which I appropriate myself as experiencing, as 'comporting' or 'relating' (*Verhaltenen*) to, the world. 'I am as this comporting' belongs always and immediately to 'the given in comportment' of 'world'. God, as one of the things possible to be 'given in comportment', is separate from my 'I am as comporting' only in one sense, because I am already there in the 'given in comporting'. It is only in this sense that 'I' as my phenomenological self-holding lie 'prior' or apart from what is to be given or is 'atheistic'. It is 'atheistic' only in the sense that I do not experience myself as God, though when I experience God (in prayer, in sacrament, in preaching – only some of the modes of being like Christ), it is 'I' who have this experience and therefore 'I' am also given in the experience. God comes to me as a way of making me who I am. As I speak in a Godly way, God comes to me *as* me, *with* me, revealed *in* me.

The difficulty of making sense of this lies partly in how ἀρχέ is to be understood as futural. Kant's struggle in the *Opus Postumum* had been in part to discover the inner unity and ground of 'God, human-being and world'.[49] This conceives the world as already-there, already-grounded, ἀρχέ as the 'prior', what lies behind me. If, however, world is conceived as what comes from out of the future to me, so that 'I' am determined from out of the future, and this futural 'eventing' is structured by my being-with that might otherwise be named as λόγος, then the problem of the groundedness of the world as independent from me and prior, or its ground-edness as only in consequence of me (the 'will to power') disappears, because the world never comes to me as an object or domain of objects except where I extract myself from it in that metaphysics that carries out the subject–object distinction. Ἀρχέ is then always what lies before me, never what founds me. In this sense the world, and even the past, always lies ahead of me as regions into which I enter, but I enter them because I am constitutive for them. I make them. I co-create them (with the others whom speaking always presupposes). The question is not *whether*, but 'how'. The 'how' of my co-creating will disclose who I am.

Who 'I' am reveals me to be a conversation, one which takes place *in* creation (which means *in creating*) *with* God. I 'am' when I am in God in this sense, always prayerful. What underlies this must be the recognition that there can be no experience of God except and 'insofar' as God meets with me in the realm of being. In this sense all theological discourse is both a discourse concerning faith, and already a revealed theology. Still more important, any claims to a purely 'private' or 'personal' experience of God apart from 'world' are shown to be nonsensical. This does not mean I cannot pray privately; it means that even when I pray on my own, in the privacy of my room, I pray in a 'world' as a being whose coming about is as lingual or even 'λόγος-ed'. I pray *as* a worlded being, never in some interior, subjective or 'noumenal' space. I pray as already-related, already in being, already in the manifold saying of being. 'Insofar' means 'existential' as a being who, having my being, experiences it *as* different modes, directednesses and so forth. Here, the sacramental is then that mode of being which reveals me to be already-related ecclesially, as one to whom God is revealed by the divine-revealing aspect of world (perhaps here recalling *die Göttlichen* as one aspect of the fourfold mirror-play of Heidegger's later work).

In this essay nothing is decided for faithfulness, which is to say that the *content* of faithfulness cannot be given by an investigation into being, but only as revelation. What has been carried through here (as merely an outline) is what in other terms might be called an anthropology, although I hesitate to use the term. Being decides nothing for God, and yet is simultaneously intimately involved in God. Considered still more strictly, the 'being' of God (God's existence) is human-being – God, insofar as God meets with us in the realm of being, in creation. The 'essence' of God lies beyond what can be said, what can be spoken about. The only possible fulfilment of what is said here is a fully worked out Christology.

The difficulties for theology to think these things through have partly been in consequence of a lack of clarity in the distinction made between so-called 'natural' and 'revealed' theology: an over-determination of the relationship between God and God's creation, the realm of (finite) being. The problem partly comes to light if I consider that no one who claims to be an 'atheist' ever carries out a natural theology which is then subsequently shown to be propædeutic to a Christian 'revealed' theology. Every natural theologian is already working from out of a situation of faith. So what is going on? The construction of a 'natural theology' is intended to explain how 'conversion' is possible. In other words it is intended to do two things:

one, to protect the freedom of anyone not (or not yet) gripped by the truth of the Gospel; and, two, to explain who I am prior to my being taken up in Christ. It is in this sense carried out as a theoretical project subsequent to my being Christian. It articulates my separateness from God as an already-belonging. It becomes problematised at precisely that point when it appeals to a 'universal' time as opposed to being understood to unfold in the time of any given human-being, or '*Dasein*'.

The word 'natural' can now, in consequence of Nietzsche, be understood only as the 'constructed', to the extent that it is arguably no longer possible or even desirable that the word 'natural' can be used uncritically to articulate the pious expression of faith. Construed in one way, 'natural theology' is no different from claiming that 'nihilism is a normal state of affairs'. Nihilism is that situation from out of which I am called to redemption, it is the experience of world apart from God. Understood like this, nihilism is that place from out of which I come and into which I fall in the continuing desire to be faithful, the continuing need to redeem the place in which I find myself. Ethics, then, is shown to have no ground apart from revealed theology, because ethics as God-less is only that which is of God and falls out into nihilism. There is no grammatological necessity to a 'moral' life, which is why 'ethics' apart from redemption is always revealed to be in consequence of the will to power. It is always a self-founding – the only question being, 'who' is the self who, in demanding I 'am' in a certain way, is founding himself or herself.

It is necessary to note for a moment how 'negative theology' might be understood. If negative theology is understood as in some sense disclosive of the essence of God – if, in other words, it has the pretension to be a philosophical discourse which is in some sense totalising, and more totalising than 'positive' theology because it already includes it (if, in other words, it conforms to Jean-Luc Marion's understanding of negative theology as idolatrous), then negative theology is simply a vaster metaphysic. If, however, 'negative theology' is understood fundamentally as *my* prayerful comportment towards a God of whom one may not speak, a way of being in the direction of God that does not seek to comprehend or dominate God's essence, then it might make sense. It is in this sense that pseudo-Dionysius means the negative – 'knowing' as 'unknowing' (ἀγνωσίον), 'being' as 'beyond being' (ὑπερουσίας), and which Eckhart is also groping towards (in, for instance, the sermon *Quasi Stella Matutina*),[50] where language is subverted into a speaking which is 'un-speaking' – silence, not as the never-said, but as the beyond-said which provides for saying.

These are no more than outlines, and, moreover, they indicate a theology not at all out of step with much that has been and is being said already, sometimes in a surprisingly orthodox voice. In conclusion, a sacramental theology with a strong emphasis on the symbolic as disclosive (where 'I' am determined faithfully from out of the future) is not in the least bit ruled out by taking seriously nihilism's claims about God, faith and theology. On the contrary, taking nihilism seriously means being able to turn into the modern situation of nihilism and proclaim there that redemption in Christ which is to be proclaimed and faithfully kept. One might ask, what does it mean to bear God in my life, which means as 'I' come about in the worlding of world to find God worlding with me and so speaking and revealing God with and as me?

Ich muß Maria seyn, und Gott auß mir gebähren
Sol Er mich Ewiglich der Seeligkeit bewehren.[51]

Notes

1 Although cold water has to some extent been poured on this 'consensus' that Christianity, in Britain at least, is in a slow but inevitable and irreversible decline by more measured considerations of the topic, not least Adrian Hastings' *A History of English Christianity 1920–1990* (London, SCM, 1991).

2 *Kirchliche Dogmatik I: Die Lehre vom Wort Gottes 2*, §15, 4. Barth indicates clearly that the working out of the meaning of the term Θεοτόκος was in consequence of the working out of Christology, and, most particularly, that aspect of Christology which relates the nature of being human to the nature of being divine from the perspective of what Jesus received from Mary.

3 *Der Wille zur Macht: Sämtliche Werke* (Stuttgart, Kröner, 1996), §23.

4 In *Nihilism before Nietzsche* (Chicago, University of Chicago Press, 1995).

5 *Ibid.*, p. 16.

6 *Ibid.*, p. 18.

7 If we understand 'radical dependence' as 'valuation', then it becomes clear how remarkably Ockham's God prefigures the Nietzschean Subject as *that one* who, in the revaluation of all values gives value to things and so makes them what they are. This is not so extravagant a claim if one recalls Gillespie's suggestion that, for Ockham, we are no more than ideas in the mind of God. If such a God is declared dead, then we are the ones who undertake the valuation.

8 Gillespie, *op. cit.*, p. 19.

9 In *Duns Scotus: Philosophical Writings*, with a translation by Allan Wolter (Cambridge, MA, Hackett, 1987), pp. 1–13.

10 In *Gesamtausgabe* (Band 33), *Aristoteles, Metaphysik Θ 1–3*, (Frankfurt, Klostermann, 1981), p. 46.

11 In the 1929 lecture course published as *Gesamtausgabe* (Band 29/30), *Die Grundbegriffe der Metaphysik* (Frankfurt, Klostermann, 1983), §14.

12 *Summa Theologiæ* I Q. 3 A. 4.

13 I am aware that the Blackfriars' translation renders the phrase [I Q. 3 A. 4 ad 2] '. . . alio modo, significat compositionem propositionis, quam anima adinvenit coniungens prædicatum subiecto' as '. . . or it may mean the composition effected by the mind in joining a predicate to a subject'. The translation does not, I think, do full justice to the breadth of meaning intended by the two terms *adinvenit* and *anima*. I would contend that Aquinas is describing more than a simply mental act, although certainly that is included.

14 *Ibid.*, ad 2.

15 Sermon 9 in Kohlhammer's schema, in *Werke* (Band I), *Predigten* (Frankfurt, Deutscher Klassiker Verlag, 1993). A further indication of how close Eckhart is to this understanding of Aquinas can be found in Sermon 62: 'God *becomes* when all creatures say "God" – then God comes to be.'

16 This is here only a sketch, but becomes eminently intelligible when understood in relation to those texts which articulate an ascent into darkness as a knowing of God, as in pseudo-Dionysius' *Mystical Theology* or even Gregory of Nyssa's *Life of Moses*.

17 This is, I grant, a slight simplification. Pseudo-Dionysius resolved this question in the

Divine Names and *Mystical Theology* by speaking of God as ὑπερουσίας (beyond being) in order to avoid bringing God under the determination of (created) being. Dionysius does, however, continue to say that in some sense God 'is' and to speak of God as being 'beyond being'. This distinction is maintained by Aquinas in his separation of the common being-caused (*esse commune*) of all things from the being of God (*ipsum esse subsistens*). It is in this sense that David Burrell and others have argued that Aquinas' understanding of *ens increatum* is not in any sense 'a' being.

18 This rather reads Gillespie's argument against himself. His contending thesis is that Nietzsche misunderstood the origins of nihilism, a misunderstanding which resulted in his declaration 'God is dead'. While wishing to accept many of Gillespie's arguments and conclusions, I remain unconvinced that Nietzsche's insight differs so greatly from the origins he traces and so fails to describe the essence of nihilism in its unfolding. Indeed, Nietzsche's brilliance is that he presents not simply an historical insight, but the essence of what can also be explained as a history in a figure – of a madman, or of Zarathustra.

19 *Einführung in die Metaphysik* (Tübingen, Max Niemeyer Verlag, 1953), p. 6, the published text of a lecture course entitled 'Einführung der Metaphysik' and given in 1935. Translated as *An Introduction to Metaphysics* by R. Manheim (New Haven, CT, Yale University Press, 1959), p. 7.

20 Later published as *Schellings Abhandlung über das Wesen der menschlichen Freiheit* (1809) and translated by Joan Stambaugh as *Schelling's Treatise on the Essence of Human Freedom* (Ohio, University of Ohio Press, 1985). Also published as volume 42 of the *Gesamtausgabe* in a re-edited form. For other places where *ontotheology* as a term appears, see the 1942/3 text *Hegels Begriff der Erfahrung*, in the 1949 'Vorwort' to the 1929 lecture on the nothing, 'das Nichts', entitled 'Was ist Metaphysik?' in 1957 in *Identität und Differenz*, and in 1962 in *Kants These über das Sein*.

21 *Schellings Abhandlung*, p. 61.

22 *Ibid.*, p. 62.

23 An accusation made first by Karl Löwith, explicitly in relation to Heidegger's *Habilitationsschrift* on a text, then thought to have been authored by Scotus, of 1916. Cf. Löwith's *Heidegger – Denker in dürftiger Zeit*, first published in 1953. Revised and republished in 1960 in *Sämtliche Schriften* (Band 8, Stuttgart, Metzler, 1984), p. 170; English translation in *Martin Heidegger, European Nihilism* ed. R. Wolin, New York, Columbia, 1995, pp. 75ff. A footnote (on p. 254 of the English text, p. 139 of the German) refers to pp. 348–351 of Heidegger's 1916 work *Die Kategorien – und Bedeutungslehre des Duns Scotus*, published in *Frühe Schriften* (Frankfurt, Klostermann, 1972), and suggests that terms relating to God in the 1916 text are immediately interchangeable with reference to being (*das Sein*) in several post-war texts. Löwith supplies no supporting scholarship for this argument.

24 Cf *Dieu sans l'Etre* (Paris, Fayard, 1982), especially pp. 68f; translated as *God without Being* by T.A. Carlson (Chicago, University of Chicago Press, 1991).

25 *Aristoteles Metaphysik Θ 1–3*. Heidegger notes this is the thinking of the early Eckhart, and possibly the Eckhart of the *Quæstiones Parisiensis*. It is arguably not the Eckhart of the *Prologi* to the *Opus Tripartitum*, with its opening '*Esse est Deus . . .*' (*Opera Latina, II: Opus Tripartitum Prologi*, ed. H. Bascour (Rome, Sancta Sabina, 1935), p. 12).

26 *Gesamtausgabe* (Band 15), *Seminare* (Frankfurt, Klostermann, 1986), p. 436.

27 *Ibid.*: 'Ich glaube, daß das Sein niemals als Grund und Wesen von Gott gedacht werden kann . . .'.

28 What happens when faith is explained solely in terms of metaphysics, and is therefore determined by and out of the unfolding of the history of being, is explained in some depth by Heidegger in his *Die Metaphysik als Geschichte des Seins*, published in *Nietzsche*, II, pp. 399–458.

29 Cf. for instance, St Athanasius, *De Incarnatione*, 3.

30 *Gesamtausgabe* (Band 65), *Beiträge zur Philosophie (Vom Ereignis)* (Frankfurt, Klostermann, 1989), §253, pp. 405–420.
31 *Ibid.*, p. 411.
32 *Nietzsche* (Band I, Pfullingen, Neske, 1961), p. 183. Translated by D.F. Krell as *Nietzsche by Martin Heidegger*, 4 volumes (San Francisco, Harper Torchbooks, 1979).
33 *Ibid.*, (Band I), pp. 435f.
34 *Ibid.*, (Band I), p. 421.
35 *Ibid.*, p. 323.
36 *Ibid.*, pp. 433f.
37 *Die Grundbegriffe der Metaphysik*, p. 30.
38 *Identität und Differenz* (Pfullingen, Neske, 1957), p. 46.
39 *Ibid.*
40 'For the same is for knowing (thinking) as is for being.' The dictum, which Heidegger names in *Being and Time* as Parmenides' 'ontological thesis' (and which he translates and re-translates with different emphases throughout his work) formed the basis for Heidegger's last seminar in 1973 at Zähringen. (*Seminare*, pp. 401ff.) It is worth noting that in *Being and Time* Heidegger connects the working out of Parmenides' dictum explicitly with Aquinas, in which he connects Aquinas' understanding of the soul with *Dasein*. This 'soul' has nothing to do, he says, 'with the vicious subjectivising of the totality of beings'. We know from what has been said above, that this 'totality of beings' viciously 'subjectivised' is nothing other than the metaphysical conception of God. Once again, Heidegger is keen to draw a sharp distinction between Aquinas and metaphysics. (Cf. *Sein und Zeit*, p. 14.)
41 *Sein und Zeit*, p. 14, quoting Aquinas' *Quæstiones de Veritate*, q. I, a 1 c.
42 *Aristoteles Metaphysik* Θ, p. 151.
43 Cf. *Vom Wesen und Begriff der* φύσις, *Aristoteles' Physik B 1* in *Wegmarken* (Frankfurt, Klostermann, 1967), pp. 309–372, especially p. 343; first published in Milan in 1958 in *Il Pensiero*, vol. III; translated by T. Sheehan as *On the Being and Conception of Physics. Aristotle's Physics B 1*, in *Man and World*, vol. 9 (The Hague, 1976).
44 *Einführung in die Metaphysik*, p. 95.
45 *Ibid.*, p. 348.
46 Cf. for instance *ibid.*, p.147.
47 *Ibid.*
48 In, for instance, the 1949 lectures 'Das Ding' and 'Die Kehre', published in *Vorträge und Aufsätze* (Pfullingen, Neske, 1954), p. 179 and *Die Technik und die Kehre* (Pfullingen, Neske, 1962), p. 44; translated as 'The Thing' in *Poetry, Language, Thought* (New York, Harper, 1971), p. 180, and *The Question Concerning Technology* (Harper, New York, 1977), p. 45. In both cases 'worlding of world' relates to the being of God and to *das Geviert*, the 'fourfold'.
49 Section 21.
50 *Op. cit.*
51 Angelus Silesius, *Cherubinischer Wandersmann* (Kritische Ausgabe), (Stuttgart, Reclam, 1985), I, 23: 'Mary must I be, and bear forth God from me, should Ever blessedness be borne to me.'

5

DESIRE

Augustine beyond Western subjectivity

Michael Hanby

I

Can there be a non-possessive desire? Are all claims to knowledge intrinsically violent? These sorts of question, disguising their contingent origins and formal presuppositions, present themselves to our age with utmost urgency, as if inevitably and transcendentally inscribed into the very nature of things. And it is in response to these questions that much of (post?)modern theology, in the long wake of Christendom's collapse, now seems eager to constitute itself. But of course these questions take as transcendentally normative the consequences of that collapse, the parceling up of an ancient theological consensus into various abstract mathematical and atheistic oppositions distributed among analytical and continental preoccupations, whose metaphysically inevitable excesses modern liberal politics is meant to tame. Among them: the ratios of finitude to infinitude and immanence to transcendence; the abstract relation governing the opposition of a self-asserting subject to its objects and the subjects it converts into objects; the despair for the subject of having to buck up in the face of its own self-negation in the limiting face of the 'other'; and the subsequent relations between intellect and will and descriptive and evaluative language, to name a few.

Michael Allen Gillespie rightly traces the origins of nihilism, not to Nietzsche who largely misunderstood it, but to the possibility of divine deception engendered by Scotus' and Ockham's reconfiguration of God's omnipotence and infinity, conceived now as the arbitrary exercise of a divine will unqualified by its other essential predicates, and not intelligibly and iconically manifest by the arrangement of the created order.[1] The quest for certain foundations, which resulted in Descartes' *cogito* and the principles of his science, produced what was at once a participation in and security against this exigency by an assertive human will, similarly conceived. Gillespie is thus right to locate the birth of modernity in the ascendancy of an account of the will deviant to the antecedent Christian tradition. However, Gillespie evinces little understanding of that earlier notion of will from which the nominalists departed, its relation to intellect, or its own principle. His own liberalism, which both owes to and differently perpetuates the original nihilist assumptions, blinds him to the anachronistic nature of the dichotomies – intellect and will, reason and revelation, rational philosophy and theology are examples – which he employs to narrate the pre-Scotist tradition[2] and prevents him from seeing how he remains confined to that which he is attempting to critique. Obscured in the process is how, for Aquinas for instance, the charity in-formed virtues and thus a will ordered doxologically from its end entered inextricably into the very notion of rationality. For the forms, apart from virtues so in-formed, do not guarantee the correctness of their own apprehension. Hence Gillespie is led to imply a sort of liberal stop-gap solution to nihilism which shares the latter's historical precursors, presuppositions, and *telos*, and he is thus prevented from reaching the sort of MacIntyrean conclusion to which his otherwise excellent research should have led: the story of nihilism is still the story of the death of God, for the God from which nihilism emerges is still-born, an idol. As a mistaken deviation from Augustinianism, the problems engendered by the variations in the modern concept of will must remain intractable, the questions, premissed on this mistake, unsolvable. Moreover, if this account is true, the discourse of philosophy as it has come to be practiced and institutionally embodied must prove – and as MacIntyre claims, is proving – inadequate to the job.[3] For if Augustinian Christianity is true, and if the antinomies plaguing modernity are in his work somehow forecast and resolved, then the genre of the *Confessions* and its ecclesial outworking are less pious or manipulative accidents than they are intrinsically expressive both of what it is to raise and in some measure to answer the question of being, for they exemplify what it is doxologically to participate in it. If Augustinian Christianity is true, then should modernity wish to escape the imprisonment of its fly-bottle, it will find only one exit – the hole by which it flew in. The answer will thus not be, as it is for Gillespie,[4] finally to escape the Christian God, but to return to him.

The question which theology should therefore address is not whether all is violent, but whether an account of the will or subjectivity not Christologically mediated and doxologically ordered to participation in the life of the Trinity through the Church can be anything else (and whether, apart from a nature so understood, the concept of violence has coherent application[5]). Using primarily Augustine's *De Trinitate* and *Confessions*, I shall henceforth articulate the contours of an account of the doxological subject iconically constituted within the normativity of orthodox Christology, an account which mandates confession and the historic ecclesia as ontological modalities, and which exposes modern attempts to fix the ratio of finitude to infinitude and activity to passivity as simply secular variations on the Pelagian and Nestorian heresies.[6] My concern is not to answer the nihilist questions, whose admission already requires ceding as common too much metaphysical ground. Though I, like Wittgenstein, seek that 'the philosophical problems should completely disappear,'[7] the very terms of the account which I put forth, and its acknowledgment of the institutionalized force of habit, recognize that it will take more than a philosophical event, as this might commonly be understood, to bring that about. The best I can do is to begin to explicate an account without whose perversion and rejection such problems need never arise.

<h2>II</h2>

As Conor Cunningham observes, all the logics of exponential negations must, by virtue of the formal elements of the terms employed in expounding the logic,[8] presuppose something about the character of what there is on hand to negate. Be it the nihilation executed by a willing subject on the inert other, the other's necessary negation of his exertion, or that which dissolves both by virtue of the transcendental conditions of possibility for their interaction, all must assume some measure of that for which they attempt to account, some sort of stable, albeit oppositional, relationship between immanence and transcendence, between activity and passivity, and the like. It is, after all, only within some sort of positive metaphysical prejudice about these ratios that one can conceive of all passivity, reception or extension as incursions against consolidated ground or projections into an indeterminate abyss. However, I intend to show, perhaps against the dualistic sound of Augustine's conceptual tools, that the substance of Augustine's thought is decidedly anti-metaphysical (in the secular sense) for its refusal to fix these borders, save his implicit deference to the ratio harmoniously cohering in the two natures of Christ, which is itself unique precisely in that it remains both intrinsically and extrinsically borderless at the same time as the natures remain distinct.

If Augustine has such prejudices they should be revealed in the answer which he gives to the question posed just before the recollection of his baptism in the *Confessions*: 'who am I, and what am I?'[9] It is a question that recurs in various forms throughout the remaining chapters,[10] and one whose answer will mirror that posed in Book VIII of *De Trinitate*: how the man not yet righteous can know the righteous man whom he loves.[11] And given the history of interpretation of the *vestigia trinitatis*, it is here we should probably begin. For it is a commonplace, as Rowan Williams notes, to assume that Augustine, as a sort of proto-Cartesian, will locate the answer to the *Confessions'* question in the establishment of a triadic resemblance in the mind from which to argue his way to the Trinity.[12] As Williams indicates, this misses the significance of Book XV's insistence of the mind's *unlikeness* to the Trinity, a point to which we shall soon return, but it also elevates (and misinterprets) Book XIV at the cost of making the arguments of Books II–IV a *non sequitur* to the purpose of the work. Whereas I would wish to maintain that these arguments concerning the manner of the divine appearances to creatures not hypostatically assumed and glorified by the person of the Son as was Christ[13] indicate the concern which controls the meaning of *imago dei*. It is a concern expressed in the question which prefaces the work's conclusion in *De Trinitate*, XV: 'how does the Trinity manifest itself?'[14] In short, Augustine is less concerned to establish the resemblance of substantially sufficient man to God, and even less to argue by way of 'self-awareness' to God, than he is to display how God is made manifest in and through the creature and how, through God, the creature whose perfection, and thus true *nature*, awaits in the glorified Christ, is mediated and made manifest to himself. The self, in other words, is fundamentally iconic for the objects of its desire.

In all of those instances, in the later books of the *Confessions*, in which Augustine might be interpreted as attempting substantially to establish and possess himself, he fails. His pursuit of the question of Book IX, 'who and what am I?', follows a technique familiar in both texts. He presses the issue in various forms till he reaches seeming *aporia*, the memory of his forgetfulness, the duality of his distention in time, his distention of a spaceless present, and the incontinence of both his desire and materiality with time's passage,[15] such that in each instance he is rendered incomprehensible to himself and invokes God's mediation,[16] until finally the story of Augustine the self becomes an icon for the story of the creation, the separation of light from darkness prefigured in Genesis, and now, through the mediation of the New Adam, recapitulated in the Church.[17]

As we shall see, Augustine's nearest approach to the abyss comes when the will most clearly resembles Pelagian, nominalist, or Cartesian self-assertion and insinuates their attendant metaphysics, that is to say when it is conceived as a self-sufficient origin, intelligible in itself, capable of spontaneous reduction from a prior indeterminacy.[18] Will becomes nihilistic, that is, when it is taken outside its paradoxically infinite determination in the Trinity. Here the point of *De Trinitate* XV, that one can be an image of the Trinity only by virtue of one's *unlikeness* to it, becomes crucial. It is not that the two ways of interpreting *imago dei*, as resemblance or as iconic participation, are mutually exclusive alternatives, but that the former is dependent upon the latter. There *is* an analogue in the creature to Augustine's clearly delineated anti-nominalist insistence that the various predicates in God can neither be subdivided among the trinitarian persons, nor 'caused' from an essence existing before or behind the Father's generation and spiration of the second and third persons[19] – the Father is never not Father of the Son, nor the Son wisdom of the Father so as to exclude the Father from being his own wisdom, nor the Holy Spirit the love of the Father, nor the Father the begetter of his greatness. Rather each is simultaneously fully his own love and wisdom and one love and wisdom and a love that is wisdom and convertible with one greatness.[20] Just as the person of the Father is not a 'self-positing subject out of whose indeterminate plenitude flow the Son and the Spirit,' but rather 'Sapientia exists *by* generating an other,'[21] so neither do intellect, will, or memory in the creature subsist (if they can be said to 'subsist' at all) in discrete hypostatic priority to each other.

There is no act either of memory, intellect, or will which does not immediately and indivisibly implicate the others. Rather to think, or to love, is always necessarily a trinitarian act which indivisibly invokes the other distinctions, since it is a linguistic impossibility either to separate one's intention from the mnemonic description under which it is rendered or to render it unintentionally. To think, to Gillespie's chagrin, is thus still to will, but to will is neither to project oneself into an unintelligible mathematical void nor to negate oneself as security against this void's possible capriciousness. For will, in God or in creatures, names neither a spontaneous arbitrary reduction from indeterminacy, nor even, strictly speaking, the relation of cause to effect.[22] Will, which cannot be in a composite or contingent relation to God's essence, rather names, paradoxically, the infinite *determination* of the Trinity *to* itself,[23] the threefold determination of Love to the *act* of Love: the lover's loving the beloved who himself fully and simply *is* the lover loving the beloved. The determination of love, to love, *ad infinitum*, is itself the *plenitudo* and *finis* of the law,[24] and is unintelligible apart from the formal entailment, the equally infinite determination of a word of knowledge (for the mind, to love anything, must know that which it loves).[25] It is the intrinsic relation to this law which constitutes the creature and determines her will, and thus the difference consists in the fact that the creature exists as an effect, insufficient in herself, of that *plenitudo*. And it is this very unlikeness to God – or, better, this analogical likeness in unlikeness – that makes it possible for a creature to be an image of God at all, for it is this unlikeness which opens the possibility of her doxological participation in the infinite doxology of the Trinitarian life.[26]

How do I know and love the righteous man when I am not yet righteous?[27] It is a question as least as old as Plato's *Meno* as well as being the question of how one can love a God whose essence is not yet visible to our eyes.[28] It is one question with two aspects, for we cannot love anything without knowing it, and there is no knowing anything that is not at the same time an act of love for some intentional object.[29] Hence, in loving the righteous man while I am unrighteous, I must nevertheless know both that he is righteous and what righteousness is. The question is, how? Proceeding through various possibilities Augustine concludes that it is by virtue of a form within him that is not him that he is able to know and love the righteous mind; by virtue of his participation in the form of love and righteousness he is able to know and to love one who is righteous by that same form.

Of course, this all looks very suspect: first, because we are formed by a world wherein there is institutionalized a nominalist prejudice against the possibility of ever knowing any such form; second, because it seems bound to an unregenerate idealism and dependence upon 'presence' and re-presentation; third, because the seeming contrast between interior and exterior knowledge seems simply to foreground a Cartesian subject; fourth, because of this subject he has been destroyed by the recognition that it is always already located in the historical instability of language. However, I wish to suggest that Augustine's accounts of subjectivity end in just the opposite conclusions and can Christologically sustain the *aporias* without lapsing into the nihilistic metaphysical oppositions of Pelagianism or its later secular counterparts.

When Augustine discerns in his love of the righteous man a form which is not him, he does not discern a stable idea, but rather his *act* – whose origin he cannot coherently isolate – of loving the righteous man, who is 'loved through that form and truth which he who loves discerns within himself, but that very form and truth itself cannot be loved from any other source than itself.'[30] That is to say, his active love of the righteous man, indivisibly entailing memory, intellect, will and their objects, simply *is* the form of the good understood as an actual *plenitudo* of love. One's knowing and loving is thus an intelligible participation through time in the ecstatic actuality of God's eternally self-differentiated love and wisdom. As such, these are not two discrete movements with discrete objects, but are rather formal inherents of a single motion which formally entails its object. This further dispels the charge of an idealism bound to a self-negating presence. For all knowledge is a bringing forth from memory[31] through a love intrinsically bound to and *generated by* its extrinsic object in a posture whose ecstatic intentional form, in seeking the end which is knowledge, must implicitly assume the shape of hope.

The 'gaze' of knowledge is thus not to be understood as a totalized comprehension of a 'present' object, but as a desire for an object determined by that object, which is itself formally desire.[32] Thus 'a word is knowledge together with love,'[33] and the intentional structure of the word's generation, its openness to an 'extrinsic' end which it seeks, means that language and knowledge in their very form are doxological and thus situated within the constative actuality of that doxology which *is* Trinity. The 'moment' of knowledge thus situated is *not* a discrete moment subject to isolation from a prior indeterminacy, and so is not a representation and does not circumvent the flux of time at all. For Augustine's gaze on the form of eternal truth does not differ essentially from his urging the love of love: they are the same form attained through the same temporal practice determined from the same end. It is by virtue of this form that the will confirms that which is not the will and implies that the description under which the intentional object is rendered does not exhaust the actuality of the signified.[34] And it is from the relation to this form that Augustine can resolve, without negation, the seeming *aporia* of the word's generation: that the thoroughly intentional *act* of generating the 'inner word' of knowledge,[35] is determined by the activity of the doxological object.

For in defining the self's love and knowledge of the righteous man by virtue of his participation in a form which is not him, and which yet contains him, and by making the end of one's intention intrinsic to the soul as its principle, Augustine, despite the dualistic nature of his language, has in fact confounded one of the fundamental metaphysical borders of modernity. He has turned the self inside out and defined interiority in terms of an exteriority which is imparted entirely as gift, but which the subject must nevertheless entirely perform.[36] Or, rather, the conclusion is that the border between interiority and exteriority is no longer intelligible as a border. Thus to confound that line even further by subjecting Augustine's language to Wittgenstinian therapy is in the end only to make Augustine *more* Augustinian. For it simply takes to its logical conclusion the claims of *De Trinitate*. To say that nothing can be loved that is not known, and that every knowing necessarily entails loving, is both to make acts of intellect and will indivisible and to implicate the *activity* of the intellect in the necessary intelligibility of the acts of the will, and – conversely – to make the proper objects of the will intrinsic to the very definition of reason.[37] The act of will is not available apart from or behind the description under which it is willed, nor is the description available apart from the act, itself inseparable from description, of calling it to recollection.[38] Contrary to our Scotist inheritance, the intellect no more lies passively latent to the activity of

114

the will than does the Son to his own generation from the Father.[39] Just as the Father, though he eternally begets the Son, does not out of his indeterminate priority posit the Son who lies dormant, such that one cannot discretely distinguish the Father's act of begetting from the *Son's own act* in being begotten, so neither can one discretely distinguish the activity of intellect or will from the relative passivity of the other. Rather the activity of the one rational appetite is always triadically differentiated and indifferentiable from its verbum or its lateral substitutions. Augustine thus anticipates rather than conflicts with Wittgenstein on this anti-Cartesian point.

Likewise the inseparability of love and word, and particular words, from the act of their generation from memory resists the move to abstract a univocal phenomenon or mental event occurring 'behind' the analogous significations of the words 'knowing' and 'loving'.[40] Rather it simply insists that all intentional events are linguistic and vice versa, which of course binds love and its objects into the kinds of narrative description given by particular historical polities. (And this reinforces more fully the conclusion of the *Confessions* and *De Doctrina Christiana*'s. proto-Wittgenstinian anticipation of the assimilation of meaning to use.[41]) The creature's 'nature' is not primarily an indeterminate self-positing given, subsisting behind its intentions, but rather is finally determined through its intentions by the company she keeps and the objects of her worship, expressed through the descriptions she gives of herself and the world. Again, despite the many 'trinities' that can be discerned in the mind's activity, it can only be an *image* of God, only manifest God in creation, insofar as it doxologically participates in God's charity through the historic ecclesia.[42] The self, who serially *is* through activity which is formally doxological, is an icon for the 'object' of its worship, by which that 'object' and the self are in turn made manifest. Seduced by 'the concupiscence of the flesh, the concupiscence of the eyes, and the ambition of the world', and so seduced ultimately by himself, Augustine becomes distended in a perverse image of the Trinity, undone by the ravages of time and misdirected desire.[43] By contrast Augustine finds himself only as he is continent in respect of that ultimate object,[44] as he is recapitulated as an actor in the ongoing drama of creation, now mediated through the Church, by which God separates light from darkness.

III

The doxological self is thus able to participate in the life of the Trinity by virtue of a doxological character which it cannot escape, but can only pervert. It is nevertheless fair to ask at this point how such oppositions as those between activity and passivity and finitude and infinitude, which variously manifest themselves in the nihilism of modern metaphysics, are to be avoided here. What is the metaphysical setting of this doxological exchange? How can the subject's acts be her own if her will is determined by its end? How, in other words, can such an incursion not result in a *de facto* negation of the subject? It must be noticed, first, that Augustine has shifted the contents of what there might be on hand to negate, and so has radically altered the possibility of a logic of negation ever arising. The subject begins to be negated or negates itself only as it mistakenly assumes itself substantially to suffice as its own end, whereas it *is* only as it participates in the ever-arriving gift of its dox-ological – which is to say, teleological – existence. Thus a nihilist metaphysical logic can arise only once the subject and its willing begin mistakenly to be construed within the *Pelagian* void, within the implicit priority of possibility over actuality, wherein either the God whose willing is a projection into the void or the subject who exists in reserved distinction and relative autonomy from its reception of grace must effect a merely conjunctive (and thus Nestorian) relation between sub-ject and object, principle and end, through the mechanisms of choice, projection, or duty.[45] A nihilist logic can arise, in other words, only from a transcendental per-spective outside of, and juxtaposed to, the Trinity. This option then becomes a self-fulfilling prophecy. For in positing itself, which apart from its gifted, participated existence ultimately *is* nothing, the will effectively performs a perverse *desire for noth-ing* as a positive object.[46] In contrast, the ecstatic openness with which the doxological subject is ontologically configured rules out the idea that every recep-tion is an *a priori* incursion, because the subject is always receiving *itself* as a gift, and indeed through confession being recapitulated truly as itself, from out of the future. Thus on Augustine's terms, nihilism can arise only when doxology fails, and *all that is not doxology is nihilism.*

Yet it is crucial to see that, while the end which is not the subject is intrinsic to the subject's activity, this reception is simultaneously the subject's *own* activity. This fails to be paradoxical precisely because the doxological subject, who is *actively* constituted *as* receiving, can only *be* herself insofar as the 'distance' between her temporal and concupiscential distension and the object of her intention is medi-ated, and recapitulated, by Christ. This brings us at once to the matter of the ratios between activity and passivity and between finitude and infinitude, a question to which Augustine provides answers by disclosing confession and the Church, bap-tism and eucharist, as ontological modalities.[47] Indeed the iconic self which opens out into the penultimate moment of creation in the ecclesia is constituted, and can only be constituted within a Christology which makes the distinction between the temporal and eternal, the finite and the infinite, both necessary and unmappable, and which refuses to turn that distinction into a border or opposition. It is only within what will later be called the hypostatic union and its mediation to the pneu-matically dispersed ecclesial body that these oppositions can be avoided.

To ask, as Augustine does in *De Trinitate* XV. 5, 'how does the Trinity manifest itself?,' is to ask how created things signify their creator, a matter painstakingly attended to in the case of the Old Testament theophanies, the number six, and so on. We see in the *Confessions* how, upon his conversion, his whole past life is made retrospectively to signify the achievement of closing books, when, graced with continence, his life in the Church is made to signify the events figured in Genesis, and vice versa. I want now to suggest that Augustine carries through this program, in his explication of the trinitarian operations of the mind, and that in the relation between memory, intellect, and will, which again requires participation in the trinitarian love in order to be an image of God, there is polyphonically manifest both the life of the Trinity and its ecclesial perfection of creation in the figures of Jesus and Mary. Here, and only here, the dichotomous oppositions are resolved.

Augustine begins Book IX of *De Trinitate* with that which is most excellent and without which all the other trinities fail – what things there are in love when the mind loves itself. From this he derives the familiar threesome of lover, love and beloved, and turns again to the concern of Book VIII, the relation between love and knowledge, and explores the necessary interrelation of each with the other. He is driven to a parallel *aporia* to the earlier one concerning how one begins to see righteousness, and to parallel conclusions. The human mind, in knowing and loving itself, does not know and love anything unchangeable; hence in defining or discussing the mind generically or abstractly one speaks from having 'gazed' on the eternal form of truth which is not itself the mind.[48] The end, as it were, is again incorporate as a principle.

I have already suggested that dramatic linguistic, ontological, and ecclesial implications follow from the fact that the determination of the will's principle by its end effectively relocates the soul within the mediate activity of the form, rather than the reverse. I raise this again in relation to Book IX, not to contest these issues further, but to show how the active–passive problem upon which negative logic must be premissed simply does not arise here. Augustine has presupposed that the form which is not the will, but which the will loves in loving itself, is intrinsic to the soul itself. The determination of the form is dependent upon the end which functions as the principle of its conception.[49] Thus the word born in language is codetermined with the presupposed object of desire and the intention's coming to rest in that object.[50] And yet, immediately upon such recognition, in IX. 7. 12–13, he conceives of the bringing-to-be of this form in the word of knowledge as wholly *our* activity.

Augustine has here given an account, not simply of how the mind resembles the Trinity, but of how through its action, determined by its objects, it participates in time in the trinitarian economy. Insofar as his account tends in the former direction, the mind in its operation resembles and, depending upon the object of its operations, manifests in time the eternal generation of the Son and spiration of the Spirit. Insofar as it exemplifies the latter, it manifests the Father's sending and the Spirit's bringing forth of the Word, and indeed the Word's bringing forth itself, in the person of Mary. Augustine thus teleologically orders intellectual intention to the activity which he himself displays narratively, through the reversal of his solipsism into the penultimate moment of creation in the Church.[51] In either case, the reception simply renames another form of activity, without a negative interchange, just as the Son's being sent is also the Son's sending of himself.[52] Indeed because he reads John's Gospel as effecting just the sort of displacement of the Body of Christ for which Graham Ward argues in this volume, because he does not conceive of the relation of Jesus to his antagonists negatively as that of an atomistically passive object over against active subjects, Augustine does not even conceive of Christ's passion as a negative passivity, but rather as his own volitional activity.[53]

Hence Augustine has established how one and the same act, if it is doxologically ordered and thus mediated by Christ, can be both wholly mine and entirely from God.[54] This is again paradoxical only if one has made a metaphysical decision in advance which fixes in opposition the ratio between our finitude and God's infinity and conceives the latter in terms of a perverted version of the former, as a subject over against its objects and projecting into a stark and depthless void modeled on a *mathesis* undetermined by 'qualitative predicates.' We have seen how God's will, convertible as it is with God's indivisible love, wisdom, and goodness and infinitely determined to itself, names an actuality in which no 'space' for such a void of indeterminacy can arise. And we can now see that, in the Christological mediation of doxological action, the relation of finitude to infinitude, though hierarchical in terms of desire and insusceptible to exhaustive mapping, is not negative *a priori*.

It is true that Augustine often seemingly juxtaposes the flux of time to the stability of eternity, and, consequently, the wisdom which contemplates eternity with the knowledge that pertains to action in time.[55] However, such a reading assumes just the sort of post-Cartesian negative infinite which I am at pains to refuse and trades too much on the post-Heideggerian move of assimilating being to a transcendental deduction of time, both of which position Christ's mediation within the allegedly neutral constraints set by time and its obfuscating opposition to eternity, rather than the reverse. On this score the relation of *Confessions* XI to the rest of the work appears unclear, and the invocation of Christ's mediation in *Confessions* XI. 29 looks like a pious *non sequitur* to the antecedent reflections on temporality. But Augustine could presume no such transcendental deduction. For if the preceding reflections are correct, and if Augustine is concerned to show in both texts how creatures exhibit the truth, beauty, and goodness of their creator, then the ratios of time to eternity and of finitude to infinitude cannot simply be the neutral, negative relation of a quantitative *mathesis* (which does not fully emerge until the nominalists), but is rather, in a sense, *moral*, inasmuch as the infinity in which finite creatures intentionally participate and exhibit is convertible with the Goodness which is at once the form, principle, and object of the act of love which God is. Time, as Catherine Pickstock argues, has an 'aesthetic' and 'moral' density, which are ontologically convertible with its 'numerical' density.

James Wetzel is thus right to argue that the dual meaning of *distentio* in *Confessions* XI consists not in the first instance in Augustine's capacity to possess a durationless present.[56] Rather, as all of the 'moments' of knowledge by which he in-habits the present are the work of memory intended by a love seeking 'rest' in its intended 'object,' the problem of the extensionless present is the problem of incontinence in his *attention*, itself the work of memory, with respect to that object.[57] It is, in other words, the recurrent problem of 'concupiscence of the flesh, and the concupiscence of the eyes, and the ambition of the world.'[58] Therein lies the sense of the second meaning of distention, the concupiscent dissolution of that attentive power in the passage of time, and the meaning of his mediated, confessional resolution. The integrity of Augustine's time-bound life is contingent upon his continence toward the proper object of his desire, which as we have seen is not just 'extrinsic' to him as an end, but 'intrinsic' to him as a principle. His integrity is thus contingent upon a continence which *he cannot*, but nevertheless *must*, supply. Hence the work of continence, the integrity of his self-hood, must needs be a work of *mediation*, actualized in what is indeed doubly a work of confession, of love in memory.[59] (Lest it be thought that memory here is simply a disembodied mental feat, it needs to be noted that the overcoming of his tripartite dissolution, seamlessly achieved in the garden, without pause for either choice or moment, finds its expression in baptism.[60]) Confessional memory and practice are thus the re-unification of his selfhood through the recapitulation, in time, of time, an anticipation of the resurrection, and an act intended forward toward continent attentiveness – in short, prayer. It is thus likewise the recognition, paralleling that of his necessary unlikeness to the Trinity, that his unified selfhood is in fact mediated to him, and was always already mediated to him, even when he was wrong about himself. The 'moment' of grace can thus no more be confined to the ever vanishing trace of an extensionless present, its origin can no more be isolated from a prior indeterminacy, than the Son, in being sent, can be said to arrive where he previously was not. However, it can be recapitulated in a unified vision by a confessional memory which revises and makes continent the perpetual activity of attention. In other words the 'moral' solution to the active–passive problem is the same for the ratio of finitude to infinitude. It is, in short, the entire cosmological drama of salvation in miniature. Both are cast, in the figure of Augustine's life, within the problematic that defines salvation as it is Christologically executed – the reconciliation of man and God. The question of the very relation of time to eternity, and the problem of bridging it, will demand just the sort of mediation of his own activity from the end that is set forth in the doxological will's relation to its principle in *De Trinitate*. In other words, Augustine's account of will is set within a ratio of finitude to infinitude that can *only* be Christological (and consequently Mariological also), and devolves toward entropy whenever it ceases to be. The solutions to that entropy are now mediated Christologically through his recapitulation of creation effected confessionally in his dispersed body. Confession and the Church, baptism, penance, reconciliation and eucharist, are now ontological modalities.

Hence the ratio of finitude to infinitude is a hierarchical one which corresponds to the order of ends manifest in the ontological order of doxology. And both the hierarchy and harmony are exhibited in the way that the potential opposition of time to eternity is converted into a means–end relationship in the relations adhering between vision and use, wisdom and knowledge in *De Trinitate* XIII–XIV. Inasmuch as wisdom pertains to the contemplation of things eternal, and knowledge to action, the latter is subordinate to the former and yet a means to it, just as the Son in becoming incarnate becomes less than himself, to return all to himself. And so it is only in wisdom (which is worship) that one properly has an image of the Trinity.[61] However, this seeming antagonism is unveiled within the context of a larger meditation on the incarnation, according to which Augustine ascribes wisdom to the eternal Word, and knowledge to that Word incarnate indivisibly in the man Jesus. 'Therefore Christ is our knowledge, and the same Christ is also our wisdom.'[62] That is to say, in the hypostatic union of Christ, Augustine dissolves any antagonism between immanence and transcendence and any possibility of metaphysically fixing their ratio behind determinable boundaries. In so doing he has dissolved any rigorous distinction between vision and use, seeing and making,[63] such that he restores the possibility of time being the medium of mediated recreation, through ecclesial recapitulation, in the image of eternity.[64] Augustine recognizes, in other words, that Christ's temporal mediation restores to creation its status as gift, and frees the gift at last to be the *creation* which it always was.[65] And to be restored as creation is to be restored to that doxology which is both the activity of the Good and the Good itself, to harmonize the past under the activity of this formality in confessional recapitulation.[66] Thus the very form of creation, its means and its end, is Church – the body to the head of that recapitulation. To raise in Jesus a border between immanence and transcendence, and between passivity and activity, is to ask how the divine and human natures are conjoined, a subject which Augustine does not broach, a question whose form and presuppositions the Church would soon reject. It is to conflate all forms of causality to efficient causality between discrete Pelagian units and thus to require just the sort of mechanism, performed by just the sort of self, which is notably missing from the key moment of Augustine's own conversion.[67] The only borders now between immanence and transcendence, finitude and infinitude, activity and passivity, are those erected by a perversion of this gift, by wills which defectively presume themselves sufficient to their own mediation and idolatrously attempt to establish themselves as God.

IV

On Augustinian terms, the presumption which gives rise to such dichotomies must be susceptible to just such a diagnosis, through its verification, retrospective and historical. If Augustine's speculations on the interrelation of justice, charity, doxology, truth and goodness are right, then one could expect at the end of a century and era so horrific as ours, that our intentions, for not having been good, are shown not to be true.

Gillespie locates the originative moment in the nominalist assertion of a purely theological knowledge, grounded in an account of God's arbitrary omnipotence, which paradoxically made modes of non-theological knowledge possible. What he does not explore, but which I suspect more accurately holds the key to the origins, is the extent to which the fateful course set by the Condemnation of 1277 was itself a reaction to the assertion, already present in, and well before, the time of Aquinas, of such non-theological modes, and which had begun to effect the institutional disjunction of intellect and will in the relative autonomy of the emerging universities, and the reactionary subordination of the former to the latter.[68] That is to say, the prior possibility of a non-theological knowledge already begins to fit the Augustinian diagnosis.[69]

That such knowledge now seems to have no real object 'behind' the endless manipulations of signs, and that the restless will with which such objects are now intended finds nothing wherein it seeks, should thus come as no real surprise. It testifies only to the failure of those seemingly benign strategies of security – like political liberalism – which attempt to straddle and mask the fundamentally gluttonous and abyssal character of their (non-)commitments. For any failure to recognize – to desire and confess – the substantive doxological good as the principle and end of political and philosophical life is, in effect, to desire *nothing* as a positive object. Thus the various conundra which characterize the modern philosophical problematic, which arguably articulate only the strange superficial mix of despair and glee which is modern capitalism, shall in the end be granted just that nothing for which they have so long been seeking. For they are predicated upon a mistake from which there is only one exit.

Augustine has in some sense foreseen our Pelagian disaster, diagnosed all that which is not doxology as nihilism, and left us but one alternative. Only within the doxological and confessional practices of the historic ecclesia is the alternative desire possible. It is only within the intelligibility of the will's material, cultic participation in a charity which precedes it, in the confessional admission that we have been wrong about ourselves, that nihilism, not simply the 'existence' of nothing outside subjectivity, but the *desire for nothing* as the subject's eternal home, can be staved off.

Notes

1 Michael Allen Gillespie, *Nihilism Before Nietzsche* (Chicago: University of Chicago Press, 1995), pp. 1–63. Gillespie does not sufficiently distinguish the new 'neutral' infinity from its predecessors. For Aquinas, for instance, the term would be analogically applicable to God only inasmuch as the material division and quantity which number implies in its primary meaning is not really applicable in God *(Summa Theologica I* 30 a.3 resp.). Catherine Pickstock better diagnoses the now naked concept of infinity, which consists not simply in the reduction of causalities to an efficient quantitative *mathesis*, but in a sense in the 'de-qualification' of number.

2 See Milbank (this volume), pp. 21–37. Significantly, Gillespie's mentions of both Augustine and Aquinas amount to little more than caricatures. See particularly p. 49 for his misreading of *De Trinitate*.

3 Alasdair MacIntyre, *Three Rival Versions of Moral Inquiry: Encyclopaedia, Genealogy, and Tradition* (Notre Dame: University of Notre Dame Press, 1990), pp. 149–69.

4 Gillespie, pp. 254–57.

5 The logic here, articulated in *De Libero Arbitrio* III.14–17, that one can only condemn a flaw on the supposition of the nature of which it is a flaw, extends to the application of such privatives as 'violence'. The logic implies that language cannot get on without the supposition of something like formal and final causes (or at least formal elements formally determined from intentional objects), and the logic issues in consequences such as MacIntyre notes relative to such terms as 'watch' and 'farmer.' 'Such concepts are functional concepts; that is to say, we define both "watch" and "farmer" in terms of the

purpose or function which a watch or farmer are characteristically expected to serve. It follows that the concept of a watch cannot be defined independently of the concept of a good watch nor the concept of a farmer independently of that of a good farmer.' Augustine, *On Free Choice of the Will* (Indianapolis: Hackett, 1993); MacIntyre, *After Virtue* (Notre Dame: University of Notre Dame Press, 1981), p. 58.

6 This is conceptually, not historically, the case, as *De Trinitate* predates Nestorianism and the ecumenical councils in Ephesus, Chalcedon, and Constantinople.

7 Wittgenstein, *Philosophical Investigations* (New York: Macmillan, 1958), 133.

8 For a clear exposition of how the 'formal elements' of our terms work in this regard, see Julius Kovesi, *Moral Notions* (London: Routledge, 1967).

9 St Augustine, *Confessions*, trans. John K. Ryan (New York: Doubleday, 1960), IX.1.1.

10 *Ibid.*, X.2.2; X.8.15; X.17.26; X.32.48; XI.29.39; XIII.14.15.

11 St Augustine, *De Trinitate*, in Philip Schaff (ed.), *The Nicene and Post Nicene Fathers of the Christian Church* (Edinburgh: T. & T. Clark, 1993), 8.7.

12 Rowan Williams, 'Sapientia and the Trinity', in B. Bruning *et al.* (eds), *Collectanea Augustiniana*, Melanges T.J. von Bavel (Leuven University Press, 1990), p. 319. This is also how Gillespie understands it. Gillespie, p. 49.

13 *De Trin.*, II.

14 *Ibid.*, XV.5.7. This is prefaced by the preceding article wherein he announces: 'the whole nature of the universe itself which surrounds us, and to which we also belong, proclaims that it has a most excellent creator . . .'.

15 *Conf.*, X.16.24–5; XI.26.33; XI.29.39; XII.15.21. The technique is mirrored in *De Trin.*, VIII–IX.

16 *Conf.*, X.32.48; X.33.50; XI.29.39; XII.10; XIII.14.15.

17 *Ibid.*, XII.15.21; XIII.11.12; XIII.12.13; XIII.18.22; XIII.21.29; XIII.24.29; XIII.24.49.

18 *Ibid.*, XIII.1.1.

19 'For it is an impiety to say that God subsists, and is a subject in relation to his own goodness . . .'. *De Trin.*, VI.5.10.

20 *De Trin.*, VI.1.1; VI.7.9; VI.8; VII.1.1–2; VII.2.3.

21 Williams, p. 328.

22 This is not to deny causality to God, but rather to argue that as 'his only motive [in creating] was goodness,' the principle and end from which God creates is the plenitudinous act of love which he is (creation is *in* the Son), such that the economy of created effects only *is* as is determined to the Father and Son's determination for each other, a point recognized and instantiated liturgically in the prayers of the Mass. The point of the inappropriateness of cause–effect description applies to creatures *theologically*, because, on this reckoning, they exist not in a primary state of indeterminacy, but of actually intrinsically being determined by desire according to the form of the first or second Adam, thus defining will relative to the objects which determine it; and *philosophically*, because will is unintelligible rendered in the form of a cause and effect description, as it is only intelligible described in terms of what it is thought to have caused. Augustine, *De Civitas Dei* (London: Penguin, 1984), XI.24.

23 *De Trin.*, VI.X.12.

24 Augustine, *De Doctrina Christiana* (New York: Macmillan, 1958), l.xxxv.39.

25 *De Trin.*, VIII.4.6, IX.3.3.

26 D.B. Hart's argument, from Gregory of Nyssa, that the creature's analogical difference from God is actually constitutive of God's gift, is also applicable to Augustine. See Hart, 'Beauty, Violence, and Infinity: A Question Concerning Christian Rhetoric', Dissertation, University of Virginia, pp. 227–311.

27 *De Trin.*, VIII.6.9.

28 MacIntyre, p. 92.

29 The thing known can be a proximate good partially known for the sake of an end whose

excellence is more fully known (*De Trin.*, X.2.4). It is no coincidence that Augustine him-self fills this proximate role in the order of intention in the *Confessions*, for it is the order for the mediation of the proximate good by the end.

30 *De Trin.*, IX.6.9.
31 The essentially mnemonic, and embodied, character of knowledge is exemplified in its perverse aspects in the importance Augustine attributes to the *fomes* of carnal habit in his anti-Pelagian exegesis of Romans 7. See J. Wetzel, *Augustine and the Limits of Virtue* (Cambridge: Cambridge University Press, 1990), pp. 161–97.
32 *De Trin.*, IX.6.11–IX.7.12; IX.12.18; Williams, pp. 321–31.
33 *De Trin.*, IX.15.15.
34 Catherine Pickstock has also noted the doxological structure of language and its modern alienation from itself in her *After Writing: On The Liturgical Consummation of Philosophy* (Oxford: Blackwell, 1997), Chapter 1.
35 *De Trin.*, IX.7.12–13.
36 *Ibid.*, XI.6.10: 'Look no longer for the moment when God should will, as if you would offend him by willing before he did. At whatever time you will, you will with God's help and by his work. His mercy undoubtedly goes before you, that you may will. But when you do will, it is you in particular who wills.' From the *Epistula ad Firmum 2*, cited in Wetzel, p. 195. For a similar argument, to which I am much indebted in comparing Augustine to Gregory of Nyssa on this point, see Milbank, *The Word Made Strange* (Oxford: Blackwell, 1996), pp. 194–216.
37 *De Trin.*, XI.7.12.
38 Stanley Hauerwas, *Character and the Christian Life: A Study in Theological Ethics* (San Antonio: Trinity University Press, 1985), pp. 23–24. Hauerwas is here more concerned to estab-lish the priority of intelligible action, as I am trying to establish the always intentional character of intelligibility. From an Augustinian perspective, these are two sides of a single coin.
39 See MacIntyre, *Three Rival Versions*, p. 155; Gillespie, pp. 14–47. The post-Scotist position of subordinating intellect to will is anticipated and refused by Augustine, for it implies the will's univocal paternity, whose analog in the Trinity would presumably both confuse the order of generation and spiration and divide the work *ad intra*. (*De Trin.*, XI.7.12). On Augustine's terms the Son's begottenness must also be his *activity*, just as, economi-cally speaking, he is both sender and sent. This, and not a priority of essence from which three derivations come, is the meaning of the indivisibility of the work of the three per-sons, a conclusion he takes as warranted by John 5:19–24. As the Son is the Son in being begotten of the Father, so also he is Son in the very act of seeing the Father (*De Trin.*, II.1.3). Similarly, 'in speaking that co-eternal word, He is not understood singly but with that Word itself, without whom he certainly does not speak' (*De Trin.*, VII.1.1).
40 Rowan Williams demonstrates a proto-Wittgenstinian affinity in Augustine's *nosse–cogitare* distinction, by which Augustine claims 'it is one thing not to know oneself, another not to think of oneself' (*De Trin.*, X.5.7). The self-knowledge which Augustine seeks differs from Descartes' and resembles Wittgenstein's in that it is not inferential, and thus does not construct self-awareness as an object transparent before the rational gaze. Quite the opposite is the case in both *De Trinitate* and *Confessions* – there is no self-knowledge not mediated by the Trinity, and the self-knowledge Augustine seeks, and failures in it, are failures in respect of his desire. Williams, 'The Paradoxes of Self-Knowledge in *De Trinitate*' in Leinhard *et al.* (eds), *Collectanea Augustiniana: Augustine, Presbyter, Factus Sum* (New York: Peter Lang, 1993), pp. 128–33.
41 William Babcock notes the distinction between enjoyment and use in *De Doctrina Christiana* and Augustine's doctrine of the formal determination of predicates by the ends which a 'language game' serves, and comments on Augustine's method that 'his procedure . . . defines in advance what the terminus of the scriptural signs is and thus establishes the control in the light of which we are to interpret those signs.' What goes

unanalyzed, however, is *why* the givenness of the end of charity, the *plenitudo* of the law, does not foreclose on meaning but rather generates for more possible meanings than is often admitted by exegetical methods which claim no advanced prejudice over what they will find. It is, I would venture, because the desire-of-the-good form of 'the method' is that of both the trinitarian *plenitudo* which creates and of those effects when they are truly themselves; that the typological and allegorical outcomes of such exegesis do not express merely an exegetical method or literary genre but are ontological variations of, and commentary upon, that form which confounds the *signa–res* distinction. It expresses, in other words, an ontology of creation *ex nihilo*, and the exegete's location within the activity of the Trinity informs her craft. This can be seen in *Confessions* XIII. I am increasingly convinced that the form of Patristic exegesis is crucial to understanding the Christian transfiguration of pagan ontology (and its rebuttal of the neo-pagan). And this, I would argue, is how one could begin to resolve on Augustinian terms, without necessary mediation by Aristotle, MacIntyre's diagnosis (*Three Rival Versions*, p. 100) of the problem 'which arises for every type of Platonism. If to understand any particular is to understand it in its relationship to a form or universal in the light of which alone that particular can be made intelligible, what is the nature of that relationship?' See Babcock, 'Caritas and Signification', in Arnold and Bright (eds), *De Doctrina Christiana: A Classic of Western Culture* (Notre Dame: University of Notre Dame Press, 1995), pp. 145–63.

42 I qualify charity with doxology because charity between persons, inasmuch as it is convertible with justice, always has the worship of God as its end.

43 *Conf.*, X.30.41; XI.29.39. James O'Donnell argues that throughout the *Confessions* these three vices depicted in I John 2:16 operate as a perversion of the trinitarian image, which, if true, corroborates the interpretation below of the second meaning of distention. O'Donnell, *Augustine Confessions: Commentary in Three Volumes* (Oxford: Clarendon Press, 1992), vol. 1, p. xxxv..

44 *Conf.*, VIII.10.22–VIII.11.27.

45 The suggestion is that Pelagius is proto-modern in his metaphysical implications and the possibilities he engenders. For a brief evaluation and an acquittal of Ockham's 'semi-Pelagianism,' see Gillespie, p. 23. Yet it seems that Ockham escapes only by effecting a 'double-Pelagianism,' which conceives of God in terms similar to the Pelagian self, much as Milbank suggests neo-orthodoxy construes God on the model of man without God. Augustine himself knew precisely that Pelagianism usurps divinity for humanity. Ironically this is the opposite of what the nominalists later hoped to achieve. Inevitably, construing the will (human or divine) primarily in terms of choice (fiat, projection) establishes the sort of juxtaposition between creator and creature which requires the invention of a deontological 'ought' to force the submission of the will to an external imperative which must operate in addition to the directive of the good, an 'ought' both promoted and resisted by philosophy from Descartes to Kant and furthered by the Levinasian attempt to ground an imperative in the encounter with the 'other.' For a contrast between Augustine and Pelagius which unwittingly foreshadows this modern problematic, see Wetzel, p. 202. For Pelagius' own position and the implicit metaphysical priority of possibility, see Pelagius, *Pro libero arbitrio* cited in J. Stevenson (ed.), *Creeds, Councils, and Controversies* (London: SPCK, 1995), pp. 232–3. For Scotus and the two 'oughts' see MacIntyre, *Three Rival Versions*, p. 155.

46 *De Trin.*, X.5.7. As Wetzel notes (p. 213), and as the pear-tree episode illustrates, sin is finally, or retrospectively, unintelligible, though it may prospectively result from a misapprehension of the good.

47 *Conf.*, X.26.37; X.43.68; XI.29.39; XIII.5.6; *De Trin.*, XIII.19.24.

48 *De Trin.*, IX.6.9. To Augustine the gaze in the sense of representation would be an idolatrous assimilation of corporeality to the metaphor. The rationality of the gaze for Augustine is inseparable from its affective, i.e. its doxological and liturgical, character.

49 The soul can miscarry in birthing this form, depending upon its object – as immediately evidenced in *De Trin.*, IX.8, where he distinguishes the conception of the word in *cupiditas* from that conceived in *caritas*.

50 Augustine thus distinguishes the spiration of the Spirit from the generation of the Son (*De Trin.*, IX.12.18).

51 Augustine himself does not allude to this figuration in this example. However, it would be consistent with the principles of Augustinian exegesis, as it is executed in *Confessions* XII–XIII, to read it thus.

52 *De Trin.*, II.5.7–10. See also, Milbank, *The Word Made Strange*, p. 195; William S. Babcock, 'Augustine on Sin and Moral Agency', *Journal of Religious Ethics* 16 (1988), p. 46.

53 *De Trin.*, II.5.7; IV.13.16. From the commonplace of 'volitional condescension' which Ward notes among the Church Fathers, by which "Christ straddles humanness in pre- and postlapsarian modality" and which Ward, like the Fathers, spots *before* Christ's glorification, one concludes that the categories of activity and passivity, presupposing the modern juxtaposition and circumscription of subject and object, are inadequate to describe the relation of Christ to his antagonists. Rather Christ, in his locality within the flesh of Jesus, nevertheless somehow *encompasses* his opponents, who minimally depend upon their participation in him *to* oppose him, and recapitulates their opposition in the resurrection, just as Jesus ontologically recapitulates Israel in the Jordan and the wilderness, and, as in miniature, Augustine's opposition is recapitulated in the *Confessions*. The argument is that only in Christ can these oppositions be undone in a non-oppositional way. And only thus can Jesus actually be understood to assume all of human nature and recapitulate all creation in his flesh. Only this displacement combined with Jesus' volitional obedience, i.e. his *doxological* exchange with the Father, can avoid making death and the cross, rather than Jesus' continence and innocence, the meaningful moment in God. Together they allow one to think an atonement theory wherein Jesus can both undercut and redeem that opposition, refuse salvific efficacy to the violence itself, and leave the hope, relative to justice for instance, that the resurrection does not simply 'transcend' evil, but reverses and 'undoes' it. I take the politics of such a recapitulation, in the context of discussing the *Confessions*, to be somewhat obvious – and daunting. I am indebted for these thoughts to Hart, pp. 424–538 (see above, note 26).

54 Indeed my doxological activity is the very activity of God. *Conf.*, XIII.31.46.

55 *De Trin.*, XII.14.22–23.

56 *De Trin.*, IX.4.4. This knowing and loving oneself fully and proportionately would be a matter of justice and so relative to the 'referral' of this knowledge beyond its proximate status to its ontological and doxological status in the worship of God. '[W]e love ourselves so much the more, the more we love God' (*De Trin.*, VIII.8.12).

57 See Wetzel, pp. 17–44, though his lack of attention to the intentional structure of Augustine's trinitarian participation causes him, I think, to err too much on the side of representation.

58 *Conf.*, X.30.41.

59 Wetzel, p. 215.

60 O'Donnell, pp. xxviii–xxxv; *Conf.*, VIII.11.25ff.

61 *De Trin.*, XIV.1.1.

62 *De Trin.*, XIII.19.24; Colossians 2: 1–3.

63 I have similarly argued in a paper, as yet unpublished, for the undoing of any disconnection between moral and intellectual virtues in Aquinas, insofar as they are disconnected.

64 See especially *Conf.*, XII.20.29; XIII.12.13–XIII.29.44.

65 This phrasing is Hart's. Hart would likely find Augustine somewhat antagonistic to the soteriology of analogically practiced recapitulation which he develops from Gregory of Nyssa, whereas I have tried to show that a similar recapitulation is effected in Augustine's self-revision and his exegesis of Genesis.

66 This is not a Nietzschean tragic harmony which gives justification and intelligibility to evil, but rather the opposite. The harmony effected by bringing the past under a doxological formality deprives the tragic of its conceit. Under the glare of judgment it unmasks the prospective conceits as without retrospective warrant, as the pear-tree meditation in *Confessions* II illustrates.

67 As Wetzel writes (p. 191), 'Those who come to the scene of their conversion expecting to encounter God for the first time come too late.'

68 I suspect these have their origins in part in Abelard's philosophy of intention and in the 'pre-philosophical' penitential changes wrought by Lateran Council IV. See MacIntyre, *Three Rival Versions*, pp. 82–104. See Jacques Le Goff, *Intellectuals in the Middle Ages* (Oxford: Blackwell, 1993), and *The Birth of Purgatory* (Aldershot: Scolar Press, 1990); Mary C. Mansfield, *The Humiliation of Sinners* (Ithaca: Cornell University Press, 1990).

69 Although this process is extremely complicated, in part because the logic of Augustine's position, though it remained remarkably consistent throughout his career, was transfigured by the changing polemical contexts of its encounter with a Stoicized Aristotelianism in the Pelagian controversy. The result was the transmission of a somewhat Pelagianized Augustine, made the more so by its reception in Gaul and subsequent synthesis with John Cassian by Gregory I. As a consequence, the high Middle Ages witnesses the spectacle, put very crudely and misleadingly, of an Augustinianized Aristotelianism, in the work of Aquinas (truer to Augustine than its subsequent rivals), confronting an Aristotelianized Augustine in the persons of Scotus and Ockham.

6

FRIENDSHIP

St Anselm, *theoria* and the convolution of sense*

David Moss

I

Perhaps, one should barely speak of friendship. For if to speak of one's own friendships would be to risk an immeasurable exposure, then to speak of another's would amount to a most primitive trespass. Friendship reveals as it retires, illumines as it withdraws; in this, one can say, it is much like love.[1]

But we should not be too delicate here for, as Francis Bacon reminds us in his famous essay *Of Friendship* (27), on the verge of friendship we are as 'cannibals'; cannibals ready to consume our own and other hearts. And this, according to St Anselm, and somewhat bizarrely, with that particular organ of friendship: 'the mouth of the heart'. Friendship no doubt has always eaten us up; but is friendship of its very self a strange and possibly impossible consumption?

Still, and as Bacon continues, the man who would be without friendship 'taketh it of the beast, and not from humanity'. For 'No receipt openeth the heart but a true friend'[2] – and a weary but still passionate saint, St Augustine, would no doubt agree. Of a long and tumultuous life he would reflect:

> [W]hat consolation have we in this human society, so replete with mistaken notions and distressing anxieties, except the unfeigned faith and mutual affections of genuine, loyal friends?[3]

No doubt on an axis of the 'modes of moods' – from despair to ecstasy – friendship enjoys a particular power. For, as Bacon has it, friendship has 'two contrary effects . . . it redoubleth joys, and cutteth griefs in halfs'. Such a gift then, in shortening the abysmal measure of human existence – of halving descent and redoubling ascent – has been cause enough to attract holy investiture. And in a living and thinking so unfamiliar to us now – in which one listened for a play of

* I am indebted to Lucy Gardner and Laurence Hemming for comments made on an earlier version of this essay.

127

resonances and sympathies descending through all the gradations of being (truly an 'analogical imagination') – friendship was freighted with divine intensity. Moreover, friendship was a way of return to the happiness of paradise.

Thus Cicero famously in *De amicitia*: 'With the single exception of Wisdom, I am inclined to regard [friendship] as the greatest of all the gifts the gods have bestowed on mankind.'[4] But more than this, in the 'Great Tradition' it is from and within the encounter with friends that *theoria* arises. *Theoria* – that is to say the proper contemplation of the transcendental properties of Being itself: goodness, truth and beauty. Friendship then was *the scene* – the place of appearance as the appearing place – for an originating and originary speculation: the ascent of *theoria* as a shooting for the gods. And vigilant no doubt to the discontinuities of translation, of at least Greek across Hebrew, it is at a meal shared between friends – the *caritas christiani* of the Last Supper – that eternal truth is not so much sighted as consumed. Friendship, one could reasonably suggest, in magnetising to itself a theatrics of thinking which would chart a passage to a redemptive paradise, illumined the world of Western Christianity up until at least the twelfth century.[5]

My purpose in this essay is by and large limited to revisiting this configuration of *theoria* with friendship as it is presented in the 'Great Tradition'; or at least a tributary of this tradition: the friendships that St Anselm enjoyed as witnessed to in his letters to fellow monks. This rehearsal of the tradition will be the main concern of the third and fourth sections of this essay in which I endeavour to show how a *theoria* set upon divine contemplation is released through the convolution of the senses experienced in friendship. This exquisite attention to a sensuous reception of the friend marks no doubt a moment within Christianity's re-imagining of the body in the medieval world; however, the sociology or history of these practices will not be my concern here.[6] What will be the point of this argument, and here my intention travels beyond attentive exegesis, is to suggest a space in which this 'performance of the tradition' could begin to address a current obsession in 'high theory' today with the status and absenting presence of 'the Other'.[7]

In short, the most radical issue with which this essay is concerned is the ancient and orthodox demand of the Fathers of the Church (a demand Anselm repeats against Roscelin) that it is only when one is perfected in *praktike* that one can undertake *theoria*. That is to say, between faith and insight comes the experience of life. And in this most dislocating and abysmal of experiences – friendship – do we not come upon a trembling between the manner of regarding and being regarded, the manner of holding and being held, the manner of embracing and being embraced, which speaks of the openness and ecstasy of the creature? It is perhaps within *this* perpetual differencing, and so on the other side of modernity's dialectics of identity, that a conjecturing or analogical wager upon our friendship with God may reoccur.

II

Could the experience of friendship return a certain humility to the discourses of the capitalised Other in 'high theory' today: the capping of a real inflation that has too much attended our demands for and of the Other here? In the endless deconstruction of logics of colonisation and identity, what contortions must the theories of this demand (as the abysmal demands of theory) enact in pursuit of such a pure phenomenality – an untouchable other? Perhaps there is much to be welcomed here, but still one wonders: how do we recognise *the* Same in our perpetual negotiations between an 'I' and an 'Other'?

To give only an indication of this, after the thought of Husserl and Heidegger had been carried back to France in the 1940s, what do we discover in the philosophical ferment released by the reception of phenomenology? In Jean Paul Sartre's dire existentialism, the *otherness* of otherness as an epistemological monstrosity which can only send us back into a nauseous apprehension of the inscrutable subjectivity of others. While in the work of Emmanuel Levinas, who with Sartre had effected the translation to France, we find his now well-worn meditations upon the pure epiphany of the Face which purportedly sends one naked into the rhythms of eternity but which in fact ends up entangled in a more severe (because elided) 'initial' projection of the 'I'.[8]

One could remark, as a largely arbitrary index of this point, that in Michael Theunissen's magisterial study of the social ontologies of Husserl, Heidegger, Sartre and Buber, entitled *The Other*, the theme of friendship appears only in a passing reference to Aristotle's famous meditations in Books VIII and IX of the *Nicomachean Ethics*. And this to suggest only that the I–Thou relationship of modern philosophy should not – following Aristotle's reflection on the fluid relationship between the intimacy of friendship and the alienness of public encounter – be understood as merely 'private'.[9]

I am unsure whether any of this fits particularly well with our experience of others around us, where 'experience' is precisely that certain readiness or receptivity to the world that phenomenology would have us investigate. But perhaps this is all at one with our attachment to the infernal regions today – to a fascination with the claustrophobia of *Inferno* rather than the ascent to *Paradiso*. There is no doubt good reason for this, but in the early centuries of the Christian West this was not so, for what preoccupied men's minds was a promised and desirable paradise. And in the writing that this ecstasy provoked – a writing on and of the heart – references to paradise were repeatedly figured in and from *a scene of friendship*.

These introductory remarks though should not be misunderstood. It is not that the theory of dialogical encounter, or discourse of the capitalised Other, requires leavening with the warmth of a long-lost wisdom concerning the intimacy of friendship. No, it is something other that I am suggesting here, in attention to the allegories of *theoria* in the Tradition.

In the *Phaedrus* the love of friends enables the 'philosophical lover' – the theoretician – to acquire wings (249A) that begin to grow in the presence of the beloved (251B). And when fully winged the soul soars upwards, attaining again the primeval vision of truth and beauty. Friendship is that 'mania' which transforms us upon a 'winged splendour, capable of soaring to the contemplation of eternal verities'.

And so this motif runs on throughout Christian literature up until the Middle

Ages. St Jerome will write of friends flying to one another, their feet winged with *caritas*, as Hermes before. And St Gregory the Great in his commentary on Ezekiel will interpret the wings of the animals in his vision of the chariot of Yahweh as representing the love of God and love of man. Aelred of Rievaulx, whose *On Spiritual Friendship* in many ways sets the high water mark of this tradition, will speak of the movement of friendship as flight and as an ascension made by friends together on the ladder of *caritas* to the embrace of Christ.[10]

Amicitia – friendship – then is a way to the happiness of paradise symbolised as a winged flight, an ecstatic ascension, in which one is drawn to the source of all truth, goodness and beauty. As such, friendship is the occasion, the scene, for the appearance of an impassioned *theoria* that will rise to eternity.

However, if we are to suggest that friendship provides the proper site for *theoria*, then we should recognise that this involves no mere extrinsic exchange – the swapping or laying out of notional or acquired truths. The classical definition of friendship, and the one that was to have so important an influence on the monastic ideal of friendship in the twelfth century, was given by Cicero in his *De amicitia*. Friendship, he wrote, is the 'complete identity of feeling about all things in heaven and earth: an identity that is strengthened by mutual goodwill and affection.'[11] A briefer and more popular definition than this first appears in the writings of Gregory the Great and was then popularised in the medieval encyclopedia, the *Etymologiae* of Isidore of Seville. According to Gregory and Isidore, a friend is a guardian of one's soul, a *custos animi*. The definition thus suggests a responsibility for the other's well-being along with a concern for their ultimate salvation by way of a knowledge of the friend's own interior life.

What is apparent in both these definitions is some form of *interiorisation* of the other in the self which yields a grammar of identity – a felt experience of unitive recognition and purpose. Thus in the epistolatory correspondence that this essay will examine further, St Anselm will refer to his friend Gandulf as 'his other self', indicating the measure in which the souls of friends are 'consolidated' in one.[12]

Friendship then involves the *vie intérieure*, and its exegesis in the exchanges between friends is repeatedly metaphorised in a language of fire, light and, above all, sweetness *(dulcedo)*. It is now no doubt too misleading to call this language 'mystical', but we should at least be prepared to grant that it suggests a certain *fluidity* with respect to the construction of the subject.

To borrow a phrase from the French theoretician Julia Kristeva, friendship is the logic of the person-in-process but not, I will argue, through any dialectical labour of the negative. The reference here is to that adversarial moment in the construction of the self and its knowledge of itself which is 'the insight that fuels Hegel's entire discussion of the Lord and the Bondsman' in the *Phenomenology*.[13] This becoming-self, while no doubt translating a dialogic economy of sorts between self and other, nevertheless stands on the *other side* of the Cartesian *intuitus: a* certainty of certainty from which the mastering gaze will lay out the world with clarity and distinction.[14] And while the 'separatist moment' in the negotiation of identity is now deeply installed into our metaphysics and politics, if the ancient divine and cosmological laws, as well as traditional rhetorical and moral rules, have been superseded by a self-regulating constitution and 'gaps' for internal governance, can we not still claim for friendship a moment of *uncanniness* in our inscrutable universe? A moment of togetherness? In friendships and in friendship, are we not struck by that something almost unnameable that would not only *not* have us post no entry signs to our souls in the name of an infinite otherness but actually welcome thought in an ascending ecstasy?[15]

Luce Irigaray would remind us of an ancient orthodoxy, thus:

> [C]ontrary to the usual methods of dialectic, one should not have to give
> up love in order to become wise or learned. It is love that leads to knowl-
> edge whether in art or more metaphysical learning. It is love that both
> leads the way and is the pathway and is the path.[16]

What path of ascent this would chart for the soul is perhaps always to be re-discovered, but if the question of the linkage of thought and Otherness has come so to inflate contemporary high theory that it has become a 'theoria of its own height',[17] then perhaps the radical testimonies of friendship within the tradition may suggest scenes for other dispossessing convolutions and paths on high. As John Milbank comments regarding the tradition of thought which flows from Gregory of Nyssa and Augustine concerning our 'conjecture' upon God, we here encounter a

> mode of ascent which receives something of the infinite source so long as
> it goes on receiving it, so constituting, not a once and for all theory . . . but
> an endlessly repeated-as-always-different theoretical claim which is noth-
> ing other than all the biographies of every ascent, and the history of
> human ascent as such.[18]

III

The scenes of St Anselm's life (1035–1109) were many and varied. Anselm: the novice monk under Lanfranc at the Abbey of Bec in Normandy during a century of great monastic renewal. Anselm: the anguished contemplative whose malady in prayer yielded his *Proslogion*, and a proof of the existence of God that was to provoke ontological fever in the centuries to follow. And Anselm: Archbishop of Canterbury mired in the investiture crisis of 1103 at the end of his life in which he fought for the spiritual jurisdiction of the Roman Pontiff. These, though, are but occasional moments in a long life. Perhaps less well-known was Anselm's gift for friendship.

In friendship Anselm's intimates were fellow monks, and a considerable episto-latory archive to this fellowship remains.[19] There is no doubt much of historical interest here; however, what will concern me in these scenes of friendship is not the history of these relationships so much as their grammar: of the configuration of lover and beloved in these performances of friendship. Moreover, it is the staging of these scenes – of the logic of Anselm's appearance to his friends and of his friends' to him – that, I will suggest, *(con)figures* in a certain aspect his account of the ascent of reason towards God that he describes in the *Proslogion* – what he calls 'The rousing of the mind to the contemplation of God'. In short, Anselm's 'Aesthetic Reason'[20] inclines *(inclinare)*, in Augustinian fashion, towards God by way of a participation in the rhythm of the exchanging of sense; that is to say, of the experience of sense making sense in love, that is in friendship. In attending to Anselm's words on friendship, then, what we have to reckon with is the manner in which *theoria* crosses the logic of encounter, where the common point in all of this, or rather the point of crossing or turning whereby friendship yields the wings of ascent to *theoria*, is, in good Platonic and Augustinian fashion, the figure of the image.

Anselm studied Augustine for ten years as a monk of Bec and his thought is profoundly marked by Augustine, the theologian of love. The marks of this passionate tradition are there to discover in Anselm's letters. Friendship as love, as ascent, as belonging, as interior experience and above all, and to this we will return, as sweetness *(dulcedo)*. And if all this has a guiding and generative intuition then it is in recognition of the fact that the soul is as a mirror, and that in this mirror is reflected the human and the Divine face: a gesture which obviously intimates the Son of God as the most immediate coincidence of the Divine face seen always (and only) in a human face. The doctrine of the Image then – an iconography – is central to Anselm's thought.[21]

One of Anselm's more substantial correspondences was with Gandulf, a fellow monk at Bec, later to become Bishop of Rochester, which began following Anselm's move to England. Anselm's understanding of friendship can be discerned from this correspondence and, following the work of Adele Fiske, we may sketch out a brief phenomenology of Anselm's grammar of friendship in terms of five notes which perpetually interleave one another.

The *first*, and constantly recurrent, note in these letters is Anselm's appeal to Gandulf's *consciousness* of their mutual love; a consciousness which, Anselm claims, *is* love itself, and so, in a certain way, makes their correspondence, as indeed their physical presence to one another, unnecessary. Friendship is love, *affectus* – a love which is mutual and of which friends are mutually conscious.[22] He writes to Gandulf:

> You have my consciousness always with you. If you are silent, I know that you love me; when I am silent, you know that I love you. You are conscious that I do not doubt you and I give witness to you that you are sure of me. We are then conscious of each other's consciousness.[23]

This double note of reciprocity and conscious awareness indicates an experience which according to Anselm produces an interior presence of the friend – a certainty of love as mutual possession. Thus, Anselm will tend to minimise the value of corporeal presence and suggest rather that the very separation of friends is their means of being together.[24] But how is this possible?

The answer to this, which amounts to a *second* note of friendship, is given in Anselm's deployment of Augustine's image doctrine. In short, Anselm's 'consciousness' corresponds to the image doctrine, for the image of the friend loved is *in* the soul of the friend who loves. Spiritual presence then is no 'presence by absence'; rather it is, according to Anselm, an *inhering* and not merely a co-hering. It is an inscription of image-likeness in 'the heart': Augustine's *cubiculum*– a dwelling place for the friend.[25] Thus: 'One whom you bear in your bosom is interior to you, you can in no way leave him; indeed you are not able to forsake that deep presence of one who follows you wherever you go, and who, wherever he may be, is always embracing you.'[26]

So Anselm speaks expressly of an 'image' of love as *impressed* deeply on the soul by its embrace of love, and as *expressed* clearly in the act of loving. This image is of the friend himself, imprinted on the heart like a seal in wax 'formed' in the interior of the mind. This is a passage of *interiorisation*: a theme to which we will need to return. Moreover, and this is crucial, as the Image of God is to be discovered by its reflection in one's own soul which provokes reflection, so also is the image of the friend to be found in this exchange – and the two, one could further suggest, are never apart.

Third, Anselm claims, it is precisely this specular exchange that makes friendship's mutual insight uniquely sure.[27] He writes: 'Indeed I do not deceive, for I am a friend; certainly I am not deceived, for I have experience.'[28] He will constantly repeat the refrain 'I am certain, I do not doubt' in relation to the unity of love perceived and experienced in friendship. Thus, friendship provokes an *infallible intuition* that is like or analogous to the love of God – an infallibility which should more properly be understood as the faithfulness to a love that neither slumbers nor sleeps (Psalm 120: 4). This infallible intuition is of the manner of spiritual presence which is known – again as by Augustine before him – as sweetness.

Sweetness (*dulcedo*) is the *fourth* note of friendship, and is perhaps the dominant trait of friendship.[29] As such it will demand a little more consideration than we have so far given to the other aspects. For Anselm, as much as for Augustine, presence is *dulcedo* – it is vision and hearing. We need to remark with care the translation or exchange suggested here, for I will claim it is the key to Anselm's thought, and perhaps also to the tradition in which he stands. Love is sweet but as presence it is also convoluted into (and by no means as secondary) vision; for the manifestation of love known in sweetness is precisely the appearing of the image in the heart. Sweetness is vision, *and critically sight is told as touch*. Here then we begin to witness a meeting and crossing – an exchange – of the senses as sight and sound are told in terms of taste and smell.

Anselm speaks of a 'rational delight and delightful reason' that friends enjoy in one another. In short, he speaks, or writes, of an exchange of the presence of the friend experienced in sweetness. But what does this mean? It means that friendship is configured in a *crossing of the senses*, such that the image of the friend – his

133

presence to me – is always already an image in exchange as it were: a coming to know in the movement of exchange; in, we could say, the differencing of the senses as the difference of sense.

But what is exchanged here? The answer, I would suggest, is precisely nothing; or nothing other than exchange itself. To explain. In friendship, I see, and I see you always: in short, I see you in love. In friendship, I touch, and touch you always: in short, I touch you in love. Thus, it is the exchange between seeing and seeing you (this mobile difference – the difference love makes) that is to be exchanged in the exchanging of the senses: between sight and touch, between as it were speculation and materiality. In seeing and seeing the friend, then, in this difference, which is as it were nothing, I taste and touch the sweetness of you.

This is the differencing of love and, I will go on to suggest, the origin of *theoria* as originating passion and the passion of origin: a logic of that sense of sense making sense, which is but one way of explaining the fact that the Great Tradition has always understood that love and knowledge belong together.

However, to turn to the *fifth* and final note of friendship. The image doctrine is fundamentally a doctrine about *participation*. However, in this, there is a limit imposed on our mutual possession each of the other which coincides precisely with our own possession of ourselves. For as we do not possess ourselves wholly, neither can we possess our friends wholly. We may belong to our friends as we belong to ourselves, but never, according to Anselm, entirely, for it is to God alone that we belong entirely.

This is no more than a brief sketch or phenomenology of friendship that Anselm sets forth. Our task is now to examine further the clues that these notes of friendship set before us, reflecting in particular on the enigmatic translation or exchange which attends to Anselm's characterization of presence as *dulcedo*.

Could we perhaps suggest, ratcheting through the gears somewhat abruptly, that the privilege of friendship for Anselm operates as something like Heidegger's existential analytic, which is to say, as something like a privileged moment of onto-logical revelation?

To explain. The originally impassioned gesture of *theoria* steps forward from the scene of friendship in that from the intimacy of an encounter meaning comes to itself – as word (*logos*) touching itself. Friendship is this privileged moment: the provocation of the hermeneutical ascent of an aesthetic reason. By this I mean that at the scene of friendship – which is no mere place where things appear but *the* appearing place – *logos* or meaning is transcribed through a touching of itself – Anselm's 'infallible intuition' – in the existential encounter with otherness: the friend known in sweetness. And here I want to urge again that we avoid interpret-ing this encounter as the occasion for dialectical development. Of course, we come to learn in friendship, and in this 'the dialectics of lived experience' are implicated; but in friendship we come to re-cognise that encounter never 'occurs' before or without meaning, as it were – in some sort of languorous solitude. Is it that friend-ship intimates something of a remainder of touch, an excess – as Bernard of Clairvaux so clearly recognised – which precedes this event of encounter? And if this is the case then perhaps we can mark this in terms of a perpetual exchanging: of the experience of Word becoming flesh (in the event of friendship) in which flesh becomes words. It is towards an explanation of this suggestion that the rest of this essay is concerned.

IV

Meaning enjoys, as Kant would have it, a rhapsodic beginning – a sense of coming to itself in a shuddering recognition. And if the process of this recognition, of thought, is therefore originally impassioned, this does not mean that thought is a particular passion arising from a particular place or origin, but rather that this passion is the ever-turning origin of thought itself. What does this involve? How can we describe this event? I would suggest, by attending to the – at least – triple sense of the meaning, or making, of *sense*.

That is to say: first, a making sense of or coming to understand something; second, a sensing something to be so, a feeling or touching; and third, although only as the crossing of these two, the exchanging of these two senses of sense in *sense understood as reason*. In this way, then, we can suggest that the experience of meaning is inscribed as the crossing of thought and touch, the immaterial and material. What makes sense about meaning is that it senses itself making sense and so moves on in its gathering ex-centricity. Meaning touches itself and is as such an aesthetic impassioned experience from the first. If we can begin to understand this of meaning, what then of friendship?

Anselm's notion of friendship always moves in a circle thus: to be a friend I must have a friend, and to have a friend I must be a friend in an exchange ever motivated by love as the recognition of virtue, and of virtue as the fruit of love. This is fundamentally Augustinian, but this moving in a circle should not be understood as the spinning of a duality – a dialectical conferring of selfhood as either a duplication or a distancing of self towards infinity. Rather, the grammar of friendship we have already examined suggests a movement, or the drawing open of a space, which is delineated precisely by the notes or traits that are here drawn forth in friendship: that is to say, intuition, certainty and sweetness. Moreover, it is of note that these are all marks of the movement of faith seeking understanding that Anselm will describe in the *Proslogion*. They are, we could suggest, the marks of *theoria*.

In short, then, one can discover a clear analogy between the grammar of friendship and the grammar of *theoria* as depicted by Anselm. But is this the end of the matter? I would suggest not, for what we have to reckon with here is not simply a homology between the grammars of friendship and *theoria* as set forth by Anselm, and indeed by the Tradition, but more fundamentally the thought of a translation of the two – perhaps an originary exchange in the exchange of exchange; that is to say, of *theoria* as the ascent towards a contemplation of the transcendentals – the ex-centricity of the passion of meaning – brought to view at the scene of friendship – the scene of an intimacy with the other recognised in love.

The scene of friendship then unfolds, as it were, the hermeneutical path of intelligibility and meaning – as an encounter with Otherness – and this it does as passion and in passion – as, one could say, bidding, appeal, request, supplication, thanksgiving, and precisely not in the fulfilment of any prior transcendental conditions.

Rather fancifully, one could suggest, then, that if Heidegger's way to thought was in meditation upon the concrete and universal 'Here I am', and Descartes' upon the abstract universal 'I am a thinking ego', then what we are set to think with Anselm is the thought: 'We are friends'. But what would this mean?

It means that Anselm's thought of friendship, in friendship, is not to be understood as a thinking of the friend (comparable to a thinking of another) with whom I come into relation. Nor is Anselm's thought to be construed (which amounts to the same thing) as the scene for a dialectical interplay between the two. The thought 'We are friends' is to be thought not as the difference of one to another, but as the *differencing* 'between' friends as it were – the differencing of friendship. The thought of friendship is always the thought of a plurality.

Friends arrive, appear as it were in the plural. Friendship provokes an *undecidability* concerning the differences between holding and being held, regarding and being regarded, and this as no measure of a recollected distance between two, however configured. This issue can be illustrated in a phenomenology of the other's gaze which must reckon always with that unfigurable density of one's appearing in another's eyes.

You appear in my eyes, an appearance that you cannot see, as indeed I appear in your eyes in an appearing I cannot see. And yet, it is *through* my eyes, through the image of you in my eyes, that I both see you and you appear to me, in the appearance that love makes. The differences here are manifold: they are plural and not to be elided. I glance, I notice when a friend enters the room; I look for you, and for you looking towards me, for me in your glance. This is the complexity of the gaze – of the world, of you, of me (and perhaps of more), always appearing in this interval of sight, broken only by the blink or the stop.[30] However, this complexity of our crossing looks does not mark out friendship. For sure, one needs to get pretty close to another's face in order to see this – one's appearance in another's eyes – but still friendship is not the only occasion to provoke such intimacy. One can just as well be face-to-face with one's enemy. And here, of course, we can note a fascination with the manner in which enmity and hatred will mimic love – in some sort of corrupted (corrupting) *mimesis*.

What then is the difference of friendship? What is the difference to which Anselm points? It is an *interiorisation* – it is, or is marked by, a passage through the pupil.[31] It is through my eyes that you will travel. You, that is, your appearance, your image, is imaged, translated in my heart as a result of a passage through the senses. And this passage is a reflecting by the senses upon themselves and a reflecting upon that which they reflect. *It is a moment of touch.*

Thus for Anselm it is the interiorisation of vision and a translation, an exchange into touch, that is the remarking of friendship. Friends gaze with the eyes of the heart, the heart that is as the mobile waxen surface upon which your image will appear. But more than this, friends taste with the eyes of the heart in a beyond of sight and sound. Thus Anselm writes:

> But what of this that neither eye has seen nor ear heard but only into the heart of man has it entered. . . . My witness is the experience of my consciousness, that the taste of this affection is not perceived by any sight or hearing, save inasmuch as it is conceived in the mind of each. Since therefore that you know that the sweetness of love is recognised, neither by eyes nor ears, but tasted delightfully by the mouth of the heart, with what words or letters shall my love and yours be described? Let our own consciousness suffice for us, by which we are conscious to each other of how much we love each other.[32]

Let us put it like this. In the mirror-play of vision I scan the world, catching occasional sight of myself; but in the interiorization of the image in friendship, what I come to hold, to behold, to taste, is the image of the one who holds my image. This is the acute mutuality of friendship, according to Anselm. In the friend I see me; in me I see the friend – and it is this that I taste.

But the question arises: is this not to provoke an infinite regress and duplication? For if I hold a mirror in my heart in which I see you holding a mirror in which I see me, do I not see, in that mirror again, a mirror in which I see you holding a mirror of me, and so on and so forth? What is this miracle of recognition in and through the image which presages no reduction, which does not turn friendship into a scene for the appearance of a bad infinite? It is for Anselm touch; more precisely, taste.

In friendship it is, as it were, the tain of the image, or the mirror, that is touched. And in this, touching *gives* an infallible intuition, a certainty, in the exorbitant sweetness of love. It is love which allows this passage, this exchange to occur. To enable this image of you in my eyes to become the image – the icon – of you touched in my heart requires attentive love. Love has that which *withdraws* in order to make an opening for entry and passage. *This crossing of the senses is love's exchange.*

And again, this miracle of recognition – of me, of you, of me in you and you in me, precisely the plurality of the differencing proper to friendship – is no simple exchange. Rather it is the event or the occurrence of the *exchange of exchange*. And by this I mean that our passing glances, one to another, become as it were freighted with a weight of love, indeed even glory, eliciting from them the peculiar passion of *theoria*: of sense reaching out to touch itself in ascent/assent to the truth, beauty, goodness and unity that I experience in this encounter.

The interiorisation of the gaze that Anselm describes, then, is precisely a reflection upon reflection; it is the passage to this touching place, this taste of sight, which is the origin of figuration, the sweetness of love. To speak of the exchange of exchange in this miracle of recognition is not to suggest, therefore, that the path of interiorisation involves a simple metaphoric translation from sight to touch. This is not the exchange evoked. Rather, to speak of the exchange of exchange here is to try to indicate that the passion of thought – sense making sense – originates, or springs up from the crossing of the senses, in dispossession: of their belonging together, as learnt only and always in friendship; that is to say, in love.

V

A patient reading of Anselm, one that is attentive to the ever present–absent bodies of friends in words of friendship, reveals, I have argued, a chiastic configuration of friendship and *theoria as configuration* which has endowed friendship with a particular privilege in the Christian tradition. The differencing of friendship involves the interiorisation of the gaze which, in provoking a reflection upon reflection, is told as touch. In this logic, then, *friendship is theorised*, but not, as I have stressed, as the exchange of one thing for another – as, for example, the abandonment of the particularity and materiality of things for a contemplation of pure ideas. Rather, the crossing of friendship with *theoria* is precisely that which evokes the idea of the exchange of exchange told as a bodily convolution of the senses which does not abandon the creature and its corporeality in order to speak of its proper ecstasy. Moreover, friendship gives a pedagogy in the attributes of Being – a teaching in the experience of truth, unity, goodness and beauty – which is, at the same time – I want tentatively to suggest – *a pedagogy in analogy*.

In order to conclude this reflection I want to indicate a further path for investigation which I believe this logic provokes. This would involve a somewhat eccentric reading of Anselm's thought, which – in some proximity to Balthasar's brilliant reading of Anselm's 'Aesthetic Reason' – would give particular attention to the implications of an odd temporality that Anselm describes in the *Proslogion*. This concerns the occasion of a coincidence – the 'simultaneous' presence–absence of God in recollection.

To explain. Popularly, Anselm's words-towards, *pros-logion*, are but the enactment of the *fides quaerens intellectum* – of a faith seeking (perhaps then reaching out towards) understanding – which wondrously has always already been granted admittance to that which it seeks. The tortured contemplative in prayer discovers, like a bolt from the blue, that that which he seeks has no longer to be pursued. The pursuit – if pursuit it is to remain – is apparently not for the lost but in the excessive thought of an ever-greater God (Augustine's *semper maior*). But still in this pursuit Anselm's abysmal reflection continues, for *(and upon this everything now turns)* Anselm writes: 'But if you have found [Him], why is it that you do not feel what you have found? Why, O Lord God, does my soul not feel You if it has found You?'[33]

This is a perplexing admission: a discovery that has not been felt? A touching without touching? Anselm bewails the 'absence' of a God who is yet believed to be present, precisely when this knowledge cannot by itself effect the act by which He would be made present. What are we to make of this? Is it that Anselm's words-towards stall, short of their intended target, precisely because the interiorisation of the *logos* as felt experience fails to secure the touch of reflection's reflection which would propel it into an ascent to the heavens (*theoria*)? Thus, the exchange of exchange – the event that would bring the *delectatio* and *dulcedo* of God's presence and which is *theoria's* only fuel – fails to occur? In this sense, does Anselm's abysmal longing amount to a recognition of the fact that friendship with God cannot be theorised? Or does it say something other: that this theorisation *occurs otherwise*, that is to say, is timed otherwise in an impossible simultaneity? At this turning, the questions proliferate – inevitably, impossibly.

The 'event' of the *Proslogion* is structurally – temporally – *traumatic*: a knowing which is equally the felt experience of never knowing, of never being able to know. It is a dual event which involves both pleasure and prohibition; a convolution which 'occurs', as it were, in the differencing of time itself – across a moment that can never be present. It is in this recognition that our reading would draw near to that of Henri de Lubac, who has argued that the line of the *Proslogion* is deeply broken: broken in that Anselm's intellectual satisfaction at the discovery of the proof of God's existence is not at all the joy in God promised by Christ. However, in this reading it is a recognition, an *aporia*, that is saturated by the *delay of time*, the delay that time is: neither the *punctum* nor the *nunc stans*.

In recognition of something like this, Balthasar draws to a close his own assessment of both the *Proslogion* and *Monologion* with this judgment:

> And then there comes a final thought. The joy of aesthetic reason, which contemplates the harmony of God's work of salvation, is founded on the suffering of the Son of God. This casts a long shadow over the whole theological aesthetic.[34]

What sort of shadow? A reversal that would explode every perceptible proportion in the existential structures of mortal life, friendship included? This is the question that the concluding and disturbed chapters of the *Proslogion* bring us to ask: what catastrophe would this bring to the friendship of God with his creature? The question is freighted with theological implication, for if the convolution of friendship with *theoria* resides in an exchanging of sense which raises speculation to the heavens, then what of an exchange in which God offers himself *in friendship* to His creation in the unheard of descent of the *Logos*? There can be no doubt that the pattern of the exchange of exchange is for Anselm, as for all orthodox theology, 'prefigured' in the Son, the Word, the *Logos* of God; but to take these thoughts further would demand, no doubt, a new intervention in, and engagement with, Anselm's famous satisfaction theory of the Atonement: the timing of an exchange of the first order, if ever there was one.

To conclude this reflection, I would hazard the following speculation. If the ontological privilege of friendship amounts to a delay of the crossing of word becoming flesh and flesh becoming word in the exchanging of senses, then *theoria's* ascent will properly never involve an unshackling of itself from body: as merely flesh become word and word leaving flesh. But it will perhaps always demand a figuration and reiteration of this exchange of exchange as the delay of love's withdrawal of itself – the delaying withdrawal which is necessary in order for love to love. It is only this withdrawal that will allow love to give itself completely without exhausting itself and without the end of the giving ever being reached. But it is precisely in this withdrawal that love reflects upon itself – in a flash – and so is crossed by thought.

For thought to hold – to touch, to reach out for – itself (and thought is nothing other than this) then it must always be held together; held, that is, by and in the body, learning the (withdrawing, delaying) differences of the love in friendship. And, of course, it is itself subject to this same delay – this is its passion, and its pain, its opening in the exchange of exchange. That which has become flesh has lit the flesh through, such that it can hold, must perhaps hold back, withdraw, if words are to come forth: a gesture we could name *kenosis*. *Theoria*, like love, must reflect upon this, its own movement; but it can do so only by continuing to participate in it. For *theoria* to recognise, to reach out and touch, it cannot be anything other than *theoria*. And yet it may repeatedly mistake itself in this very recognition, as it strives to forget the together of love and knowledge in its desire to be carried beyond being carried.

Would, then, friendship give the site for a most radical recollection today: a remembering of the *analogia entis*?

Notes

1 The Latin root word in *amicitia* (friendship) is *amo* – I love.
2 Quoted in Edward Carpenter, *Iolaus, An Anthology* (Author's Edition, MCMII), p. 137.
3 *City of God*, Book XIX, Ch. 8.
4 *On the Good Life*, trans. Michael Grant (London: Penguin Classics, 1971), p. 187.
5 See for example Brian Patrick McGuire, *Friendship and Community – The Monastic Experience 350–1250* (Kalamazoo: Cistercian Publications Inc., 1988).
6 For a further examination of these themes see Philip A. Mellor and Chris Shilling, *Religion, Community and Modernity* (London: SAGE Publications, 1997), Ch. 3.
7 In this breath I cannot avoid mentioning Jacques Derrida's recent and formidable essay *Politics of Friendship*, trans. George Collins (London: Verso, 1997). For Derrida it is a destined identification of friend with brother in an ever returning politics of 'fratriarchy' that must now yield to the deconstructive energy released by the grief of Aristotle aporetic 'O my friends, there is no friend'. It is this that speaks to Derrida today of 'an unheard of friendship'. Any further development of my argument could not avoid these traces; and most especially in terms of the reduction of the many to the one of which Aristotle remarks.
8 See the comments of John Milbank in his 'Only Theology Overcomes Metaphysics' in *New Blackfriars* (vol. 76 No. 895, July/August 1995), p. 327.
9 *The Other: Studies in the Social Ontology of Husserl, Heidegger, Sartre, and Buber*, trans. Christopher Macann (Cambridge, MA: MIT Press, 1986), pp. 371–72.
10 *Spiritual Friendship*, trans. Mark F. Williams (London: University of Scranton Press, 1994), III. 134, p. 90.
11 *On the Good Life*, trans. Michael Grant (London: Penguin Classics, 1971), p. 187.
12 *The Letters of Saint Anselm of Canterbury*, vol. 1, trans. Walter Frolich (Kalamazoo: Cistercian Publications, 1990), Letter 7, p. 87.
13 Rowan D. Williams, 'Interiority and Epiphany: A Reading in New Testament Ethics', in *Modern Theology* (vol. 13 No. 1, January 1997), p. 31.

14 One could suggest that the Cartesian deduction fails to heed the enigma of its own beginning, for while Descartes wants to begin with the security of the *cogito*, the *cogito* itself relies upon an earlier starting point in doubt. There is then a certain ambiguity and duplicity in the Cartesian philosophical beginning.

15 Raissa Maritain offers compelling witness to this in the record of her life with the great Thomist philosopher of this century, Jacques Maritain, *We Have Been Friends Together* (Garden City: Image Books, 1961), pp. 84–85:

> We were alone in my parents' living room. Jacques was sitting on the rug, close to my chair; it suddenly seemed to me that we had always been near each other, and that we would always be so. Without thinking, I put out my hand and stroked his hair; he looked at me and all was clear to us. The feeling flowed through me that always – for my happiness and my salvation (I thought precisely that, although then the word 'salvation' meant nothing to me) – that always my life would be bound up with Jacques'. It was one of those tender and peaceful feelings which are like a gift flowing from a region higher than ourselves, illuminating the future and deepening the present.

16 *An Ethics of Sexual Difference*, trans. Carolyn Burke and Gillian C. Gill (London: Athlone Press, 1993), p. 21.

17 Vassilis Lambropoulos, *The Rise of Eurocentrism: Anatomy of Interpretation* (New Jersey: Princeton University Press, 1993), p. 325.

18 'Only Theology Overcomes Metaphysics', p. 335.

19 My examination of Anselm is indebted to the scholarly work of Adele M. Fiske on friendship in the monastic tradition: *Friends and Friendship in the Monastic Tradition* (Cuernavaca: Centro Intercultural de Documentación, 1970), 'Saint Anselm' (Ch. 15). While I have used Walter Frolich's recent translations of Anselm's letters, I have also, where indicated, depended on Fiske's renditions.

20 See Hans Urs von Balthasar, *Glory of the Lord, Vol. II: Studies in Theological Style: Clerical Styles* (Edinburgh: T. & T. Clark, 1984), pp. 213f.

21 *The Letters of Saint Anselm of Canterbury*, Letter 41, p. 144.

22 *The Letters of Saint Anselm of Canterbury*, Letter 16, p. 103.

23 *Friends and Friendship in the Monastic Tradition*, p. 15. Also *The Letters of Saint Anselm*, Letter 4, p. 81.

24 *The Letters of Saint Anselm of Canterbury*, Letter 41, p. 144.

25 *The Letters of Saint Anselm of Canterbury*, Letters 7, p. 87, 16, p. 103 and 41, p. 144.

26 *Friends and Friendship in the Monastic Tradition*, p. 15. Also *The Letters of Saint Anselm of Canterbury*, Letter 4, p. 81.

27 *The Letters of Saint Anselm of Canterbury*, Letter 28, p. 121.

28 *Friends and Friendship in the Monastic Tradition*, p. 15.

29 *The Letters of Saint Anselm of Canterbury*, Letter 4, p. 81.

30 See David Appelbaum's remarkable book *The Stop* (New York: SUNY Press, 1995).

31 In the original version of this paper I went on to reflect upon the configuration of this journey through the pupil as it is presented by Luce Irigaray in her remarkable meditation 'La Mysterique' (in *Speculum of the Other Woman*, trans. Gillian Gill (New York: Cornell University Press, 1985)). The juxtaposition here of Anselm with Irigaray was provoked by the theme of the touching of sense and the fate of this convolution when placed under the 'patriarchal' ban – 'Do not touch'. It is of further note that in *Politics of Friendship* Derrida will ask what would happen to friendship and the politics of brotherhood – fratriarchy – should the friend no longer be 'like the brother', but be, perhaps, a sister.

32 *Friends and Friendship in the Monastic Tradition*, p. 15.

33 *St. Anselm's* Proslogion, trans. M. J. Charlesworth (Oxford: Oxford University Press, 1965). The translation is modified in order to indicate that Anselm's *sentis* (translated by

the unlocatable idea 'experience' in Charlesworth) elicits, rather, a quite explicit reflection upon the trauma of the fallen creature, 'bereft of the *sensorium* appropriate to the living God' (Balthasar) The issue here is precisely what I have called the convolution of the senses; although it now 'occurs' more fundamentally within the problematics of time.

34 *The Glory of the Lord*, vol. II, p. 236.

7

EROTICS

God's sex

Gerard Loughlin

Erotic parodies

'It is clear' – Georges Bataille (1897–1962) asserts at the beginning of his 1927 essay 'The Solar Anus' – 'that the world is purely parodic, in other words that each thing seen is the parody of another, or is the same thing in a deceptive form'.

> Ever since sentences started to *circulate* in brains devoted to reflection, an effort at total identification has been made, because with the aid of a copula each sentence ties one thing to another; all things would be visibly connected if one could discover at a single glance and in its totality the tracings of an Ariadne's thread leading thought into its own labyrinth.
> But the *copula* of terms is no less irritating than the *copulation* of bodies.[1]

For Bataille's parodic thought everything in the world is ultimately relatable to everything else; everything can be substituted for another thing, in a ceaseless process of metaphoric exchange. It is the circulation of language that makes this possible; and since it is possible in language it is possible in the world(s) that language constitutes. The coupling of words performs the copulation of bodies. For Bataille, parody utterly eroticises the world, so that in the running of the 'locomotive's wheels and pistons' he sees the world's 'two primary motions' of 'rotation and sexual movement'. In the image of the steam engine's pounding pistons and turning wheels, Bataille sees the coupling of animals and the movements of the planets, always moving from 'their own position in order to return to it, completing their rotation'. These 'two motions' – the thrusting of sexual frenzy and the circling of the stars – are 'reciprocally transformed, the one into the other', so that the turning of the earth 'makes animals and men have coitus' and – since 'the result is as much the cause as that which provokes it' – the coupling of animals and men turns the earth.[2] For Bataille, the earth and its motions are enfolded in the erotic embrace of the cosmos:

> The simplest image of organic life united with rotation is the tide. From the movement of the sea, uniform coitus of the earth with the moon, comes the polymorphous and organic coitus of the earth with the sun.
>
> But the first form of solar love is a cloud raised up over the liquid element.
>
> The erotic cloud sometimes becomes a storm and falls back to earth in the form of rain, while lightning staves in the layers of the atmosphere.
>
> The rain is soon raised up again in the form of an immobile plant.[3]

In this essay I attempt to trace the similar parodying of the erotic in the work of Hans Urs von Balthasar (1905–1988). While Bataille couples the sun and moon with the sea, with clouds and plants, with the coitus of animals and the 'amorous frenzy' of men and women,[4] Balthasar couples the processions of the divine Trinity with the birthing of a maiden's child, with the kiss of a bride and groom who are also mother and son – bone of bone and flesh of flesh – with the embrace of every couple in Christ, and of every soul with God. Balthasar's 'copulations' are no less startling than Bataille's 'torrid and blinding sun' that 'exclusively loves the Night and directs its luminous violence, its ignoble shaft, toward the earth', whose 'nocturnal terrestrial expanses head continuously toward the indecency of the solar ray'.[5]

By thinking the parallels between the 'motions' of Trinity, Christ and Church (Mary) as parodic transformations, I want to unveil the 'body' – the ancient cultural biology – that Balthasar both exposes and conceals in his 'suprasexual' erotics. By talking of parodies rather than of metaphors, symbols or analogies, I do not intend to deny the propriety of such terms for the linkages and connections, including the copula(tion)s of human bodies, one with another, and with divine 'flesh'. Rather, in speaking of parodies – as metaphoric substitutions (in the quite precise and somewhat peculiar sense offered by Bataille) – I want to disturb the ease with which we tend to pass over such exchanges in theology and, as it were, to disenchant us of analogy – at least for the duration of this essay. If one thinks of simile as metaphor footnoted and explained, rendered less provocative and dangerous, one can think of analogy as simile extended, elaborated, intensified, stressing the greater dissimilarity (*maior dissimilitudo*) of the analogously conjoined, copulated similars.

Analogy – as John Saward puts it – sets a 'certain likeness' within a 'greater unlikeness'.[6] But since such analogy – particularly in theology – does not measure the distance between the analogues, one is left with only the 'certain likeness', which then gains in intensity from the silence of the unmeasured space – the 'greater unlikeness' – in which it is set. The shock of calling analogy 'parody' may remind us that in using analogies – even one as hallowed as the Fatherhood of

144

God – we do not escape the historical and the cultural, that from which the 'certain likeness' is taken.[7] Thus I do not intend to entirely divest 'parody' of burlesque, which is certainly still present in Bataille's usage, when he couples the polite with the vulgar, the metaphysical with the indecent.

The 'dance of dispossession'

By means of the parodic copula Bataille relates sexual rhythm with planetary motion; Balthasar – in what may be considered a no less surreal manner – relates the economic with the immanent Trinity. It is not the relation as such – baldly stated – that constitutes the surreal in Balthasar, for as much is asserted by other theologians, most notably Karl Rahner, for whom it is axiomatic that the '"economic" Trinity is the "immanent" Trinity and the "immanent" Trinity is the "economic" Trinity'.[8] Christian theology can hardly say otherwise, unless it is to entertain a second God, hidden and undisclosed beyond the one who in Christ acts for the salvation of the world.

Balthasar's surreal move is to suppose that in the economic Trinity, in the scriptural story of Christ's ministry, death and resurrection, we see the inner economy of the immanent Trinity, its fundamental dynamic, a drama that has, as it were, always-already occurred before its expression in the history of the world. Thus the mission of Christ is the historical concretion of the Son's procession from the Father, and Balthasar's 'great insight', as John Saward puts it, is to see that 'the "kenosis" of the Incarnation is made possible by and lays open a preceding and underlying kenosis within the Trinity'.[9] Thus the incarnation as kenosis – as a radical donation of the self, the self-gift of Christ unto death, an utter dispossession – is the non-identical repetition or parody of the intratrinitarian kenosis, the Father's eternal dispossession and donation of himself to the Son.

It is the nature of God to be endlessly abundant, perpetually effusive, overflowing with fecund love; an unceasing donation of self to an other – 'not another God but an other in God'.[10] The one who is thus given – eternally – is constituted as gift and reception, and thus can only in turn give again, thereby establishing the circulation, the rotation, of the eternal charity. This spinning love, as it were, is the act of the Trinity, spinning so fast, with such joy, that – for no other reason than its sheer goodness – there flows the world, which, caught in the circling draft, is to be drawn back into the eternal rotation:

> The life of the Trinity is an eternally self-fulfilled circle, which does not
> need the world . . . The act of creation has its source in the freedom of the
> Trinity; it is a 'selfless' sharing of [the Trinity's] life of blessed selflessness
> with needy creatures.[11]

It is, then, out of this circling dynamic, this 'dance of dispossession', as John Saward calls it[12], that there flows a series of relationships, each one of which, like the figures or sets of a dance, differently repeats the preceding one, joined only by a parodic copula. This is the flow of the divine mission which repeats, *ad extra* and non-identically, the preceding procession of the Son from the Father.

Continuum and indeterminacy

I now wish to introduce two related objections to the foregoing description of Balthasar's trinitarian reflections as kenotic parody. First, Bataille's parodic copula presumes a continuous domain in which to operate. No matter how fanciful or shocking his connections, they take place within the single space of the cosmos; they do not presume a radical discontinuity between any of the terms, such as the infinite distance that theology presumes to separate the creator from the creature, and which requires some concept of analogy for its bridging, if not indeed a strategy of negation. Bataille's parodic world is the pre-Christian cosmos that Balthasar describes as the 'all-embracing context' of 'being as a whole, which always includes the *theion*'.[13] This ancient cosmos – as in Plato's *Republic* – is already one of parodic substitution, in which the rightly ordered soul is the rightly ordered polis is the rightly ordered cosmos, exhibiting what Balthasar terms a 'fluid *analogia entis*'. He notes that such a cosmos – embracing both human and divine being – 'survived, in a Christian transposition, right into modern times, in spite of the fact that now there was a far more abrupt distinction between the divine, absolute world and the contingent world freely created by God'.[14] However, it would seem that one has to assume the survival of such a cosmos in Balthasar's theology, if his kenotic repetitions are to be read as a continuum of parodic substitutions, as I have suggested. But this is to raise my first question to Balthasar: How far do his analogies have to travel? What is the distance between the terms that his copulas hold together?

The second objection that I wish to raise with regard to my application of Bataille to Balthasar concerns the reversibility or inversions of Bataille's parodies, since on Bataille's account the pistons drive the wheels and the wheels power the pistons; copulation turns the planet and the planet moves the copulators, and so we are asked to imagine a perhaps perpetual motion with an indeterminate cause. In an economy of radical substitution, there can be no fixed priority or stable hierarchy. But then this raises my second question to Balthasar. Is it so certain that he can establish the priority presumed in his parodic account of trinitarian kenosis? Might the procession of Son from Father be the parody of creation, or of incarnation, or of redemption, or of the relationship – which I have yet to discuss – between man and woman, rather than that they are parodies of a prior intra trinitarian kenosis? In short, are matters not more fluid, more 'uncanny', as in the way of ancient cosmology?[15]

It is these two questions – how analogical is Balthasar's *analogia entis*, and how can he preserve the Trinity from contamination by its human parodies – that I now want to bring to a consideration of Balthasar's body theology.

Sexual womb

Mary Timothy Prokes's *Toward a Theology of the Body* (1996), while it makes only passing reference to Balthasar – acknowledging a more immediate debt to John Paul II: 'the leading advocate for the development of Body Theology'[16] – nevertheless displays Balthasarian themes, so that we may approach his body theology by way of hers.

Prokes defines human sexuality as the capacity 'to enter into love-giving, life-giving union in and through the body in ways that are appropriate'.[17] Human sexuality is not 'animalistic', but *'person-al*, involving the giving and receiving of person-gift'. As a 'capacity', this self-giving is not 'restricted to certain bodily organs and activities, nor is it confined to a certain portion of life'.[18] It pervades all of life. Like Balthasar, Prokes sees this bodily capacity to give oneself, and in return to receive the self of the other, as the result of our 'being created in the image and likeness of God', thus parodying, as it were, 'the Trinity of Persons who are in constant perichoretic union through total Self-Gift to the other Persons'.[19] She adds that

> The theology of God's inner life (and thus, of human life in that image) is a 'gift theology', a faith reflection upon the irrevocable givenness and receptivity among the divine Persons. Faith-based understandings of human sexuality take their starting point in the trinitarian mystery.[20]

Prokes pictures both the inner trinitarian relations, and the relations between divinity and humanity, after the pregnant body: the body of the woman with child. For Prokes, the child in the womb experiences sexuality in 'an elemental but profound manner', in the sense that at 'no time in later life will there be the same capacity to *reside – to live within another physically* or to share flesh and blood with such an enduring immediacy'.[21] The intimate residence of the child in the womb is for Prokes an image of that residence in Christ to which all Christians are called:

> Womb-life is a prelude to the mature capacity of living within one another in the manner that Christ prayed for in his Last Discourse: 'May they be one in us, as you are in me and I am in you, so that the world may believe it was you who sent me' (John 17. 21).[22]

In a similar way, Balthasar pictures the triune circumincession as like that of the Christ-child in the womb of his mother; so that Mary's consciousness of the child growing within her is 'like an imitation, within the economy of salvation, of the mystery of the Trinity, and, no less, like an imitation (the first and closest imitation) of the mystery of the two natures in the one Person'.[23] She feels the child within her, as she is felt by the child. And just as this circumincession of mother and child is an imitation of the triune life, so also is it of the individual soul in relation to

147

God, the experience of 'oneself and the burgeoning Word of God, which at first seems to be growing in the self until in this growth it becomes evident that it is rather the other way around and that it is the self that is contained in the Word of God'.[24]

Prokes, who with Balthasar is surely correct in stressing the intimacy of persons in the sexual relation, is nevertheless so concerned to distance human sexuality from the animalistic – from the itch and yearning of sexual organs – that one might think the attraction and desirability of the body – its physical comforts and excitements – had nothing to do with human sexuality. Prokes offers a peculiarly passionless, unsexy, sexuality. In short she fails to think the erotic. The same, however, cannot be said of Balthasar.

Enraptured bodies

Many Christian theologians have wanted to draw a sharp distinction between the love that is proper to God and the Christian imitation of God, and that which enthrals the flesh, which elicits touch, caress and embrace, the stroking of skin and the meeting of lips.[25] For Karl Barth this latter love (*eros*) is but a rapacious 'intensification and strengthening of natural self-assertion':

> It is hungry, and demands the food that the other seems to hold out. This is the reason for its interest in the other. It needs it because of its intrinsic value and in pursuance of an end. As this other promises something – itself in one of its properties – there is the desire to possess and control and enjoy it. . . . For all the self-emptying on the part of the one who loves, union with the beloved as the supreme goal of this love consists in the fact that this object of love is taken to himself, if not expressly swallowed up and consumed, so that even in the event he alone remains, like the wolf when it has devoured, as it hopes, both Red Riding Hood and her grandmother.[26]

Barth contrasts *eros* – ravenous desire – with *agape*, the properly Christian love which 'turns to the other purely for the sake of the other':

> In Christian love the loving subject gives to the other . . . that which it has, which is its own, which belongs to it. It does so irrespective of the right or claim that it may have to it, or the further use that it might make of it. . . . It does so with a radically unlimited liberality. For in Christian love the loving subject reaches back, as it were, behind itself to that which at the first it denies and from which it turns away, namely, itself: to give itself . . . away; to give up itself to the one to whom it turns for the sake of this object. To do this the loving man has given up control of himself to place himself under the control of the other, the object of his love.[27]

There can be little doubt that the opposition Barth posits between *agape* and *eros* is overwrought. From the point of view of classical philosophy it ignores the fact that, as R. E. Allen notes, the 'concern for the other is an element in the analysis of Eros' offered in Plato's *Symposium*:

> It makes Eros selfish or self-interested at the expense of ignoring happiness as consisting in justice and friendship, the works of Eros as issuing in creation not only according to the body but the soul, and the termination of Eros in contemplation of the *summum bonum*.[28]

From the theological side, Barth's account pays insufficient attention to what he nevertheless notes, namely that *eros* 'can claim some of the greatest figures in the history of the human spirit'.[29] And indeed, in an earlier part of the *Church Dogmatics* than that from which I have been quoting, Barth does envisage, if not a synthesis of *eros* and *agape* – as he thinks was attempted in the medieval concept of *caritas*[30] – at least the possibility of locating *eros* within *agape*; desire ordered by self-giving ordered by understanding:

> As the desire of love, of true *eros*, desire is legitimate . . . when it is preceded by self-giving and thus controlled, not by the need of the other, but by the joy of being his and of willing to belong to him, the confidence of being well-placed with him, the willingness to make common cause with him. Again, this self-giving, as that of love, of genuine *eros*, is legitimate, because free, when it is preceded by understanding, so that it is not a blind surrender to the other, but he is seen in his totality to be [a] partner to whose being in its totality one can honourably give oneself, and whom one may honourably desire in the totality of one's being.[31]

For a more enthralling, passionate, desire – one that might just get carried away with the object of its love – we have to turn back to Balthasar. For the ordering of *eros* by *agape*, of desire by dispossession, is one of his central concerns, not least because he is much more open than Barth to being instructed by some of those figures in the 'history of the human spirit' who have been claimed by divine and human *eros*, namely Dante and before him the pseudo-Dionysius.

For Balthasar, the content of dogmatic theology is the divine *ekstasis*, the venture of God to us and us to God, the traversal of the infinite distance between human and divine, understood as *rapture*, as a transport of delight at the beauty of the divine glory.[32] For the Pseudo-Dionysius, the transport of delight is *eros*, drawing God out into creation, revelation and incarnation, and in turn drawing us into God:

> We must dare to affirm (for this is the truth) that the creator of the Universe himself, in his beautiful and good Eros towards the Universe, is,

through his excessive erotic Goodness, transported outward of himself in his providential activities towards all things that have being, and is overcome by the sweet spell of goodness, Love and Eros. In this manner, he is drawn from his transcendent throne above all things to dwell within the heart of all things in accordance with his super-essential and ecstatic power whereby he nonetheless does not leave himself behind. This is why those who know about God call him 'zealous', because he is vehement in his manifold and beneficent Eros towards all beings, and he spurs them on to search for him zealously with a yearning eros, thus showing himself zealous for love inasmuch as he allows himself to be affected by the zeal of all beings for which he cares.[33]

Acknowledging that this may appear too neoplatonic for some, Balthasar nevertheless insists that it is consistent with the 'most authentic covenant-theology of either Testament', and that there is simply nothing to be done for those who fail to see that all revelation is 'impregnated' with 'enthusiasm', that the Pseudo-Dionysius simply points us to the 'jealous and consuming love of the divine Bridegroom doing his work in his bride in order to raise her up, invite her, and bring her home to the very same answering love'.[34]

It is, however, Dante, above all, who performs the 'daring act of taking before the throne of God the earthly love between man and woman and of purifying Eros so as to make of it something akin to Agape'.[35] In the *Divine Comedy* the love of man and woman is made the means, rather than the obstacle, of ascent to God. 'This is utterly unprecedented in the history of Christian theology.'

The principle is established for the first time, and never again so magnificently: for the sake of infinite love, it is not necessary for the Christian to renounce finite love. On the contrary, in a positive spirit, he can incorporate his finite love into that which is infinite – but at the cost of terrible sufferings, of course, as Dante shows us.[36]

Male and female he created them (Genesis 1. 27)

The riddle of humanity is constituted by a threefold polarity, of spirit and body, man and woman, and individual and community. These constants are part of the human essence, 'three fundamental human tensions'.[37] 'In all three dimensions, man seems to be built according to a polarity, obliged to engage in reciprocity, always seeking complementarity and peace in the other pole'.[38] Here I am concerned with the second polarity – sexual difference – but it cannot be treated completely separately from the other two.

The polarity of spirit and body suggests two models, one of a natural process ascending to spirit, the other an incursive descent already realized by spirit into nature. The human person, 'formed out of existing clay by the hand of God *and* directly endowed with the breath of divinity', couples these alternatives together.[39] But for Balthasar the two – earthly clay and heavenly breath – are not simply conjoined, but set against one another. The human condition is essentially dirempted, torn, broken. Or, to put it another way, it is that of being on and of the boundary, the *metharion* between two regions. This opens us to three possibilities: to remain in this condition or to seek to move beyond it, upwards or downwards. For Plotinus, life on the boundary can have only a negative meaning, for the soul, midway between the intelligible and the sensible, is unable to obtain precise knowledge of either.[40] For Gregory of Nyssa, however, it is possible and necessary to choose, and the right choice is the spiritual; but that which so chooses is, Balthasar reminds us, 'unthinkable apart from its physiological infrastructure'.[41] In choosing the spiritual, therefore, we cannot wish to leave behind the physical. 'Pure spiritualization . . . must appear as hubris, as wanting to be like God. And yet the fundamental demand must be for an upward movement, involving control of the physical and embodied, the natural and mediate'.[42] There is then, a need for an almost impossible synthesis of the contrary movements, and this, Balthasar insists, is possible only in terms of a 'dramatic engagement' (Balthasar 1990a: 364). Again, for Balthasar, we are not absolved from the need to fashion ourselves as 'responsible spiritual–physical' beings,[43] yet in order to become such beings, inhabiting, as it were, a middle, which is not poised between two extremities but where both extremities interpenetrate, folded upon and inside one another, we need a model – a 'blueprint' – which can be only Christ:

> Such a blueprint would have to execute fully both movements without hubris and without degeneration: it would have to come down into flesh 'from above', as the pure breath of God, plumbing the dimensions of 'world' and 'flesh' to the very bottom. And this descent must not imply a (Buddhist, Platonic or Gnostic) 'fall' from God: rather, it must undergird and embrace every possible declension from God. And from below, on the basis of a perfected fleshly being, it must go beyond the realm of the 'world' so as to bring both world and flesh with it, in its transcendence, up to God, 'transfiguring' it, not 'spiritualizing' it in some incorporeal manner.[44]

The tension between the two movements, upward and downward, is repeated in the second fundamental polarity of human existence, that of man and woman, which at the same time introduces the tension between individual and community, since, following Genesis, Eve is created in order to establish community for Adam, as his helpmate, counter-image and complement.[45]

One might think that Eve is but a second, though differentiated, Adam, since Adam recognizes her as bone of his bones and flesh of his flesh (Genesis 2.23), and Balthasar insists that they share 'an identical human nature'. Nevertheless, Balthasar also insists on their near absolute difference. Their identical nature does not, as Balthasar puts it, 'protrude, neutrally, beyond the sexual difference, as if to provide neutral ground for mutual understanding'. Therefore

> The male body is male throughout, right down to each cell of which it consists, and the female body is utterly female; and this is also true of their whole empirical experience and ego-consciousness. . . . Here there is no *universale ante rem*, as all theories of a nonsexual or bisexual (androgynous) primitive human being would like to think.[46]

Thus, just as Balthasar wants to think body and spirit as a unified difference, and to do so by way of the incarnation, so also with man and woman, individual and community. The poles of all three tensions are not denied or synthesized, but held within a differentiated unity, which must be thought according to the drama of the incarnation – which, as we have seen, is already the drama of the Trinity, and which also must be understood as the drama of the Church. The unified difference of Christ and Church is variously parodied: as head and members of one body, as the nuptial embrace of bridegroom and bride, and as mother and child. Here it is Mary who attains to the pitch of parodic substitution, since she is both the mother of Jesus and, as Mother-Church, of each member of his body; but as the Church she is also the bride of Christ, not only the mother but the wife of her son. (Here we are reminded that what I have been calling parodic substitution allows Christianity to place at its symbolic centre certain cultural taboos – against cannibalism, incest and homosexuality – and there break them.)

But how successful is Balthasar's attempt to think difference-in-unity, and in particular the differentiated unity of man and woman? I will propose that Balthasar finally fails to think sexual difference, and suggest that he fails, not because he stresses unity at the expense of difference, but because the unity he does stress is finally, and only, male: constituting a difference within the male. Needless to say, this failure is also present in his account of the Trinity.

Masculine (relative) priority

Balthasar's insistence – in which he is followed by John Paul II (1981: 155–6) – that sexual difference is to be traced 'right down to each cell' of the male and female body, so that one can speak of male and female cells, is a particularly modern notion, dependent – as Thomas Laqueur has shown – on the invention, at some time in the eighteenth century, of two human sexes; a model which gradually replaced the more ancient idea – dependent on Aristotle and Galen – of one sex with two genders.[47] More specifically, Balthasar's notion of male and female cells may be traced to the eminent nineteenth-century biologist Patrick Geddes (1854–1932), who argued that males are constituted of *catabolic* cells, that expend energy, whereas females are composed of *anabolic* cells, that conserve energy. On the basis of this evolutionary difference Geddes maintained the typical gender roles of his day, arguing that what 'was decided among the pre-historic Protozoa cannot be annulled by an act of Parliament'.[48] Whatever the origin of the idea in Balthasar, it would seem – when taken with his opposition to the idea of an androgynous human being – to indicate a firm resistance to a monological account of humankind. Nevertheless, as I hope to show, it is possible to read Balthasar as finally purveying a covert androgyny.

Yes – for Balthasar – human being is dipolar, but one of the poles has priority. In the order of creation they do not arrive simultaneously, but sequentially; and in this they parody the order of incarnation: 'Jesus Christ can only enter the human sphere at the one pole, in order, from that vantage point, to go on to fulfil the other pole'. As he continues

> This becomes concrete in the man/woman relationship: because of the natural, relative priority of the man (given an equality of both persons), the Word of God, on account of its absolute priority, can only enter the world of the human in the form of a man, 'assimilating' the woman to itself (Ephesians 5. 27) in such a way that she, who comes from him and is at the same time 'brought to him' by God, is equal to him, 'flesh of his flesh'.[49]

This text is tense with the indeterminacy of parodic direction, just keeping in check the potential of each parody to turn around and go in the opposite direction to that to which it is here marshalled. Balthasar wants equality of male and female but the text displays the priority of the male; he wants the priority of the male but the text insinuates an equality with the female, so we have the 'relative priority of the man', which only whispers the relative equality of the woman. The Word has absolute priority and so must have the (relative) priority of the man, rather than the posteriority of the woman; but if the Word's priority follows that of the man, whose priority does the man's follow? Who gives priority to the man if not the Word? The priorities would seem to rotate, chasing one another. Why can the Word enter the world of the human only as a man, why can it not adopt the form of a woman, the posterior position? Surely the Word is not constrained by the created order which is but a parody of a preceding heavenly one? Or if it is so constrained – constrained by itself, by its 'nature' – must we not suppose the Word already masculine?

Imagine reversing the order of creation – of Adam and Eve, man and woman – so that Adam comes from Eve and is brought to her, and the Word can enter the world of the human only in the form of a woman; so that Ephesians 5. 21–27 now reads:

> Be subject to one another out of reverence for Christ. Husbands, be subject to your wives, as to Christ. For the wife is the head of the husband as Christ is the head of the church, her body, and is herself its saviour. As the church is subject to Christ, so let husbands also be subject in everything to

their wives. Wives, love your husbands, as Christ loved the church and gave herself up for him, that she might sanctify him having cleansed him by the washing of water with the word, that she might present the church to herself in splendour, without spot or wrinkle or any such thing, that he might be holy and without blemish.

In keeping with the overall reversal, I have changed the gender of the Church's pronoun, so that instead of a male Christ with a female body, as in Ephesians, we have a female Christ with a male body. The reversal allows us to imagine a different world. But does it require us to imagine a different theology, different kinds of relationship between the persons of the Trinity (Mother, Daughter and Holy Spirit), different kinds of relationship between the Daughter and her Church? If the answer is yes, then I think it is clear that we are thinking the Trinity a parody of creation; change the order of the sexes, the relative priority of one to the other, and we have to change heaven. But if the answer is no – as it surely is – then we can see that creation is properly a parody of the Trinity, a non-identical repetition in the order of created being of the trinitarian relations, which are now seen to be determinative of human bodies, but not of human sexes.

Eve's flesh

Here is another take on the problem: Does Eve have her own flesh? Adam recognizes her as bone of his bones, flesh of his flesh (Genesis 2. 23). In short, she has the bones and flesh of a man, and Balthasar does not demur from this. His reference to male and female cells is only a gesture, as also his appeal to genetics as providing a supporting parody for the idea that human being is understood more properly as feminine than as masculine, as Marian rather than Christic. For according to the flow of the trinitarian parodies, Marian flesh is already male flesh, since as the bride of the groom – the second Eve – Mary is – as in the passage I have already quoted – flesh of his flesh.[50]

This is confirmed by another passage in the *Theo-Drama*, in which Balthasar follows Augustine, and couples the coming forth of the Church from Christ through the death of the latter on the cross – the second Eve from the second Adam (the mother–bride from the son–husband) – with the coming forth of Eve from the wound in Adam's side, the extracted bone. This confirms the eternal (relative) priority of the masculine:

> The reciprocal fruitfulness of man and woman is surpassed by the ultimate priority of the 'Second Adam', who, in suprasexual fruitfulness, brings a 'companion', the Church, into being. Now the 'deep sleep' of death on the Cross, the 'taking of the rib' in the wound that opens the heart of Jesus, no longer take place in unconsciousness and passivity, as in the case of the First Adam, but in the consciously affirmed love-death of

the *Agape*, from which the Eucharist's fruitfulness also springs. The relative priority of the man over the woman here becomes absolute, insofar as the Church is a creation of Christ himself, drawn from his own substance. All the same, the first account of creation is over-fulfilled here, for in the mind of God the incarnate Word has never existed without his Church (Ephesians 1. 4–6).[51]

However, perhaps Christ's flesh is itself womanly, since as I have already mentioned, the Christ of Ephesians is transsexual, a male with a female body. The answer to this supposition is already given in Genesis, where, as we have seen, there is really only one kind of flesh – Adam's – from which Eve's flesh derives, thus parodying – or being parodied by – the ancient biology which posited two genders upon one sex, the female being a cooler version of the male. It is, I suggest, this biology that really informs Balthasar's theology (rather than the more recent nineteenth-century, biology of Patrick Geddes), and it is this ancient biology which – I now want to suggest – he parodies in the Trinity.

Why 'Father'?

As we have seen, Balthasar understands God's intratrinitarian being according to two reciprocal acts, the giving and receiving of love, the outpouring of divine *agape* and its return, so constituting the eternal circulation of charitable desire, which is endlessly repeated, non-identically, in the incarnation and creation. Giving and receiving are parodied as masculinity and femininity, informing both human flesh and trinitarian being, so that sexual difference is parodied in heaven. But since there is no sex in God – to suppose which would be to fall into Gnostic mythology – heavenly masculinity and femininity are suprasexualities: supramasculinity and suprafemininity.

David L. Schindler, one of Balthasar's American disciples, notes that 'Balthasar's carefully qualified treatment of the question of gender in God follows the processions in God':

> That is, the Father, as the begetting origin-with-out-origin, is primarily supramasculine (*übermännlich*); the Son, as begotten and thus receptive (*der Geschehenlassende*) is suprafeminine (*überweiblich*); but then the Father and the Son, as jointly spirating the Spirit, are again supramasculine; the Spirit then is suprafeminine; finally, the Father, who allows himself to be conditioned in return in his begetting and spirating, himself thereby has a suprafeminine dimension.[52]

Here masculinity is associated with giving, as begetting and spirating, as generating; whereas femininity is associated with receiving; in other words – and according to a certain biology – masculine and feminine parody the active and passive partners in the act of insemination or fertilization. As Schindler notes, the trinitarian processions or relations, which are represented temporally, must be understood simultaneously, so that both supramasculinity and suprafemininity are 'somehow shared' by all the divine 'persons'; in other words – and again according to a certain biology – the Trinity is parodied as a self-inseminating, self-fertilizing, womb.

Balthasar, who warns us against the error of projecting 'the difference between the sexes upon God', so that we might see the Spirit as feminine, 'the 'womb' in which generation occurs', nevertheless allows that for those who wish to 'go further', the feminine is best sought in the Son, who in his earthly existence 'allowed himself to be led and "fertilized" by the Father', while yet at the same time representing the 'originally generative force of God in the world'. And since the Son – the inseminated icon of the inseminator – proceeds from the Father, 'the different sexes are, in the end, present in the latter in a "preternatural" way'.[53] It is only at the end of this remarkable passage form Balthasar's meditations on the Apostles' Creed – in which he has imagined the incestuous homosexual coupling of Father and Son – that he reminds us that God remains 'more dissimilar than similar to everything created'.[54]

In more prosaic terms, Schindler notes:

> It is not the case that the Father and the Spirit each possess one 'gender' to the exclusion of the other, or that the Son alone possesses both 'genders'; it is rather the case that all three persons share both 'genders' (share in some sense both generativity and receptivity), but *always by way of an order that remains asymmetrical.*[55]

Thus, as Schindler brings out, the Son is both supramasculine and suprafeminine. He is suprafeminine in relation to what he receives from the Father, yet supramasculine in what he gives, both to the Father and the Spirit, and to the world, in creation and incarnation. And what he gives is his own receptivity, his suprafemininity, given both to Mary and, in her, to the Church. Yet at the same time he is the icon also of the Father's supramasculinity, which he has received by way of his preceding suprafemininity, which suggests to Balthasar and Schindler a certain priority of the suprafeminine, in Christ and in creation. Yet, as before, I want to suggest that this supposed precedence of the suprafeminine conceals an always-prior supramasculinity. This is inevitable when one has, like Balthasar, a hierarchical Trinity in which everything is ultimately traced back to a primal origin who, in himself, always-already, gives and receives, and who is always and only 'Father'.

This is what remains truly remarkable in Balthasar and Schindler, especially Schindler, who, in the essay I have been quoting, does not even raise the question: why 'Father'? Neither does he, or Balthasar, ask, why – given the name – the Father's primary act is considered supramasculine rather than suprafeminine. Why not think donation suprafeminine and reception supramasculine? In a sense, of course, Balthasar has already done this, in that both Father and Son are alike suprafeminine and supramasculine, that is, conceived androgynously or hermaphroditically. Nevertheless, in Balthasar, they are male hermaphrodites. Balthasar – for whom theological agnosticism is almost utterly foreign – does try to say why the simple origin of all is 'Father':

> That he is Father we know in utmost fullness from Jesus Christ, who constantly makes loving, thankful, and reverent reference to him as his Origin. It is because he bears fruit out of himself and requires no fructifying that he is called Father, and not in the sexual sense, for he will be the Creator of man and woman, and thus contains the primal qualities of woman in himself in the same simultaneously transcending way as those of man.[56]

Needless to say, the Father's bearing of fruit out of himself without need of fructifying, does not explain why he is named 'Father'. On the very same ground, one might as well, if not better, name him 'Mother'. Balthasar's *non sequitur* is, I think, indicative of a failure to maintain the 'greater unlikeness' between God and humankind. In the passage just quoted we are told that God's fruitfulness, his self-fructifying nature, is not to be understood in a sexual way. Elsewhere, as we have seen, he refers to the suprasexual. But, that the addition of 'supra' fails to measure the infinite distance between ourselves and the Trinity, whose relations Balthasar describes in such resolutely sexual terms, is indicated by the ancient biology that, I suggest, informs Balthasar's Trinity, and which the latter parodies. The man gives to the woman, who is but an extension of himself. She takes what she is given and returns it, enhanced, to his greater glory, having become the mother of his child. This is the drama of the Trinity, of its processions and missions.

Cultural biology

Breandán Leahy, in his study of the Marian principle in Balthasar's theology, has a curious footnote, in which he tells us that Balthasar 'guards' against any 'false implication' arising from his identification of God with 'the 'masculine' active principle . . . while human creaturehood is seen as the organ of feminine receptive, dialogical and maternal fecundity'.

> Von Balthasar writes [Leahy does not tell us where] that, prescinding from any and every social system, be it patriarchal or matriarchal, and from all theories of procreation, be they ancient, scholastic or modern, it remains true that in the act of sexual intercourse the man is the initiator, the one who shapes, while the woman's active role is essentially receptive. In this act the woman is awakened to the fullness of her feminine self-awareness.[57]

It would seem that our culture always takes us unawares. Balthasar is unaware of the masculinist culture that shapes his understanding of sexuality, of masculinity and femininity. Despite his advocacy of 'dramatics' he is unaware that sexuality is culturally constituted and performed.[58] Here my argument – which I can now state only briefly – is similar to that of Graham Ward in relation to Karl Barth.[59]

For Ward, Barth fails to recognize the import of his understanding of the trinitarian relations for the sexual relations of human bodies. This is because Barth is too influenced by what Luce Irigaray calls the culture of hom(m)osexuality, or as one might say a homosociality. Balthasar, because of his failed *analogia entis*, is – even more than Barth – unable to realize the fluidity of sexual symbolics when applied to the bodies of actual men and women.[60] The ancient masculinist biology he nowhere questions is indeed both product and producer of a hom(m)osexual culture. Indeed it may be suggested that only when theology begins to think sexual difference starting from the homosexual couple as its paradigm of sexual difference will it be possible to think the difference not in crudely biologistic terms, as in so much of Balthasar, but in more properly theological ones. This thinking of sexual difference is indeed already present in both Barth and Balthasar as the relationship of donation, reception and return; but it needs to be thought more radically, as that which establishes sexual difference, so that whether it plays between Father and Son, man and man, woman and woman, or woman and man, it remains, as Ward argues, always constitutive of (hetero)sexual difference. In this way, what our culture may dictate as our sex and gender will no longer be determinative of our freedom to give and receive love. For truly in Christ there is no male and female, only the reciprocation of bodies; beautiful parodies of the trinitarian donation. In this way we may also discover that Mary has not only a womb, but – as Tina Beattie has suggested in a recent essay[61] – a uterus and a clitoris also.

It may seem, that however wonderful and complex is Balthasar's weaving together of the trinitarian processions, with agapeic expenditure and erotic return, with donation and dispossession, with masculinity and femininity, supra and mundane, producing what Rowan Williams has called a 'superbly integrated pattern of Christian symbols',[62] it nevertheless remains an esoteric fable, with little contact or relevance for the life of the Church today and tomorrow. But, of course, this is not the case. On the one hand, Balthasar's theology is too rich and provocative, too productive of insights into the Christian symbolic – and precisely through what I have been calling its parodic substitutions – for us to deny Catholic theology the good fruit of his imagination. On the other hand, his theology gives rise to an ecclesiology, an understanding of the Christian *polis*, that is already being put into practice. Even though – as I have found myself arguing – Balthasar's Trinity, at least in part, parodies an ancient masculinist biology, the Church is already enjoined to parody this Trinity's suprasexuality in such a way that men beget and women receive what they are given.

Thus David Schindler can write in all seriousness and, as it were, without blushing, that 'the question of gender in its more acute form today' is 'the question of the sense in which the "feminine" is a matter of perfection' (Schindler 1993: 203). It seems to me that, on the contrary, the acute question of gender today – with regard to Balthasar and the ecclesial polity to which his theology gives rise – is the question of the 'masculine', and the question of *distance*.

Conclusion

I began this essay with Bataille's 'locomotive', the thrusting pistons of copulating animals turning the world, a parody, if you will, of the love (*amor*) that in Dante 'moves the sun and the other stars' (*l'amor che move il sole e l'altre stelle*).[63] Gustave Doré's illustrations of Dante's *Commedia*, first published in 1861, include wonderful images of the celestial wheels that empower the world's pistons.

The heavens through which Dante – with Beatrice – ascends, are forever in motion, forever turning and circling, filled with rotating lights, with saints and angels performing round-dances, 'measure with measure, strain with strain'.[64] Dante attains sight of God's throne, at the centre of the celestial rose, the encircling flower of the redeemed. Doré gives us a picture of Dante, with a figure standing by his side – perhaps Beatrice just before she slips away to take her seat

> In the third circle from the highest place,
> Enthroned where merit destined her to be[65]

or perhaps St Bernard, sent by Beatrice to guide Dante's sight, first to the Virgin and then, with the Virgin's aid, to the dazzling, unapproachable, 'light supreme'[66] of the three-fold God. I would like to think it is a picture of Dante with Beatrice, before his gaze sees into the light.

We can think the picture a parody – an analogy – of the heart's yearning, of its desiring, for that divine donation and dispossession which already gives to the heart its restless want of beatitude: *eros* in the order of *agape*. Dante and Beatrice stand in the foreground, looking towards the rose; Dante transfixed, standing at a distance, fallen into a silent stupor before the 'living light'.[67] It is the moment before Beatrice merges, as it were, with the light, taking her place in the circling glory; the moment before Dante begins his final ascent that will lead him to see into the light, to see the 'three spheres, which bare/Three hues distinct' and occupy 'one space', the first mirroring the next, 'as though it were/Rainbow from rainbow', and the third seeming 'flame/Breathed equally from each of the first pair'.[68]

The image of Dante with Beatrice, their love ordered by and toward the celestial charity, in the moment before Dante presumes to see into the living light itself and not find there an ever greater darkness, is also, if one likes, a parody or analogy of the argument in this essay: that we will think *eros* better the more we remember that there stretches an infinite distance between the clouds on which Dante and Beatrice stand and the rotating glory of the celestial rose.

Notes

1 Georges Bataille, *Vision of Excess: Selected Writings 1927–39*, tr. Allan Stokel *et al.* (Minneapolis: University of Minnesota Press, 1985), p. 5.
2 *Ibid.*, p. 6.
3 *Ibid.*, p. 7.
4 *Ibid.*, p. 5.
5 *Ibid.*, p. 9.
6 John Saward, *The Mysteries of March: Hans Urs von Balthasar on the Incarnation and Easter* (London: Collins, 1990), p. 18.
7 John Milbank, *The Word Made Strange: Theology, Language, Culture* (Oxford: Blackwell, 1997).
8 Karl Rahner, *The Trinity*, tr. Joseph Donceel (London: Burns & Oates, 1970), p. 22. See also C. M. LaCugna, 'Reconceiving the Trinity as the Mystery of Salvation', *Scottish Journal of Theology*, 38 (1985), pp. 1–23.
9 Saward, p. 28.
10 Hans Urs von Balthasar, *Credo: Meditations on the Apostles' Creed*, tr. David Kipp (Edinburgh: T.&T. Clark, 1989), p. 31.
11 Cited in Saward, p. 31.
12 *Ibid.*
13 Hans Urs von Balthasar, *Theo-Drama: Theological Dramatic Theory. Vol. 2: The Dramatis personae: Man in God*, tr. Graham Harrison (San Francisco CA: Ignatius Press, 1990), p. 347.
14 *Ibid.*, p. 348.
15 *Ibid.*, p. 352.
16 Mary Timothy Prokes, *Towards a Theology of the Body* (Edinburgh: T.&T. Clark, 1996), p. x.
17 *Ibid.*, p. 95.
18 *Ibid.*, pp. 95–6.
19 *Ibid.*, p. 96.
20 *Ibid.*, p. 96–7.
21 *Ibid.*, p. 97.
22 *Ibid.*, p. 97.
23 Hans Urs von Balthasar, *The Glory of the Lord: A Theological Aesthetics. Vol. 1: Seeing the Form*, trs. Eramo Leiva-Merikakis, ed. Joseph Fessio and John Riches (Edinburgh: T.&T. Clark, 1982), p. 339.
24 *Ibid.*
25 Anders Nygren, *Agape and Eros*, tr. Philip S. Watson (London: SPCK, 1982).
26 Karl Barth, *Church Dogmatics IV.2: The Doctrine of Reconciliation*, tr. G. W. Bromiley (Edinburgh: T.&T. Clark, 1958), p. 734.
27 *Ibid.*, p. 733.
28 *The Dialogues of Plato: Vol. 2: The Symposium*, tr. R. E. Allen (New Haven: Yale University Press, 1991), p. 97 (Allen's commentary).

29 Barth, p. 735.
30 *Ibid.*, pp. 737–8.
31 Karl Barth, *Church Dogmatics III.3: The Doctrine of Creation*, tr. A. T. Mackay *et al.* (Edinburgh: T.&T. Clark, 1961), p. 219 (adapted).
32 Hans Urs von Balthasar, *The Glory of the Lord: A Theological Aesthetics. Vol. 1*, p. 126.
33 Cited in *ibid.*, p. 122.
34 *Ibid.*, p. 123.
35 Hans Urs von Balthasar, 'Another Ten Years – 1975', in John Riches (ed.), *The Analogy of Beauty: The Theology of Hans Urs von Balthasar* (Edinburgh: T.&T. Clark, 1986), pp. 222–33.
36 Hans Urs von Balthasar, *The Glory of the Lord: A Theological Aesthetics. Vol. 3: Studies in Theological Style: Lay Styles*, tr. Andrew Louth *et al.*, ed. John Riches (Edinburgh: T.&T. Clark, 1986), p. 32.
37 Hans Urs von Balthasar, *Theo-Drama: Theological Dramatic Theory. Vol. 2: The Dramatis Personae: Man in God*, tr. Graham Harrison (San Francisco CA: Ignatius Press, 1990), p. 358.
38 *Ibid.*, p. 353.
39 *Ibid.*, p. 359.
40 *Ibid.*, p. 360.
41 *Ibid.*, p. 362.
42 *Ibid.*, p. 363.
43 *Ibid.*
44 *Ibid.*, p. 364.
45 *Ibid.*, p. 365.
46 *Ibid.*, pp. 365–6.
47 Thomas Laqueur, *Making Sex: Body and Gender from the Greeks to Freud* (Cambridge MA: Harvard University Press, 1990), pp. 149–92.
48 Patrick Geddes and J. Arthur Thompson, *The Evolution of Sex* (London: W. Scott, 1889), p. 266. Quoted in Laqueur, *op. cit.*, p. 6. See also Lacqueur, 'Orgasm, Generation and the Politics of Reproductive Biology', in Catherine Gallagher and Thomas Lacqueur (eds), *The Making of the Modern Body: Sexuality and Society in the Nineteenth Century* (Berkeley CA: University of California Press, 1987), pp. 1–41.
49 Hans Urs von Balthasar, *Theo-Drama: Theological Dramatic Theory. Vol. 2*, p. 411.
50 *Ibid.*
51 *Ibid.*, p. 413.
52 David L. Schindler, 'Catholic Theology, Gender and the Future of Western Civilization', in *Communio*, 20 (1993), pp. 200–39.
53 Hans Urs von Balthasar, *Credo*, p. 78.
54 *Ibid.*, p. 79.
55 Schindler, p. 207.
56 Hans Urs von Balthasar, *Credo*, p. 30. For a similar *non sequitur* 'explaining' why the Word is Son and not Daughter, see also p. 37.
57 Breandan Leahy, *The Marian Principle in the Church in the Ecclesiological Thought of Hans Urs von Balthasar* (Frankfurt am Main: Peter Lang, 1996), p. 85, n. 187.
58 Judith Butler, *Bodies that Matter: On the Discursive Limits of 'Sex'* (London: Routledge, 1993).
59 Graham Ward, 'The Erotics of Redemption: After Karl Barth', *Theology and Sexuality*, 8 (March 1998).
60 See also Gerard Loughlin, 'Baptismal Fluid', *Scottish Journal of Theology*, 51 (1998).
61 Tina Beattie, 'Carnal Love and Spiritual Imagination: Can Luce Irigaray and John Paul II Come Together?', in Jon Davies and Gerard Loughlin (eds), *Sex These Days: Essays in Theology, Sexuality and Society* (Sheffield: Sheffield Academic Press, 1997), pp. 160–83.
62 Saward, p. ix.

63 Dante Alighieri, *The Divine Comedy Vol. 3: Paradise*, tr. Dorothy L. Sayers and Barbara Reynolds (Harmondsworth: Penguin, 1962), XXXIII, l.145, p. 347.
64 *Ibid.*, XII, l.6, p. 6.
65 *Ibid.*, XXXI, ll.68–9, pp. 68–9.
66 *Ibid.*, XXXII, l.67, p. 67.
67 *Ibid.*, XXXI, l.46, p. 46
68 *Ibid.*, XXXIII, ll.116–23, pp. 116–23.

8

BODIES

The displaced body of Jesus Christ

Graham Ward

Karl Barth announced that theology is always a post-resurrection phenomenon working within an eschatological horizon. Theology reads Scripture, the traditions of the Church and the world in the light of the glory of the Risen Christ in the space opened between that resurrection and our own. While not wishing to contradict that, I want to argue for the place of the ascension in Christianity, its practices, its Scriptures and its theological task. This nascent theology of the ascension will begin by investigating the gendered body of that Jewish man, Jesus the Christ. It will begin, therefore, not with those concepts philosophically and theologically honed by the ante- and post-Nicene Fathers, but with the gendered body as scripture presents it to us and as the Church has reflected upon it. It will attempt to demonstrate, through this approach, how questions such as 'Can a male Saviour save women?'[1] and modern investigations into the sexuality of Jesus,[2] which simply continue the nineteenth-century rational search for the historical Jesus, fail to discern the nature of corporeality in Christ. For these approaches take the human to be a measure of the Christic. What happens at the ascension, theologically, constitutes a critical moment in a series of displacements or assumptions[3] of the male body of Jesus Christ such that the body of Christ, and the salvation it both seeks and works out (Paul's *katergomai*), become multi-gendered. I wish to argue that, since none of us has access to bodies *as* such, only to bodies that are mediated through the giving and receiving of signs, the series of displacements or assumptions of Jesus's body continually refigures a masculine symbolics until the particularities of one sex give way to the particularities of bodies which are male and female. To that end, this essay examines the presentation of the male Jesus in the Gospels and its representation in the life of the Church. It examines both the performance of Jesus the gendered Jew and the way that performance has been scripted, reperformed and ventriloquized by the community he brought to birth. It traces the economy of the deferred identity of the body of the Messiah;[4] an economy which becomes visible in a series of displacements. The ascension marks the final stage in the destabilized identity of the body of the Messiah.

163

Incarnation and circumcision

In a recent book on the sexed body of Jesus, Leo Steinberg writes: "from Hilary and Augustine to Michelangelo, the humanity of the Incarnate is perceived as volitional condescension", and in this condescension Christ straddles 'humanness in pre- and in postlapsarian modality'.[5] In what follows, then, I am not denying the credal statement that Christ is both fully God and fully man, but pointing up this pre- and post-lapsarian corporeal ambiguity. Tertullian, writing one of the earliest treatises on the body of Jesus Christ, *De Carne Christi*, situates the very ambiguity of Christ's flesh (as opposed to other forms of flesh, including spiritual flesh and the flesh assumed by angels) in the fact that it is flesh like ours, and yet: "As, then, the first Adam is thus introduced to us, it is a just inference that the second Adam likewise . . . was formed by God into a quickening spirit out of the ground – in other words, out of the flesh which was unstained as yet by any human generation."[6] This is "the flesh which was made of a virgin" – a flesh of complex theological designation.[7] It is interesting that, later, theological figures like Augustine and Athanasius, who also embraced the full humanity of Christ, found, when describing that full humanity which Christ possessed, pre-lapsarian faculties beyond those available to human creatures in the post-lapsarian world.[8]

From the moment of the incarnation, this body then is physically human and subject to all the infirmities of being such, and yet is also a body looking backward to the perfect Adamic corporeality and forward to the corporeality of resurrection. The materiality of this human body is eschatologically informed. We will be examining such materiality in more detail later. For the moment, it is sufficient to emphasize how the specificity of Jesus's male body is made unstable from the beginning. This is made manifest by the absence (in Matthew and Luke) of a male progenitor; by the way that, in Mark, Jesus issues without a past into the emptiness of the wilderness (like John before him), and by the manner in which John's Gospel relates how the Word became flesh and dwelt (Eskēnōsen – tabernacled) among us. The paternity of God is formal, rather than material. But this formality informs substance, such that our notions of 'materiality' itself become unstable. The nature of paternity is redefined – Ephesians 3: 14–15[9] – in a way which points up the inseparability of what Judith Butler calls 'bodies that matter'[10] from a doctrine of creation. The XY chromosomal maleness of Jesus Christ issues from the XX chromosomal femaleness of his mother as miracle, and so this male body is unlike any other male body to date. Its materiality is, from its conception, unstable; though, with the circumcision, its specifically sexed nature is affirmed.

Patristic theologies of both the incarnation and the circumcision emphasize the instability of Jesus's gendered corporeality. Augustine's description of the baby Jesus – "His appearance as an Infant Spouse, from his bridal chamber, that is, from the womb of a virgin"[11] – demonstrates this. The baby boy is husband and bridegroom, spouse and prefigured lover of the mother who gives him birth, whose own body swells to contain the future Church. The bridal chamber is the womb which the bridegroom will impregnate with his seed while also being the womb from which he emerges. The material orders are inseparable from the symbolic and transcendent orders, the orders of mystery. The material orders are caught up and become significant only within the analogical orders. And so here Jesus's body is brought within a complex network of sexualized symbolic relations that confound incest and the sacred. Augustine further makes plain that the infant Jesus was not born helpless and ignorant like other children: "that such entire ignorance existed in the infant in whom the Word was made flesh, I cannot suppose . . . nor can I imagine that such weakness of mental faculty ever existed in the infant Christ which we see in infants generally".[12] Again, the logic here is theological – Augustine makes these suggestions on the basis of a doctrine of creation revealed through the incarnation in which materiality participates in God. Matter itself is rendered metaphorical within the construal of such a logic. Since creation issued from the Word of God, then, seen from the perspective of God's glory, all creation bears the watermark of Christ.[13] The material orders participate in theological orders such that they are rendered both physical and symbolic.

And so one finds that the theology of circumcision – developed from the early Fathers through to the sermons preached in Rome on the Feast of the Circumcision (1 January) in the fifteenth century – interpreted this one action upon the body of Jesus as prefiguring the final action in the crucifixion: the first bloodletting becoming the down-payment on the redemption to come. The circumcision takes place on the eighth day, and so it is linked also to resurrection, the perfection of creation and of corporeality. The body of Jesus is, once more, stretched temporally, the baby body prefiguring the adult body, the adult body figuring the ecclesial body, in its march to its resurrection. The physicality of the body, its significance as a body, and the acts with which it is involved, are figured within an allegorical displacement.

Transfiguration

Throughout the Gospel narratives Jesus the man is viewed as a man unlike other men (or women). This man can walk on water. This man can sweat blood. This man can bring to life. This man can multiply material so that 5,000 are fed from a few loaves and fish. This man can heal by touch; and not just heal but create – wine from water, the eyes of the man born blind, the ear of the Temple guard. But it is the explicit displacements of his own physical body which interest me, the various assumptions or trans-figurations that occur in which the divine is manifested in the sexed and corporeal, and the implications of these trans-figurations. In these assumptions Jesus is not alone. Tertullian, besides remarking that human flesh is made from the earth and the earth is made *ex nihilo*, points out that angels frequently "changed into human form" and the Holy Spirit "descended in the body of a dove".[14] The displacements of Jesus's body simply give Christological significance to the nature of embodiment. John's Gospel is emphatic about these assumptions, with its repetitions of ontological scandal – I am the way, the life, the truth, the Temple, the bread, the light, the vine and the gate into the sheepfold. But in the Gospels generally, in those stories which focus on the body of Jesus, there are five scenes where these displacements are dramatically performed: the transfiguration itself; the eucharistic supper; the crucifixion; the resurrection; and, finally, the ascension. Each of these scenes, in an ever-deepening way, problematize the sexed nature of Jesus's body and point towards an erotics far more comprehensive and yet informing the sexed and the sexual.

The pre-lapsarian body of Adam (and Eve) is erotically charged – perfect in its form, its goodness and its beauty – and naked. Fashions in the figuration of that form change. Today's cult of the firm, hard, male physique, like the various cultural pursuits it has fostered (body-building and dieting), is the result of certain conventions of masculinity which arose in Germany in the late eighteenth century – a masculinization modelled on classical sculpture.[15] But whatever the fashion of our representations, something Promethean, powerful and vulnerable, sticks close to the image of Adam in Paradise. What is glimpsed in and through his magnificence is the image of God – the trace of the uncreated in the created. In so far as in Christ human beings are restored to their pre-fallen splendour, the transfiguration scene on the Mount of Olives presents us with Jesus as the Second Adam. Not naked in any obvious sense, but nevertheless bathed in a certain translucence. What I am describing here as erotically charged is the way these manifestations of humankind glorified by God are attractive. They are incarnations of divine beauty and goodness, and as such they possess the power to attract, to draw us towards an embrace, a promise of grace. These disclosures establish economies of desire within which we are invited, if not incited, to participate. The transfiguration does not simply portray a resurrection hope, it performs it, it solicits it. Mark's account of it (9: 2–8) bears witness to the event's power to attract and engage. The Greek is simple, but subtle. It employs assonance and alliteration, the repetition of *kai* sets up a paratactic rhythm within which other verbal echoes resound *(leuka . . . leukanai; mian . . . mian; egenonto . . . egeneto . . . egegeneto; nephele . . . nepheles)*. The prose is as liturgical as are the event and the details of its setting (tents, a prophet, the lawgiver, the *shekinah* presence). The physical body of Jesus is displaced – for it is not the physical body as such which is the source of the attraction but the glorification of the physical body made possible by viewing him through God as God. We are attracted to the man and beyond him, so that the erotic economy does not flounder on questions of sexuality (i.e. is my attraction to this man as a man homoerotic, is my attraction to this man as a woman heterosexual?). The erotic economy propels our desire towards what lies beyond and yet does so in and through this man's particular body. This economy of desire does not deny the possibility of a sexual element; it does not prevent or stand in critical judgement of a sexual element. It simply overflows the sexual such that we cannot, without creating a false and idolatrous picture of Christ, turn this man into an object for our sexual gratification. This man cannot be fetishized, because he exceeds appropriation. Desire is not caught up here in an endless game of producing substitutes for a demand that can never be satisfied.

Such is the model of both Freudian and Lacanian desire; desire founded upon and furthering the aporetics of lack. The transfiguration sets Jesus outside any economy of exchange, any economy where the value of an object can be known and its exchange negotiated. The transfiguration, by contrast, sets up an economy of desire which the three witnesses (who proxy for us all) cannot accommodate. This transfigurability, and its subsequent beauty and goodness, is not something they lack and will now strive to attain. Jesus cannot now become an ego-ideal. His figure breaks upon them as one situated within another economy, an economy of loving and beloved ("This is my beloved Son"). It breaks upon them as a gift they know not how to receive. But, by the very fact that this enactment of divine love reaches out to draw them in, receive they will. In fact, they are already receiving. Notice how, in both Matthew's account (17: 1–13) and that of Luke (9: 28–36), we focus upon the face of Christ. It is a face full of light and energy, and the descriptions no doubt allude to the shining face of Moses as he came down from the mountain, having spoken with God. But Matthew's description exceeds any allusion to the lawgiver. He writes of Jesus's face "shining like the sun". We are drawn to love the beautiful and the good in Him. His corporeality becomes iconic.[16] We are silenced, like James and John, before this Christic sublime.[17] In the presence (where 'in' is strongly locational) of the holy, we listen, we receive, we worship, we give thanks.

Eucharist

The displacement of the physical body becomes more abrupt in the eucharistic supper. The body begins its withdrawal from the narrative. Transfiguration turns into transposition: 'He took bread, and blessed and broke it, and gave it to them, and said "Take; this is my body".' Matthew adds "eat". Neither Luke nor Mark mentions the consumption, only the giving and receiving of the bread-as-his-body. It is the handing-over of himself that is paramount. He places himself in the hands of the disciples who then hand him over to the authorities. It is the surrendering that is important. It is effected by that demonstrative indicative – "*this* is my body". These words perform the transposition. They set up a logic of radical re-identification. What had throughout the Gospel story been an unstable body is now to be understood as an extendable body. For it is not that Jesus, at this point, stops being a physical presence. It is more that his physical presence can extend itself to incorporate other bodies, like bread, and make them extensions of his own.[18] A certain metonymic substitution is enacted, re-situating Jesus's male physique within the neuter materiality of bread (*to arton*). The 'body' now is both sexed and not-sexed.

The narrative logic for this transposition is the mutability of the body throughout; the theo-logic for this transposition is Christ's lordship over creation (such that the wind and waves obey him) and yet his identification with and participation within it: Jesus as God's Word informing creation.

With the eucharistic displacement of the physical body, a new understanding of embodiment is announced. Bodies in Greco-Roman culture, according to Dale

Martin, were not viewed as discrete auto-defining entities. They were malleable; and, because they are made of the same stuff as the world around them, "the differentiation between the inner and outer body was fluid and permeable".[19] Physical bodies were mapped onto other bodies – social, political, cosmic. Hence

> for most people of Greco-Roman culture the human body was of a piece with its environment. The self was a precarious, temporary state of affairs, constituted by forces surrounding and pervading the body, like the radio waves that bounce around and through the bodies of modern urbanities . . . the body is perceived as a location in a continuum of cosmic movement.[20]

Even so, the displacement of Jesus's body at this point is somewhat different, more radical. It begins with a breaking. It is not just a blurring of the boundaries between one person and another – though it effects that through the handing over and the eating of the 'body'. The bread here does mediate the crossing of frontiers. But more is involved in what Jesus does and says in that upper room. For 'This is my body' is not a symbolic utterance. It is not a metaphorical utterance. The bread is not the vehicle for significance, for anthropomorphic projections. The bread *is* also the body of Jesus. That ontological scandal is the epicentre for the shock-waves which follow. For it is actually the translocationality that is surprising – as if place and space itself are being redefined such that one can be a body here and also there, one can be this kind of body here and that kind of body there. Just as with the transfiguration, the translucency of one body makes visible another hidden body, so too with the eucharist, although in a different way, the hidden nature of being embodied is made manifest. Bodies are not only transfigurable, they are transposable. In being transposable, while always being singular and specific, the body of Christ can cross boundaries – gender boundaries, for example. Jesus' body as bread is no longer Christ as simply and biologically male.

Crucifixion

The crucifixion develops the radical form of displacement announced in the eucharistic supper. The breaking of the bread is now relocated in the breaking of the physical body of Jesus. The handing over is taken one step further. The male body of Christ is handed over to death. The passivity of Jesus before Jewish and Roman authorities, and the two scenes of his nakedness (stripped by the Roman guards, according to Matthew and implied by Luke, then reclothed to be stripped again for his crucifixion), set this vulnerable body to play in a field of violent power games. The sexual charge is evident in the delight taken by the soldiers in abusing his body and in the palpable sense of power created through the contrast between Pilate's towering authority and Jesus's submissiveness. The quickening pace of the narrative, the breathless surge of activity which propels the body of Christ towards the resting-place of the cross, bears witness to the energetic force-field within which this body is placed and its power to effect, to draw in. The violent acts by which bodies touch other bodies – beginning with the kiss by Judas, moving through the slapping 'with the palm of his hand' by the Temple guard in the house of Caiaphas, to the scourging by the Roman soldiers and the nailing on the cross, and on finally to the piercing of the side with the lance – are all sexually charged manifestations of desire in conflict.[21] The whipped-up hysteria of the crowd shouting 'crucify' reveals the generative power of such violence – what Girard has analysed as the 'mimetic nature of desire' which seeks out a surrogate victim and marks the approach of sacrificial crisis.[22] It climaxes with the strung-up nakedness of Christ on the cross.

Throughout the play of these erotic and political power games the actual maleness of the body of Jesus is forgotten. This is a man among men; no sexual differentiation is taken account of. It is no longer 'this' body or 'my' body, but 'that' undifferentiated body. The body becomes an object acted upon at the point when the dynamic for the narrative is wrenched from Jesus' grasp and put into the hands of the Jewish and the Roman authorities. The displacement of Jesus' body is accentuated through the displacement in the direction of the storytelling, the displacement in the responsibility for the unfolding of events. The body as object is already being treated as mere flesh, a consumable, a dead, unwanted, discardable thing, before Jesus breathes his last.

There is a hiatus at this point. The orgiastic frenzy abates and there is the shaping of a new desire. Each Gospel writer shapes this new desire by relocating Christian witness within a scene that, since Peter's betrayal, has lacked it.[23] Matthew reintroduces the women who had followed Jesus from Galilee; Luke, who also frames this scene with the women, first effects the shaping of a new desire through the thief on the cross; Mark introduces his famous centurion; and John inserts into the Passion narrative a conversation between Jesus and John concerning Mary. John's Gospel testifies, proleptically, to the nature of this reorientation of desire when he has Jesus state: "And I, if I be lifted up from the earth, will draw all men unto me" (12: 32). The desire is no longer libidinal, but issues from a certain pathos. The iconic status of the body of Jesus re-emerges, but the manner in which it draws us is configured through an identification with the suffering of the body, rather than earlier, at the eucharist, through the feeding and the sharing, and the being nurtured by the body of Christ. The displacement of the body at the eucharist effects a sharing, a participation. We belong to Jesus and Jesus to others through partaking of his given body. We exist in and through relation. The displacement of the body here effects a detachment, a breaking of that relation. Displacement is becoming loss, and with the loss a new space opens for an economy of desire experienced as mourning. The affectivity of the one displacement can come about only through the other – without the sharing and participation there cannot arise the sense of a coming separation and loss. With the sense of loss comes also, paradoxically, the recognition of an identification, but an identification now passing. The space of this pathos heightens the iconicity of the crucified one. It emotionally colours a certain liminality within which the affectivity of this object is offered to us – the *inter alia* between dying and death, presence and departure; and between death and burial, departure and removal of the departed one. The liminality reinforces the sacredness of the space. Through it the crucifixion is already ritualized.

The transitional nature of Jesus's body at this point is dramatised further by the silence of Holy Saturday which deepens the hiatus effected here;[24] a hiatus made profoundly theological because it is interpreted as the Trinity at its most extended; the moment when the Father is most separated from the Son and the distance between them embraces the lowest regions of hell. The displacement here is mapped onto the eternal displacements of the trinitarian processions; the trinitarian differences: between Father and Son and then between Father–Son and Spirit. Displacement of identity itself, the expansion of the identified Word to embrace all that is other, becomes the mark of God within creation.

Iconicity transcends physicality. It does not erase the physical but overwhelms it, drenching it with significance. The maleness of Christ is made complex and ambivalent, in the way that all things are made ambivalent as their symbolic possibilities are opened up by their liminality. Victor Turner remarks about liminal *personae* that they become 'structurally, if not physically, "invisible" . . . They are at once no longer classified and not yet classified.'[25] The symbols used to represent bodies which are not outside of established categories cross or conflate distinctions – social, racial, or sexual.[26] In what Turner calls their "sacred poverty" of all rights and identifications, such bodies become floating signifiers. The medieval Church bears witness to this ambivalence in finding it appropriate to gender Jesus as a mother at this point, with the wounded side as both a lactating breast and a womb from which the Church is removed.[27] The pain and suffering of crucifixion is gendered in terms of the labour pains of birthing. There is a logic to the mothering symbolism, at this point where the economy of desire is triggered by the withdrawing of the body. A logic, that is, if Freud *et al.* are right is that all withdrawal and subsequent mourning is a reminder of the primary break from, and the libidinal desire to return to, self-unity established in and through that primary separation from the body of the mother. The symbolic template of Jesus's crucified body, and the empathy with human suffering which it invokes, draws forth deeper awarenesses of our human condition and of the primary levels of desire which constitute it. His body becomes the symbolic focus for all bodies loved and now departed: real, imaginary and symbolic mothers; real, imaginary and symbolic fathers.[28] His body calls forth all the cathectic objects of our past desires which have been abjected to facilitate our illusory self-unity.[29]

The allure of the abject, and the mourning which now will always accompany Christian desire, manifests an internalization of displacement itself. That is: the lack will now foster an eternal longing and will structure our desire for God. The economy of our salvation is triggered by this event, for, as Augustine understood, we reach 'our bliss in the contemplation of the immaterial light through participation in his changeless immortality, which we long to attain, with burning desire'.[30] It is not simply that the physical body of Jesus is displaced in the Christian story; our bodies, too, participate in that displacement in and through the crucifixion. At the eucharist we receive and we are acted upon: now, having been brought into relation and facing the acknowledgement of the breaking of that relation we recognize displacement of the body as part of Christian living. Our bodies too, sexually specific, will perform in ways which transgress the gendered boundaries of established codes. Men will become mothers – witness the writings of Bernard of Clairvaux and Aelred of Rievaulx;[31] women will become virile – witness the writings of Mechthild of Magdeburg and Hadewijch.[32] The eucharistic fracture, repeating differently the crucifixion, disseminates the body – of Christ and the Church as the body of Christ. The dissemination sets each body free to follow (and both be transposed and transfigured) within the plenitude of the Word which passes by and passes on. What initiates the following after is the awareness of our being involved, of our having been drawn into the ongoing divine activity. Our being involved is a tasting of that which we know we long for; we drink of eternal life in that participation.

The 'lack' which draws us on, and reorientates all our desiring, differs from the structural function of lack in the economies of desire in Hegel, Freud and Lacan. The economies of desire in the work of these people are circular. A moment of integration and wholeness is posited at the beginning, which is followed by the event of a break or a fall into what is other. This event constitutes the recognition of lack. In Hegel this is the fall into self-consciousness which moves out and towards itself in a dialectical sublation of what is other. In his demythologized reading of Adam's eating of the fruit of the tree of knowledge of good and evil, Hegel declares: 'What it really means is that humanity has elevated itself to the knowledge of good and evil; and this cognition, this distinction, is the source of evil, is evil itself. . . . For cognition or consciousness means in general a judging or dividing, a self-distinguishing within oneself.'[33] This is following a line of thinking opened up by Kant.[34] In Freud and Lacan, the break comes with the separation from the body of the mother. For Freud, the recognition of exile from 'the mother's womb, the first lodging, for which in all likelihood man still longs',[35] and of the loss of the mother's breast, propel the libidinal drive towards substitute pleasures and consolations. Eventually this drive then enters the Oedipal triangle which stages sexual development. Lacan is far more metaphysical. The desire of the mother is the origin. Her desire founds the economy of desire itself.[36] Her desire is for the phallus, and the child comes to recognize her as Other through the event of the father which splices the symbiosis of mother–child. The mirror stage spatially performs the alienation. But the desire of the mother is itself a desire structured around lack – the lack of the phallus. The origin, then, itself is a hole which nurtures a nostalgia for presence. The search for identity and presence is therefore a search for the nothing into which all that is folds.

In none of these foundational origins which bring about separations or alienations (which, in turn, set up the endless circulation of desire), do we ever consciously participate. They are events belonging to pre-self, pre-linguistic consciousness. They are speculative moments which provide the conditions for the possibility of what is and which yet lie outside it, as Freud (who attempted to map the morphology of the infant psyche onto primal man and the development of civilization itself) understood. They provide undemonstrable 'intuitions' of wholeness and immediacy both irrecoverable and unremembered. They are moments belonging to the metaphysics of idealism – aprioricity. The experiences they provide the condition for are loss, bereavement and the need to find consolations. 'Lack' here characterizes a kenotic economy of self-emptying *en abîme*, a *via negativa* – the endless search for the beginning which culminates in death. For Freud, the death instinct is inseparable from the libidinal drive, and what characterizes both is the desire to return to the primal condition.[37] The 'lack' is a figure of death haunting the whole economy and the immanence of its libidinal logic. Lacan writes: 'This lack is real because it relates to something real, namely, that the living being, by being subject to sex, has fallen under the blow of individual death.'[38] The libidinal logic has no exterior, no memory of that founding wholeness (or nothingness) which governs desire's subsequent teleology. And since it has no conclusion either, for its desires can never be satisfied – 'The programme of becoming happy . . . cannot be fulfilled',[39] 'man cannot aim at being whole'[40] – these economies of desire announce the vicious logic of Narcissus: pursuing one's own shadow until either one's energies are exhausted or one kisses oneself in some act of suicide. Lacan again: 'The subject says "No!" to this intersubjective game of hunt-the-slipper in which desire makes itself recognized for a moment, only to become lost in the will that is the will of the other.'[41]

This is not the structure of lack as it functions in the economy of Christian desire. The structure of Christian desire is, significantly, twofold – not only my desire, but God's desire for me. It is this twofoldedness which characterizes participation. The self is fissured in such participation, and fissured endlessly. It never had the unity of the Hegelian and Freudian ego living in and for itself;[42] it never will. Its completion lies outside, before and after it. This fissuring, and the historical events which make it possible, are performed and reperformed in the eucharist, and in the *kenosis* which constructs the Christian self in every practice of the faith. The lack, and the mourning, which issue from the radical displacement of the body of Christ in the crucifixion feed a positive regeneration. They bear the charge of resurrection, for in the pain of their present they bear the seed of the future glorious body. Not-having the body of Christ is not a negative because Christ's withdrawal of his body makes possible a greater identification with that body. In fact, the Church in its identification becomes the body of Christ. This identification is not of the logic of A = A – ultimately the vicious logic of Narcissus. It is the identification of analogy – a participation in and through difference that enables a co-creativity. The displacement does not operate within an economy of death-bound subjectivity, but within eternal trinitarian life.

The theological implication of this is that the displacement of the body in the crucifixion is not cancelled out by the resurrection, as if the tragic moment of the broken is swept into a comic finale of triumphant reconciliation. The resurrection only expands the kenotic movement of displacement effected through the crucifixion. It does not reverse it and yet neither does it constitute, by its

equiprimordiality, the paradox of crucifixion–resurrection. The death of the physical body is not the end of, but rather the opening for further displacements – the
eucharistic fracturing promoted through the Church. It makes brokenness and lack
a *sine qua non* of redemption. This redemption is not an emptying of oneself into
nothingness (*à la* Lacan); but a recognition of the lack of foundations within oneself which requires and enables the reception of divine plenitude. Lacan returns
the subject to the *nihilo* and denies that God made anything out of it. The Christian
awareness of the absent body of Christ, and of death itself, returns us to our createdness – to the giftedness of creation out of nothing.

Resurrection

The resurrected body of Jesus sums up all the modes of displacement that were
seen in evidence before his death. The life of Christ continues, playing out the glorified body of the transfiguration, the broken body of the eucharist and the
unstable physicality of the body which walked on water. The ability to disappear,
walk through walls, occupy other bodies (which causes so many misidentifications
of who he is), is countered by a corporeality which is tangible and able to eat.
Displacement opens up a spiritual *topos* within the physical, historical and geo-
graphical orders. Displacement is figured in the narrative, first, through the empty
tomb. This emptiness is emphasized in John's Gospel by the presence of two angels
at either end of where the body had been (20: 12). It is not emptiness as such;
rather it is akin to that space opened by the two angels on either side of the ark of
the covenant in the Holy of Holies: the emptiness announces the plenitude of
God's presence.[43]

The displacement is figured, second, in the actual body of Christ. It is no longer
recognizable. The two on the road to Emmaus talk to him for hours, but it is only
when he breaks the bread they will eat for supper that they recognize him. John
records Mary at the tomb turning from the angels, seeing Jesus and not knowing
that it was Jesus, supposing him to be a gardener even when he had spoken to her.
She recognizes him only when he calls her by her name. Later in the same Gospel
the disciples, out fishing, saw Jesus walking on the shore and they did not know it
was Jesus, even though he spoke to them. It was only after they had obeyed the
instruction to fish on the other side of the boat and the nets were drawing in the
heavy load that Peter said: "It is the Lord". These narrative details cannot be
taken, as they have been by some, as disfigurations which follow the almost atomic
power of the resurrection. Such an explanation assumes what Mary Douglas calls
a 'medical materialism'.[44] The misidentifications are part of the unfolding logic of
displaced bodies, bodies which defer or conceal their final identity; bodies which
maintain their mystery. In each case, from the hiddenness comes the revelation, the
realization which has the structure of an initiation – the move from what is familiar to what is strange, to what is once again familiar albeit in another guise. These
bodies of Jesus bear analogical resemblance to each other, but they are not literally
identical. The body is analogical by nature – it moves through time and constantly

changes, and yet all these changes are analogically related to each other.[45] With the new identifications ("It is the Lord"; "Their eyes were opened"; "Rabboni") a new relationship and understanding are opened up. The logic of the displacement—deferral of the Word is a pedagogical logic.

The third figuration of displacement, opening a spiritual topos, is the structure of the narrative itself. The Gospel narrative, which had previously followed Jesus Christ wherever he went until his disappearance into the tomb, now can follow him no longer. A series of appearances, visitations or epiphanies occur. The body of Christ keeps absenting itself from the text. Where does it go to? What the body is replaced by is the witness of the Church. First the angels pass on the news that he is risen, and then Mary bears witness. Finally, several other disciples narrate their experiences (those on the road to Emmaus, the disciples in the upper room to Thomas). Jesus's presence is mediated through the discourses of those who will comprise the early Church.

Patristic and medieval theology announced this creation of a new body, through the displacement of Christ's physical body, in gendered language: through the wound in Jesus's side the Church is brought to birth. Jesus makes manifest the motherhood of the divine. Caroline Walker Bynum has exhaustively researched this material. In her *Speculum of the Other Women*, Irigaray too alludes to the wounding of Christ that marks a femininity within him.[46] There is much more material, and much less explored material, in the writings of the Syrian Fathers, like Ephraim: material which speaks profoundly of the wombs from which creation and the Church issue. The water and the blood which flow from the side of Christ are the sacramental fluids which nurture and nourish his child-bride, the Church. What I wish to emphasize – and to some extent Michel de Certeau has emphasized it before me[47] – is the textuality of these bodies. The body of Christ crucified and risen, giving birth to the ecclesial *corpus*, the history and transformations of that ecclesial body – each of these bodies can materialize only in, through and with language. The continual displacement of their bodies, the continual displacement of their identities, is not only produced through economies of signification, it is a reflection (a *mimesis* or repetition) of an aporetics intrinsic to textuality itself. To adopt a Derridean term, the logic of Christ as Logos is the logic of *différance* – deferral of identity, non-identical repetition which institutes and perpetuates alterity: this is not that, or, more accurately, this is not only that. Thus, the absenting body of Christ gives place to (is supplemented by) a body of confessional and doxological discourse in which the Church announces, in a past tense which can never make its presence felt immediately: "We have seen him. He is risen." The testimonials cited in the Gospels provide a self-conscious trope for the writing of the Gospel narratives themselves. For we had only the mediated body of Jesus Christ throughout. We have been reading and absorbing and performing an ecclesial testimony in the fact that we have the Gospel narratives (and Pauline Epistles) at all. The confessions and doxologies staged within the narratives are self-reflexive moments when the narratives examine that which makes the Gospels possible: the giving and receiving of signs.

The appearance–disappearance structure of Christ's resurrected body serves to emphasize the mediation of that body – its inability fully to be present, to be an object to be grasped, catalogued, atomized, comprehended. The appearance–disappearance serves as a focus for what has been evident throughout – the body as a mystery, as a materiality which can never fully reveal, must always conceal, something of the profundity of its existence. In Mark's Gospel a young man sits astride the head of the empty tomb and tells the women: "He is risen. He is not here. He goes before you to Galilee." Galilee was where the story began and will begin, when the story is retold (at least by Mark). The young man points them back to the beginning of their discipleship. The beginning is doubled. In Matthew's Gospel the young man is an angel *(aggelos,* a messenger *par excellence).* In Luke's Gospel there are two angels, and the story proceeds to narrate the testimonies of the disciples who saw the Risen Christ appear on the road to Emmaus, noting also the testimony of Simon Peter (whose story of Christ's visitation does not appear in the text). In John's Gospel it is Mary Magdalene who communicates the news, who becomes an angel (and envoy); Jesus subsequently appearing to confirm the news. Meditation, the dissemination of messages, the narration of stories, the communication in one context being transposed and reported in another – these constitute the poetics of the New Testament itself, the letteral Word of God which supplements the incarnate Word of God. The practices of Christian living parse the divine grammar: in our words and our worlding we are adverbial in the sense Eckhart gives that part of speech when he prays: 'may the Father, the Verbum, and the Holy Spirit help us to remain adverbs of this Verbum'.[48]

Communication confers communion and creates community.[49] From the dispersal of the disciples on the point of Christ's crucifixion, a new collectivity of relations begins to form following the resurrection. People are sent to each other – by the young man, by the angels, and by Jesus. The resurrection play of appearances and disappearances triggers a series of relational relays. These are performed across various geographic, gendered and socially symbolic spaces: across the city of Jerusalem; from Emmaus to Jerusalem; from Jerusalem to Galilee; across the sea of Galilee; across the divide between women and men, believers and doubters, Jews and Gentiles (maybe rich and poor, the skilled and the unskilled, the labourer and the academic, the Temple and the people of the land, slave and freeborn, for all we know about the contexts within which these narratives were composed). Relationality and spatiality, the new collectivity born within and borne across the distensive absence, a new collectivity issuing from the divinely driven imperative to bear witness to the appearance and disappearance of Jesus Christ – all come to an apex in the scene of the ascension.

Ascension

The ascension is the final displacement of the body of the gendered Jew. The final displacement rehearses the logic of the eucharist: the body itself is transposed. A verse from Colossians elucidates this: 'The Church is his body, the fullness of him

175

who fills all in all.' I will avoid entering into the ambiguities of both the Greek syntax and the authorship of this letter. Scholars have debated long. It is sufficient to point out that the Church is now the body of Christ, broken like the bread, to be food dispersed throughout the world. The final displacement of the gendered body of Jesus Christ, always aporetic, is the multi-gendered body of the Church. A new spatial distance opens up with the ascension – a vertical, transcending spatiality such as divides the uncreated God from creation. There will be no more resurrection appearances. The withdrawal of the body is graphically described. The emptiness is emphasized by the angels: "Why stand ye gazing up into heaven?" It is a moment of both exaltation and bereavement.

Michel de Certeau, following Hegel, views the loss of the body of Jesus as the beginning of the community of faith. The Church proceeds because of lack.[50] Certainly, with Christ's departing words concerning the Holy Ghost to come and the angels' pronouncement that Jesus himself will return, a desire is installed as they who 'continued with one accord' are now orientated towards the future, towards a deferred *eschaton*. Certainly, the gap which now opens up between the Ascension and Pentecost has a similar structure to the gap between Good Friday and Easter Sunday: as if something important is going on behind the scenes. The disciples are caught between memory and anticipation. But the absenting is not a decisive break. I have argued throughout that the body of Jesus Christ is continually being displaced so that the figuration of the body is always transposing and expanding its identity. That logic of displacement is now taken up in the limbs and tissue of his body as the Church. Poised between memory and anticipation, driven by a desire which enfolds it and which it cannot master, the history of the Church's body is a history of transposed and deferred identities: it is not yet, it never was, and still it will be. Furthermore, the absenting does not culminate in bereavement. The new body of Christ will not promulgate and live out endless simulacra for fulfilment. The loss of the body of Jesus Christ cannot be read that way. The logic of the ascension is the logic of birthing, not dying. The withdrawal of the body of Jesus must be understood in terms of the Logos creating a space within himself, a womb, within which *(en Christoi)* the Church will expand and creation be recreated.[51] In this way, the body of the Church and the body of the world are enfolded through resurrection within the Godhead. The body of Jesus Christ is not lost, nor does it reside now in heaven as a discrete object for veneration (as Calvin thought and certain Gnostics before him).[52] The body of Jesus Christ, the body of God, is permeable, transcorporeal, transpositional. Within it all other bodies are situated and given their significance. We are all permeable, transcorporeal and transpositional. 'There is neither Jew nor Greek, there is neither bond nor free, there is neither male nor female, for ye are all one in Christ *(eis este en Christoi)*' (Philippians 2: 12). This theo-logic makes possible, as I mentioned at the beginning of this essay, an understanding of the omnipresence or ubiquity of God.[53]

We have no access to the body of the gendered Jew. So all those attempts to determine the sexuality of Jesus are simply more recent symptoms of the search for the historical Christ – which Schweitzer demonstrated was pointless at the beginning of this century.[54] It is pointless not only because it is a human attempt to give Christianity an empirically verifiable foundation and because the metaphysics implied in believing that project to be possible are profoundly anti-Christian (atomism, positivism, atemporality, immanentalism, access to the immediate and subjectivism). It is pointless because the Church is now the body of Christ, so to understand the body of Jesus we can only examine what the Church is and what it has to say concerning the nature of that body. The Church dwells in Christ and in Christ works out its salvation and the salvation of the world. The body of Christ is a multigendered body. Its relation to the body of the gendered Jew does not have the logic of cause and effect. This is the logic which lies behind such questions as 'Can a male saviour save women?' This is the logic of Hegel's description of the relationship between God and the Church. God in Christ dies and the Church is born. One gives way to the other, without remainder. The relationship between Jesus and the Church is processional, as the relationship between the trinitarian persons is processional. One abides in and through the other. The body of the gendered Jew expands to embrace the whole of creation. That body continues to expand by our continual giving and receiving of signs. This is the textuality of Christian time, made up, as it is, of doxological words and liturgical practices. The expansive bloom of the flower is not the effect of the bud, but its fulfilment.

Those theologians framing questions such as 'Can a male saviour save women?', or engaged in investigating the sexuality of Jesus, fail to discern the nature of the body of Christ; fail to understand the nature of bodies and sex in Christ. As Gregory of Nyssa points out in his thirteenth sermon, on *Song of Songs*: 'he who sees the Church looks directly at Christ. . . . The establishment of the Church is re-creation of the world. . . . A new earth is formed, and it drinks up the rains that pour down upon it. . . . [B]ut it is only in the union of all the particular members that the beauty of [Christ's] Body is complete.'[55] The next step in understanding the body of Christ is to investigate the Church, that Spouse 'wounded by a spiritual and fiery dart of desire (*eros*). For love (*agape*) that is strained to intensity is called desire (*eros*).'[56] To continue would be to detail and discuss the body of the Church as the erotic community.

Notes

1 I am quoting a question that forms the subtitle of a chapter in Rosemary Radford Ruether, *Sexism and God-Talk: Towards a Feminist Theology* (London: SCM, 1983), pp. 116–38. I do not intend this essay to be an attack on Ruether herself. Rather I am attacking the biological essentialism which lies behind many of the recent moves by feminists towards a post-Christian perspective, and attempting to show how a masculinist symbolics can be refigured in a way which opens salvation through Christ to both (if there are only two, which I doubt) sexes.

2 The question was opened, and the investigations undertaken, because sexuality and Christianity had become so divorced from one another. The topic had become taboo, as Tom Driver suggested at the outset of his article 'Sexuality and Jesus', *Union Seminary Quarterly Review*, 20 (March 1965), pp. 235–46. Stephen Sapp, in a chapter of his book

Sexuality, the Bible, and Science (Philadelphia, 1976) entitled 'The Sexuality of Jesus', developed the discussion. Driver and Sapp, in their attention to this sexuality – and by calling into question dogmas such as the virgin conception and birth – employ medical materialism to offset a potential docetism. Both of them needed to go back to Tertullian and a cultural epoch when *eros* could still be theologically valued beyond its implications for sexuality. Ruether joined in with her own note 'The Sexuality of Jesus', published in *Christianity and Crisis*, 38 (29 May 1978), pp. 134–37.

3   I employ this word because of its associations with patristic theologies of Christ's flesh. These patristic theologies understood bodies more fluidly than we who have inherited notions of 'body' following the nominalist (and atomistic) debates of the late Middle Ages, the Cartesian definition of bodies as extended things (*res extensae*), the seventeenth-century move towards unequivocation, and Leibniz's understanding of the individuation of matter. See Amos Funkenstein, *Theology and the Scientific Imagination* (Princeton: Princeton University Press, 1986), pp. 23–116; although even Leibniz developed 'a doctrine of semi-substances in order to lend precise meaning to Christ's real presence in the Host' (p. 109).

4   The deferral of this corporeal identity can be related to the diverse names and titles given to Jesus, most particularly in John's Gospel. Attention has frequently focused on the title 'Son of Man' – its relation to Daniel 7 (Schnackenburg), the Gnostic Saviour (Lindars), the humanity of Christ (Pamment), the Primal Man (Borsch). But the appellation 'Son of Man' stands, especially in John's Gospel, alongside a series of other titles: *Logos*, Light, Only-Begotten, Jesus Christ, King, Lamb, Lord, Rabbi, Teacher, Jesus of Nazareth, Son of Joseph, Son of God, Messiah, *ego eimi*. Furthermore, as scholars of John's Gospel have pointed out, Jesus performs actions which are explicitly associated with his Jewish forefathers: he is compared to Jacob, Moses, the heavenly Adam, the Suffering Servant. The deferral of corporeal identity is paralleled, therefore, by the plethora of names and designations for this man, such that his identity is always excessive to any single appellation. For an examination of these titles in relation to the early formation of doctrine, see James D. G. Dunn, *Christology in the Making: An Inquiry into the Origins of the Doctrine of the Incarnation* (London: SCM, 1989).

5   *The Sexuality of Christ in Renaissance Art and Modern Oblivion* (Chicago: University of Chicago Press, 1996), p. 296.

6   *De Carne*, xvii. Tertullian, polemically engaging with various Gnostic heresies – the Ebionites, Valentinians and Marcionites – suggests that copulation changes corporeality. He speaks of sinful flesh, angelic flesh and virginal flesh, besides spiritual flesh (or 'flesh from the stars'). Gregory of Nyssa will make a distinction between true human nature and the post-lapsarian human nature which is forced to wear a *garment of skin*; that is, a corporeality subject to mortality and corruptibility. See *de Anime et Resurrectione*. Christ's body wears a *tunic of incorruptibility*.

7   Tertullian notes that Mary is both virgin and not a virgin, a virgin and yet mother, a virgin and yet a wife, married and yet not married (De *Carne*, xxxiii).

8   For Augustine see notes 4 and 5; for Athanasius (who Frances M. Young understands as 'Apollinarian in tendency' – *From Nicaea to Chalcedon* (London: SCM, 1983), p. 80), see *de Incarnatione Verbi Dei*, 17: "The Word was not hedged in by His body, nor did His presence in the body prevent His being present elsewhere as well. When He moved His body He did not cease also to direct the universe by His mind and might."

9   "[T]he Father from whom [out of whom, *ex ou*] every fatherhood in the heavens and upon the earth is named".

10   *Bodies that Matter: On the Discursive Limits of 'Sex'* (London: Routledge, 1993). While Butler sees how the material is informed by the way in which we represent it, she does not take this further to ask: what then is the nature of materiality itself? She does not relate it to a wider genealogy to show the way in which representations of the corporeal,

the philosophical notion of substance itself, are historically situated and theologically indebted.

11 *Sermons*, IX.7.

12 *On the Merits and Remission of Sins and on the Baptism of Infants*, pp. 63–64.

13 The doctrine of the ubiquity or omnipresence of God starts here. For the way in which these theological notions change and become secularized (becoming the feared omnipotent God of the nominalists, see Funkenstein and Michael Allen Gillespie, *Nihilism Before Nietzsche* (Chicago: University of Chicago Press, 1996), pp. 1–32.

14 *De Carne*, iii.

15 See George Mosse, *The Image of Man: The Creation of Modern Masculinity* (Oxford: Oxford University Press, 1996), pp. 17–39. The Renaissance architect Vitruvius is a forerunner. The geometric perfection of the cosmos is mapped onto the body of a well-built male adult, as his famous diagram of the outstretched limbs of a naked man embraced by a circle demonstrates. See 'Utopic Rabelesian Bodies', in Louis Marin, *Food for Thought*, trans. Mette Hjort (Baltimore: The Johns Hopkins University Press, 1989), pp. 84–113.

16 For a phenomenology of the invisible within the visible, the iconic beyond the idolised, see Jean-Luc Marion, *La Croisée de visible* (Paris: La Différence, 1991), pp. 11–46.

17 This form of the sublime differs from the sublime as it features in Romantic aesthetics and, more recently, in the work of Jean-François Lyotard. The sublime here is not registering the *frisson* of the unpresentable, the abyssal, the ineffable. The sublime here is more like Longinus's sublime: it elevates, its ennobles the soul, it leads to reflection and examination, it 'exerts an irresistible force and mastery'. *On the Sublime*, trans. T.S. Dorsch (London: Penguin Books, 1965), pp. 99–113

18 Gregory of Nyssa makes a similar claim while simultaneously distinguishing Christ's body as immortal from the mortality of our own: 'that body to which immortality has been given by God, when it is in ours, translates and transmutes the whole into itself' (*The Great Catechism*, 37). See also my essay 'Transcorporeality: The Ontological Scandal', in Grace Jantzen (ed.) *Representation, Gender and Experience*, special issue of *The John Rylands Bulletin*, June 1998.

19 *The Corinthian Body* (New Haven: Yale University Press, 1995), p. 20.

20 *Ibid.*, p. 25.

21 Cinematographic accounts of the crucifixion scene enable us to appreciate the erotic charge of the action, because they place us (as none of the disciples were placed) as voyeurs, observing the playful abuse perpetrated. See Franco Zeffirelli's *Jesus of Nazareth*.

22 See *Violence and the Sacred*, trans. Patrick Gregory (Baltimore: The Johns Hopkins University Press, 1977), p. 169. For the libidinal nature of this desire, see Chapters 5–7, pp. 119–92.

23 In bringing back this Christian witness, we too, as readers, are no longer voyeurs; for we identify with this witness and claim it as our own.

24 My thinking here has been profoundly influenced by the work of Hans Urs von Balthasar. See, particularly *Mysterium Paschale*, trans. Aidan Nichols OP (Edinburgh: T. & T. Clark, 1990).

25 *The Forest of Symbols* (Ithaca: Cornell University Press, 1967), pp. 95–96. Turner recognizes how 'novel configurations of ideas and relations may arise' (p. 97) from such liminality – the liminal space opens up the potential for new births.

26 *Ibid.*, p. 98.

27 See the work of Carolyn Walker Bynum.

28 The terms real, imaginary and symbolic are Jacques Lacan's. I am not using them in his technical sense (particularly his understanding of *réel*), but more in the looser manner of Moira Gatens in *Imaginary Bodies: Ethics, Power and Corporeality* (London: Routledge, 1996). The real bodies are the empirical and historical, medical and material ones to which we have no access other than through the 'images, symbols, metaphors and representations . . . the (often unconscious) imaginaries of a specific culture: those ready-made

images and symbols through which we make sense of social bodies and which determine, in part, their value, their status and what will be deemed their appropriate treatment' (Gatens, p. viii).

29 See Julia Kristeva, *Power of Horror: An Essay on Abjection*, trans. Leon Roudiez (New York: Columbia University Press, 1982); and, specifically on the relation of abjection to Christ's death and resurrection, *In the Beginning Was Love: Psychoanalysis and Faith*, trans. Arthur Goldhammer (New York: Columbia University Press, 1988).
30 *City of God*, trans. Henry Bettenson (Harmondsworth: Penguin Books, 1972), XII.21.
31 Caroline Walker Bynum, *Fragmentation and Redemption: Essays on Gender and the Human Body in Medieval Religion* (New York: Zone Books, 1992), pp. 158–60.
32 See Barbara Newman, *From Virile Woman to Woman Christ: Studies in Medieval Religion and Literature* (Philadelphia: University of Pennsylvania Press, 1995), and Elizabeth Castelli, '"I Will Make Mary Male": Pieties of the Body and Gender Transformation of Christian Women in Late Antiquity', in *Body Guards: The Cultural Politics of Gender Ambiguity*, eds Julia Epstein and Kristina Straub (London: Routledge, 1991), pp. 49–69. Of course this trans-gendering or making women virile – which goes back to the Gnostic *Gospel of St Thomas* – is part of a masculine ideology. I do not wish to suggest that in late antiquity or the medieval period there was a cultural openness such that men being figured as women and women being figured as men were equally valued.
33 *Lectures on the Philosophy of Religion*, ed. Peter C. Hodgson, trans. R. F. Brown *et al.* (Berkeley: University of California Press, 1988), p. 443.
34 See Kant's 'Speculative Beginning of Human History', in *Perpetual Peace and Other Essays: on Politics, History, and Morals*, trans. and ed. Ted Humphrey (Indianapolis: Hackett, 1983). Kant reads the Genesis story again, albeit differently, in *Religion Within the Limits of Reason Alone*, trans. J. R. Silber (New York: Harper, 1960).
35 'Civilization and its Discontents', in *The Complete Psychological Works of Sigmund Freud*, trans. and ed. James Stratchey (London: Hogarth Press, 1961), volume XXI, p. 91.
36 *Seminar VII: The Ethics of Psychoanalysis*, trans. Dennis Porter (New York: Norton, 1992), p. 283.
37 Freud, pp. 118–22.
38 *Four Fundamental Concepts of Psycho-Analysis*, trans. Alan Sheridan (Harmondsworth: Penguin Books, 1979), p. 208. Lacan writes about *objet à* which symbolizes lack. This is where the subject, in order to constitute itself, posits an object outside itself. The *objet à* substitutes for the lack of the phallus. With this substitution, the entry in the symbolic, Lacan (more than Freud) views the death instinct as encoded within libidinal desire. In *Écrits*, trans. Alan Sheridan (London: Tavistock Publications, 1977), he writes: 'what is primordial to the birth of symbols, we find . . . in death. . . . It is in effect as a desire for death that he [the subject] affirms himself for others' (p. 105). For an excellent discussion of the nihilistic metaphysics governing Lacan's project, see Henry Staten, *Eros in Mourning* (Baltimore: The Johns Hopkins University Press, 1995), pp. 166–85.
39 Freud, p. 83.
40 *Écrits*, p. 287.
41 *Ibid*, pp. 104–105.
42 Freud: 'there is nothing of which we are more certain than the feeling of our self, of our own ego. This ego appears to us as something autonomous and unitary, marked off distinctly from everything else' (pp. 65–66).
43 Luce Irigaray refers to the holiness of this spacing, which she likens to the sacred hiatus which is constituted by sexual difference, in her essay 'Belief Itself', in *Sexes and Genealogies*, trans. Gillian C. Gill (New York: Columbia University Press, 1993), pp. 25–53. 'Those angels . . . guard and await the mystery of the divine presence that has yet to be made flesh' (p. 45).
44 *Purity and Danger* (London: Routledge, 1966), p. 37.
45 Gregory of Nyssa uses the Greek term *scopos* to describe the growth here through all its

stages. He distinguishes this growth or movement from the cyclical one, which is inferior and immanent to the orders of creation. This second movement is a movement of expansion or *epectasis* – the perpetual growth in goodness as the human nature is redeemed. For a more detailed examination of *epectasis*, see Jean Danielou's 'Introduction' to Herbert Musurillo, *From Glory to Glory: Texts from Gregory of Nyssa's Mystical Writings* (London: John Murray, 1961), pp. 56–71.

46 *Speculum of the Other Woman*, trans. Gillian C. Gill (New York: Cornell University Press, 1985), pp. 199–200.

47 Certeau writes: 'Thus, through community practice and Trinitarian theology, the death of Jesus becomes the condition for the new Church to arise and for new languages of the Gospel to develop. The true relation of Jesus to the Father (who gives him his authority) and to the Church (he 'permits') is verified (i.e. manifested) by his death. The Jesus event is extended (verified) in the manner of a disappearance in the *difference* which that event renders possible. Our relation to the origin is in function of its increasing absence. The beginning is more and more hidden by the multiple creations which reveal its significance.' ('How Is Christianity Thinkable Today?', in *The Postmodern God*, ed. Graham Ward (Oxford: Blackwell, 1997), pp. 146–47.

48 Quoted by Jacques Derrida in his essay 'Comment ne pas parler: dénegations', in *Psyché* (Paris: Galilée, 1987), p. 578.

49 See the narrative theologians for a more detailed exposition of this: the work of George Lindbeck, Ronald F. Thiemann and Gerard Loughlin. See also Paul Ricoeur, 'Eighth Study: The Self and the Moral Norm', in *Oneself as Another*, trans. Kathleen Blamey (Chicago: University of Chicago Press, 1992), pp. 203–39.

50 See *The Mystic Fable*, trans. Michael B. Smith (Chicago: University of Chicago Press, 1992), pp. 79–90.

51 Gregory of Nyssa writes: 'Participation in the divine good is such that, where it occurs, it makes the participant ever greater and more spacious than before, brings to it an increase in size and strength, in such wise that the participant, nourished in this way, never stops growing and keeps getting larger and larger.' *De Anime et Resurrectione*.

52 Calvin, *Institutio* IV. 17, 'The Sacred Supper of Christ and What it Brings to Us'.

53 This ubiquity is not compromised by what appears to be the mutability of assuming other bodies. God is immutable. But the displacements of the body involved in transcorporeality must be understood as variations on a single theme, as moments within the *scopos* of the divine unfolded love. Creation – and human nature as part of the created order – is placed within the operation of the Trinity, such that the Trinity informs embodiment.

54 *The Quest for the Historical Jesus*, trans. W. Montgomery (London: A. & C. Black, 1922).

55 *Comm. on the Cant.*, 13, 1049B–1052A.

56 *Ibid.* 13, 1048A. Herbert Musurillo comments, significantly : 'In this passage *eros* would seem to be merely[!] a more intense, less satisfied form of *agape*', *From Glory to Glory*, p. 297.

9

THE CITY

Beyond secular parodies*

William T. Cavanaugh

Can you draw out Leviathan with a fishhook . . . ?
(Job 41:1)

Humankind was created for communion, but is everywhere divided. For the purposes of this essay, this opening statement will serve as a somewhat bold – though I hope not inaccurate – summary of the Book of Genesis, Chapters 1–11. The reader will recognize an intentional parallel with one of the most famous opening lines of modern intellectual history, that of Rousseau's *The Social Contract*: 'Man was born free, but is everywhere in bondage.'[1] Although at first glance Genesis and *The Social Contract* seem to be about quite different tasks, both are similarly engaged with foundational stories of human cooperation and division. Modernity is unaccustomed to regarding political theory as mythological in character. The modern state is, however, founded on certain stories of nature and human nature, the origins of human conflict, and the remedies for such conflict in the enactment of the state itself. In this essay I will read these stories against the Christian stories of creation, fall, and redemption, and argue that both ultimately have the same goal: salvation of humankind from the divisions which plague us. The modern state is best understood, I will attempt to show, as a source of an alternative soteriology to that of the Church. Both soteriologies pursue peace and an end to division by the enactment of a social body; nevertheless I will argue that the body of the state is a simulacrum, a false copy, of the Body of Christ. On the true Body of Christ depends resistance to the state project. The Eucharist, which makes the Body of Christ, is therefore a key practice for a Christian anarchism.

I use the term 'anarchism' to alert the reader to the radical nature of the orthodoxy in question. By it I do not mean no government, but rather no state. By 'state' I mean to denote that peculiar institution which has arisen in the last four centuries

---

* I would like to thank Frederick Bauerschmidt, John Berkman, James Fodor, Michael Hollerich, and D. Stephen Long for their insightful comments on an earlier draft of this essay.

in which a centralized and abstract power holds a monopoly over physical coercion within a geographically defined territory. I am aware of the danger in ignoring the differences between actual states, or between states in theory and states in practice. Nevertheless, I think it is a useful exercise to consider in general terms the pathologies which modern states seem to share – especially that of atomization of the citizenry – and the common stories which serve to enact these pathologies.

I begin by telling, in the first section, the Christian story of creation, fall, and redemption – as interpreted by Paul, John, and various patristic writers – as the loss and regaining of a primal unity. In the second section, I offer a reading of Hobbes, Locke, and Rousseau as attempts to save humanity from the pernicious effects of disunity through the mechanism of the state. In the third section, I suggest why this project has failed. In the final section, I explore the Eucharist as a practice of resistance to the binding discipline of the state.

The Christian story

Cain's fratricide, the wickedness of Noah's generation, and the scattering of Babel can be understood only against the backdrop of the natural unity of the human race in the creation story of Genesis 1. The supernatural unity effected in the Body of Christ rests upon a prior natural unity of the whole human race founded on the creation of humankind in the image of God (Genesis 1: 27). 'For the divine image does not differ from one individual to another: in all it is the same image,' says Henri de Lubac, summing up patristic anthropology – 'The same mysterious participation in God which causes the soul to exist effects at one and the same time the unity of spirits among themselves.'[2] Such is this unity based on participation in God that, as de Lubac comments, we can no more talk of humans in the plural than we can talk of three Gods. Not individuals but the human race as a whole is created and redeemed. This essential unity in our creation is the natural source of a Church truly Catholic into which all people regardless of nationality are called. Thus Clement of Alexandria:

> This eternal Jesus, the one high priest, intercedes for all and calls on them: 'Hearken,' he cries, 'all you peoples, or rather all you who are endowed with reason, barbarians or Greeks! I summon the whole human race, I who am its author by the will of the Father! Come unto me and gather together as one well-ordered unity under the one God, and under the one Logos of God.'[3]

It is because of this unity that Paul is able to explain to the Romans that 'sin came into the world through one man, and death came through sin, and so death spread to all because all have sinned' (Romans 5: 12). Adam is not merely the first individual, but represents humanity as a whole.[4] The effect of Adam's disobedience to God, however, is to shatter this created unity. The disruption of the harmonious participation of humanity in God by Adam and Eve's attempted usurpation of God's position – 'when you eat of it your eyes will be opened, and you will be like God' (Genesis 3: 5) – is accompanied necessarily by a disruption of human unity, since through the *imago dei* our participation in God is a participation in one another. This disruption begins with Adam's attempt to blame Eve for the sin (3: 12). Genesis 4–11 then narrates the effects of the fall as division and strife: Cain murders Abel, and the 'earth was filled with violence' (6: 11). The story of Babel sums up the dynamic of the fall from unity; because of the attempt to usurp God's position, the human race is scattered abroad (Genesis 11: 1–9). This sequence of stories is fully comprehensible only against the assumption of a primal unity in the creation story.

In his great work *Catholicism*, de Lubac follows this theme through the writings of the Fathers. Maximus the Confessor sees the fall as the dispersal of a created unity in which there could be no contradiction between what is mine and what is thine. Cyril of Alexandria writes: 'Satan has broken us up.' Augustine pictures Adam almost as if he were a china doll, falling and shattering into pieces which now fill the world.[5] De Lubac comments on these passages and others:

> Instead of trying, as we do almost entirely nowadays, to find within each individual nature what is the hidden blemish and, so to speak, of looking for the mechanical source of the trouble . . . these Fathers preferred to envisage the very constitution of the individuals considered as so many cores of natural opposition.[6]

In other words, the effect of sin is the very creation of individuals as such, that is, the creation of an ontological distinction between individual and group.

If sin is scattering into mutual enmity – both between God and humanity and among humans – then redemption will take the form of restoring unity through participation in Christ's Body. The salvation of individuals is only through Christ's salvation of the whole of humanity. Christ is the new Adam because he assumes the whole of humanity. In the incarnation God takes on not simply an individual human body but human nature as such, for, in the slogan of the Alexandrian School, 'that which is not assumed is not saved.' Christ is incorporated in a human body, but likewise humanity is saved by being incorporated into the Body of Christ. The Body of Christ is the locus of mutual participation of God in humanity and humanity in God.

In the Body of Christ, as Paul explains it to the Corinthians (I Corinthians 12: 4–31), the many are joined into one, but the body continues to consist of many members, each of which is different and not simply interchangeable. Indeed, there is no merely formal equality in the Body of Christ; there are stronger and weaker members, but the inferior members are accorded greater honor (12: 22–25). Furthermore, the members of the Body are not simply members individually of Christ the Head, but cohere to each other as in a natural body. The members are not 'separate but equal,' but rather participate in each other, such that 'If one member suffers, all suffer together with it; if one member is honored, all rejoice together with it' (12: 26).

Incorporation into Christ's Body restores the tarnished image of God in humanity: 'you have put on a new self which will progress towards true knowledge the more it is renewed in the image of its Creator; and in that image there is no room for distinction between Greek and Jew, between the circumcised and uncircumcised, or between barbarian and Scythian, slave and free' (Colossians 3: 10). Ephesians expresses this in terms of the enmity between Jews and Gentiles:

> For he is our peace; in his flesh he has made both groups into one and has broken down the dividing wall, that is, the hostility between us. He has abolished the law with its commandments and ordinances, that he might create in himself one new humanity in place of the two, thus making peace, and might reconcile both groups to God in one body through the cross, thus putting to death that hostility through it.
>
> (Ephesians 2: 14–16)

This reconciliation of Jews and Gentiles is an anticipation of the eschatological gathering of all the nations to Israel, in whom all the nations will be blessed (Genesis 12: 3). Jesus dies for the nation, 'and not for the nation only, but also to gather together into one the scattered children of God' (John 11: 52).

This eschatological gathering is neither an entirely worldly nor an entirely otherworldly event, but blurs the lines between the temporal and the eternal. The individual soul is indeed promised eternal life, but salvation is not merely a matter of the good individual's escape from the violence of the world. We await, rather, a new heaven and a new earth (2 Peter 3: 13; Revelations 21: 1), which are already partially present. The heavenly beatific vision is the full consummation of the unification of the human race begun on earth. As Augustine says:

> We are all one in Christ Jesus. And if faith, by which we journey along the way of this life, accomplishes this great wonder, how much more perfectly will the beatific vision bring this unity to fulfillment when we shall see face to face?[7]

In Augustine's vision of the two cities, the reunification of the human race depends on Christians locating true citizenship beyond the confines of the earthly empire. We journey through the *civitas terrena* always aware that our true home is in heaven. This communion with our fellow-citizens in heaven is not, however, an escape from this-worldly politics, but rather a radical interruption by the Church of the false politics of the earthly city. Thus Augustine contrasts the fellowship of the saints in heaven – and on earth – with the violent individualism of the Roman empire, the virtue of which is based on a self-aggrandizing *dominium*, the control over what is one's own. It is the Church, uniting earth and heaven, which is the true 'politics.' The earthly city is not a true *res publica* because there can be no justice and no common weal where God is not truly worshipped.[8]

The state story

The primeval stories told by the classical theorists of the modern state begin from a state of nature. Whether or not this state of nature can be characterized as pre- or post-lapsarian depends on the thinker. Rousseau, not identifiably Christian, assumes an original state of freedom, but is agnostic on the cause of its loss: 'How did this change *from freedom into bondage* come about? I do not know.'[9] Neither Hobbes nor Locke makes any effort to describe a pristine pre-fall state; both treat of the state of nature as ordained by God, beginning with Adam. For Hobbes, God establishes a system of rewards and punishments, under which Adam's sin would presumably fall: 'The right of nature, whereby God reigneth over men, and punisheth those that break his laws, is to be derived, not from his creating them, as if he required obedience as of gratitude for his benefits; but from his *irresistible power*.'[10] Participation in God is therefore ruled out. As John Milbank has argued, modern politics is founded on the voluntarist replacement of a theology of participation with a theology of will, such that the assumption of humanity into the Trinity by the divine *logos* is supplanted by an undifferentiated God who commands the lesser discrete wills of individual humans by sheer power.[11] The older theology rather declared that Adam and Eve acted against their true good, which God commands not from sheer will but because God cannot command in any other way than for the good of humanity. In other words, God's will is inseparable from the good. The loss of a theology of participation is a loss of teleology, the intrinsic ends of human life. Thus Hobbes will interpret Adam's disobedience as punishable simply because it contradicts God's arbitrary will. Locke too assumes that the state of nature is already characterized by formal mechanisms of will and right, subject to the superior will of God. It follows that in the state of nature, each individual is formally discrete and equal, 'unless the lord and master of them all should, by any manifest declaration of his will, set one above another.'[12]

It is important for our purposes to see that this *mythos* establishes human government not on the basis of a primal unity, but from an assumption of the essential individuality of the human race. When Rousseau says that humanity was born free, he means free primarily from one another; by way of contrast, in the Christian interpretation of Genesis, the condition of true human freedom is participation in God with other humans. Hobbes famously posits a natural state of *bellum omnis contra omnem*, which conflict he derives precisely from the formal equality of all human beings,[13] but the more liberal and sanguine Locke agrees on the essential individuality of humanity in the state of nature.

> To understand political power aright, and derive it from its original, we must consider what estate all men are naturally in, and that is, a state of perfect freedom to order their actions, and dispose of their possessions and persons as they think fit, within the bounds of the law of Nature, without asking leave or depending upon the will of any other man.[14]

Hobbes, Rousseau, and Locke all agree that the state of nature is one of individuality; individuals come together on the basis of a social *contract*, each individual entering society in order to protect person and property.

The distinction between mine and thine is therefore inscribed into the modern anthropology. Indeed the early modern theorists of the state depended on a redefinition, according to Roman law, of Adam's *dominium* as sovereignty and power over what is his. As Milbank tells it, *dominium* was traditionally bound up with the ethical management of one's property, and was therefore not a sheer absolute right but was based on ends, namely upon what was right and just. In Aquinas' thought, Adam's right of property was based on *dominium utile*, justified by its usefulness to society in general. Under the influence of Roman law in the early modern era, the Aristotelian suspicion of the right of exchange over use gave way to an absolute right to control one's person and property. This movement was the anthropological complement of the voluntarist theology: humans best exemplify the image of God precisely when exercising sovereignty and unrestricted property rights.[15]

Locke will say, in countering Robert Filmer's deduction of absolute monarchy from Adam, that 'God gave the world to Adam and his posterity in common,'[16] but he then hastens to explain how it is that property is not held communally. This is not the result of some fall from grace, but of God's gift of reason which is necessary for individuals to derive benefit from the goods of nature: 'Though the earth and all inferior creatures be common to all men, yet every man has a "property" in his own "person."'[17] Individuals appropriate goods from the as-yet-unclaimed abundance of nature and mix their labor or 'person' with it, giving them an exclusive property right to it. According to Locke, God's command to subdue the earth and have dominion over it necessitates the development of private property rights, since it is human labor which both makes nature beneficial to humanity and establishes property as one's own.[18]

Although the essential individualism of the state of nature contrasts with the created unity of the human race found in the Christian interpretation of Genesis 1–2, both accounts agree that salvation is essentially a matter of making peace among competing individuals. It is in soteriology, in other words, that the ends of the Christian *mythos* and the state *mythos* seem to coincide. Hobbes paints this competition among individuals in the starkest terms: two people in the state of nature, by nature equal, will want what only one can have. From the natural equality of humans therefore arises the war of all against all, from which Leviathan – enacted by social contract – saves us. Rousseau denies that humans are 'natural enemies;'[19] Locke distinguishes between the state of nature and a state of war.[20] Nevertheless, both Rousseau and Locke agree with Hobbes that individuals are compelled into the social contract by the need to defend one's property and person from encroachment by other individuals. According to Locke, 'the pravity of mankind being such that they had rather injuriously prey upon the fruits of other men's labors than take pains to provide for themselves' obliges individuals to enter into society with one another.[21] For Rousseau, the social contract comes from the need 'to defend and protect, with all the collective might, the person and property of each associate.'

The state of nature cannot continue: 'humankind would perish if it did not change its way of life.'[22]

As in Christian soteriology, salvation from the violence of conflicting individuals comes through the enacting of a social body. The metaphor of body is most obvious in Hobbes' figure of the great Leviathan, the artificial man, the commonwealth or state, in which sovereignty is the soul, the magistrates the joints, reward and punishment the nerves, and '[l]astly, the *pacts* and *covenants*, by which the parts of this body politic were at first made, set together, and united, resemble that *fiat*, or the *let us make man*, pronounced by God in the creation.'[23] Leviathan, then, is the new Adam, now of human creation, which saves us from each other. Although less famously than Hobbes, Rousseau and Locke also employ the metaphor of a social body. For Rousseau, a 'collective moral body' is the result of the social contract, which he characterizes in the following terms: 'Each of us puts into the common pool, and under the sovereign control of the general will, his person and all his power. And we, as a community, take each member unto ourselves as an indivisible part of the whole.'[24] Locke deduces his argument for majority rule by employing the metaphor of body, for once the consent of each individual has produced a body, 'it being one body, must move one way,' and that way is 'whither the greater force carries it.'[25]

Thus far I have been treating the Christian story and the state story as parallel accounts of salvation. The soteriology of the modern state is incomprehensible, however, apart from the notion that the Church is perhaps the primary thing from which the modern state is meant to save us. The modern secular state, after all, is founded precisely, the story goes, on the need to keep peace between contentious religious factions. The modern state arose out of the 'Wars of Religion' of the sixteenth and seventeenth centuries, in which the conflicts inherent in civil society, and religion in particular, are luridly displayed. The story is a simple one. When the religious consensus of civil society was shattered by the Reformation, the passions excited by religion as such were loosed, and Catholics and the newly minted Protestants began killing each other in the name of doctrinal loyalties. ('Transubstantiation, I say!' shouts the Catholic, jabbing his pike at the Lutheran heretic. 'Consubstantiation, damn you!' responds the Lutheran, firing a volley of lead at the papist deviant.) The modern secular state and the privatization of religion were necessary, therefore, to keep the peace among warring religious factions. As Jeffrey Stout tells the story, 'liberal principles were the right ones to adopt when competing religious beliefs and divergent conceptions of the good embroiled Europe in the religious wars. . . . Our early modern ancestors were right to secularize public discourse in the interest of minimizing the ill effects of religious disagreement.'[26]

For Hobbes, Locke, and Rousseau, there could be no question but that the state body would have to solve the question of the Body of Christ before there could be true peace. Hobbes' solution, not yet liberal, is for Leviathan to swallow the Church whole; a commonwealth is a church is a state. The sovereign not only makes religious laws but teaches doctrine and authorizes the interpretation of Scripture.

This absolute identification of Church and state means that there is no one Church, but exactly as many Churches as there are states. The transnational Church produces conflict by dividing people's loyalties between sovereign and pontiff: 'there must needs follow faction and civil war in the commonwealth, between the *Church* and *State.*'[27] Absolute unity of Church and state is therefore necessary to emerge fully from the state of nature and into the peaceful embrace of Leviathan. 'Religion' therefore becomes a means of binding the individual to the sovereign. According to Hobbes, religion is a universal impulse which arises in the state of nature from anxiety and the need for security, the very same source of the social contract. Religion is therefore particularly apt to produce obedience to laws.[28]

Rousseau has a similar concern for the unity of the state. He asks why the pagan world had no 'religious wars.' The answer is that each state had its own religions and its own gods. Rather than produce division, Rousseau argues, such an arrangement meant that the gods of one nation had no power over the people of another nation, and therefore the gods were not imperialist or jealous. The Romans eventually adopted the wise policy of tolerating the gods of vanquished peoples, and so paganism in the Roman empire could be considered a 'single, homogeneous religion' despite the diversity of gods and religions:

> Thus matters stood when Jesus made his appearance, bent on estab-
> lishing a spiritual kingdom on earth – an enterprise which forced a
> wedge between the political system and the theological system, and so
> undermined the unity of the state. Hence the internal divisions that –
> *as we are about to see* – have never ceased to plague the Christian peo-
> ples.[29]

Christianity produces divisions within the state body precisely because it pretends to be a body which transcends state boundaries. 'What makes the clergy a body . . . [is] communion among churches. Communication and excommunication – these are the clergy's social compact.' Priests in communion are 'fellow-citizens' even though they come from different parts of the globe.[30] This system, 'so obviously baneful' precisely because it 'impairs social unity,' must be remedied by the creation of a civil religion to bind the citizen to the state. Although Rousseau congratulates Hobbes for clearly diagnosing both the problem and the cure to the Church question, Rousseau insists on the tolerance of a diversity of religions, provided they have to do only with the 'purely inward worship' of God, do not interfere with the duties of citizens to the state, and tolerate other religions. Intolerant religions such as Roman Catholicism are not to be tolerated.[31]

In Locke we find a more recognizable form of liberal tolerance, but it is essential to see the fundamental agreement between Hobbes, Rousseau, and Locke on the need to domesticate the Body of Christ in order to produce unity. Locke's concern, again, is the division produced by the 'Wars of Religion' which have plagued England and the Continent:

> I esteem it above all things necessary to distinguish exactly the business of civil government from that of religion. . . . If this be not done, there can be no end put to the controversies that will be always arising between those that have, or at least pretend to have, on the one side, a concernment for the interest of men's souls, and, on the other side, a care of the commonwealth. The commonwealth seems to me to be a society of men constituted only for the procuring, preserving, and advancing of their own civil interests.[32]

Locke makes no attempt to bind together, as do Hobbes and Rousseau, these self-interested individuals through any mechanism of public religion, ecclesiastical or civil. Nevertheless, the victory over the Church is the same; his principle of tolerance for all religion, provided it be a private affair, eliminates the Church body as a rival to the state body by redefining religion as a purely internal matter, an affair of the soul and not of the body. This, indeed, the story goes, is a Glorious Revolution. We are saved bloodlessly from the most serious cause of division among people, and all religion is tolerated. All religion, that is, except those forms which continue to consider the Church a transnational body. Locke's principles served as the basis for the Toleration Act of 1689, from which Catholics were explicitly excluded.

Extra respublicam nulla salus?

In the modern age, Christians have tended to succumb to the power of the state soteriology I have just sketched, and they have done so often on Christian grounds. It is not enough to see what is called 'secularization' as the progressive stripping away of the sacred from some profane remainder. What we have instead is the substitution of one *mythos* of salvation for another; what is more, the successor *mythos* has triumphed to a great extent because it mimics its predecessor.[33] In the dissociation of the Church from the sword, many Christians have seen the God of peace emancipated from captivity to the principalities and powers; and in national unity, despite religious pluralism, many have glimpsed the promise of the original Christian quest for unity and peace. It will be my task in this section of the essay to suggest that state soteriology offers a false unity and a false peace which are fundamentally at odds with the Christian story.

As I have argued at greater length elsewhere,[34] the story told of the modern state's salvation of Europe from the violence of the 'Wars of Religion' is simply not true. Catholics and Protestants often found themselves fighting on the same sides in the so-called 'Wars of Religion,' and just as often co-religionists battled each other in the name of more significant loyalties. To cite a few examples: in the French civil wars of the late sixteenth century, the Catholic League was opposed not only by Huguenots, but by another Catholic party, the Politiques; in German territory, Catholic Habsburg wars against Lutherans in both 1547–1555 and 1618–1648 were opposed by the German Catholic nobility, and in both cases the

French Catholic king came to the aid of the Lutherans; the Thirty Years' War – the most notorious of the 'Wars of Religion' – became a contest between the Habsburgs and the Bourbons, the two great Catholic dynasties of Europe.

To call these 'Wars of Religion' is anachronistic, because what was at stake in these wars was the very creation of 'religion' itself. The word *religio* derives from *religare*, to bind together. *Religio* is found in Thomas' *Summa Theologiae* as a virtue which directs a person to God by means of bodily ritual practices.[35] *Religio* is a habit of appropriate disposition of body and soul toward God, a habit which governs the person's behavior without regard to distinctions of 'public' and 'private.' For Aquinas, *religio* – as external and bodily and not merely interior – presupposes an entire context of communal practices by which the person is bound to others in the Body of Christ. In the late-fifteenth and the sixteenth century, however, 'religion' in the modern sense is created as a universal human impulse buried within the recesses of the individual heart. As religion is therefore removed from its specific ecclesial context, Christianity becomes for the first time 'a religion,' one of a genus of religions, a system of beliefs rather than a virtue located within a set of theological claims and practices which assume a social form called Church.[36] The crucial move, as we have seen in Hobbes, Locke, and Rousseau, is the separation of religion and Church (unless the Church is absorbed by the state, as in Hobbes). If religion was to remain as a practice of *religare* at all, it would serve only to bind the individual to the state.

The wars in question, then, were not fought as between members of two different 'religions.' What was at stake was rather the aggrandizement of the centralizing territorial state over the remnants of the transnational ecclesial order and the remnants of local privilege and custom. The rise of the state was not necessitated by the 'Wars of Religion'; rather, these wars were the *birthpangs* of the state, in which the overlapping jurisdictions, allegiances, and customs of the medieval order were flattened and circumscribed into the new creation of the sovereign state (not always yet nation-state), a centralizing power with a monopoly on violence within a defined territory.

Essential to state soteriology is the unity and uniqueness of the sovereign; the sovereign is a jealous god. The Church above all must be defeated in order for salvation to take place, but more generally any association which interferes with the direct relationship between sovereign and individual becomes suspect. It is no coincidence that the royalty–nobility cleavage was the most determinative in the wars of the sixteenth and seventeenth centuries. At stake in all of the major 'Wars of Religion' was the attempt by the nobility to protect local prerogatives against the assertion of centralized royal or imperial control. When Hobbes and Rousseau theorized the emergent state in the seventeenth and eighteenth centuries, they understood quite clearly the imperative to defeat the lesser associations within the state body in order to vanquish multiplicity. Locke was less clear on this point, but in practice the modern sovereign state has been *defined* by its usurping of power from lesser communal bodies. The view that the state is a natural outgrowth of family and community is false. As Robert Nisbet points out, the modern state arose from *opposition* to kinship and other local social groupings: '[t]he history of the Western State has been characterized by the gradual absorption of powers and responsibilities formerly resident in other associations and by an increasing directness of relation between the sovereign authority of the State and the individual citizen.'[37]

Examples of this process are innumerable: the intervention of the state in matters of kinship, property, and inheritance; the conception of the law as something 'made' or legislated by the state rather than 'disclosed' from its divine source through the workings of custom and tradition; the abolition of ecclesiastical courts and the transfer of sole judicial proprietorship to the crown; the replacement of local duties and privileges by the rights of interchangeable individuals; the enclosure of common lands; the state's securing of a monopoly over legitimate violence.[38] Undergirding these and countless other instances is the use of Roman law on the Continent to arrogate to the state the sole privilege of recognizing the existence of lesser associations; such associations become endowed with a purely 'fictitious' personality, a *nomen juris* given from the center by royal fiat rather than developed organically.[39]

State sovereignty and the debilitation of other associations were meant not to oppress but rather to free the individual; even more state-centered theorists such as Hobbes and Rousseau are quite clear on this point. As Nisbet makes plain: 'The real conflict in modern political history has not been, as is so often stated, between State and individual, but between State and social group.'[40] Indeed, the rise of the state is predicated on the creation of the individual. The realization of a single unquestioned political center would make equivalent and equal each individual before the law, thereby freeing the individual from the caprice of local custom and subloyalties which would divide them from their fellow-citizens. For example, the dissolution of the medieval guild system and the endless 'interventions' of religious custom in economic matters is what unleashes the 'free' market.[41] The power of the state grew in concert with the rise of capitalism, because of direct state subsidies for business and international trade, the development of state-sanctioned standardized monetary and taxation systems, and the emergence of a centralized legal system which made possible the commodification and contractualization of land, goods, and especially labor. In other words, the impersonal and centralized state accompanied the invention of the autonomous individual liberated from the confines of the traditional group and now relating to other individuals on the basis of contract. Property – including one's own self in the form of one's labor – became *alienable*. Thus were born both the capitalist and the wage laborer.[42]

Why has the state failed to save us? Let me outline the argument of this section in three points.

1   The state *mythos* is based on a 'theological' anthropology which precludes any truly social process. The recognition of our participation in one another through our creation in the image of God is replaced by the recognition of the

other as the bearer of individual rights, which may or may not be given by God, but which serve only to separate what is mine from what is thine. Participation in God and in one another is a threat to the formal mechanism of contract, which assumes that we are *essentially* individuals who enter into relationship with one another only when it is to one's individual advantage to do so. The mechanism of contract is purely 'formal' in the sense that it has no intrinsic relationship to ends – the providential purpose of God – but is definable only as a means. The state can never truly integrate the individual and the group because there is nothing transcending the two-dimensional calculus of individual–aggregate through which individual and group are related.

2   State soteriology has tried to unify humankind by incorporation into a body of a perverse sort. Beginning with an anthropology of formally equal individuals guided by no common ends, the best the state can hope to do is to keep these individuals from interfering with each other's rights. While this can serve to mitigate the conflicting effects of individualism, it cannot hope to enact a truly social process. The body that is enacted is a monstrosity of many separate limbs proceeding directly out of a gigantic head. Hobbes foresaw this with his usual clarity: in a true commonwealth the members cohere, not as in a natural body to one another, but only to the sovereign.[43] Rousseau too anticipated a perfect panopticon, such that 'each citizen should be completely independent *vis-à-vis* each of the others, and as dependent as can be *vis-à-vis* the city.'[44] This arrangement is not an accident of Hobbes and Rousseau's 'overemphasis' on the state, but proceeds logically from the anthropology of individual *dominium* on which the liberal state is founded. Because of this, modern politics is centripetal; talk of '*the* healthcare debate,' for example, means attempts principally to exert influence over the bureaucratic organs of the state with regard to healthcare. Rather than 'cohere' directly to one another, we relate to each other through the state by the formal mechanism of contract. Paul's image of the Body – internally differentiated yet suffering and rejoicing as one – is supplanted by a formal interchangeability of each individual with any other.

In this type of body, local communities of formation and decision-making are necessarily subsumed, as we have seen, under the universal state. Those who hail 'globalization' as the demise of the nation-state fail to see that globalization is simply the logical extension of the state project's subsumption of the local under the universal. Although it is certainly true that capital has become almost infinitely mobile, and multinational corporations have succeeded in transcending national allegiances, the state project of achieving a 'smooth' space of interchangeable individuals is just now being fulfilled by those who admonish us to recognize the 'global village' of which we are all supposedly part.[45] Amid images of happy Bolivian peasants, London stockbrokers, and sub-Saharan tribespeople all linked up in cyberspace, Microsoft advertisements ask us to ponder if utopia has been reached, ignoring the fact that a Bolivian peasant with malnourished children is not likely to buy a modern, especially when there is no place to plug it in. To imagine that the London stockbroker and the Bolivian peasant inhabit the same social space–time is to obliterate the particularities of localized and oppositional spaces such as that occupied by peasants in Bolivia. Globalization is an extension of the state project of smoothing over local politics, local histories, and local resistance. This signals not the acceptance but the obliteration of the identity of the other.

3   The state has promised peace but has brought violence. The wars of the nineteenth and twentieth centuries seem sufficient *prima facie* evidence to demonstrate this, and yet the bogus myth of the 'Wars of Religion' persists. If my argument is correct, however, the 'Wars of Religion' were provoked– not peaceably resolved – by the centralization of the state over against local forms of governance. Apart from the violence resulting from the process of securing a monopoly on legitimate force within a defined territory,[46] the establishment of territorial borders with a single authority within each assumes a 'state of nature' between territorial states, heightening the possibility of war.[47] Our fellow-citizens are limited to all those currently living English, Americans, French, etc. The dominance of state soteriology has made it perfectly reasonable to drop cluster bombs on 'foreign' villages, and perfectly unreasonable to dispute 'religious' matters in public.

In the absence of shared ends, individuals relate to each other by means of contract, which assumes a guarantee by force. Hobbes was of course clear on this, but Locke too assumed, as we have seen, that the state body moves in whichever way the greater force compels it. Max Weber rightly perceived that the modern state cannot be defined by ends, but only by its peculiar means, which is a monopoly on the legitimate use of force.[48] Internally, such force is necessary to keep the mass of individuals from interfering with each other's rights. Externally, the violence of war is necessary to provide some unity – albeit a false one – to a society lacking in any truly social process. As Raymond Williams and others have argued, war is for the liberal state a simulacrum of the social process, the primary mechanism for achieving social integration in a society with no shared ends.[49] In a word, violence becomes the state's *religio*, its habitual discipline for binding us one to another.

Toward eucharistic anarchism

If it is true that the modern state is but a false copy of the Body of Christ, then it should be obvious that state power is the last thing the Church should want. To overcome the privatization of Christianity through attempts, direct or indirect, to influence the state is worse than futile as long as what is meant by 'politics' remains centripetal. Fortunately, in the making of the Body of Christ, Christians participate in a practice which envisions a proper 'anarchy,' not in the sense that it proposes chaos, but in that it challenges the false order of the state. In this final section, I suggest that the Eucharist is the heart of true *religio*, a true practice of binding us to the

Body of Christ which is our salvation. My comments – necessarily brief – will follow on the three points of the state *mythos* I addressed above.

1   The Eucharist defuses both the false theology and the false anthropology of will and right by the stunning 'public' *leitourgia* in which humans are made members of God's very Body. 'Just as the living Father sent me, and I live because of the Father, so whoever eats me will live because of me' (John 6: 57). Augustine envisions Jesus saying 'I am the food of the fully grown; grow and you will feed on me. And you will not change me into you like the food your flesh eats, but you will be changed into me.'[50] The contrast with Locke's explanation of property – that through labor one assimilates things from the state of nature to the property in one's person – is extremely suggestive. Indeed, in the Eucharist the foundational distinction between mine and thine is radically effaced (cf. Acts 2: 44–47). Christ's restoration of the *imago dei* in humanity is consummated in individuals in the Eucharist, in which our separateness is overcome precisely by participation in Christ's Body.

   The Body of Christ which overcomes the scattering of humanity through Adam's sin is not enacted by any social contract but is always received as gift: 'the free gift is not like the effect of the one man's sin' (Romans 5: 16). The Eucharist undercuts the primacy of contract and exchange in modern social relations. For, as we have seen, the state enacts the formal interchangeability of the subject, removed from true community and relating to others according to laws of exchange (abstract labor): the gift is privatized. Property is commodified and thus made alienable. In contrast, as Jean-Luc Marion stresses, what is transubstantiated is not *ousia* understood as property, a substance available for possession; the Eucharist is enacted by the pure gift of God, requiring only that we be disposed to receive it anew.[51] Milbank provides a corrective to Marion in pointing out that a certain kind of exchange does take place in the divine gift. Although it is true that we can never make a return to God, 'since there is nothing extra to God that *could* return to him,'[52] in the economy of the divine gift we participate in the divine life, such that the poles of giver and recipient are enfolded into God. In a capitalist economy, gifts are possible only privately, where the recipient is rendered passive and the giver experiences giving as an alienation of property. In the divine economy of gift, in contrast, as in pre-capitalist economies, the gift is not alienated from the giver, but the giver is in the gift, goes with the gift. For this reason in pre-capitalist economies a return is expected, but this is never a mere contract, since the return is not pre-established, but comes in an unpredictable form at an unpredictable time, bearing the character of the counter-giver. In the divine economy, this type of giving is perfected as the dualism of giver and recipient are collapsed; Christ is the perfect return of God to God. In the Eucharist, we receive the gift of Christ not as mere passive recipients, but by being incorporated into the gift itself, the Body of Christ. As members of the Body, we then become nourishment for others – including those not part of the visible Body – in the unending trinitarian economy of gratuitous giving and joyful reception.[53] Property and *dominium* are thus radically questioned.

2   The Eucharist aims to build the Body of Christ, which is not simply centripetal: we are united not just to God, as to the center, but to one another. This is no liberal body, in which the center seeks to maintain the independence of individuals from each other, nor a fascist body, which seeks to bind individuals to each other through the center. Christ is indeed the Head of the Body, but the members do not relate to one another through the Head alone, for Christ himself is found not only in the center but at the margins of the Body, radically identified with the 'least of my brothers and sisters' (see Matthew 25: 31–46), with whom all the members suffer and rejoice together (I Corinthians 12: 26). Christ is the center of the eucharistic community, but in the economy of the Body of Christ, gift, giver, and recipient are constantly assimilated, one to another, such that Christ is what we receive, He who gives it, and 'the least' who receives the gift, and we are assimilated to Christ in all three terms. Whereas in the modern state the center either vindicates the rights of property against the marginalized or takes direct concern for the welfare of the marginalized out of our hands, in Christ the dichotomy of center and periphery is overcome.

The unity of the state body depends, as we have seen, on the subsumption of the local and the particular under the universal. This movement, and especially its extension under the new globalization, is a simulacrum of true catholicity, in which the antithesis of local and universal is effaced. The Eucharist gathers the many into one (cf. I Corinthians 10: 16–17) as an anticipation of the eschatological unity of all in Christ, but the local is not therefore simply subordinated to the universal. Indeed it is in the local community that the Eucharist is found. As John Zizioulas points out, it was therefore possible for the early Church to speak of 'catholic Churches' in the plural, and to identify the 'whole Church' with the local church. Each Eucharist performed in the local community makes present not part of Christ but the whole Christ, and the eschatological unity of all in Christ. For this same reason, however, there can be no mutual exclusion between local eucharistic communities. From the early centuries this principle was represented by the necessity for two or three bishops from other communities to participate in the ordination of any bishop. The Eucharist made it necessary to see the whole Christ in each local community, which at the same time united the communities, not through a single external center or structure superimposed on the local, but through the presence of the whole Christ in each.[54] The one Christ, then, is the center of each eucharistic community, yet the center appears in many different places. Here we might apply Alan of Lille's comment about absolute Being to the Body of Christ: it is an 'intelligible sphere whose center is everywhere and whose circumference is nowhere.'[55]

3   The Eucharist transgresses national boundaries and redefines who our fellow-citizens are. Rousseau was right to note that communion among churches is a

threat to the unity of the state. The eschatological breakdown of divisions between Jew and Greek – and all other natural and social divisions – is pre-eminently made present in the eucharistic feast. Patristic writers tended to emphasize the eschatological dimension of the Eucharist,[56] regarding it as a foretaste of the heavenly banquet in which 'people from east to west, from north and south, will come and sit down at the feast in the kingdom of God' (Luke 13: 29). Thus St John Chrysostom, in his commentary on Hebrews, displays the early Church's conviction that at the Eucharist the heavenly banquet irrupts into earthly time:

> For when our Lord Jesus lies as a slain Victim, when the Spirit is present, when He Who sits at the right hand of the Father is here, when we have been made children by baptism and are fellow-citizens with those in heaven, when we have our fatherland in heaven and our city and citizenship, when we are only foreigners among earthly things, how can all this fail to be heavenly?[57]

This is a fundamental disfigurement of the imagination of citizenship in the territorial state. One's fellow-citizens are not all the present English or French, but fellow members (and potential members) of the Body of Christ, past, present, and future.

The Eucharist is not simply a promise of future bliss outside of historical time. In the biblical and patristic witness we find the Eucharist as an earthly practice of peace and reconciliation. Paul reprimands the Corinthians for continuing divisions between rich and poor, and suggests that some of them are sick and dying *now* because they have partaken of the Eucharist without first reconciling these divisions (I Corinthians 11: 17–32). Where peace is lacking, the Eucharist appears as an eschatological sign of judgment requiring that people reconcile before a true Eucharist can take place. For this reason *The Didache* requires that anyone who has differences with another should not participate in the Eucharist until the two parties have reconciled[58] (see also Matthew 5: 23–26). From the earliest times Christians have exchanged a kiss of peace before the Eucharist as an indication that the Eucharist demands reconciliation. This practice is a sign of the peace which cannot be specified through the formal adjudication of contractual obligations, but can be constructed only in the direct encounter of human beings who consider themselves members of one another and of the Prince of Peace.

This brief display of a few central eucharistic themes is not intended to idealize the actual practice of the Eucharist in our divided churches. Clearly Christians have, to an alarming degree, adopted the salvation *mythos* of the state as their own, and submitted to the state's practices of binding. We submit to these practices, even give our bodies up for war, in the hope that the peace and unity promised by the state will be delivered. What I have tried to show is that the state *mythos* and the state *religio* are distortions of our true hope, and that the Christian tradition provides resources for resistance.

For the most part, Christians have accepted the integrating role of the state on the assumption that the state is a 'secular' and therefore neutral apparatus for the working out of conflict among disparate interests. To see the state instead as an alternative soteriology is to begin to notice the inherent conflict between state practices and the practices, such as the Eucharist, which Christians take for granted. True peace depends not on the subsumption of this conflict, but on a recovered sense of its urgency.

Notes

1 Jean Jacques Rousseau, *The Social Contract*, trans. Willmoore Kendall (South Bend, IN: Gateway Editions, 1954), p. 2 [Book I, Ch. 1].

2 Henri de Lubac, *Catholicism: Christ and the Common Destiny of Man*, trans. Lancelot C. Sheppard and Sister Elizabeth Englund OCD (San Francisco: Ignatius Press, 1988), p. 29.

3 Clement of Alexandria, *Protreptic*, c. 12, cited in de Lubac, pp. 32–33.

4 The view I am developing in this section does not necessarily depend on the historical existence of a single set of biological ancestors, although recent discoveries of 'Eve' and 'Lucy' by anthropologists raise interesting questions about monogenism.

5 de Lubac, pp. 33–34. In this regard, de Lubac also mentions Origen's dictum 'Where there is sin, there is multiplicity,' but this opposition of unity and multiplicity has possible 'fascist' overtones which are avoided in Paul's account of unity through multiplicity in the Body of Christ.

6 *Ibid.*, p. 34.

7 Augustine, *In Galat. Expositio*, n. 28, quoted in de Lubac, p. 112.

8 Augustine, *The City of God*, trans. Marcus Dods (New York: Modern Library, 1950), pp. 686–709 [XIX, 11–28]. See also John Milbank's discussion of Augustine's thought in his *Theology and Social Theory* (Oxford: Blackwell Publishers, 1990), pp. 389–92, 398–411.

9 Rousseau, p. 2. [Book I, Ch. 1].

10 Thomas Hobbes, *Leviathan: Or the Matter, Forme, and Power of a Commonwealth Ecclesiasticall and Civil* (New York: Collier Books, 1962), p. 262 [Ch. 31].

11 Milbank, *Theology and Social Theory*, pp. 12–15.

12 John Locke, *Two Treatises of Government* (New York: Dutton, 1924), pp. 118–19 [Book II, §4].

13 Hobbes, pp. 98–99 [Ch. 13].

14 *Ibid.*, p. 118 [Book II, §4].

15 Milbank, *Theology and Social Theory*, pp. 12–15.

16 Locke, *Two Treatises of Government*, p. 129 [Book II, §25].

17 *Ibid.*, p. 130 [Book II, §27].

18 *Ibid.*, p. 132 [Book II, §32-34].

19 Rousseau, p. 9 [Book I, Ch. 4].

20 Locke, *Two Treatises of Government*, pp. 126-27 [Book II, §16–19].

21 John Locke, *A Letter Concerning Toleration* (Indianapolis, IN: Bobbs-Merrill, 1955), p. 47.

22 Rousseau, p. 13 [Book I, Ch. 6].

23 Hobbes, p. 19 [Author's Introduction].

24 Rousseau, p. 15 [Book I, Ch. 6].

25 Locke, *Two Treatises of Government*, p. 165 [Book II, §96].

26 Jeffrey Stout, *The Flight from Authority: Religion, Morality, and the Quest for Autonomy* (Notre

Dame, IN: University of Notre Dame Press, 1981), p. 241. For similar invocations of the 'Wars of Religion' as the founding moment of the modern state, see Judith Shklar, *Ordinary Vices* (Cambridge, MA: Harvard University Press, 1984), p. 5; John Rawls, 'Justice as Fairness: Political not Metaphysical,' *Philosophy & Public Affairs* (Summer 1985), p. 225.

27 Hobbes, pp. 340–41 [Ch. 39].
28 *Ibid.*, pp. 87–90 [Ch. 12].
29 Rousseau, p. 151 [Book IV, Ch. 8].
30 *Ibid.*, p. 153 [Bk. IV, Ch. 8].
31 *Ibid.*, pp. 153–62 [Book IV, Ch. 8].
32 Locke, *A Letter Concerning Toleration*, p. 17.
33 I am indebted here to John Milbank's argument which frames his *Theology and Social Theory*; see especially pp. 9–12.
34 William T. Cavanaugh, '"A Fire Strong Enough to Consume the House": The Wars of Religion and the Rise of the State,' *Modern Theology* 11:4 (October 1995), pp. 397–420.
35 St Thomas Aquinas, *Summa Theologiae*, II–II. 81.
36 See Wilfred Cantwell Smith, *The Meaning and End of Religion* (New York: The Macmillan Company, 1962), pp. 31–44.
37 Robert A. Nisbet, *The Quest for Community* (London: Oxford University Press, 1953), p. 104.
38 *Ibid.*, pp. 102–108.
39 On this development see John Neville Figgis, 'Churches in the Modern State' in *The Pluralist Theory of the State: Selected Writings of G.D.H. Cole, J.N. Figgis, and H.J. Laski*, ed. Paul Q. Hirst (London: Routledge, 1989), pp. 111–27. Figgis points out that, although Roman law as such was never adopted in England, an equivalent doctrine of state recognition of associations developed as part of the general trend toward centralization in the sixteenth century and after; *ibid.*, p. 114. Ironically this nominalist doctrine, which would be used to reduce the Church to a purely 'voluntary association,' was first borrowed from Roman law by Pope Innocent IV; see Nisbet, p. 113.
40 Nisbet, p. 109.
41 See, for example, Adam Smith, *The Wealth of Nations* (New York: The Modern Library, 1937), pp. 740–65, 775–77 [Book V, Ch. 1, Part III, Art. III]. Smith details how the rise of commerce was accompanied by the dissolution of 'the ties of interest' which bound the classes to one another, as facilitated by the Church.
42 Anthony Giddens, *The Nation-State and Violence* (Berkeley: University of California Press, 1987), pp. 148–71.
43 Hobbes, p. 418 [Ch. 42].
44 Rousseau, p. 58 [Book II, Ch. 12].
45 Although capital has become more flexible and decentered, the state is still essential to the neutralization of opposition to globalization and its acceptance as natural and inevitable. The US congressional debate over NAFTA, for example, was conducted in such a way that nationalism wholly occluded the issue of class, such that the terms of the debate became 'Is it good or bad for America?' Absent was the possibility that the agreement eliminating the last trade barriers between North American nations might be good for *some* Americans (or Mexicans, etc.), namely the owners of capital, and bad for *some* Americans, namely the workers. While in one sense, then, nationality becomes less relevant to globalizing capital, the state is alive and well, and has been essential to the promotion of 'free' trade.
46 See Charles Tilly, 'War Making and State Making as Organized Crime', in *Bringing the State Back In*, ed. Peter B. Evans, Dietrich Rueschemeyer, and Theda Skocpol (Cambridge: Cambridge University Press, 1985), pp. 169–91.
47 See Giddens, pp. 50–1, 86–90.
48 Max Weber, 'Politics as a Vocation,' in *From Max Weber: Essays om Sociology*, trans. H.H. Gerth and C. Wright Mills (eds) (New York: Oxford University Press, 1946), pp. 77–78.

49 See Raymond Williams, *Towards 2000* (Harmondsworth: Penguin Books, 1985), pp. 218–40.
50 Augustine, *Confessions*, trans. Henry Chadwick (Oxford: Oxford University Press, 1991), p. 124 [Book VII, Ch. 10, §16].
51 Jean-Luc Marion, *God Without Being*, trans. Thomas A. Carlson (Chicago: University of Chicago Press, 1991), pp. 95–101, 161–82.
52 John Milbank, 'Can a Gift Be Given?: Prolegomena to a Future Trinitarian Metaphysic,' *Modern Theology* 11 (1995), p. 133.
53 *Ibid.*, pp. 119-61. See also, John Milbank, 'Socialism of the Gift, Socialism by Grace,' *New Blackfriars* 77: 910 (December 1996), pp. 532–48.
54 John Zizioulas, 'Eucharist and Catholicity,' in *Being as Communion: Studies in Personhood and the Church* (Crestwood, NY: St Vladimir's Seminary Press, 1985), pp. 143–69. Catholic and Orthodox ecclesiologies provide a valuable check to each other on this point. The papacy guards against a tendency to Caesaropapism, but Pope must be seen as Bishop of Rome, *primus inter pares*.
55 Alan of Lille, quoted by St Bonaventure, in *The Soul's Journey into God*, trans. Ewart Cousins (New York: Paulist Press, 1978), p. 100 [Ch. V, §8].
56 For documentation of this connection, see Geoffrey Wainwright, *Eucharist and Eschatology* (New York: Oxford University Press, 1981).
57 St. John Chrysostom, *In Heb. Hom.*, XIV, 1, 2. The translation is from Dom Gregory Dix, *The Shape of the Liturgy* (London: Dacre Press, 1945), p. 252.
58 *The Didache*, §14.

10

AESTHETICS

The theological sublime*

Frederick Christian Bauerschmidt

Versions of postmodernity

Readings of the postmodern are legion, and these legions seem locked in perpetual combat.[1] In this essay I will attempt to distinguish two among the many versions of the closure of modernity – postmodernity as the end of 'metanarratives' and postmodernity as the end of 'suspicion' – and sketch a theological version of the latter as a genuine path forward. Postmodernity is too easily identified with nihilistic accounts of truth, for such an association presumes an identification of modernity with truth and reason. In this essay I will gesture toward a theological account of truth – an account that belongs neither to modernity nor to premodernity or postmodernity – that can begin to acquire new force as the end of the reign of modern 'clear and distinct ideas' comes into view. In this sense, postmodernity can be a propitious moment for theology. Still, postmodernity in no way constitutes the condition for the possibility of theology; the possibility of speech about God can be founded on nothing less than God's own speaking.

In perhaps its most common usage, associated with Jean-François Lyotard's *The Postmodern Condition*, the 'postmodern' marks the end of the master narratives of modernity, indeed the end of *all* grand narratives. This, at its extreme, is the idea of postmodernity as the death of meaning and the triumph of wild and unregulated interpretation. In this reading postmodernity is a time in which strong poets assert their will to power without regard to such eternal values as truth, goodness, unity, or beauty; in which the deconstruction of signs negates all stable meanings from within; in which modernity's universal narrative of human reason is shattered into micro-narratives of race, class, and gender through which the previously suppressed Other is presented to us with a new force. A corollary of all this is the end of the modern subject, conceived as gnoseologically stable and morally self-possessed.[2] Lyotard declares: 'A *self* does not amount to much, but no self is an island; each exists in a fabric of relations that is now more complex and mobile than ever before'(p. 15). The self becomes a pastiche of fragments collected around

* My thanks to James Buckley, Bettina Bergo, and William Cavanaugh for their comments on this essay.

nothing more than the remote control that connects it to the cable television with its 57 channels (and nothin' on).

But before we get too excited or worried, I would note that this seemingly apocalyptic version of postmodernity is in fact in substantial continuity with the modernity that preceded it. The modern turn to the subject has been intensified as the subject turns on itself, so that what we have in this purported death of grand narratives is actually the triumph of the modern narrative of emancipation. Traditionally, for Christians, submission to the master narrative of scripture, as Augustine knew so well, meant the surrender of our *free* will (our capacity to choose) so as to possess a *freed* will (our capacity to do the good). Part of the modern project – and perhaps its *defining* feature – has been the valorization of the contentless freedom of the will, the sheer capacity of human self-assertion against any external imposition.[3] Postmodernity, as the end of master narratives (which seem always to be construed as heteronomous), then becomes simply the intensification of modernity's quest for autonomy – freedom without terminus or telos. For the ultimate in contentless freedom is the negation of any stable, narratively given, identity. This may be the apocalypse, or it may be more of the same.

In a later essay entitled 'Answering the Question: What Is Postmodernism?' (published as an appendix to *The Postmodern Condition*) Lyotard gives us a second, somewhat different, account of the postmodern. In this account, postmodernity is marked by a particular mode of figuring the sublime. Following Kant, Lyotard understands the aesthetics of the sublime to be grounded in 'the incommensurability of reality to concept' that occurs when 'the imagination fails to present an object which might, if only in principle, come to match the concept' (pp. 78–79). In other words, the sentiment of the sublime arises from the gap between our ability to conceive of, for example, totality, and our inability to imagine (to present ourselves or others with an image of) that totality. Thus the imagination presents to itself not the unpresentable idea, but the very unpresentability of the idea. Kant notes: 'it can never be anything more than a negative presentation – but still it expands the soul.'[4] Or, as Gilles Deleuze puts it: 'The feeling of the sublime is experienced when faced with the formless or the deformed (immensity or power). It is as if the imagination were confronted with its own limit, forced to strain to its utmost, experiencing a violence which stretches it to the extremity of its power.'[5]

According to Lyotard, the modern aesthetic of the sublime is a 'nostalgic' one, in which a unified form is used to present the missing content (Proust is his example). The postmodern aesthetic, on the other hand, is one that 'denies itself the solace of good forms' and presents the unpresentable in the deformation of the signifier itself (Joyce is his example).[6] In other words, immensity and power are registered not simply as absent from representation, but as the very twisting and bending of beautiful forms into what are, by previous standards, hideous and grotesque forms. One might say that the modern and the postmodern mark two distinct modes of negation of form. And in postmodernity, this deformation of forms has no terminus, but is an ongoing process driven by the ceaseless and insatiable desire to convey a sense of the unpresentable.

What is of particular interest for my purposes is Lyotard's way of distinguishing the modern from the postmodern and how this relates to what is perhaps the pre-eminent modern virtue: suspicion. Lyotard notes that modernity carried with it the destruction of belief and the discovery of the 'lack of reality' of all representations of reality (p. 77). The Kantian problematic of the sublime is indicative not only of a suspicion of all received representations (and thus in continuity with Kant's reading of enlightenment), but also of a profound pessimism about our ability to produce *any* adequate image or account. Reality is the unpresentable, which can be put forth only as the 'missing contents' of the form from which all superfluous ornamentation has been stripped away. Yet this aesthetic is still 'nostalgic' for the real, and thus seeks a kind of clarity and distinctness of form – one might think of the functionalism of the so-called 'international style' of architecture or, for that matter, of Descartes' *Meditations*.

The postmodern shares with the modern a sense of the lack of reality of all rep-resentation, but it is no longer suspicious of received representations, for it realizes that a lack of reality only warrants suspicion if one presumes that there is a 'real' to which one has some sort of (at least negative) access. Rather the postmodern 'puts forward the unpresentable in presentation itself' by a proliferation of forms created out of those received representations (p. 81). The spareness and function-ality engendered by modernist suspicion is replaced in postmodernity by a baroque superficiality. In modernism the corrosion of suspicion strips away all exterior decoration – whether in art or philosophy – to reveal the sublime as what cannot be indicated by the bare form, while in postmodernity the sublime is the ever-shifting figuration of the surface. This flux creates a fantastic space in which the unpresentability of the sublime may be presented.

In some ways Lyotard's second account of postmodernity is, like his first, still fundamentally grounded in a hyper-modern master narrative of emancipation. The relationship of this second account to the first can be seen in its concluding clarion call: 'Let us wage war on totality; let us be witnesses to the unpre-sentable . . .' (p. 82). There is the same questioning of any unified discourse or presentation of such sublime concepts as totality or simplicity. Having finally thrown off the dead hand of the past, the self need not fear or be suspicious of that past; it is freed to use whatever fragmented forms of the past it wishes. Rather than being suspicious of those forms, the postmodern self is ironic about them, and thus is no longer so threatened. Forms no longer possess us, but rather we them. A clas-sical column here, a snatch of Gregorian chant there, an image of Elvis thrown in for a smile – all are assembled by the ironic subject into a pastiche. Thus in his ironic path beyond modern suspicion, Lyotard seems to retain at least enough of a centered subject to provide a locus for the ironic gaze, to act as a *bricoleur*.[7] Suddenly, ironic pastiche does not seem so 'postmodern,' for while it renounces sus-picion, it partakes of an essentially modern view of the subject as a contentless freedom that constructs the world, a freedom into which the powerful tonic of irony has been infused, so that it is no longer threatened by (and therefore suspi-cious of) the forms of the past.

While Lyotard does not himself fully distinguish them, he still presents us with at least two distinguishable ways in which we might think about 'postmodernity.' On the one hand, we have the end of metanarratives, the end of all totalizing schemes, the decentering of meaning and the self. On the other hand, we have the end of suspicion through a refiguring of the sublime, so that metaphors of depth are replaced with those of superficiality and unpresentability becomes a quality of figuration rather than something lurking behind figuration. The first, as I have argued, seems more an intensification of the modern project of emancipation than a surpassing of it. The second, particularly when tied to the first, can also – though it need not – be understood as a consequence of the emancipatory project.

The claim that all metanarratives have become incredible is of course simply an assertion, and one about which we might have well-founded suspicions, particularly given the way in which the emancipatory metanarrative of modernity seems to be smuggled back in. We might well turn suspicion and even irony back upon themselves and ask: 'Incredible to whom?' Whose interests are served by the disembedding of the subject from any and all metadiscourses so as to bounce through cyberspace? If one questions both modern suspicion and the postmodern assertion of the end of master narratives, then one is presented with the possibility of a true (or real) metanarrative presentation (or presence) of the sublime. The self is decentered – not in the sense of being fragmented, but of being unlocked from its Cartesian isolation – so as to discover truth in the concrete objects of the world.

The two versions of postmodernity that we find in Lyotard have their theological analogues. On the one hand, some theologians (or atheologians), such as Mark Taylor, have taken up the idea that we are living at the end of all metanarratives and argued that in such a situation the very notion of God must be jettisoned.[8] Similarly, there are those who conceive of the postmodern as the end of metanarratives, but are not willing to go quite as far as Taylor, arguing instead for a postmodern Christian theology that rejects the universal and totalizing pretensions of much traditional Christian theology in favor of some more modest version. The Christian story can no longer be understood or presented as the world's true story; it is at best simply the story that Christians tell about the world, and which they cannot impose upon the world or even preach to the world in the hope that the world might turn and be converted. Such theologians point to the contemporary awareness and tacit acceptance of religious pluralism as creating a new situation in which such notions as the necessity of Christ for salvation or the Church as the locus of grace are simply incredible and should be abandoned.[9] Indeed, they must be abandoned, for they inevitably wage war against the Other. Instead, we are given a Christianity that understands its mission as one of service to a world that has become increasingly secular, emancipated, and autonomous. In this version of postmodern theology the Church's task is to bring the Reign of God, now glossed as the modern project of emancipation, to its completion.[10]

On the other hand, there is a way of conceiving a theological closure of modernity that corresponds to the understanding of postmodernity as the end of suspicion. In this understanding, modernity is characterized by the 'ugly broad ditch' that Lessing saw stretched between the 'accidental truths of history' and the 'necessary truths of reason.'[11] In modernity these necessary truths could never be represented in historically contingent facts. With the closure of modernity and the jettisoning of the modern account of 'necessary truths of reason' understood as Cartesian 'clear and distinct ideas,' however, it once again becomes possible to put forward the notion of the sublime presented through the contingent and historical. It is to such an understanding of the task of theology after modernity and beyond suspicion that I now turn.

Beyond suspicion

Christianity of course has its own form of suspicion – a suspicion of representation inherited from Israel's strictures against idolatry. As is clear from the charges of 'atheism' lodged against the early Christians by their pagan opponents, Christianity antedates modernity in its destruction of belief and the discovery of the 'lack of reality' of all representations. However, just as postmodernity moves beyond the suspicion characteristic of modernity in its ironic appropriation of representations through pastiche and bricolage, so too (though without irony) Christianity moves beyond suspicion in its proclamation of faith in Jesus Christ as God incarnate, the image of the invisible God (Colossians 1: 15).

In recent theology it is Hans Urs von Balthasar's theological aesthetics that is best known for stressing the importance of the 'form' (*Gestalt*) of revelation. Less well known is the historiographic scheme in which Balthasar locates his theological project.[12] According to Balthasar, the gospel first took root in a world that was viewed by its inhabitants as fundamentally sacred. The approach of the early apologists (e.g. Justin Martyr and Clement of Alexandria) was not to preach God's Word to a godless world, but to gather together into unity the fragmentary manifestations of the Word in the world (the *logoi spermatikoi*) through the proclamation of the personal incarnation of that Word in Jesus Christ. This provides an organizing and form-imparting center to the sacred cosmos of antiquity. As Balthasar puts it:

> All the unifying principles of the ancient world – such as the Logos of the stoics, the Neoplatonic hierarchy of being rising from matter to the supraessential One, the abstract majesty of the unifying power of Rome – all these were regarded as baptizable anticipations of the God–Logos in person who entered Israelite history, filled the whole world, in whom were the Ideas which were the pattern by which the world was made, and in relation to whom the world could be understood.
>
> (Balthasar 1968: 12–13)

In such a scheme the line between philosophy and theology, between faith and reason, could be extremely blurred, or indeed non-existent. This situation, and therefore this form of Christian theology, persists throughout the Middle Ages and into the Renaissance in such writings as Thomas More's *Utopia*, in which, says Balthasar, the 'natural' religion of the inhabitants of Utopia is 'a reduction of Christianity to its simplest, most luminous truths' (p. 18).

Yet in Renaissance humanism the seeds are sown for a new worldview, and therefore a new fundamental approach for theology. Balthasar declares that:

> In place of the world-immanent Logos of the ancient world there slipped in unnoticed 'natural' religion, ethics and philosophy, corresponding to the nature common to all races, peoples and ages; one part of revelation was regarded as belonging to this natural religion . . . while the other part was regarded as belonging to the 'positive' religions (Christian and others), so that these positive religions were more and more insistently called upon to justify themselves before the judgement-seat of the religion of mankind.
>
> (Balthasar 1968: 20)

In other words, in a world disenchanted by human reason, it is the human being rather than the cosmos who becomes the backdrop against which revelation takes place. Thus, as Balthasar writes, 'the attempt was made to transfer the locus of verification from a cosmos becoming more and more godless (and so having less and less in common with Christianity) to man as the epitome of the world' (p. 25). Such a shift is implicit in the sixteenth century – e.g. in Luther's question: 'How can I find a gracious God?' – but comes fully into view with the post-Kantian theology of Schleiermacher. Balthasar notes that in Schleiermacher's theology Christology is subsumed under the consciousness of salvation as its precondition, so that '[o]nly in relation to the pious consciousness are dogmatic propositions in general to be called scientific' (p. 31). Theological propositions no longer find their intelligibility in the context of the cosmos, but become descriptions of human self-consciousness. Consequently their 'reality' becomes questionable: is the source of the feeling of absolute dependence – the absolute subjectivity that stands in tension with our finite subjectivity – simply, *à la* Fichte, the formal and transcendental structure of the human person? Is it not the case, as Feuerbach argued, that talk about God is a fundamentally alienated and deceptive mode of speaking about human beings? What compelling reason can one give to move beyond the anthropological referent to some purported divine referent? Thus, even apart from any postmodern critique of the notion 'man' as, in Foucault's famous words, 'an invention of recent date' that is perhaps destined to 'be erased, like a face drawn in sand at the edge of the sea,'[13] there are strong theological grounds for being wary of the attempt to ground theology in anthropology.

After the desacralization of the cosmos coincident with the modern turn to the subject, and after the modern subject's theological collapse upon itself, what is left? It is at this point that Balthasar puts forward what he calls 'the third way of love,' which can be approached from two different paths. The first is the path of 'personalism' – the confrontation of the 'I' with the irreducible otherness of 'thou' (p. 38) – and the second is the path of aesthetics – the confrontation of the perceiver with the 'inner, unfathomable necessity' of the beautiful object (p. 44). Both of these modes of encounter indicate a kind of thinking, a *logos*, that neither simply reads truth off of the surface of the cosmos nor discovers it in the depths of the self, but which dwells in a space of interlocution between self and other. Still, these modes of encounter are insufficient in themselves, for they 'can at most provide us with a pointer, a signpost suggesting the direction in which to look for the specifically Christian' (p. 45). And that toward which they point us is the Word that God speaks to humanity, 'the Son interpreting the Father through the Holy Spirit as divine love' (p. 47).

Thus the third alternative that Balthasar presents us with is a theological aesthetics in which the sublime unrepresentability of God is taken up with full seriousness. Though ancient and medieval writers are mined for insights that have been lost in modernity, no appeal is made to the premodern sacred cosmos that transparently radiates divine wisdom. Balthasar accepts, at least on a certain level, the brute opacity of modernity's mechanized and quantified universe, in which 'all the evidence. . . seems to point to a world devoid of love' (p. 115). Balthasar seeks not a path backward, prior to suspicion, but a path forward, beyond suspicion, to a kind of Kierkegaardian 'immediacy after reflection.' It is simply facile to consign him, as David Tracy does, to the dustbin of 'antimodernity.'[14] The modern destruction of the ancient sacred cosmos is seen by Balthasar (rightly or wrongly) as a *fait accompli* of intellectual history, and one that should be accepted on Christian grounds as giving a clarity previously lacking to the distinction between creator and creation.

It is true, however, that the path forward that he seeks is not one that accepts as enduring achievements the speculative and emancipatory master narratives of modernity, for to proceed with these as baggage is to continue the self-defeating project of modern theology.[15] One might say that just as modern aesthetics sought to register the sublime by stripping away superfluous ornamentation in the pursuit of pure functionality, so too the modern theological project has been to seek the 'essence' of 'religion' by clearing the ground of dogmatic, ritual, and narrative accretions. And when this essence is found, it is found as a certain kind of experience, just as for Kant the sublime is registered as a certain expansion of the soul. Once this essential experience is distilled, it may be left bare or the 'ornaments' of doctrine, ritual, and narrative may be brought back in, but the basic impulse with which one starts is still the same as in modern aesthetics: a reduction to that which is essential. And granted that basic impulse, it is difficult not to treat doctrine, ritual, and narrative as 'mere' ornamentation. This can be seen in the theology of Karl Rahner. He clearly stresses the importance of categorical experience of God associated with doctrines, rituals, and narratives as 'the necessary but historical and objectifying self-interpretation of the transcendental experience which constitutes the realization of man's essence.'[16] However, when it comes to the '*reductio in mysterium*' of the Christian life, Rahner considers that while a Christian does indeed live a tangible and ecclesial life . . . the ultimately Christian thing about this life is identical with the mystery of human existence. . . . And to this extent to be a Christian is simply to be a human being, and one who also knows that this life which he is living, and which he is consciously living, can also be lived even by a person who is not a Christian explicitly and does not know in a reflexive way that he is a Christian.[17]

It is difficult to see how one could avoid a certain ironic stance toward the contingent particularities of Christian story and practice once one has glimpsed the truth that the Christian life is ultimately the same thing as authentic human existence. Perhaps the best one could hope for would be to maintain a sentimental attachment to those particularities.[18]

Balthasar's theological aesthetic is fundamentally different, for he seeks the unrepresentable mystery of God not through abstraction from particular categorically apprehended forms, but precisely *in* those forms, viewed in light of the glory revealed in the Christ-form.[19] He declares:

The distinctive Christian factor is that here we not only 'start from' the corporeal and the sensory as from some religious material on which we can then perform the necessary abstractions; rather, we abide in the seeing, hearing, touching, the savouring and eating of this flesh and blood, which has borne and taken away the sins of the world.[20]

One does not move beyond the particularities of the presentation to their essence. In this sense, a true theological aesthetic, like Lyotard's postmodern aesthetic, 'puts forward the unpresentable in presentation itself', because it proclaims Christ as the filial image of the paternal *archē* – an image that is 'equal' to that which it images. As Balthasar expresses it: the form of revelation does not present itself as an independent image of God, standing over against what is imaged, but as a unique hypostatic union between archetype and image' (1982: 432). The sublime archetype is in the form; one might say that the form is the 'real presence' of the archetype.

Further, one might say that for Balthasar, as for Lyotard, the sublime is put forward through the *shattering* of aesthetic form: 'it is only through being fragmented that the beautiful really reveals the meaning of the eschatological promise it contains' (1982: 460). But before we effect a *rapprochement* between Balthasar and Lyotard, it is important to mark a crucial difference, one that in fact makes any reconciliation between the two impossible. As I said earlier, Lyotard's aesthetic remains one that is bound to an emancipatory narrative and therefore, I have argued, fundamentally a modern one. The sublime that is presented in presentation itself is in fact the rapturous tremors of the strong poet's will to power as it shatters and reassembles previous forms. For Balthasar, on the other hand, it is *one particular* fragmented form that reveals the eschatological promise of the beautiful:

what he calls the Christ-form. One might put this in Lyotard's terms by saying that for Balthasar there is in fact a master narrative that speaks the truth of the world. This is a fragmented, *crucified*, narrative, but it is still *one* narrative, which presents the glory of the triune God's differentiated unity.

Balthasar notes that 'Christ's mediating form is multiple . . . in its very exercise, and yet this multiplicity can ever give expression only to the one form' (1982: 529). In explaining this multiplicity Balthasar appeals to the ancient notion of the *corpus triforme*, or the three-fold body of Christ: his 'natural' body that was born of the Virgin Mary and ascended into heaven, his ecclesial body; and his eucharistic body (in which Balthasar includes also Christ's scriptural 'body').[21] In what follows I will not follow Balthasar's specific discussion of the three-fold body of Christ. Rather, I will take it as a pattern that can help us understand Jesus Christ as the sacrament of God, the Church as the sacrament of Christ, and the Eucharist as the sacrament that, in Henri de Lubac's phrase, 'makes the Church.' In presenting this three-fold body I attempt to sound themes that I have alluded to earlier, which are sometimes thought of as distinctively 'postmodern' – negation, bricolage, and alterity. The theological reading of these themes, however, can perhaps move us beyond suspicion toward a theological realism.

The threefold *corpus Christi*

Negation: the body of Jesus

The primary referent of the phrase *corpus Christi* is the human flesh of Jesus, his natural body, and by extension his human nature as a whole. This human nature is the 'primordial sacrament' because it is the sign and instrumental cause of human salvation.[22] As Aquinas says, it is the 'flesh [*caro*]' of Christ 'and the mysteries accomplished therein [*et mysteria in ea perpetrata*]' that is both instrumental and exemplary cause of grace (ST III.62.5.ad 1). In what Jesus does and suffers in his human history – the intention-laden events of his flesh – we are presented with nothing less than the life of God, and through the instrumentality of the action and passion of that history divine life is communicated to us.

This notion of Christ as the sacrament of God is the foundation of any Christian theological aesthetic that seeks to move beyond the modern *aporia* of the sublime. Jesus is the 'effective' or 'causal' sign of the saving presence of God. His death and resurrection are the 'sign of Jonah,' the only sign that is given (Matthew 12: 38–40), and they present us with the reality of God as triune love, and not simply a representation of that reality. This is not to collapse the distinction between visible sign and fundamentally invisible referent, for to do so would be to obliterate the gracious distance between God and creation (thus the distinction between the immanent and economic Trinity remains a relevant one). But it is to claim that the sign (the human nature of Christ) is 'assumed' by the reality (the Word of God) into a personal union in which there is, in the words of Chalcedon, difference without division or separation. This distinction or 'distance' between sign and referent is not a division only if it is, to borrow a phrase from Jean-Luc Marion, 'saturated' by the referent, and this is in part what the Christian tradition has meant by 'hypostatic union.'[23]

As befits a visible presentation of that which is fundamentally beyond presentation, Christ is a sign of contradiction (Luke 2: 34) – the form (μορφή) of God become the form of a slave (Philippians 2).[24] Jesus is a sign *sous rature*; his whole life is one of negation of himself so as to be a sign that is transparent to the will of the Father (John 4: 34; 14: 7). Thus it is the cross and resurrection that have been the focal points for understanding the saving work of Jesus. It is in the fragmentation of his crucified body and the unrecognizableness, apart from his self-revelation, of his resurrected body that, from a human point of view, Jesus's human nature attains its perfection as the sacrament of the God who is beyond human representation. The cross, the tomb, the way to Emmaus: all places of negation, of vanishing. At the same time, the transparency of the sign does not make it, in all of its contingent particularities, nugatory. For it is this *particular* negation (cross and resurrection) of this *particular* sign (Jesus of Nazareth) that moves us beyond mere negation of meaning to an excess of meaning.

Of course, how we read this sign depends on the larger narrative in which we locate it. When placed within a master narrative of emancipation, even the shattering of the Christ-form could appear – as it did for Nietzsche – as a manifestation of the will to power. But when we start from the narrative of the cross – the narrative of power as the kenotic donation of being on those things that are not (Romans 4: 17) – and we let this narrative shape our perception of the sign, then its negation is not will to power but love unto death. Balthasar writes:

> God's incomprehensibility is now no longer a mere deficiency in knowledge, but the positive manner in which God determines the knowledge of faith: this is the overwhelming inconceivability of the fact that God has loved us so much that he surrendered his only Son for us, the fact that the God of plenitude has poured himself out, not only into creation, but emptied himself into the modalities of an existence determined by sin, corrupted by death and alienated from God. This is the concealment that appears in his self-revelation; this is the ungraspability of God, which becomes graspable because it *is* grasped.[25]

The sublime is not the will to power, but the outpouring in love of God's plenitude, even to the ultimate point of human sin and alienation.[26]

One might, of course, posit a different 'postmodern' reading of Christ, one that takes its cue from the proclaimed end of metanarratives. In this reading the 'decentering' of postmodernity makes the Christocentric account of God that I have sketched highly problematic. Jesus can be at best one of the plurality of manifestations of the divine; his self-negation includes his negation as privileged sign. As Paul Lakeland puts it, 'the particularity lies in the messenger, not the message.'[27] In other words, Jesus is a particular messenger who bears a universal message – one borne by many others. From this perspective, claiming the identity of message and messenger, the hypostatic union of referent and sign, makes the human history of Jesus into a master narrative. Yet this putatively postmodern Christology sounds quite similar to the liberal theology of Harnack and others (the Gospel *of* Jesus, not the Gospel *about* Jesus), which might lead us to ask whether such an approach really takes us beyond the master narratives of modernity.[28] In particular, it retains the modern suspicion of representation, the sense that there is some obscured message lurking *behind* its various messengers, and that there is some standpoint from which we can discern the fact of such a message, if not its content.

But the event of the cross presents us with a path beyond suspicion. It is not the path of the strong poet's Nietzschean confidence in his ability to master any and all master narratives through irony. Rather it is the hope that is given paradoxical voice in Christ's cry of dereliction, the hope given birth by the cross seen as a trinitarian event in which God's very being is extended to encompass even the ultimate alienation of hell and damnation, the hope beyond death that is awakened by Christ as he breaks bread with the disciples at Emmaus. We are no longer (or at least no longer take ourselves to be) citizens of the ancient cosmos imbued with the divine; our experience of the world is an experience of godlessness. But in the cross we are presented with a God who is present even in godlessness, and in the resurrection we are promised that godlessness shall not have the last word.[29]

This provides a ground of critique by which we might distinguish false representations of God from true or, perhaps more precisely, by which we might distinguish 'idols' (our representations of the divine) from 'icons' (God's self-presentation in revelation).[30] The 'cruciform' life of Jesus – and his life is cruciform in that it is lived in its entirety 'toward' the cross – serves as the norm of holiness, and all other claims to righteousness must fall under its critique. The cross and resurrection, in their very negativity and obscurity, become the icon by which God presents to us God's own unpresentable trinitarian life, and we are called not to irony, but to adoration and participation.

Bricolage: the ecclesial body

Yet we must take a further step. For the presentation of God in the negated sign of Jesus on the cross and in the resurrection – the shattering of the Christ-form by which it 'reveals the meaning of the eschatological promise it contains' – is an event that cannot be confined to a single moment in time, but is eucharistically extended through history in the Church. In John's Gospel Christ's side is pierced to bring forth sacramental water and blood (John 19: 34), a healing river flowing from the Lamb who reigns from the throne of the cross down through the middle of God's new city (Revelation 22: 1–2). Just as the postmodern sublime is figured through both the fragmentation of form and a (pseudo) regathering of that form through pastiche or bricolage, so too the Christian sublime involves both the shattering of the Christ-form upon the cross, and a regathering of that form through the resurrection, a regathering that has as an intrinsic element the regathering of the scattered disciples into an *ekklesia*, which is fused by pentecostal fire to become part of the form.[31] Balthasar affirms that: 'the Christ-form attains to its plastic fullness only through the dimension of the Holy Spirit – and this means also through the Church.'[32] Or, as Gregory of Nyssa put it even more boldly, 'he who sees the Church looks directly at Christ – Christ building and increasing by the addition of the elect.'[33]

Said differently, the Church is 'the universal sacrament of salvation.'[34] Though this notion of the Church as a sacrament has patristic roots, it owes its modern articulation not least to Henri de Lubac, who wrote in his 1938 book *Catholicism*: 'If Christ is the sacrament of God, the Church is for us the sacrament of Christ; she represents him, in the full and ancient meaning of the term; she really makes him present.'[35] The Church is the sacrament of Christ, according to the Dogmatic Constitution on the Church, in that it is 'a sign and instrument' of salvation understood as both 'union with God and . . . the unity of the whole human race.'[36] Otto Semmelroth notes that 'a sacrament is something eschatological in the sense that the "eschaton," the heavenly salvation we are yet to reach, has already invaded this world in the sacramental sign.'[37] It is an effective sign – not simply representing salvation but bringing it about. Again, the gap between sign and referent is saturated through the self-giving of the referent. Not, in this case, a hypostatic or personal union of two natures, but a union in love between head and members to form one communion in love. This union fills the gap that might call into question the veracity of the sign, so that, as John Zizioulas puts it, 'Christ Himself becomes revealed as truth not *in* a community, but *as* a community.'[38] It is the quality of life of those who are in Christ that manifests – or fails to manifest – the truth of Christ.

We might put this also in terms of the *totus Christus* of which Augustine wrote in his *Homilies on 1 John*. Because of the union of love between Christ and the Church, to speak of the whole Christ is to speak of both head and body.[39] Reflecting on the statements in 1 John that 'God is love' (4: 8) and that 'no one has even seen God' (4: 12), Augustine notes that the fundamentally invisible reality of God manifests itself not simply in Christ, the Word made flesh, laying down his life for us, but also through the manifold concrete acts of *caritas* enacted within the Body of Christ – gifts of alms and instruction, acts of adoration and attentiveness.[40] And acts of charity are not simply a way of showing forth the reality of God, but are themselves acts of seeing God: 'Love your brother; in loving your brother whom you see, you will see God at the same time. For you will see charity itself, and there within is God dwelling.'[41]

In the Church that is one yet is spread over all the earth, the invisible God becomes visible in a multitude of acts of charity, not as some original that is imitated – even for those who do them there is no way of seeing the original apart from these acts – but as the sublime that is presented in that multitude. As Lewis Ayres puts it, to live in ecclesial charity is to 'see' the Trinity; moreover, it is to become a mirror of the self-transcending *caritas* of Father, Son, and Spirit.[42] And this charity remains 'christomorphic,' judged and determined by Christ as the primal sacrament of God (and here one might speak properly of imitation). Thus pre-eminent among those actions that manifest the invisible reality of God are acts of forgiveness, particularly forgiveness extended to our enemies, by which we see them as the brothers and sisters for whom Christ died. This, for Augustine, is perfect love, for it enacts and manifests the charity shown by Christ on the cross.[43]

Again, if one takes the end of master narratives as the key feature of postmodernity, then one might argue for a different account of the Church from the one I have sketched here. The myth of the *totus Christus* would be simply one more example of a totalizing master narrative that, of its very nature, eradicates difference.[44] For it makes the Church, if not the sole locus of salvation, at least the point out of which salvation flows into the world. And if one accepts a 'polycentric' view of the world, then this is clearly unacceptable. A more truly postmodern role for the Church, on this reading, would be as the servant of the world. Rather than imposing its story on the world – or even proclaiming it to the world as the world's true story – the servant Church places itself at the world's disposal. Not, of course, uncritically. The Church must retain its prophetic role, but that prophetic role cannot be the preaching of Christ crucified or any other such particularistic story. For the story by which the Church lives is, at its very core, a partial one, and thus not in itself the source of the Church's critical judgements with regard to the world. What then can be the source of those judgements? It seems it would have to be some constellation of 'thin' human values, such as autonomy and self-determination. Again, as Paul Lakeland puts it, 'Prophecy today . . . is not a matter of presenting a substantive message to an uncomprehending multitude, but rather of demanding – through acting out – an uncompromising openness to the future revealed through unconstrained discourse.'[45] And thus it seems that we have returned to the emancipatory master narrative of modernity.

In what I am proposing, in contrast, the Christian community is called to be 'light to the world,' to speak and enact the story of Christ so as to give back to the world the story it has lost through sin. One might go so far as to say that because of the unity of the *totus Christus* the Church simply is that (eucharistically) enacted story. This story is complete, because perfectly enacted in the life of Christ, and at the same time yet to be fulfilled, as the sinful and repentant Church of tears journeys toward its eschatological wedding with the Lamb. It is thus in one sense a 'master narrative,' yet one that is pneumatologically constituted (or 'edified') by the sheer diversity of the gifts of the Spirit (1 Corinthians 12) and is fragmented into a multitude of eucharistic enactments – the Church in its fullness being present in each eucharistic community.[46] Similarly, the closure of the narrative awaits its eschatological consummation; final knowledge of who has in fact enacted that story and who will constitute the multitude gathered around the throne of the Lamb is deferred (Matthew 25: 31–46; Revelation 7: 9–17). It is for this reason that Henri de Lubac says of the Church that it is 'one living being' that is 'vivified by the one Spirit,' yet 'its scope remains God's secret.'[47]

Thus rather than having recourse to facile (and fundamentally deceptive) claims about the 'end of master narratives,' we may look to the narrative of the *totus Christus*, the narrative of the particular historical figure of Jesus of Nazareth raised in power to God's right hand, and of the body that claims that same Jesus as its head, the body animated by the Spirit with the diversity of gifts. This is the Spirit who, as Gerard Manley Hopkins put it, 'delights in multitude,' yet who is always the Spirit of Christ, and thus conforms that multitude to him. Hopkins wrote that

> as the breath is drawn from the boundless air into the lungs and from the lungs again is breathed out and melts into the boundless air so the Spirit of God was poured out from the infinite God upon Christ's human nature and by Christ, who said: Receive the Holy Ghost: as my Father sent me so I send you, was breathed into his Apostles and by degrees into the millions of his Church, till the new heavens and new earth will at last be filled with it.[48]

The Spirit is the ecclesial *bricoleur*, that blows where it will, along whose errant path the *ekklesia* is gathered from the world into Christ's body, only to be impelled forth again by that same Spirit, to dwell in peace among the nations.

Alterity: the eucharistic body

We must take one final step. If Christ is the sacrament of God, and the Church is the sacrament of Christ, then the Eucharist is the sacrament of the Church, since it is the 'sign and cause' by which the Church is constituted in union with Christ its head. Again to quote Henri de Lubac, 'the Eucharist makes the Church.'[49] A certain 'eucharistic realism' is a corollary of an 'ecclesial realism' that sees the Church as the *corpus verum*, the true body of Christ.[50]

The Eucharist is thus not simply a reproduction, whether psychological or metaphysical, of a past reality, but it is a genuine production – an 'edification' or building up – of the present and future reality of the Church.[51] Here again we have a complex play of depth and surface or, in scholastic language, of *res* and *sacramentum*. The reality (*res*) which is to be signified is the unity in love of the *totus Christus* – the unity of the members among themselves and with Christ as their head. But this reality is not, as it were, self-subsisting, but is produced through the instrumentality of the sign (*sacramentum*) of bread and wine, through which the power of Christ's eucharistic body, which is both reality and sign (*res et sacramentum*), is exercised.[52] This odd category of that which is both reality-and-sign seeks to articulate the coinhabitation of depth and surface: it is through the Church's visible ritual action with bread and wine that the Church herself is produced as body of Christ: the agent is produced as it 'exteriorizes' itself in action. But this is the case only because something quite *other* than either simply sign or reality intervenes – the reality-and-sign of the eucharistic Christ. Only if Christ is present in the eucharist as *res et sacramentum* can the skeptical gap between reality and signs be bridged. Again, the gap between sign and referent is 'saturated' by that which is both sign *and* referent.

A similar point has been argued by Jean-Luc Marion in his defense of the traditional doctrine of transubstantiation in the face of various attempts to refor-mulate it in 'nonmetaphysical' terms, such as transignification. His fear is that attempts to articulate the eucharistic event in terms of meaning will end up reduc-ing the eucharistic presence to a matter of the consciousness of the celebrating community.[53] Though he does not put it this way, one might say that he fears that transignification in the end capitulates to Feuerbach: the Eucharist is finally a matter of humanity's coming to consciousness of itself. In contrast, for Marion the doctrine of transubstantiation means that 'the consecrated host imposes, or rather permits . . . the irreducible exteriority of the present that Christ makes of himself in this thing that to him becomes sacramental body.'[54] The irreducible exteriority of the doctrine of transubstantiation makes it possible to understand the Eucharist according to a 'christic temporality,' in which real presence is the present, under-stood not (metaphysically) as the stable given of the here-and-now, but as the gift of the present, both memorial (or, perhaps better, *anamnesis*) of the covenant pledged in the past and a stretching out in hope toward the eschatological future.[55]

Whether or not one agrees with Marion's argument that *only* the doctrine of transubstantiation secures the irreducible exteriority of the eucharistic Other,[56] he makes a compelling case for the claim that only if the Other who is encountered in the Eucharist is not determined by human consciousness, but rather determines human consciousness – *saturates* human consciousness – can the Eucharist be any-thing other than idolatry and the eucharistic community anything other than one more human community. Of course, for those who would see postmodernity as the end of metanarrative, all that the Church *should* claim to be is one human response in faith to the experience of the divine although one may suspect that it is merely a human mystification of the workings of power.[57] Similarly, to claim that eucharis-tic worship is more than simply one human language game among others, to claim that it is an act of divine speech through the priest acting *in persona Christi*, which brings about a 'substantial' change, seems thoroughly 'metaphysical.' But if Marion is correct, only a divine discourse that breaks into and breaks apart human speech can in fact rupture the totalizing discourse of metaphysics; it is only such a claim that can in fact confront us with a God who is truly other, without delivering that Other to us as an effect of our consciousness.[58]

Thus, perhaps oddly, eucharistic discourse as master narrative does not obliter-ate otherness but in fact instantiates it as 'irreducible exteriority.' It recalls to us that the Church is not simply the body of Christ, but also the bride who receives as gift the body of her divine spouse. Separated from 'eucharistic realism,' 'ecclesial real-ism' can domesticate the relationship between Christ and the Church into a kind of auto-eroticism that makes the self-donation of one to the other impossible. The gap between bride and spouse must be saturated by the Spirit who only intensifies the bride's longing for the return of her bridegroom: 'The Spirit and the bride say, "Come." And let everyone who hears say, "Come."' (Revelation 22: 17).

But the story does not end here. The union of bride and spouse is not simply an ecclesial romance, but the occasion for a banquet to which countless particular human 'others' are invited. The mutual hospitality of bride and spouse toward each other opens out to become coextensive with hospitality toward all who hunger or thirst or are naked or imprisoned (Matthew 25: 34–40). Thus it is that the bride's invitation to her spouse overflows immediately into an invitation to all: 'And let everyone who is thirsty come. Let anyone who wishes take the water of life as a gift' (Revelation 22: 17).

Conclusion

If the claim to be living at the end of modernity means that modern confidence in human reason's capacity to tell the world's true story has come to an end, and that we are thus at the end of all master narratives, of all attempts to articulate the *one* true story of the world, or even of the attempt to construe the world as *having* a single story, then theology must say 'yes' and 'no' at the same time. Inasmuch as modernity has been the attempt to ground human reason in itself and has sundered 'necessary truth of reason' from 'accidental truths of history,' theology may welcome claims to its demise as opening a path beyond suspicion. And such characteristically postmodern notions as negation, bricolage, and alterity may prove tactically useful in preaching and understanding the gospel. But theology cannot tie its fate to postmodernity, for modernity has also been an exercise in human self-assertion and in this sense much of so-called postmodernity is simply a nihilistic intensification of the modern project. The claim to be at the end of all master narratives may simply be a covert way of liberating the self from any claims upon it. Theology, however, is the language given to a community, the *ekklesia* that exists only insofar as it is called and claimed by God. It is this call and claim that beckons the bride on her pilgrimage to the banquet of the Lamb, passing from premodernity through modernity to postmodernity . . . to whatever lies beyond.

Notes

1 For a partial catalogue of instances of the use of the term 'postmodern' (or 'postmodern') dating back to 1934, see Margaret A. Rose, *The Post-Modern and the Post-Industrial: A Critical Analysis* (Cambridge: Cambridge University Press, 1991), pp. 171–175. For a genealogy and analysis of the postmodern in relation to theology (including the distinction between 'postmodernity' and 'postmodernism') see Graham Ward, 'Introduction, or, A Guide to Theological Thinking in Cyberspace,' in *The Postmodern God: A Theological Reader*, ed. Graham Ward (Oxford: Blackwell Publishers, 1997).

2 According to Lyotard, the narrative form of knowledge is the most basic form, and even science has recourse to narrative for its legitimation. See *The Postmodern Condition: A Report on Knowledge*, trans. Geoff Bennington and Brian Massumi (Minneapolis: University of Minnesota Press, 1984), p. 29 (parenthetical references in what follows are to this text). However, the modern master narratives by which knowledge was legitimated – which he describes as the speculative (Hegel) and the emancipatory (Kant, Marx) – have been fragmented into a multitude of language games that cannot be 'unified or totalized in any metadiscourse' (p. 36). What we are left with is *local* knowledge, fragmentary knowledge, knowledge of how to go on in this or that particular instance, but not of how to go on 'in principle.'

3 See Hans Blumenburg, *The Legitimacy of the Modern Age*, trans. Robert M. Wallace (Cambridge, MA: The MIT Press, 1983). Reading human self–assertion as the defining trait of modernity suggests how thinkers as different as Descartes and Nietzsche can both properly be called 'modern.'

4 Kant, *The Critique of Judgement*, §29.

5 Deleuze, *Kant's Critical Philosophy*, trans. Hugh Tomlinson and Barbara Habberjam (Minneapolis: University of Minnesota Press, 1993), p. 50.

6 See *The Postmodern Condition*, pp. 80–81.

7 For the post-structuralist appropriation of Levi-Strauss' notion of *bricolage*, see Jacques Derrida, 'Structure, Sign and Play in the Discourse of the Human Sciences,' in *Writing and Difference*, trans. Alan Bass (Chicago: University of Chicago Press, 1978), pp. 278–293.

8 Or so it seems. In 'Denegating God', *Critical Inquiry* 20:4 (1994), pp. 592–610, Taylor seems to want to retain 'the sacred' as that which remains after the death of God, 'a lack that leaves us wanting' (p. 609). However, Taylor's account of the sacred strikes me as simply atheism in vestments.

9 In its accession to the givenness of the 'situation' which determines what is and is not possible for theology, such a view resembles Rudolph Bultmann's famous statement: 'We cannot use electric lights and radios and, in the event of illness, avail ourselves of modern medical and clinical means and at the same time believe in the spirit and wonder world of the New Testament' ('New Testament and Mythology: The Problem of Demythologizing the New Testament Proclamation' (1941), in *New Testament and Mythology and Other Basic Writings*, ed. and trans. Schubert M. Ogden (Philadelphia: Fortress Press, 1984), p. 4.

10 For such a self-described 'weak' postmodern position, see Paul Lakeland, *Postmodernity: Christian Identity in a Fragmented Age* (Philadelphia: Fortress Press, 1997). We will have recourse to Lakeland later as an example of one understanding of postmodernity, though of course there is a perhaps infinite variety of positions that might claim this name.

11 Gotthold Friedrich Lessing, 'On the Proof of the Spirit and of Power' in *Lessing's Theological Writings*, trans. Henry Chadwick (Stanford, CA: Stanford University Press, 1956).

12 This is most fully spelled out in *The Glory of the Lord: A Theological Aesthetics*, volume 4, *The Realm of Metaphysics in Antiquity*, and volume 5, *The Realm of Metaphysics in Modernity*. However a more succinct – and therefore clearer – presentation of Balthasar's historiography can be found in the first three chapters of his little book *Love Alone: The Way of Revelation*, trans. Alexander Dru (London: Burns & Oates, 1968). Parenthetical references in what follows are to this text.

13 *The Order of Things: An Archeology of the Human Sciences* (New York: Random House, 1970), p. 387.

14 See David Tracy, 'On Naming the Present,' in *On Naming the Present: Reflections on God, Hermeneutics, and Church* (Maryknoll, NY: Orbis Books, 1994), pp. 3–24.

15 In this sense there clearly *is* a distinction between the postmodernity of Tracy or Lakeland (see above, notes 10 and 14), which has affinities with Habermas's call to 'complete' modernity, and that of Balthasar, which takes more seriously the need to sublate 'epic' (the speculative narrative) and 'lyric' (the emancipatory narrative) into 'drama.'

16 *Foundations of the Christian Faith: An Introduction to the Idea of Christianity*, trans. William V. Dych (New York: Crossroad, 1987), p. 153.

17 *Ibid.*, p. 430.

18 It is possible to read Rahner's transcendental method as more an *ad hoc* technique. See Fergus Kerr, *Immortal Longings: Versions of Transcending Humanity* (Notre Dame, IN: University of Notre Dame Press, 1997), pp. 173–184.

19 For an admirably clear and balanced examination of the philosophical roots of the

disagreement between Rahner and Balthasar, see Rowan Williams, 'Balthasar and Rahner,' in *The Analogy of Beauty: The Theology of Hans Urs von Balthasasar*, ed. John Riches (Edinburgh: T. & T. Clark, 1986), pp. 11–34.

20 *The Glory of the Lord: A Theological Aesthetics*, volume I: *Seeing the Form*, trans. Erasmo Leiva-Merikakis (San Francisco: Ignatius Press, 1982), pp. 313–314. Parenthetical references in what follows are to this text.

21 *The Glory of the Lord*, I, pp. 529–531. Balthasar's discussion of the *corpus triforme* is somewhat confusing, in part because he does not clearly delineate what the three bodies are (something that is not clarified by his combining the eucharistic and scriptural bodies of Christ). No doubt this lack of clear delineation is in part a witness to the ultimate unity of Christ's body, though it may testify also to a conceptual unclarity on Balthasar's part. Also, the notion of the *corpus triforme* itself has a very complex historical development, and there are in fact several, not always compatible, versions of this three-fold body of Christ, relating particularly to whether the term is used in connection with scriptural exegesis or liturgical commentary. My appropriation draws from the exegetical tradition. See Henri de Lubac, *Corpus Mysticum: L'Eucharistie et l'Église au Moyen-Age*, 2nd edn (Paris: Aubier, 1948), *passim*.

22 See Edward Schillebeeckx, *Christ the Sacrament of the Encounter with God* (New York: Sheed & Ward, 1963), p. 15.

23 Jean-Luc Marion, *God Without Being: Hors Texte*, trans. Thomas A. Carlson (Chicago: University of Chicago Press, 1991), pp. 46, 156. For a fuller development of the notion of 'the saturated phenomenon' as a philosophical concept that opens out toward the possibility of divine revelation, see Jean-Luc Marion, 'Le phénomène saturé' in *Phénoménologie et théologie*, J.-F. Courtine, ed. (Paris: Criterion, 1993), pp. 79–128. In this essay Marion sketches a phenomenology that overcomes the Cartesian and Kantian commitment to the paradigmatic status of phenomena that are 'poor in intuition' in favor of those that are 'saturated,' in particular those of historical events and revelation.

24 Note that in Philippians Paul speaks of the μορφη of God, not the ειδος. While we should not try to get too much philosophical mileage out of this, we might simply note that Paul wishes to speak of a divine 'shape' and not simply a divine 'idea' (though the relationship between μορφη and ειδος is a complicated one).

25 *The Glory of the Lord*, I, p. 461.

26 Hence the importance played in Balthasar's narrative by Holy Saturday. See *Mysterium Paschale*, trans. Aidan Nichols OP (Edinburgh: T. & T. Clark, 1990), pp. 148–188.

27 Lakeland, *Postmodernity*, p. 112.

28 See Harnack, *What Is Christianity?* trans. Thomas Bailey Saunders (Philadelphia: Fortress Press, 1986 [1900]), pp. 142–146.

29 One might compare Simone Weil's 'The Love of God and Affliction,' in *Waiting for God*, trans. Emma Craufurd (New York: Harper & Row, 1951), pp. 117–136.

30 See Marion, *God Without Being*, pp. 7–24.

31 This is not to say that the resurrection simply *is* the regathering of the community. On the relationship between the resurrection and the regathering of the disciples, see Rowan Williams, *Resurrection: Interpreting the Easter Gospel* (Harrisburg, PA: Morehouse Publishing, 1994), especially chs 3–5.

32 *The Glory of the Lord*, I, p. 408.

33 Gregory of Nyssa, *Commentary on the Song of Songs*, Sermon 13, in *From Glory to Glory: Texts from Gregory of Nyssa's Mystical Writings*, selected and with an Introduction by Jean Daniélou SJ, trans. and ed. Herbert Musurillo SJ (Crestwood, NY: St Vladimir's Seminary Press, 1995), p. 272.

34 *Lumen Gentium* (Dogmatic Constitution on the Church), §48.

35 Henri de Lubac, *Catholicism: Christ and the Common Destiny of Man*, trans. Lancelot C. Sheppard and Sr Elizabeth Englund OCD (San Francisco: Ignatius Press, 1988), p. 76.

36 *Lumen Gentium*, §1.

37 *Commentary on the Documents of Vatican II*, volume 1, ed. Herbert Vorgrimler (New York: Herder & Herder, 1967), p. 282.

38 John D. Zizioulas, *Being as Communion: Studies in Personhood and the Church* (Crestwood, NY: St Vladimir's Seminary Press, 1985), p. 115.

39 Homily 1.2 in *Augustine: Later Works*, ed. and trans. John Burnaby (Philadelphia: The Westminster Press, 1955), p. 261. In what follows in this paragraph I am indebted to Lewis Ayres's essay 'Augustine on God as Love and Love as God,' *Pro Ecclesia* V: 4 (Fall 1996), pp. 470–487.

40 See Homily 7.10 (*Later Works*, p. 317).

41 Homily 5.7 (*Later Works*, p. 299).

42 Ayres, pp. 485–487. On the Trinity as *caritas* that transcends the mutual love of one for another, so as to engender a third, the *locus classicus* is Richard of St Victor's *De Trinitate*, Book III.

43 Homily 1.9 (*Later Works*, p. 266); Homily 9.3 (p. 331).

44 For this claim about master narratives, see Lakeland, *Postmodernity*, pp. 30–36.

45 Lakeland, *Postmodernity*, p. 105. For Lakeland's 'weak' postmodern account of the Church, see pp. 101–107.

46 On the eucharistic assembly as the fullness of the Church, see *Lumen Gentium*, §26. On the Church as comprised of *charismata*, see Zizioulas, *Being as Communion*, p. 111.

47 De Lubac, *Catholicism*, p. 47.

48 *The Sermons and Devotional Writings of Gerard Manley Hopkins*, ed. Christopher Devlin SJ (London: Oxford University Press, 1959), p. 98.

49 De Lubac, *Corpus Mysticum*, p. 104.

50 *Ibid.*, p. 283.

51 *Ibid.*, pp. 79–80.

52 The historical development of this terminology, and consequently its use in any particular instance, is quite complex. See *ibid.*, pp. 189–209.

53 Marion writes: 'The immediate consciousness of the collective self hence produces the first appearance of the presence of "God" to the community. The (human and representational) present commands the future of divine presence' (*God Without Being*, p. 167).

54 *Ibid.*, p. 169.

55 *Ibid.*, pp. 172–176.

56 See Gerard Loughlin, *Telling God's Story* (Cambridge: Cambridge University Press, 1996), pp. 234–237, for a defense of what might be called transignification – or at least Herbert McCabe's version of it – against Marion's critique. It strikes me that the primary object of Marion's critique is not so much contemporary Catholic reformulations of transubstantiation (though these may fall more generally under that critique) as it is Hegel's remarks on the 'externality' of Catholicism. See Hegel, *The Philosophy of History*, trans. J. Sibree (New York: Dover Publications, 1956), pp. 377–378.

57 The former view can be found in Lakeland's understanding of the Church as one form among others of 'faithful sociality.' See *Postmodernity*, p. 60.

58 One must keep in mind that Marion uses 'metaphysics' in a highly specific way, referring to 'the system of philosophy from Suarez to Kant, as a single science concerned both with what is universal in "common being" (*l'étant commun*) and in "essence" (or "essences")' (Jean-Luc Marion, 'Metaphysics and Phenomenology: A Summary for Theologians' in Graham Ward, *The Postmodern God*, pp. 279–296, at p. 281).

11

PERCEPTION

From modern painting to the vision in Christ*

Phillip Blond

La question de la peinture n'appartient ni d'abord, ni uniquement
aux peintres, moins encore aux esthéticians. Elle appartient à la vis-
ibilité elle-même, donc à tous – à la sensation commune.
(Jean-Luc Marion[1])

I would like to begin with a claim as to what art is, or should be, for any account
of aesthetics that would seek to be equal with its object. Art, should be an account
of, and a meditation upon, our relationship to what we are given. And the given
must be that against which we measure ourselves and all of our projects, be they
theological, philosophical or aesthetic, because any departure from *what is* and its
presentation to us, in the name and pursuit of what is not, is a refusal to see,
acknowledge, or fulfill the promise of worldly creation. And, as such, any departure
from the materiality of *this* world in search of a reality beyond the reality we
inhabit is a form of metaphysics as it seeks the truth of nature beyond nature in a
realm unseen and unheard by any natural beings. A not unimportant consequence
of this metaphysics is the ubiquitous denial that *what is* conveys anything fundamental or decisive about human beings and their world at all. Consequently the
actuality of the world is stripped of any integral goodness, beauty or truth that it
might once have been thought to disclose, because for this era *what is* does not
convey what should be and what should not; it shows only one arbitary possibility,
a possibility that has no inherent right to be anything at all.

However, the question as to 'what is' as opposed to 'what is not,' and the issue of
'what should be' as opposed to 'what should not,' are perennial matters for philosophical discussion. None the less the resolution of these questions has taken
decidedly different shapes in different epochs. For example, it is only in our present
age that we have held that that which is ideal *is not*, whereas that remaining 'reality' which is not ideal *is*. Apparently, for us moderns, it is entirely appropriate to

* I would like to thank both Oliver Soskice and Conor Cunningham for conversations that I had with
them about various aspects of this essay.

separate ideality from reality, as reality has nothing of the ideal in it; the belief being that reality presents itself to us outside of and apart from any transcendent form as a simple, brute, ever-changing phenomenon, a formless appearance that has no internal temporal coherence or spatial stability. On this account modern ideality has abandoned any location or expression in the world, to reside only in the head, claiming not to lie in the things themselves but in the human mind. Nowadays ideality is thought only through the guise of modern transcendentalism, and it is thought to be that which is the precondition of there being any reality at all. Ideality is thought of as a non-empirical creation of the mind, a mental creation that alone can make reality come into being.

Ideality reduced to a merely mental existence by transcendental idealism is thought to provide form and shape to the Heraclitean flux of sensible intuitions by placing empirical sensations under the rules and sets of its own understanding, completing sensations or rather making them possible by synthesizing the diverse formlessness of materiality into those discrete informed perceptions of which the mind is able to make sense.

This modern separation of ideality from materiality has had several consequences, a number of which are now well known and much discussed. For if post-modernity represents the logical culmination of modernity – a modernity whose circular, self-validating, claims to found its rationality on an ideality reducible to itself have now been exposed – then all the requisite relativism, groundlessness and nihilism of the postmodern situation testifies to a need to re-articulate and re-describe the relation between the ideal and the real that modernity has so evidently misconstrued.

But what force or position can adequately rethink this modern separation of ideality from reality? This separation has produced only a materialism that claims to be a self-sufficient account of reality or a self-sustaining idealism that neither requires nor seeks any actuality at all. The trouble is that these seemingly opposed positions are essentially the same, as each sees no other cause of what is beyond the immediately given. As such the division of the ideal from the real reveals its true teleology and inheritance: self-sufficient immanentism. This situation then reveals to us another problematic: how can that which is ideal be restored to that which is real without collapsing the ideal into the real, or the real into the ideal ? The claim of this essay is that it is only Christianity that can now escape the modern separation of ideality from reality and their subsequent reduction to each other, because it seems that only in Christian theology does the ideal visibly and sensately persist in our reality without this ideality ever being reduced to our reception of it. For if indeed, as Christianity suggests, this material reality we inhabit is a God-given participation by us in him and his ideality, then we can never be equal to the gifts we are given, not least because we are not God and cannot engender the ideal out of ourselves and so provide our own foundation. Theology, then, re-describes the created world, not as nothing, nor indeed as any self-sufficient something, but as the real testimony and loving expression of God who donates the ideal to the real in order that we might make it so. This donation, as most fully expressed by the incarnation of the Most High in the human form and reality of Christ, has forever and for all time fused together ideality and reality and forbidden any faithful perception of the world from ever again dividing them from each other again.

If our created order is the sphere wherein the ideal and the real meet and make a world, what form of perception or aesthetic could show us that this was indeed the case? What type of vision would be adequate to ascertain the nature of such a world? Obviously it would require a higher aesthetic, an account of visibility that we have long ceased to recognise or acknowledge in our aesthetic practices, our art and our painting. But rather than begin with any assertion, it may well be better to describe where our modern alienated aesthetic has come from, to have taken us to such a nihilated and hopeless account of the material world: a world whose actuality has been stripped of any integral value or meaning by an aesthetic that shows no recognition or belief that anything ideal resides in the reality that we all inhabit.

Vision and painting

Impressionism and the path from objectivity to subjectivity

I remain in the grip of sense-perceptions and . . . riveted to painting.
(Cézanne, 27 June 1904)

What, though, of the vision in painting? If theology can sustain a visible relationship with the ideal, can painting? For if theology is intimately bound up with the visible and sensate disclosure of the ideal in the real, then surely theology would have serious problems claiming an affinity with any art that would break from, or, at the very least, distance itself from the real and its attempted representation. And, unfortunately, this break with objective accounts of reality is exactly how, we are told, modern art understands and distinguishes itself from that which preceded it.

Thus we find Roger Fry in *An Essay in Aesthetics* (1909), defining the new modernist sensibility as an emotional need of subjective imaginative life to receive aesthetic stimulation – all that matters is that this stimulation is attained; and, as a consequence, Fry would later claim that painting 'may then dispense once for all with the idea of likeness to Nature.'[2] Indeed it appears, from such accounts of aesthetic modernism, that any objective natural form was to be allowed pictorial presence in modern art only if it generated subjective approval and stimulation. This subjectivisation of aesthetics, and concomitantly the world it represents, has continued in the accounts of art provided for us throughout the twentieth century. For example Clive Bell tells us that while 'significant form . . . is the one quality common to all works of art,' the delineation of this 'significant form' is at the mercy of subjective taste since, for Bell, 'all systems of aesthetics must be based on personal experience – that is to say they must be subjective.'[3]

Now, while these figures may represent easily discounted theories, they are no less influential for that; indeed, it could well be argued that in the English-speaking world it is this peculiar account of the subjectivisation of natural form, and the consequent freedom to claim authorship of any corresponding form and content, that came to dominate contemporary descriptions of aesthetics and accounts of what art actually is. Unfortunately, however, this discourse of the pursuit of abstracted form or, as it became known, this 'formalism' allowed modern art to articulate and legitimise itself at the expense of any material world that these forms might be thought to inform.

For if someone like Michael Fried can say in 1965, in almost a melancholic fashion, that 'the history of painting from Manet through synthetic cubism and Matisse may be characterised in terms of the gradual withdrawal of painting from the task of representing reality – or of reality from the power of painting to represent it – in favour of an increasing preoccupation with problems intrinsic to painting itself,'[4] then this is why retrospective critics such as Clement Greenberg (also writing in 1965) were able to announce that art secures itself and its own modern status only by reflecting on the defining limitations of its own medium. In which case, as he put it, Cézanne's modernity can be detected insofar as 'Cézanne sacrificed verisimilitude, or correctness, in order to fit drawing and design more explicitly to the rectangular shape of the canvas.'[5]

If all these statements now strike one as both banal and, unfortunately, utterly and tragically ubiquitous, this is because as Jay Bernstein has pointed out 'part of our experience of art is its becoming only art, mere art, a matter of taste.'[6] As a result, any celebration of the subjective autonomy of modern aesthetics can but announce at the same time the alienation of art from any overarching truth or morality which it might otherwise possess. As such, aesthetic autonomy frees art not for itself but only from the obligation to represent anything but itself.

Nevertheless, in many ways, when one looks at the history of modern art, at its birth and origin, this collapsing of aesthetic reality into subjectivised accounts of form need not have occurred. In which case (positioning ourselves via a Kantian vocabulary), if modern art has become merely sublime, if it has become the sensuous presentation in intuition of the ideas of reason – that is, if art has become merely an account of the mind visibly displaying to itself its own legislative potency over intuition – then modern art needs to confront again the possibility of an intuition whose form does not arise from the mind but rather from the other side of the intelligible/sensible divide – that is, from the natural world.

However, the first sign of modern painting comes from those innovations that took place mostly in the nineteenth century when art attempted to be more 'realist,' even though it is retrospectively claimed that this is when art first departed from the real and its attempted classical depiction. And, of course, we can detect the end of 'something,' even by the early part of the nineteenth century. For long before the rise of Impressionism, we already see in France a certain rupture with the rise of Delacroix and his opposition to Ingres, the shift in interest to the shading and the landscapes of Courbet, Corot, and Rousseau, and the explicit naturalism of the Barbizon School. In England, by the way, there is a similar Impressionistic orientation even earlier with Turner (and in his case there is even already the presence of abstraction) and, furthermore, with Constable and Bonington, where human portraiture is abandoned in favor of nature and its earthly depiction as a sensate realm illuminated and colored by light and the possibility of experience.

Perhaps this is why the origin of modern art is taken to lie in a break with reality and the classical depiction of natural form. However, this is a peculiar account because if the origin of modern art can 'broadly speaking' be located in the rise of French Impressionism and Cézanne's passage through it, then modern art did not begin in any break with the real, but rather in an ever-more faithful attention to reality in all of its visual aspects. For Impressionism was an attempt to depict what we actually see when we are seeing, over and against any retrospective conceptual account of what was actually seen. Or, as Manet put it, 'I paint what I see and not what others choose to see.'[7] Impressionism was, then, a return to an almost pre-conceptual realist (as opposed to idealist) account of what the perceived world is. As such, Impressionism claims to be faithful to a visible and illuminated world – a realm, it was claimed, that is already disclosed to the eye before visibility becomes all covered over by human projection and conceptualisation. There is a truth in this account, for in the world as it is actually and really seen, sensations spill out of their forms, and color takes on adumbrations and shades, not from itself but from its immediate surroundings and context; and there is moreover an explicit attempt in Impressionism to give visible depiction and testimony to the dynamics of light as it plays upon and brings forth the very visibility of the things themselves. Perhaps this is why Impressionism first took shape in France in the summer of 1869, when Renoir and Monet were together beginning to paint the atmosphere of light and water at the lake of *La Grenouillère*, encapsulating there the Impressionistic imperative to capture every momentary disclosure of appearance, as visuality reveals itself, not for itself but only for us.

And this is where a strange and ultimately disastrous reversal takes place. For in this laudable attention to the realities of sight and vision – the inability of the eye and stereoscopic vision to focus with detail on more than one point at the same time, the inevitable blurring at the periphery of vision, the incapacity of the eye to isolate itself from the movements of the head and the body, the constant motion of sight that produces an ever-shifting inundation of sensibility – in respect of the uncovering of all these truths of perception, any realist attempt at Impressionism dissolved into an account not of an objective world but rather of a description of the subjective constitution of reality. For the ever-more attenuated attention to the foundational primacy of perception in human accounts of objective reality, uncovered (unfortunately, for the future of painting) not an account of reality but rather the great philosophical claim of modernism – that subjectivity constitutes objectivity and makes it possible.

Now I am not saying that this is all that Impressionism was, or that it is not amenable to another account (as, indeed, I think it is with the late works of Monet); but I would suggest that the true inheritance of Impressionism in terms of the future development of modern art was the loss of the possibility of an objectivity in art that was not exhausted by our reception of it. For the Impressionist pursuit of objectivity, or rather the quest for a faithfulness to what is actually perceived, produced paintings which were little more than open loops of immanent consciousness, a surround that was to be completed by the perceiver who, as a result, now controlled the very constitution of the painting itself.

For the Impressionist purifying of color from all the dark browns and blacks of the earth, the expunging of darkness from shadow via the use of primary colors in juxtaposition with their complementaries, all of this served to cause the eyes of the viewer to synthesise the visuality of the painting in an act of almost retinal consciousness whereby the very vividness we see is constituted by us through the act of sight. Now, of course, I am in a sense describing more accurately the metaphysical or rather the physical programatic of neo-impressionism, and the flirtation with science pursued by Seurat with his pointillism or divisionism. Yet this psychologistic breakdown of light into its constituent parts for reformulation by the eye, only built on recognitions already gained and painted by the Impressionists themselves.

Hermann Bahr has written: 'The Impressionist leaves out man's participation in appearance for fear of falsifying it.'[8] This is because 'to Impressionism man and the world have become completely one; to Impressionism only sense-impressions exist.'[9] Incidentally it is exactly this type of recognition that gave rise to the possibility of a Marxist critique that saw Impressionism as being merely a bourgeois validation of the status quo. And, to an extent, these remarks have a certain purchase: impressionistic phenomenalism has had the effect of privileging not the perceived world itself, but rather the subjective act of reception and constitution, whereby the now wholly phenomenal being of the world is converted into an account of its pleasurable absorption and delightful reduction by us.

Cézanne and the path from subjectivity to objectivity

It is in the light of this strange reversal of realist perception into a subsequent idealism that Cézanne's dissatisfaction and break with Impressionism can be understood (he last exhibited with them in the Impressionist exhibition of 1877). For Cézanne's late work is nothing but a visual depiction of an objectivity apart from and before its absorption by the perceiver, and in the attempt to realise this objectivity Cézanne's work steps back from any simple human reception and becomes instead an account of visual objectivity. Cézanne attempted the depiction of the overarching being of the natural world, a 'phenomenon' that is for itself and as a result not wholly for us, an objectivity whose essence exists apart from temporalised human life in a monumental, and in a sense inaccessible, eternity. Consequently there is in Cézanne's painting almost the veritable presence of a surfaced and visible world that discloses the fact that what is essential about itself is apart from us.

This separation and transcendence of nature over and above the viewer of the painting has an almost formal presence in Cézanne's work. From the relatively early painting *The Railway Cutting* in 1869–70, where the foreground separates itself via the device of a wall from the monumentality of the background, to the depiction of the Lac d'Annecy in 1896, where the water of the lake provides the collapsing vacation of the foreground in favor of the back. An inaccessibility of objectivity that is all the more present in the late paintings of Mount Saint-Victoire, where Cézanne, painting the foreground with cold hues to make it step back, and the back with warmer colors to make it approach, makes the distinction between the respective domains of the subject and the object even more apparent. In these late paintings Cézanne virtually eliminates any visual distinction in the lower third of the picture, painting the earth that sustains the mountainous objectivity of Saint-Victoire as a blank coloration that loses all character and form under the density and weight of what stands over.

But if objectivity stands apart from us, and if the task of painting, as it was for Cézanne, is in some sense to articulate the immense being and endurance of this reality apart from us, then why paint? For surely if the aim of Cézanne's art is to picture that which is permanent in the changing world of appearance and, as it were, this universality stands in a certain indifference to and reservation from us, what legitimacy can painting claim? Cézanne, though, had an answer to this, and he gave it in a letter to Gasquet in 1897 when he wrote that 'Art is a harmony which runs parallel with nature.'[10] Indeed, this discernment of art as nature's parallel makes manifest what Cézanne was trying to achieve with his painting, while also marking the limits that he believed himself to be operating under. For of course parallel lines never meet or touch, and there is little doubt, to extend the metaphor, that though such lines may begin together it is nature's line that sets the course and the edge which Cézanne's art constantly attempts to track. Moreover it was, I believe, Cézanne's unspoken contention that mind and world do not have a teleology for one another. As such, for him the human mind occurs more essentially in the form of a subservient realm parallel to a nature that it can never be equal to. As Cézanne wrote earlier, in 1879: 'Nature presents me with the greatest difficulties.'[11] He reputedly told Denis: 'I wished to copy nature but I did not succeed,'[12] since for Cézanne nature had 'a dull brilliance' that he could not capture on canvas. Consequently, for Cézanne, nature was not something to be copied or mimicked by a mind in search of resemblance, but was rather something whose transcendent surface disclosure of objectivity was to be translated into a form more amenable for take up by human sight. And, of course, it is here that we find all of Cézanne's writings on sensation and realisation (*réalisation*) in which he attempts to bring the mind into a parallel harmony (though one necessarily more diminished) with nature: a nature whose very externality and otherworldliness begin to suggest to the perceiver that man and humanity are an ephemeral and needless addition to a world where objectivity contemplates itself only and its own disclosure.

For there is, I think, a deep melancholia in Cézanne, one that is grounded in this almost pagan separation of natural objectivity from human subjectivity, a separation that is perhaps all the more foregrounded and visible when we look at Cézanne's portrayal and depiction of people and human life. Throughout, Cézanne's portraits depict people as isolated and remote individuations, creatures suspicious of their world and the objects found therein. Indeed, even as one of his finest advocates, Kurt Badt, notes: in Cézanne's early portraits (1865–1872), 'though they represent people whom Cézanne knew well – friends or relatives – something deeply reserved, inaccessible and alien adheres to them all.'[13] Moreover I would suggest that whatever resolution or change marked Cézanne's later work, the portraits we find there do not represent any fundamental reversal from the earliest accounts – for we see in these pictures of people (the 1899 portrait of Ambroise Vollard, for example) the presence of a certain romantic and tragic resignation, an acceptance of their alienation from essence and being. These human figurations are in an explicit relationship with objects but still not fully at home with them.

Now, of course, I do not want to caricature Cézanne nor downgrade his genuine and, I believe, revelatory penetration to the form and essence of nature, but what I am suggesting is that Cézanne is not adequate to what he manages to depict. For though Cézanne paints the objective form and harmony of nature he fails to realise what is actually shown there: namely, that this visibility is intended for none but *us*, that visibility does not occur more essentially apart from us than it does for us. For vision is only for us, and, as a consequence, Cézanne makes the very visibility and beauty of the world not more miraculous but rather more occult and shocking. For he fails to show or explain why this visibility occurs at all; he fails to depict why the world is visible and why it chooses to reveal its own essential form and structure on its surface, so that what is essential to it is made visible for us.[14]

Painting and theology

What do we have, then, in this picture that I have just presented? Is there not already the immanent shape and constellation of a critique of modernity and its art? For, between the subjectivity of Impressionism and the objectivity of Cézanne, what is it that has been described if not the modern separation and alienation of subjectivity from objectivity and a hopeless oscillation between the two?

In many ways subsequent painting testifies to this very oscillation. If I can suggest that the great advocates of pure abstraction in the early years of the twentieth century were Kandinsky, and Mondrian, and – a little later – Malevich (and here I exclude Picasso because, in the decisive years of the early twentieth century, Picasso was still interested in the 'representational' aspects of Cubism; in, that is, Cézanne's injunction to 'treat nature by means of the cylinder, the sphere, the cone,'[15]), then through these figures we can detect the oscillation that I spoke of earlier: unfettered subjectivity (Kandinsky), relentless objectivity (Mondrian), and, as I will indicate, a wholly unexplored Christian alternative for abstract art (an alternative which is perhaps partially exemplified in the work of Malevich).

Leaving aside for now the question as to what it is that abstract art might be abstracted from, let us briefly chart the various paths to its modern formulation. At the origin of modern abstraction we find on the one hand the subjective agenda of Kandinsky and his pursuit of the lost '*what*' of art. Indeed in 1911 Kandinsky announced that 'this "what"' will no longer be the material objective "what" of the former period, but the internal truth of art, 'something less "bodily",' something that Kandinsky rather disingenuously termed the 'soul.'[16] For Impressionism bequeathed to Kandinsky and modern art the possibility that it subsequently fulfilled, that of a relentless subjectivisation of the world, a situation where nature is drained and exhausted of all objectivity by the mind, such that this subjectivity and its art understood itself as no longer situated in a recognisable material reality that corresponds to anything that might be true, beautiful, or good. Consequently, in the absence of any orienting and enhancing externals, Kandinsky felt that the only fidelity art owed was to itself and its own 'internal necessity.'[17] A situation that leads to the wholesale abandonment of the physical world, since apparently for the anti-materialistic theo-philosophy of Kandinsky, the world does not disclose any visible salvific forms. As a result the contemporary injunction upon the artist who would liberate the 'soul' is that of abandoning the shell of objective materiality, as materiality can never capture, embody or personify the life of the spirit, since 'one cannot crystalise in material form what does not yet exist in material form.'[18] As such, and by way of example, this turn to an internalized basis for art in an ethereal 'spiritual interiority' simply culminates in a form of aesthetic solipsism: a conceptual and abstracted art whose value derives only from the constant and perpetual claims it makes to re-frame itself as its own object.

The sad thing is that Kandinsky's attempt to distance himself from spiritless materialism acted only to confirm rather than to contest an atheistic account of materiality. For though Kandinsky denounced 'the nightmare of materialism, which has turned the life of the universe into an evil useless game,' he in true Gnostic and Manicheaean fashion ceded all materiality to such an account via the dissolution of worldly form by an enervating internalised spirituality of feeling and color.[19] Moreover by denying that ideality was ever material, or that it could find its true essence expressed in a non-abstract real embodiment, Kandinsky abandoned the highest spiritual values to an account of their subjective genealogy and origin. This situation in its turn only further intensified the modern experience of the loss of the world and aided the rise of an aesthetic which sought the sublimity of internal sensation rather than any correspondence with external forms which, though present, exceed simple depiction.

Concomitantly, just as the spiritual pursuit of modern subjectivity has culminated in the loss of an external world, there lies at the birth of abstract art the pursuit of an objectivity apart from any subjective contamination at all. The origin of this quest in the modern era lies, I believe, in the technical achievement of Cézanne's art: his holding apart of a visual objectivity from subjective absorption. This refusal to mediate the universal through its particular acts of reception and perception, became in time a wish to depict the unmediated form of the universal itself.

The first and most powerful advocate of this was, of course, the Dutch painter Mondrian. And it was Mondrian who, with his now classically recognised pictures of self-referential squares and rectangles, hoped to hold in equilibrium the tension between color and non-color, in order the better to express the fundamental equivalence and indifference that universality has for any particular that would claim to instantiate it. Moreover, Mondrian's whole intellectual lineage and concern had the effect of directing him away from the particular to the universal. His earlier Calvinism (itself a doctrine that was no friend of mediation and facade) was augmented when he joined the Theosophical Society in 1909 and absorbed their doctrines of a higher non-material reality. This position was itself further refined when Mondrian finally authored his principles of neo-plasticism, which expressed the need to bring all visual relations into an equivalence with themselves and with the resultant whole that they thereby expressed.

However, just as subjectivity can absorb a world, so can objectivity deny any recognisable world to a subject. Thus this 'spiritual' concern with a universality unencumbered by real individuals or particularities also results in the loss of a world since, as Mondrian puts it, 'in art, the universal is impossible to express determinately within naturalistic form.'[20] For what Mondrian was advocating was the possibility of an aesthetic depiction of an objectivity that has nothing to do with us whatsoever. In which case, as the further developments of modern art in the twentieth century have revealed, an objectivity abstracted from human concerns and recognition produces such an extreme departure from the world that it becomes wholly unclear from what, exactly, this abstract art is abstracted. For if Cézanne bequeathed the pursuit of objectivity to modern art, then by and large this objectivity or universality when its realisation is attempted, as it was in the sublime compositions and vacated spirituality of Mondrian's mature work, is an objectivity achieved at the expense of any objects at all. See for example Mondrian's *Composition in Black and White* of 1917, or his *Composition in Black and Grey* of 1919. A point that Mondrian made quite explicit in *De Stijl* in 1917 saying 'only when the individual no longer stands in the way can universality be purely manifested.'[21] Perhaps unsurprisingly, this search for the universal and the 'superhuman' reveals itself as a hopeless and ultimately nihilistic account of form and essence, since it maintains that forms can appear apart from what they inform, and universality upholds only its self-depiction and has no necessary or obvious regard for the particulars it could instantiate.

It is in this sense that modern art has become the depiction and celebration of nothing whatsoever – nothing, that is, but the fluctuation between a subjectivity without recognisable objects and an objectivity whose pursuit renders it uncognisable for subjectivity. An oscillation between subject and object that always collapses into the *same phenomenon* – the visual celebration and depiction of a negation of any recognisable world at all, a prospect all the more encouraged by the sublime and perverse stimulation of ourselves at such a prospect.

There are, however, indications in the tradition of another possibility, a possibility where one condition of reality, be it subjectivity or objectivity, does not conspire against another. For if the aesthetic negation of the world that I have been describing has been pursued from both sides of the subject/object divide, and if these traditions have culminated in the nihilistic enthronement of nothing over the

God-given reality that we inhabit – the reality that is *of something* – then are there artists who express and paint the glorious filiation of the universal and the particular that alone creates a world? Such an artist would have to visibly show how transcendent forms are created only out of love, depicting how these existent forms exist in this world only in order to express themselves in particular objects, making these objects the singularised created beings that they are. Thence is derived the absolutely gifted and graced status of particular beings, for particulars, through being graced by the incarnation of form, have become something real and unique, an expression of that which is neither arbitary nor non-negatable and hence non-exchangeable with anything else.

Such an art would be able to show the refusal of God to let possibility run riot to produce a meaningless world where everything is possible and nothing really matters. And in isolated places we do see such an art: as early as the nineteenth century one finds Van Gogh reviving the style of realists like Millet – not, however, painting his world as one which is mundane, but rather as one which is inundated with the color of the transcendent: light itself. A world where the glory of light expresses itself, not in the erasure of delineated beings, but in a bringing to the particular and undissolved phenomena of what we actually see an ever-more wondrous realisation *that they are* (in, for example, Van Gogh's *The Sower* of 1888).

Similarly, amongst the final forerunners and advocates of abstract art there is Malevich, whose vaunted 'supremacism' (though supremacism is, in my view, a misleading term), certainly testifies to a break with representational painting but not to an atheist abstraction from the world of meaning and content. For he himself described his famous painting of a black square on a white background (the *Black Square* of 1915) 'as a totally bare icon with no frame'. In terms of theology what should a bare icon disclose – save *the inability of nothing to be anything at all*. Moreover, all of Malevich's abstractions seem precisely, and perhaps for the first time, to be genuinely *abstract*, in that they appear derived from something meaningful and something given. As such, though they are not representational, they are not unworldly. In some way, Malevich's abstract work always takes up a certain explicitness of form. His work does not endorse the arbitrary or celebrate the possible over the actual, but appears to reflect upon the definite shape of the world. In 1915, for example, we are given squares, crosses, and circles, pictures that seem to represent the inability of form to be separated from worldly exemplification. And, as a result, such shapes remain iconic because they testify, not to the absence of God, nor to any simply self-evident foundation to reality, but rather to the fact that though we do not know what something is it still nevertheless *is*, whereas nothing *is not* (for example, even the coloration of the back square red, in the *Red Square*, also of 1915, makes the whole work a negative testimony to something incredibly existent).

Later on, as Malevich added other and more varied shapes to his work, each composition increasingly expresses, not a grid-like indifference and equivalence of one shape or color to another, as with Mondrian, nor a subjective absorption of form altogether, as with Kandinsky, but rather a filiation of forms for objects and a desire for that which is ideal to become real. In these works, squares and rectangles gather together in different colors and hues as though they, too, wanted to make a meaningful world and express a language worth speaking. Given all this, it is perhaps not surprising that Malevich abandoned supremacism in the late 1920s to paint once again the human figure against a recognisable landscape. But now Malevich does not paint icons vacated of their content; rather, he depicts the attendance of ideal form in the embodied contents that now show themselves: they have taken human form again, and express themselves as differentiated and unique presentations of the same higher form. Now there is a beauty and a stunning quality to these pictures. Even where the face of a human figure is left blank, the colors surrounding it edge around and mark out in the absence of a face the shape of what might fulfill such a request (see for example Malevich's *Sportsmen*, of 1928–30 or the *Complex Premonition*, of 1928–32). In this sense all of Malevich's work was indeed iconic, a visible testament to the presence of the ideal in the real, and a belief that the artist could depict such a fact.

Unfortunately, however, and with some other notable exceptions (Chagall being the most obvious), modern art has not understood itself and its role via such an account. If modern art can be approached as a tradition that has celebrated the loss of both its subject and its object, what can restore to us and to our art the perception that we are indeed real and meaningful and that both we and our objects have, and share in, a visibly discernible world that reveals the true structure and nature of creation? No doubt surprisingly for modern art and its secular advocates, the answer has already been provided by Christ, for he *and he alone* teaches us that the Most High and the most ideal has been incarnated here in our world as the most explicit account of the union of ideality and reality that we have ever been given. Christ shows us in the form of his own worldly body that form is invisible and, for us, nothing at all, unless it informs and takes up reality; and that subjectivity is nothing, nothing at all, unless it extends beyond itself to take up that which has always been given.

Theology and vision

He was made visible in the flesh.
(1 Timothy 3: 16)

To say all this, is to say that an aesthetic practice that would evade nihilism should be re-aligned around the perception of what we are given. But modern accounts of perception do not testify to the theological relationship between the ideal and the real that I have been arguing for and that I have been attempting to suggest should lie at the basis of any proper art or aesthetic practice. If those accounts are correct, the arguments I have been advancing are without basis, because the world that would support them, it would appear, does not exist.

Yet, despite this lack of perception, the question of what *can* be seen retains a crucial importance and priority, not least because – in some as yet unascertained manner – theology can, I believe, show how sensate perception does in fact disclose and reveal the structure and nature of the world, an account and a description that can, I believe, *only be theological.* To say this is to say that only theology can, in the fullest sense of the word, *see at all,* since only theology can provide an account of what is actually seen that might be adequate to the vision and the reality of the perceptual world that we all share.

This is to suggest, then, that for theology there is something theological to see. But what is it that theology thinks has been given to it to see? And is this givenness given only to theology, and in that case can only theology see it? This last question is perhaps the most problematic, because what is indeed 'given' is, to say the least, contested; moreover, outside of any such contestment, many people simply do not see anything theological about reality at all. In spite of the problems – and the undoubted existence of profane vision – my contention is that those who do not see theologically are not really seeing anything at all. For to assume that reality does not show itself theologically is to assume both that reality is not in essence theological, and that reality is simply there either for itself or as a blank material screen for human projection. However, theology should not accept such an account, for does not the New Testament suggest that the divine phenomenon is discernible, there for those that would look? Does not Christ himself make visible what was previously hidden, and is not his sensate form *exactly* the structure of God's revelation for Christianity? Perhaps this is why, after Christ, St Paul calls for a new faculty of perception, for a subjectivity not blinded by its own potency, since for Paul, God 'however invisible has been there for the mind to see in the things he has made.'(Romans 1: 20)

However such claims encounter easy secular refusal. Those who do not see such a reality will say 'I do not see,' and there seems little weight, though every importance, in asking them to look again. Self-evidently there is only so much that one can say or show to those who have already made a decision about what they can know and what they cannot. In respect of such refusals, one experiences a strange kind of silence. A silence moreover whose dreadful acquiescence impels one to speak about it. From a theological perspective such a cognitive atheism lacks what Merleau-Ponty called perceptual faith (*la foi perceptive*): it does not understand the import of even the merest brush of sensation – that there is a world whose reality and disclosure constantly exceeds any secular attempt to describe it.[22]

Obviously, the tone of these remarks indicates that in matters of perception, ontology and theology I am a realist. However, the use of this term immediately introduces us to new dangers and problematics. For, though I am a realist, I do not think that realism is defensible or indeed desirable outside of theology. As such I am saying that one can be only a theological 'realist.' And this qualification arises because much of what constitutes modern realism allies it with atheism, as secular accounts of reality fail to capture reality's essential aspect, its dependence on and participation in God.

And this aspect of modern realism (its ability to discard God when describing the real) owes its origin to developments in theology at the end of the thirteenth century, when those who attempted to argue for knowledge of God did so by attempting to discern the nature of God from the nature of the ontic world. This 'natural theology' was, in effect, first constituted by Duns Scotus who, when wishing to give to human cognition the possibility of knowing God, elevated a neutral account of being above the distinction between the Creator and his creatures, allowing both God and finite beings to share in this being in due proportion, since for Scotus rationality required that the same substance be shared by both God and his creatures if each were to know the other.

This elevation of worldly univocal being above the distinction between God and his creatures marks the time when theology itself became idolatrous. For Scotus disregarded what Aquinas had already warned him against – that nothing can be predicated univocally of God and other things. For Aquinas that which is predicated of God can be participated in by finite creatures only via analogy. As a result, since no created effect can possess its own origin or replace and transcend its uncreated divine cause, any discernment of the origin of the natural world can and should lead us to a discernment of God, and not to any affirmation of an independent basis for the world. For theology, therefore, the very possibility of any secular realism derives from the Scotist belief that the ground of both God and created objects is the same. Whereas for theology no created object stands on the same ground as God, and as there is nothing higher than God any transcending of the Creator–creature distinction will, as Aquinas pointed out, only idolatrously posit some higher third entity which both God and creature will have to share as derivative terms.[23]

The outcome of the univocal thesis of Scotus was a twofold abandonment and scission of the inter-relation of God and creation. The univocal thesis allowed the world to abandon God, as one could now wholly dispense with God by explaining the world in terms of this higher ground whatever it might be. This thesis also led to God abandoning the world, since the assumption that both God and his creatures share in some prior term meant that God could assert himself as God only by claiming to have a greater degree of this prior quality and hence, from the perspective of man, a greater power. This situation made God like man (even though God has an infinite share of this univocal being whereas man takes only a finite proportion) since both God and man were forced to share in the same immanent being in order to be at all. Consequently this quantitative distinction between man and God, by reducing God to the level of an unequal participant in the being that man also shared in, meant that man could see God only as a greater and more powerful version of himself. Perhaps not surprisingly, God then became an object of fear and loathing for a humanity that began to wish for a usurpation of his station.

And, of course, this is exactly what happened with William of Ockham. For Ockham accepted that God was defined on the basis of his overwhelming power, and that he was so powerful that there was the real possibility of God's malignity of will and of our utter defencelessness and lack of guile in the face of such deception. He denied that there could be any universal structure to the world that was perceivable by man. Since the only source of certainty was God's omnipotent will, then all other beings (since man cannot share God's consciousness) are incapable of certain knowledge. Man has then to be content with mere conjecture and hypothesis about what he is given in intuition and experience. He can of course generalise from these intuitions, but since this intuitive faculty lies at the mercy of a God who can conjure an impression in the absence of any object, and maintain illusion instead of truth, then human experience can for Ockham yield only contingency and hopeless conjecture.

The only empirical certainty that remained for human beings as a result of this nominalist reversal was the certainty that God himself chooses to disclose, through revelation, to individuated beings. Revelation then becomes, after Ockham, not only divided from the rest of the world and all other phenomena, but re-understood, not as a general phenomenon, but as a specific solipsistic and interiorised encounter between a human being and an arbitrary or capricious deity. It was a specific revelation, moreover, whose veracity can apparently never be made evident to others or to the world but only to oneself through the 'subjective certainty' of faith and justification.

But this nominalist postulation and projection onto God of the will to power created only the conditions for subsequent modern subjectivity to usurp these powers.[24] For Ockham produced an account of a God who 'owed no debt to man,' and thus human beings after Ockham, facing the possibility that all their given reality and perception were illusory, arbitrary and liable to negation at any moment by the Creator, decided to assert themselves and make stable their values, thereby securing a world that a perverted theology had so explicitly abandoned.

Any recognition that the preceding account is in some way true should have certain consequences for Christianity. It suggests that no term can be raised above God and his creatures, in order to explain God to his creatures, other than that which God himself discloses; in which case, the question as to what God *does* give and disclose to us returns to view. Obviously, any account of God which refuses to accept that we are given anything at all cannot be a Christian one, not least because it is the essence of Christianity that the Son was indeed given and did indeed make what was previously invisible – visible. God does reveal himself in sensate word and form as the Son. And this visible invisibility is exactly what Scripture attests to: 'No one has ever seen God, it is the only son, who is nearest to the Father's heart, who has made him known' (John 1: 18).

Theology, it seems, should take seriously the issue of the senses, not only because these senses were once exposed to divinity but really and rather because the nature and message of the Son is that all creation can and does participate and share in this grace and can itself be similarly so ordered. For the message of the sensate Christ is not that of a divinity that expresses itself at the expense of the created world, but that of an explicit and utterly evident love of creation, the kenotic love of a God who wholly gives himself to that which he has created, so much so that he makes himself manifest in it. This, of course, does not mean that that which is seen or shown is itself wholly expressive or exhaustive of God. *Not at all*: there are no totalised phenomena for theology, no attempted copies or representations of other images, and no fulfilled completed phenomena. These are only actualised and temporal manifestations of creation becoming ever-more real as a result of participating in the fully realised actuality of the Father and the Son.

What, then, can be our preliminary conclusions? There is no such thing as a secular realm, a part of the world that can be elevated above God and explained and investigated apart from him. This means that the world can be understood only in terms of its relationship to God, and God can (from *our* perspective and not in himself) be understood only in terms of his relationship to the world in terms of what he gives to the world – *which is the world*. This means that for me it is worldly form as God-given (as culminated and expressed in the union of word and flesh in Christ) that is revelatory, and nothing else. For there is no division between grace and nature, no separation of revelation from all of creation, and, consequently, no possible denial that the world shows and exhibits its participation in universal theological forms that can and must be seen. For theology, any refusal to also admit the world into a revelatory economy is a form and species of Manicheanism and a separation of the God who created the world from the God who will redeem it.

This promise of a world participating in ideality is not abstract but actual; the incarnate God is not an abstract promise concerning some other realm, but rather the bringing into reality of our own fallen world. While this is not a picture or a perception that is in any way widespread or accepted, it is nonetheless my contention that this focus on perception alone brings ontology out of a fixation with a noumenal world, behind all appearances, and into a recognition and acknowledgement that a Christian account of presence is perhaps the only successful account of the phenomenal reality that we all see.

However, before I attempt any description of this situation, we require some new vocabulary. I will speak of the *visible* and the *invisible*, not only because these terms have already had some deployment in contemporary work on phenomenology and theology, but because they speak to the current perceptual situation. For most people, the higher dimensions of the visible world are quite simply invisible, not even recognised or aimed at by subjective intention. In truth, however, the invisible is not separable from the visible; in fact the visible is but a dimension of invisibility, and indeed the very clarity of the visible world rests upon the profiles and adumbrations of this higher discernible.[25]

In order to ascertain that such an account of reality is not just some religious projection, but is rather borne out by any faithful account of what phenomena really are, I would like, briefly, to focus on the work of Maurice Merleau-Ponty. For in *Le Visible et l'Invisible*, Merleau-Ponty moves to a point where he also phenomenologically acknowledges the presence of the invisible in visibility. Like most phenomenologists, Merleau-Ponty distances himself from conceptual abstraction, yet he does not denounce transcendence, as for him transcendence is not a departure from the world but an immersion in it. For Merleau-Ponty pursues the *esse* of the phenomenal world *in* the phenomenal world, and in this he determined the world to be 'one body' or flesh (*chair*), a body moreover whose being (*esse*) grants to the things themselves (*les choses elles-mêmes*) the plenitude of always being more than the look which perceives them.[26] Yet, despite being located in the heart of this immanent world, the perceiver is not absorbed by its flesh. Indeed this world flesh is that from which individuated beings segregate and singularise themselves in a reciprocal and reversible fashion. The world flesh then is unlimited (*illimité*) and, as the most terminal notion (*une notion dernière*), it sustains all subsequent beings who derive their corporeality and singularity from it.[27] Now, this visibility that Merleau-Ponty describes seems at first sight to be the most specific and compelling picture of a phenomenology that has departed from transcendence and been led to immanentism.

Yet this Deleuzian settlement does not satisfy Merleau-Ponty, as for him such a description is not true to the phenomena of the world. Merleau-Ponty begins to discern in the heart of all this massing of corporeality a disjuncture between the 'subject' and the 'objective world.' The irreducible distance between 'my flesh' and the world begins to speak to him of a form of visibility that accompanies the massiveness of flesh such that it graces it with subtlety, overlaying on the momentary body of sheer matter the discernment of a glorious body (*un corps glorieux*); this discernment brings with it the consequent implication of an order which is higher than that of mere immanence.[28] Merleau-Ponty sees in the heart of immanence that which will forever forbid sheer visibility from believing itself to be the only description of the world: he sees the higher order of the invisible.

This invisibility or ideality is for Merleau-Ponty not an absolute invisible (*qui n'aurait rien à faire avec le visible*) cut off from this world; on the contrary, it is 'the invisible *of* this world.'[29] It comes to the immanence of flesh, giving it all its dimensions, axes and depths. In earlier times the concept would claim this ideal role in respect of empirical content, but for Merleau-Ponty this invisibility is not an abstract concept of the mind but a carnal presence in the body. As a form this ideal presence enshrines itself in all singularised beings; indeed it is what allows these beings to carve out their individuated natures in the first place. Consequently the invisible ideality which covers all differentiating and plural life is not a category of conceptual subsumption or prior necessity, just as a form does stand apart from what it informs, so there is no possibility here of deducing any *a priori* knowledge of this ideal apart from its adhesion to the real. This ideal is no abstract conceptualisation by a mental life that has sundered itself from reality: it is reality at its profoundest level.

I have argued that although this ideal is not visible it is not separated from sight. Though it is in a sense invisible, this is not for it a noumenal quality: invisibility has a look. The ideal as an invisible look upholds what it sees and sustains all visibles as such. And in respect of this invisibility 'sensation is literally a form of communion' (*la sensation est à la lettre une communion*).[30] As an invisibility this *eidos* does not negate the ontic visibles that it creates. Though existent beings stand in seeming independence and brute facticity, they are all in truth enveloped in an invisible penumbra which they can either deny or acknowledge. From the perspective of ontic visibility the invisible need not be perceived, but the transcendent gratuity of the invisible, its formless donation, clings to all the singularised beings it holds together, not as an internal *ousia*, but as a transcendent form inseparable from that which it informs. Spread along the surface of each being, flowing along its contours, this *a posteriori* ideality grants creation existence through adhering to the own-most potential of each creature and carving out its reality as a result.

Merleau-Ponty is led, then, not to any immanentist account of the phenomenal world, nor again to any transcendental account of its formulation, but rather to an account of its plenitudinous creation and a curious and unexplained filiation of the invisible to the visible. What, though, can explain this commitment of the most ideal reality to that being which we exhibit and are, what can explain or capture this kenotic incarnation of the visible by the invisible? It is, of course, no accident that this language, which had sought to describe reality, is beginning to describe the incarnate Christ.; nor that Merleau-Ponty himself was considering ending *Le Visible et l'Invisible* with a chapter on God. For, finally, I can now sketch out what I have been trying to approach – the world describes only God, and as a result the world is the mediated body that shows and reveals God and God's utter overwhelming of visibility in Christ.

In consequence a theological return to the natural order does not, in spite of what distorted accounts of theology might have us believe, lead us to identify nature with God and so endorse some pantheistic account of the world. On the contrary, for us God can be only what he shows and gives to us; and what we are shown and given is a phenomenal, sensate, world that reaches its fullest height and unimaginable glory in Christ. For Christ came to grace us and our world with the highest possibility conceivable – that of full participation in eternal divine reality.

This conception of nature shows that all beings are a combination of the actual and the manifestly possible, and that which is given to us as a possibility is to become *more real*. By this I mean that God creates Being and brings beings into Being in order that they can become what they are – in order, that is, that they can fulfill their God-given form and so enter eternity with him. In which case each actualised creation hovers in its moment of formation and all the possibles, all the best possibles, are born with it and come to it. This is what one should mean by this being 'the best possible world' – not the reducing of the world to its most privated state, but an arguing for its highest power. And this is what it means for a possibility to supervene on an actuality and for it not to be a nihilation of actuality – for human beings our possibility is a higher actuality. In John we find Christ saying: 'I tell you most solemnly, unless a man is born from above he cannot see the Kingdom of God' (John 3: 3). And the glory is that *man is born from above*: he is born from the highest reality, and it is this and this alone that allows human beings to transfigure themselves and their world.

At the outset of this section I spoke of perception, and indeed perception retains its crucial importance, for perception allows us to see these higher possibles amid all the self-presencing and misreading of actuality, and in this respect the truth retains its visual component. For perception as a strange and beautiful combination of activity and passivity, spontaneity and reception, is what allows us in these denuded times not to be wholly authored by our environment. It is granted to perception to see and grasp those possibles or higher realities which are given to us at birth, as potentials that can be made actual. In the realm of the visual, then, beings retain a diaphanous quality such that the possibility of the reality of the good and the beautiful and the true can shine into them and cohere their bodies with the highest values.

This solicitude of the invisible for the visible arises only from love, and, because nothing is created so that it might die, this love does not negate what it creates. Instead it raises it to the highest level. In this way the most high utterly abandons itself to us; its kenosis consists in that 'the Word was made flesh,' (John 1: 14), and we remain forever transfigured as a result. The Johannine transparency of the Son in respect to the Father – 'The Father is in me and I am in the Father' (John 10: 38) – is an elevation that is also given to us: 'I shall draw all men to myself' (John 12: 32). Perception draws us into this harmonic – in which we participate without negation – and we embrace and see the objective because we are for it and it is for us.

Furthermore any error of natural theology is avoided by arguing that no thing is in fact determinable, that all beings, as a combination of actuality and possibility, are not capable of finite determination, not least because they are capable of so much more. And while I have avoided natural theology by denying any knowledge founded on finitude, I have perhaps reformulated the relation between nature and theology. Because we have discerned that every natural visible rests on an infinitude of participation and possibility, we have in a curious and unexpected way recovered nature for God. Since knowledge of nature no longer stands in the way of knowledge of God, and since God's glory and ideality is now revealed to cover every creature, every substantial surface and every visible body, we have perhaps recovered the correct alignment and perception of God's relationship to the world. For by accepting existent actuality, and yet simultaneously refusing the ability of this ontic actuality to determine the higher possibilities of reality, we have prevented the reduction of invisibility to visibility and preserved the qualitative uniqueness of God's transcendence beyond any reduction to immanence. Moreover, since I have held that this invisibility is not thinkable apart from visibility, we do not have a transcendence that takes place at the expense of immanence. Because I have argued that invisibility as a possibility represents a higher dimension of actuality, not fully accessible by us, we have perhaps shown immanence to be life at its lowest power. Without a cognisance of the invisible, immanence remains trapped in untruth, for it is impossible to account for visibility apart from invisibility and then claim truthful knowledge of that which is manifest. All of which is to say that the plenitude of the trinitarian harmonic retains a phenomenological presence, a presence that *can* be perceived, even if it is not *necessarily* seen.

It is Christianity, and Christ's incarnation of the Word into flesh, which alone grants us the possibility that our highest attempted descriptions might actually be the case. For Christ binds together in his own body the invisible and the visible, and as a result he incarnates the transcendent in the flesh and prevents any subsequent account of human materiality divorcing itself from theology. This is why it is so important to refuse to surrender the world and its phenomenal beauty and materiality to Gnostic and idolatrous denials of God's creation. This again is why the whole stress and hope of this essay is to say that reality is indeed spiritual, that matter is intertwined with spirit, and that matter is not a noumenal materiality but rather a wholly phenomenal futurity. For both reality and humanity have and show a futurity and a potentiality that are not reducible to each other. For theology both man and nature, mind and world, have their origin in God, and (for phenomenology) both testify to and celebrate what is possible for them as a result. Mind and world are indeed meant to come together in knowledge, but the only knowledge that can genuinely come from this union is knowledge of the Father and the Son. And it is this possibility that I have been attempting to describe. From the perspective of man this means that though 'no one has ever seen God' (John 1: 8), 'whom no man has seen and no man is able to see' (1 Timothy 6: 16), Christ is the one 'who has made him known' (John 1: 18), since as Christ himself says: 'to have seen me is to have seen the Father' (John 14: 9), for we are told that 'whoever sees me sees the one who sent me' (John 12: 45). And this inconceivable sight is possible for us because Christ represents the Word and 'the Word was made flesh' (John 1: 14), as a consequence of which our reality has forever been transfigured, because now 'the reality is Christ' (Colossians 2: 18). As a result of this unimaginable event, God has been reconciled with man such that the created world is restored in and to its mediated alignment with the Creator; and in their most truthful consort with their highest possibility, the phenomena of the world testify to nothing but their in-sitting dependence in the glory and love of God.

To say this is to re-consecrate our world; it is to say that no created thing stands apart from its Creator and that each and every existent creation reveals its origin in the Father through showing and revealing the grace that allows it such an exhibition. In respect of this I feel, then, that it is no act of idolatry to believe that theology finds its possibility here – etched in the phenomenal world of perception and in the look and appearance of the created world. Not least because this claim, that we see God in the glory of the perceptual world, necessarily prohibits any visible from being both self-determinate and determinative of God, since, as I have said, God is seen only when every being and each and every visible surrenders idolatrous self-determination to enter into the beauty and light of infinite participation. In this way a phenomenal indeterminacy reveals not nothingness but an utter dependence upon, and an absolute determination by, God.

And this is why I focus on perception, because to perception is given, as Merleau-Ponty recognised, the paradoxical and wondrous gift to see both immanence and transcendence, to discern in the heart of what is most material what is most transcendent; which is to say that perception always goes beyond its objects, because objects always go beyond themselves.[31] For immanence is founded on a transcendence that is more intimate than itself, and that which is transcendent distinguishes itself from every immanent thing only in order to give itself wholly, without noumenal reserve, to every single thing in the measure that it, as creature, can receive. And for human beings it is perception that has first encounter with this wholly phenomenal gift. But this phenomenon does not stand above us as a transcendence hovering only in negation beyond a world that it cannot embrace. No – as soon as we open our eyes, as it were, we find ourselves wholly embraced and already inscribed, we find the ideal already running over us, and the invisible already there streaming over our bodies. And all of the shapes that we see, all of the depth, perspective, color and form, are figures and contours that the invisible brings forth for the visible. It pulls visibility into attendance with its highest form and possibility, and in the end we cannot separate the one from the other: we cannot see in this kenotic consort of the invisible and the visible where one ends and the other begins. This is perhaps why perception, with its inability to separate intuition from concept, with its account of passive reception and active contribution, cannot discern where the intellectual begins and the phenomenal ends. Because, in truth, perception takes us beyond any secular opposition; it affirms us and our objects, and it affirms them both as participation in and as culmination of God, and God's glory. And, in respect of this utter reality and beauty, only a theological realism can properly acknowledge and affirm what is presented there. For God grants to perception both the invisible and the visible, and when we color-in the adumbrations and transcendent shapes of the invisible and make it seen, and when we judge that we are for it and it is for us, and when we act in the name and are named in the act, then we see the phenomenal presence of the ideal in the real. And this ideality has the effect of calling forth from us a contribution such that we might make it so, and make manifest that it is so.

For the filiation of an invisible ideal form for a real visible content is nothing less than an account of the world as precisely a reality whose stature and glorious infinite phenomenality has yet to be captured by a modern art that has thoughtlessly and carelessly abandoned the painting of the real world to the falsifications of representational art and so-called classical depiction. For all that we know is the world, and theology shows us that this earth is created in order that subjectivity and objectivity might meet, but we have yet to give an account of what this might mean, or indeed fully describe what this might look like.

Despite the failure of modern art and perception to be adequate to such a Christian vision, it is possible for a painting that would be faithful to the world to make such a presentation, because the visible is there and is never simply visible as a secular or atheistic phenomenon. The visible is always infused with transcendent intelligibility and invisible form. As a result there is always more to see, and because each unseen side of each visible object struggles to come to visibility, the invisible is not unseen but is part of what it is to see, and consequently ideality struggles to assume visible reality for our participating vision. And it is only Christian theology that teaches us that the visible world is for us, that visibility is an invisible gift that completes itself and fulfills itself in human sight. But this is not a subjectivisation of the visible world; it is impossible to make our perceptions equal with what we perceive, for the visible is always in excess over us. Its intimate commerce with the invisible is given to sight, yet always exceeds our vision. Nontheless we can still make sense of it, since the visible never goes beyond us to something else, because all of its infinitude, its invisibility, is directed at us, is *for us*, as a donation of ideality to our receiving reality.

And while this world is not abstract but actual, it is by no means clear that an abstract art might not be the best account of it; for the incarnation of form is a reality that has still to be recognised and painted by the art of this era. And art should attempt this because it is Christianity that alone brings art into a relationship with a world that it might not be adequate to. Reality is, then, all that we have; but, by the same token, we cannot fully determine or ever represent what reality is; we can never complete the account, for created life is an inexhaustible plenitude, and the role of art should be, and should be only, to give an account of what we might otherwise not know – that which we have all been given and that which we can in consequence all see.

Notes

1 Jean-Luc Marion, *La Croisée du visible*, Paris: La Différence, 1991, p. 7.
2 Roger Fry, *Vision and Design*, London: Pelican, 1937, p. 39.
3 Clive Bell, 'The Aesthetic Hypothesis,' *Art*, London: Chatto & Windus, 1931, p. 29.
4 Michael Fried, 'Three American Painters,' *Modern Art and Modernism*, eds F. Frascina and C. Harrison, London: Harper & Row, 1982, p. 115.
5 Clement Greenberg, 'Modernist Painting,' *Art and Literature*, No. 4, Spring 1965, p. 195.
6 Jay M. Bernstein, *The Fate of Art*, Cambridge: Polity Press, 1993, p. 2.
7 As quoted in Peter H. Feist, *French Impressionism 1860–1920*, Köln: Taschen, 1995, p. 36.
8 Hermann Bahr, *Expressionism*, trans. R. T. Gribble, London: Henderson, 1925, pp. 45–46.
9 *Ibid.* p. 47.
10 Paul Cézanne, *Cézanne Letters*, ed. J. Rewald, Oxford: Bruno Cassirer, 1976, p. 261. (Hereafter, *Letters*).
11 Cézanne, Letter to Emile Zola, 24 September 1879, *Letters*, p. 182.
12 As quoted in Paul Smith, *Interpreting Cézanne*, London: Tate Gallery, 1996, p. 51.
13 Kurt Badt, *The Art of Cézanne*, trans. S. A. Ogilvie, London: Faber & Faber, 1965, p. 182.
14 In a letter to Bernard on 15 April 1904, Cézanne wrote: 'nature for us men is more depth than surface' (*Letters*, p. 301); in a letter to his son on 8 September 1906, he writes: 'I cannot attain the intensity that is unfolded before my senses. I have not the magnificent richness of colouring that animates nature' (*Letters*, p. 327). Remarks such as these reveal, for me, Cézanne's evident puzzlement at the surface disclosure of ideality and form; it is as though he almost recognises that what is most objective about visibility is not nature holding itself apart from us but our inability to be perceptually adequate to the very plenitude of its visibility.
15 Cézanne, *Letters*, p. 301.
16 Wassily Kandinsky, *Concerning the Spiritual in Art*, trans. M. T. H. Sadler, Toronto: Dover, 1977, pp. 9ff.
17 As reported in Ulrike Becks-Malorny, *Wassily Kandinsky: 1866–1944. The Journey to Abstraction*, Köln: Taschen, 1994, p. 55.
18 *Ibid.*, p. 59.
19 Kandinsky, *Concerning the Spiritual in Art*, p. 2.
20 Piet Mondrian, *The New Art – the New Life: The Collected Writings of Piet Mondrian*, eds H. Holtzman and M. James, London: Thames & Hudson, 1987, p. 107.
21 *Ibid.* p. 30.

22 *Le Visible et l'Invisible*, eds C. Lefort, Maurice Merleau-Ponty, Paris: Éditions Gallimard, 1964, p. 17. (Hereafter cited as VI.)

23 *Summa Contra Gentiles*, Vol. 1, Chapter 34.

24 See for example Hans Blumberg, *The Legitimacy of the Modern Age*, trans. R. W. Wallace, Cambridge, MA: MIT Press, 1985; and M. A. Gillespie, *Nihilism Before Nietzsche*, Chicago: University of Chicago Press, 1996.

25 I have argued elsewhere that this invisibility marks the relationship of the theological to the ontological and so indicates the point at which perceptions can transcend the secular and become truly theological. See my 'The Primacy of Theology and the Question of Perception,' in *Religion, Modernity and Postmodernity*, ed. P. Heelas, Oxford: Basil Blackwell, 1998.

26 VI, p. 178. 'On comprend alors pourquoi, à la fois, nous voyons les choses elle-mêmes, en leur lieu, où elles sont, selon leur être qui est bien plus que leur être-perçu.' Indeed this discrepancy between the subject and the object in matters of perception – their always being in excess of each other – testifies to a (theological) recognition that neither side of this divide can ever foreclose on the other. The object will always have more perspectival profiles for the intending gaze of the subject, and the subject will always bring more cognitive desires to the object than the object can ever satisfy. For it will be our point that this type of disjuncture speaks to the higher *eros* of cognition, and it marks, therefore, the passage to a genuinely theological perception.

27 VI, p. 185.

28 VI, p. 195.

29 VI, p. 198.

30 Maurice Merleau-Ponty , *Phénoménologie de la Perception*, Paris: Librairie Gallimard, 1945, p. 246.

31 See Merleau-Ponty's *Le Primat de la Perception*, Paris: Verdier, 1996 [1946], p. 49. 'Il y a donc dans la perception un paradoxe de l'immanence et de la transcendance.' In English the text of this 1946 discussion can be found as 'The Primacy of Perception and its Philosophical Consequences,' in *The Primacy of Perception*, trans. and ed. J. M. Edie, Chicago: Northwestern, 1964.

12

MUSIC

Soul, city and cosmos after Augustine

Catherine Pickstock

This essay examines the metaphysical category of 'music' in the Western tradition with special reference to Augustine's *De Musica* (composed in AD 391). In his treatise on 'the science of proper modulations', Augustine codified what Boethius was later to call the *quadrivium*, the 'fourfold path', according to which mathematics was subdivided into arithmetic, geometry, music and astronomy.[1] This curricular articulation was centred upon sciences of measurement: geometry measured inert, inorganic, sublunary spaces; music measured the relationship between the soul and the body (i.e. the proportions between the psychic and the organic), and also proportions within the soul itself; astronomy measured the time and movements of the heavenly bodies (often regarded as moved by the World Soul); and arithmetic, the most abstract, was the science of numbers in themselves. The order of these disciplines – the higher liberal arts – ascended through increasing degrees of abstraction from material to incorporeal contemplation, encouraging the knower towards the vision of God.[2] However, in the tripartition of music itself, the first category, the *musica mundana*, overlapped in its concerns with astronomy, as the heavenly spheres were thought to compose through their movements and ratios a music unhearable by us.[3] Moreover, as we shall see, because musical measurement is applied by Augustine even to God, on account of the relationality between the persons of the Trinity, the supremacy of arithmetic as *transcending* measure is implicitly surpassed. In this way, music becomes the science that most leads towards theology, and it is, perhaps, not accidental that Augustine's only lengthy treatise on a single liberal art concerns music.

After the *musica mundana*, the other parts of music, according to the Boethian classification which was adopted in the Middle Ages and which blended with Augustine's analysis, were *musica humana*, which concerned the harmonies between the body and the soul as well as the musical relationships within both the body and the soul, and *musica instrumentalis*, which concerned aspects of audible music governed either by a tension upon a string, by breath, by water, or by percussion.[4] This latter category underlines the societal dimension of music as envisaged by Augustine. In keeping with this tripartition, in this essay I treat of music in three sections under the headings: the cosmic, the psychic, and the ethical. However, it is necessary to modify the rigidity of these categories to the extent that, as we shall see, the very idea of music as a science of measurements (*modulatio*) displaces the isolation of these realms as discrete edifices in favour of relationality itself.[5]

In my consideration of the *De Musica*, I suggest a three-fold contrast between the Augustinian (and Boethian) tradition which was influential for Western thinking until the Renaissance and (1) the non-Western Indian tradition; (2) the disintegration of the Western tradition after Descartes; and (3) postmodern musical ontology as exemplified by Philippe Lacoue-Labarthe and Jacques Attali, which I suggest reinvokes certain aspects of that tradition, but in nihilistic cast. I argue that this nihilism, despite its exhaustive claims as to the universality of the flux, is an arbitrary phenomenology, and that the Augustinian tradition can once again become available as a theologico-musical key to ontology, psychology and to the political order. However, for this to become a coherent possibility, it is necessary that music be understood as a metaphysical category.

Cosmic music

Dionysus and the Eastern paradigm

A comparative examination of Indian thinking about music and the Western tradition reveals two strikingly different ontological conceptions of music. The Indian paradigm for sound is a distinctively Dionysian, exclusively time-bound, flow of a continuous fluidic stream or a vital inner substance along the channels of the human body, or emergence from a tube.[6] These images combine to form the idea of *nâda* which, via the atavistic roles of gesture and respiration, construes musical sound as a recreation of ancient sacrificial ritual.[7] But it remains a conception of music as wholly immanent, centred on the human body and with the human voice as its primary model,[8] a medium which evolves a continuous drone as a symbolic representation of unceasing world process, and which is characterised by a nasal timbre which draws attention to the resonance of the facial cavities.[9] This configuration of emission and bodily expulsion, or *prâna*, articulated through serial and organic forms, is paradoxically at once both 'humanist' and 'nihilistic' since, on the one hand, the aim is to rid the self of phenomenal reality by attaining a powerful indifference to, and control over, suffering emotions and, on the other hand, the ultimate transit of the soul and the perfect degree of power is an obliteration of any separate identity via a merging of the individual self with the creative principle of the universe.[10]

Apollo and Dionysus: the Western order

The ideal attainment of such a state of Nirvana, embodied in the flattening-out of hierarchies into a flow of extended phrases which are neither differentiated from, nor subordinated to, the complete musical composition, contrasts with the Greek and medieval European paradigm for music, for which the dominant metaphor was the tensed bow-string, ready for the impact of plucking.[11] This paradigm gave rise to various consequences for the development of later musical style in the West, namely a preference for distinct impacted sounds and structural clarity, the principles of tension and release, and of numerical proportions, the caesura, and an hierarchical and syntactical articulation of form.[12] The metaphysical principle which undergirds this inclination towards an ordering of the whole, and most differentiates the Eastern from the Western conception of music, is harmony. For while, in effect, the Indian ultimacy of *nâda* aims to displace the cosmos in favour of a uniting of the self with an undifferentiated continuum, harmony (the science of proportioned sounds) was a symbol of universal order, uniting all levels of the cosmos – the four basic elements (earth, water, fire, air), human beings, angelic persons and the heavenly bodies – into a numerically proportioned whole.

Even though, for the early Greeks, there was no concept of concordant tones being sounded simultaneously, the harmonic notion of simultaneity was nonetheless presupposed in several ways.[13] First, Western harmony extends from the Antique paradigm of the unification of opposites (linked to the paradigm of the tensed bow-string) as a kind of redeemed binarity.[14] Indeed, the Greek interest in mathematical proportions in music presupposes the bringing together of successive notes into a psychically spatial ratio, in a way that seems to anticipate harmonic relations in actual sound.[15] Second, despite the absence of harmony in audible music, it was present in ancient Greek metaphysics. The notion of the cosmos itself as a balance of four elements, and of the paths of the celestial bodies, involved the simultaneity and interdependence of nonetheless distinct continua.[16] Their revolving paths suggested a harmony which, while mobile, was not subject to decay or any dissolute successiveness. Third, harmony was something that existed in the mind. For while notes could be sounded only successively by a singer, the harmonious relationship between, say, the consecutive sounding of a tonic and its dominant would have been apparent to a hearer.[17] It should be noted that this notion of a psychically apprehended harmony depends, first, upon the invocation of memory and, second, on the segmentation of a musical line into distinct units. By contrast, the continuous flow of Eastern music is more allied to the inducing of a trance-like state which is inherently amnesiac, conserving the essence of what has passed only in its dissolution into something unmediably different. In this conception, both music and selfhood are approximated to impersonal unconscious organic processes of temporal flux.[18]

In spite of the association of Western harmony with the plucking of the Apollonian lyre,[19] one should not follow Nietzsche in interpreting Greek culture in terms of an opposition between the Dionysian spirit of music and the Apollonian spirit of the visual arts (or of music rationalised) or in terms of the Apollonian as a dialectical stage or dissembling mask of the Dionysian.[20] In fact, the notion of musical harmony among the Greeks holds in tension the temporality of the Dionysian and the spatiality of the Apollonian paradigms, as can be deduced from the fact that they did not conceive of harmony as arising from a statically spatial simultaneity, but, on the one hand, from the coincidence of distinct and dynamic cosmic paths and, on the other hand, from the synthesis performed by the temporal recall in the soul.

This same balance was preserved in the later development of Western music, the audible realization of this harmonic synthesis of the spatial and the temporal with the rise of polyphony. While, formerly, liturgical plainchant obeyed the ineluctable structures of divine revelation, dictated to St Gregory,[21] polyphony, which arose around the ninth century, was an apparently more 'rationalized' musical form.[22] In Notre Dame, Magister Leoninus composed a collection of two-voice polyphonic settings (c. 1182) where a deceleration of liturgical melodies was sustained by the *tenores*, beneath the melodic arc of the *vox organica* whose line was governed by the creation of strictly ordered numerical proportions and rhythmic modes which were defined into *ordines* by the articulation of pauses or rests.[23] However, this polyphonic expression of human reason, although opposed by those who thought that music should be monodic so that its words might speak more directly to the soul unencumbered by complex musical artifices,[24] was not an *unambiguous* expression of the triumph of human reason. For despite its numerical structures, there is a sense in which polyphonic music, when it is *sounded*, lies always beyond our grasp; our assertion of human reason is a deliberate, humble, doxological abasement of the same, in honour of the superlative Reason. In fact, composers of polyphonic music made explicit appeal to the (unhearable) harmonies of the cosmos in order to counter monodistic oppositions.[25] Their arguments were anticipated in the ninth century by Johannes Scotus Eriugena who defended complex music on the grounds that the harmonies and rhythms of humanly produced music and its internal mathematical relationships could be equated with the invisible musical and mathematical relationships of the cosmos. He argued that if cosmic order is itself complex and multidimensional, those terrestrial sounds embodying numerical principles proportionate to those of the cosmos could be complex and multidimensional in comparable ways.[26] This spatial assimilation of timelessness is not an idolatrous spatialization, because the unhearable simultaneity never remains still, even for a fraction of a second.[27] The interweaving of melodic lines ensures that the vertical is always equally balanced with the horizontal, while the hierarchical character of the vertical itself ensures that the horizontal points beyond itself rather than inculcating a flattened-out spatial immanence.

Augustine's musical ontology

According to William Waite, there is a strong possibility that these architects of polyphony were influenced by Augustine's *De Musica*, since we know that many theologians of the time drew upon his definition of music as 'the science of proper modulation'.[28] Indeed, there is an almost perfect correspondence between the modal systems of the Notre Dame composers and the doctrines of rhythm enunciated by Augustine, in particular his equal stress upon the measurement of the *absence* of sound (in rests) as its presence.[29]

Whatever the case for influence may be, the same co-articulation of time and space in order to achieve the best possible representation of (and offering to) eternity is apparent in Augustine's treatise, as it is in the complex music of these composers.

In the *De Musica*, musical rhythm, which Augustine takes as applying equally or even more to poetry as it does to what we would describe as music, is characterised, first, by the classification of rhythmic patterns in proportions which remain the same regardless of length of sounding,[30] and, second, by a stress on the importance of intervals as elements which can themselves form part of a rhythmic structure, but which serve also to divide up musical sequences. This dual stress on relative proportion in abstraction from isolated units, and on unhearable intervals, is reflected by Augustine in his treatment of cosmic music, or of music as an ontological category.

Number and relationality

Any rhythmic proportion is given by Augustine the name of 'number'. Created reality itself consists, for his adapted Pythagorean view, of nothing but numbers.[31] This is equivalent to saying that it consists in nothing but relations ordered in certain regular and analogical proportions. Indeed, this is so much the case that for Augustine the entire cosmos itself is not a total 'thing' to which one could accord a size, even a maximum size. On the contrary, it is rather an assemblage of all the relations that it encompasses, in such a way that since there is nothing else with which it can be compared or to which it is related, it cannot in itself be accorded a size, measure, or rhythmic modulation. One might say that the totality of reality is not one big note, but instead, as Augustine says, a poem or song (*carmen*), and so, in other words, the total series of numerical interactions.[32]

The caesura and creatio ex nihilo

If musical rhythm is exemplified, for Augustine, on a cosmic scale, so also is the musical interlude or rest, which, as we have seen, is crucial to the entire character and development of Western music as based upon articulated phrases.[33] The alternation of sound and silence in music is seen by Augustine as a manifestation of the alternation of the coming into being and the passing into non-being which must characterise a universe created out of nothing. Augustine thus Christianises the Pythagorean view and is able to give a serious ontological role to 'nothing', in contrast to a Platonic scheme which would envisage numbers as imposing merely a *degree* of order upon chaos. To the contrary, for Augustine, creation exhibits a *perfect* order or beauty, albeit in its own restricted degree, and the nothingness intrinsic to creation on its own is a necessary part of this order.[34] Indeed, it is when human creatures fail to confess this nothingness, when their lives in time are without pauses, that this order is denied and a greater nothingness of disharmony ensues.[35] Furthermore, the 'nothings' do not for Augustine merely segment rhythmic phrases into regular metric units; they also enter into the constitution of the rhythmic units themselves. This is because, as he puts it, a line is a proportion between an unextended point and its own length; thus it is a mysterious finite measure of an infinite distance. The same structure is repeated in the case of a two-dimensional surface, which measures the distance from a line without breadth, and for a three-dimensional figure, which measures the distance from a two-dimensional figure without depth.[36] Augustine suggests, on this basis, that all spatial reality is continuously generated from something without extension by a power essentially alien to this spatial reality. He pursues this contention with examples of both artificial and natural processes. In the first place, he argues that the process of human artistic creation precedes the substantiality of its product. And in the second place, he argues that the time-spans of a tree precede its space-spans, because a tree gradually emerges from a seed.[37]

In this way, substantiality is perpetually crossed-out by temporal emergence, or creation. In the case of human artistic endeavours, Augustine notably omits here the traditional view that the completed work exists primarily as a kind of 'given' in the mind of the artist. On the contrary, he appears at the end of the *De Musica* to recognise that human art can truly create something new and, indeed, it is just this circumstance which suggests this possibility to Augustine because human beings are situated within a universe which springs from nothing. The fact that things are continuously *coming to be*, and continuously emerging from points which are nothing, implies for Augustine that it is most rational to see finite reality as having emerged in its entirety from nothing.[38] One should note that the nothingness of the 'point' indicates for Augustine at once the abyss of finitude and a participation in the plenitude of the infinite. Thus, he evacuates reality in a way that seems to include a nihilistic moment, only to affirm all the more an absolutely infinite order which, nonetheless, finitude can never fully grasp.[39]

Time, space and the 'measure' of eternity

It is this suspension of the created order between nothingness and the infinite which demands that its order be primarily a temporal and audible sequence, rather than a spatial and visible one. This might seem a paradox in that it makes time, which does not stand still, closer to eternity than space, whose permanence might more easily seem to mimic it. However, the whole point is that such mimicry risks a demonic substitution for eternity, or forced 'spatialisation'.[40] By contrast, the passage of time continuously acknowledges the nothingness of realized being, and can become the vehicle of a desire for a genuinely infinite 'permanence'. Moreover, since this genuine permanence, as infinite, is not circumscribed, the non-closure of time is in fact the best finite image of this.[41] It is just for this reason that Augustine regards only infinity, which is without measure, as the one true equal measure. It is to be noted that this claim radically redefines order as not opposed to freedom, and as no longer to be associated with fixed boundaries and unrevisable rules.[42] By comparison with eternity, created realities are, for Augustine, only imperfectly equal and only imperfectly harmonic. This is because no finite position (point, line, surface, body) is ever perfectly instantiated, since every finite point already has some extension. Thus, nothing finite is ever equal to itself,[43] nothing finite is ever perfectly one, nothing finite is ever perfectly exact or measured. And yet, for Augustine, the true unity, the infinite One, is not itself a true (univocal) unity but, on the contrary, coincides with the perfect harmonic relation in such a way that the divine Father *is* the communication of his unity to the perfect measure of his Son.[44]

Rhythm and redemption

The nearest approximation to true infinite measure is therefore the temporal striving towards greater and greater exactitude.[45] For Augustine, this is not just something which conscious rational human beings do, but in fact is what sustains every creature in being.[46] Every creature is perpetually seeking to be 'like itself' or to occupy more precisely its proper position in time and space. Every creature is a specific rhythm. However, despite this necessary primacy of time over space, Augustine exhibits also an equivalence of the balancing of time and space which we saw in the case of polyphonic music.[47] Were it the case that space is merely hierarchically subordinate to time, then the supreme ideal would be something like the pure flow of the Eastern paradigm, which seeks the dissolution and forgetting of every spatial articulation. As we have seen, such a privileging of Dionysian flow has acosmic 'nihilistic' connotations. However, just as important as the priority of time, for Augustine, is the insistence on articulation into distinct musical units or phrases, the very move which allows a stress upon the simultaneity of harmony, whether in memory or in the actuality of performed polyphony. What mediates and allows this double stress is precisely the centrality of the silent caesura, because, first, this suggests how music constantly emerges in time from nothing, and, second, it divides each musical phrase from every other, and in reality this means every creature from every other creature. This division by the point or the 'nothing' can be seen as the transcendental precondition for the possibility, not of spatial totalisation, but of spatial relationship which is to a degree simultaneous. Thus, music, although initiated by the flow, is not primarily a matter of flow 'over against' articulations. On the contrary, it is only constituted *as* flow by the series of articulations mediated by a silence which allows them also to sound together. It is on the basis of this conception that Augustine can make the astonishing assertion at the end of the *De Musica* that the salvation of every creature consists in its being in its own proper place as well as its time.[48] Both aspects are equally necessary if there is to be a cosmic poem. (This same integration of rhythmic and melodic flow with harmony implies also a possible integration of the audible and the visible in an 'operatic' unity.)

Augustine's synthesis of the spatial and the temporal, of articulation and flow, producing the best possible expression of the eternal music, is a distribution of the spiritual and the real which disallows any crude dualism, for his transcendent context, as we have seen, releases the ultimacy of such contraries by encompassing and redeeming them. However, if one examines post-Cartesian theories of music, one finds that Nietzsche's distinction between the Apollonian (spatial) and the Dionysian (temporal) now becomes relevant.

The theory of music expounded by Rameau (principally in *Génération harmonique* [1737], *Démonstration du principe de l'harmonie* [1750], and *Observations sur notre instinct pour la musique* [1754]) and the counter-theory presented by Rousseau (in his *Essai sur l'origine de langues, où il est parlé de la mélodie et de l'imitation musicale* [1761], and throughout his fictional and non-fictional writings) seem to distort the chronotope of their Augustinian inheritance in opposing, but dialectically identical, ways. For, as I will show, Rameau stresses the exclusively spatial origins of all music, while Rousseau opposes this view by focusing on the nature of music as a derationalised flow of subjective expressiveness.[49]

Rameau and the 'corps sonore'

For Rameau, the origin of music lies in the essentialised triadic chord always hearable in the sounds generated by the resonant objects of nature. He thus identified the unalterable physical laws of the *corps sonore*, i.e. the fundamental tone sounding in simultaneity with its two harmonics, and argues from this triadic disposition of resonances for the priority of a fixed spatial harmony over the more temporal flow of melody: 'Music is ordinarily divided into Harmony and Melody, although the latter is only a part of the former'.[50] This primacy of harmony, because based upon a physical law, is unalterable in historical or cultural terms. In a gesture of universalisation influenced by Descartes' *Method*,[51] Rameau sought to show that this single principle of the origins of music could be extended to become a *mathesis* for all the sciences, for 'it is in Music that nature appears to designate the Physical principle of those first and purely Mathematical notions on which all the Sciences are based; I mean, the Harmonic, Arithmetic, and Geometric proportions from which follow progressions of the same type and which are revealed at the first instant of the resonance of a *corps sonore*'.[52] Thus, while for Augustine the liberal arts ascended to a transcendent contemplation of divine ineffability, Rameau suggests that such an all-encompassing epistemological cyclopaedia can be derived from the result of a physical action upon resonant matter. The cosmic consummation of harmony is therefore immanentised to the level of air, 'stirred up by the impact of each particular *corps sonore*.'[53]

Rousseau and melodic ultimacy

Rousseau, on the other hand, stresses that monodic music ('a simple unison') is more primary than the fundamental bass suggested by the *corps sonore*. He dismisses Rameau's theory, characterising modern European (harmonic and chordal) music as a repressive distortion of an unblemished original sonority found only in the music of oriental cultures,[54] which speaks directly to the heart.[55] In keeping with this Eastern preference, Rousseau argues that the paradigm for such music is *vocal*, thus stressing the constitutive ties between language, music and culture. This drift towards orientalism was endorsed in the nineteenth century by Schopenhauer, who claimed that music was a pure unmediated force which exhibited the naked unteleological Will which is the deepest ontological reality. In consequence, Schopenhauer claimed that music is closer to the real than is poetry, being at its purest when it consists in tones without words or mediation of any kind. In these respects, Wagner was Schopenhauer's faithful disciple, and his operas sought to subordinate words to melody; indeed, as Jean-Luc Nancy argues in *Les Muses*, the final function of the musical libretto here is to theorise the supremacy of music. In addition, Wagner sought to put into practice the Rousseau-esque and 'oriental' notion of real music as pure melody, subordinating both harmony and rhythm. This attempt to achieve flow without measure is in effect a will to expiration, as measure can never finally be extirpated. And it refuses the Western primacy of *Logos* which understands flow as only expressive of, and constituted by, measure.[56]

Polyphonic resolution

In the analysis of Augustine's musical chronotope in the previous section we saw that space is represented by an implicit vertical axis by which a hierarchy of numbers links the higher to the lower, although not in such a way as to cast the lower things as quantitatively lesser counterparts of higher things. Rather, as we have seen, Augustine suggests that the lower elements have their own irreplaceable value – so much so, in fact, that it becomes possible to be *jealous* of lower things.[57] The vertical axis of space, for Augustine, complements the horizontal axis of time which is seen to represent both process and development. This model of time and space is exemplified by the structures of polyphony, in whose interweaving lines the temporal melodic component, despite its successiveness, preserves an integrity and coherence, while the hierarchy of its parts, despite its spatial distribution, must perpetually redefine its path.

Musical immanentism

In contrast to this model, the Rameau-esque chord, by essentialising a static vertical universal, paradoxically surrenders its hierarchical differentiation, because the value of each component, and historical instantiation of this 'origin', are equalised as infinitely transferable, irrespective of circumstance. Furthermore, the chord is here regarded as a purely physical phenomenon, bearing no relation to the hierarchy of soul and body. It no longer points beyond itself to a transcendent consummation of harmony, but rather to further chordal progressions, or modulations into indifferently varied inversions. Thus, the spatial hierarchy is flattened into a linear succession of interchangeable variables. On this view, melody is reduced to a regrettable necessity, occasioned by our inability to apprehend everything at once, as the only means by which harmony can be experienced in time.

And 'ideal' music is implicitly represented as a spatially simultaneous universal chord, in contrast to the Augustinian poem of the universe. This baroque or classical spatialisation of music is exhibited also in the drift towards music as 'spectacle', all the way from the court masque through public opera to the bourgeois concert.[58]

While Rameau's insistence upon harmony seems to denude the spatial axis of its hierarchical aspect, Rousseau's model of music as primarily melodic and temporal seems paradoxically to spatialise time. For, by insisting on melody as a purely temporal duration of experienced process, he reduces time to a formless flow without articulation or distinguishing parts. Such a flow seems reducible to a spatial continuum. One could say, by contrast, that for Augustine time makes space more properly space, and space makes time more properly time.[59]

The inevitable consequences of no longer regarding time as a moving image of eternity are exhibited in Kant's treatment of time in the first *Critique*. For although Kant sees both time and space as *a priori* forms of sensibility (in that neither objectively belongs to the world), he regards them as separate: space is the form of outer sense, and time is the form of inner sense. (Time is thought to be not something one can sense, but is that which links sensations through memory.[60]) He then argues that if time is the ground for comprehending both succession and simultaneity, then time as such does not change, but becomes itself the *substratum* of appearances (rather than things in themselves). As an epistemological version of substance, time is turned into the most stable (and therefore most spatial) thing that there is.

As we have seen, modern music theory, at least from the eighteenth century onwards, and (perhaps with some important exceptions) the Western tradition, broke with the synthesis of time and space that was secured by the idea of performing an adequation of eternity. So-called postmodern thought seemingly makes some attempt to overcome this modern separation and especially its spatialising of time and subordinating of space to a mere linear punctual temporality (Rameau). Thus, in the case of Heidegger, as compared with Kant, one finds a re-ontologisation of time: time is no longer simply the form of appearances, but the inseparable mode of Being itself. Time, for Heidegger, has a certain priority over space and yet in our ontological fallenness we can never fully step outside the sense of a present 'now' and its spatial concomitants.

Lacoue-Labarthe and musical autobiography

This dual stress upon a temporal flow which 'gives' Being and, at the same time, upon the occurrence of this flow only through temporal 'spacings' (which must be at once both temporal and spatial intervals) is taken up by Jacques Derrida as a theory of transcendental differentiation and deferral governing both Being *and* knowledge. Derrida's disciple, Philippe Lacoue-Labarthe, explicitly recognises that this constitutes a kind of musical ontology.[61] Thus, it would seem that we have been returned to a Pythagorean–Augustinian perspective. Moreover, Lacoue-Labarthe places an especial stress upon the inescapability of the subjective or 'autobiographical' moment, the moment of 'making music', which would provide an equivalent to Augustine's granting privileged place to the psyche in this ontology.[62] For Lacoue-Labarthe, the indeterminacy of differentiation is the site of the opening-out of subjectivity, while the 'presence' of a specific temporal–spatial ordering grants to the subject a specific rhythm, *tupos*, or character.[63] It would seem that Lacoue-Labarthe is attempting to integrate the Dionysian and the Apollonian, since the continuous flux of music, its audibility and languishing/desiring agony, cannot occur without Apollonian mimesis, by which the subject composes itself in terms of repetition of other 'musical' instances which have preceded it.[64]

The stasis of time

However, this postmodernist ontology remains immanentist. It can be demonstrated that without an Augustinian account of transcendence, it actually lapses back into modern (metaphysical) music, the very structure it apparently overcomes. First, since Heidegger does not regard time as a moving image of eternity, his diagnosis of the ecstatic character of time or the non-punctual inter-involvement of past, present and future at every moment must regress into a Kantian substantialisation of time, albeit now in ontological and not epistemological terms. (Although it is possible to argue that Heidegger remains secretly a prisoner of epistemology, because he still thinks he can determine the ontological difference according to its appearance/non-appearance to the knowing subject.[65]) According to this new substantialisation, the *aporias* of ecstatic temporality do not point, as for Augustine, to the inherent non-being of time taken by itself,[66] but rather indicate directly a paradoxical 'essence' which is the constitution of all Being by nothing, which only *is* through this constitution. Thus, nothing, the secret real, asserts itself only as Being which nonetheless immediately dissolves back into nothingness. This is a nihilistic version of Augustine's Christian–Pythagorean dissolution of finite reality through his reflection upon numbers and music or, as Derrida might say, differentiation.

Time and the audible

The same nihilism governs Lacoue-Labarthe's reflections. First, we find that there is here after all no easy co-existence of the Apollonian and the Dionysian. The mimetic and representational, although inevitable, is always contaminated for Lacoue-Labarthe by a metaphysical claim for essential identity. Thus his primary appeal is to audibility in order to sustain his dissolution of metaphysics.[67] Compared with Derrida, this does seem to constitute a new appeal to orality and, indeed, Lacoue-Labarthe insists that deconstructive differentiation occurs always and only through subjective reflection (in a sense, for Lacoue-Labarthe, difference *is* subjectivity), and that this moment of subjective intervention will include a new instance of self-characterisation which none the less will have immediately to be overcome in order to avoid a new lapse into the metaphysical.[68] This latter point shows that Lacoue-Labarthe is unable to use the notion of orality to fuse the integrity of the speaking body with the flux; it is therefore no accident that he sometimes wishes to characterise music rather as *writing* than as audibility.[69]

Text versus performance

This tension between the written and the audible paradigm of music suggests that Lacoue-Labarthe is unable to resolve the modernist hesitation between the essence of music as being in the written work, and, on the other hand, being in repeated performance (this dualism is another outcome of the breakdown of the Pythagorean inheritance – see below). In the end, he seems to opt for music as written and, therefore, for the Dionysian as an unconscious process.

Legible music

Although Lacoue-Labarthe is critical of accounts of music, such as those of Plato, Nancy and Heidegger, whose exaltation of musical form (*gestaltung*) he claims too much denies the supremacy of the flux,[70] Lacoue-Labarthe's own speculations on music are themselves belied by the same denial. In his account, the spatial is finally subordinated to that which has therefore become a new substantial 'essence', a new metaphysical substance, in such a way that time is here spatialised – because it now has an essence which is an indefinite flux, a rhythm which mourns an origin that never was, and encourages a desire destined to frustration.[71] Such flux is paradoxically spatialised, and paradoxically has an essence, since it passes from nothing to nothing and has in consequence no authentic transition. As entirely elusive, it must remain static and shares with the nihil that consummation of essence described above. Since space is subordinate, there can be no notion here of finding one's proper place in time; thus salvation is occluded from the picture. It is notable that Lacoue-Labarthe claims that if one sees a configuration of dancing couples through a sound-proofed window, one will 'see' no rhythm; only the music will provide the key to their movements.[72] This seems quite arbitrarily to deny the traditional Pythagorean truth that rhythm can be incarnate as much in the visual as in the audible, two embodiments which are integrated in poetry, which for the tradition is perhaps even more musical than music itself.[73] The paradox here is that rhythm is banished by Lacoue-Labarthe from the public spatial dance, and yet supremely located in intrinsically private spatial writing. This is because the true objective spatial substance is for Lacoue-Labarthe this impersonal flux of mutually cancelling absence and presence which is correctly and exactly measured by the arbitrary and open-ended indifference of the private subject. Thus the precise co-ordination of the isolated individual with an objectively measuring *mathesis* characteristic of modernity is hereby repeated in a nihilistic guise. Lacoue-Labarthe, like Rousseau, suppresses the spatial axis of harmony but no longer through expressive Romantic melody; instead, through the dull beat of impersonal 'pulsional' rhythm which imposes its violent writing regardless. This is his new version of music as a universal language, which perpetuates the Wagnerian error of imagining that music has a 'pure' essence, free from the mediation of verbal and symbolic convention.[74]

Psychic music

The Eastern paradigm and the burden of the self

Indian music is not concerned with the establishment of *tupos* or character. On the contrary, it is concerned with the purging of emotions and sufferings according to a process of sacrificial offering which releases the self from *care* – not into a higher care, as for Augustine (see below), but from the burden of self altogether – that it may eventually merge with Nirvana.[75] Similarly, on this view, there is no cosmos, since the world is not a site of order, but ordering rather is a progressive dissolution of the world. So, likewise, there is no microcosmic order or psyche.

The ascent of numbers

By contrast, in the West, there is psyche, and not only is music concerned with the imprinting of its *tupos*, but the psyche itself is a musical reality. It exists, as we have seen, in a musical proportion to the body and in turn to the whole cosmos. Thus music is at once a thing measured and the measure itself; it is for us supremely the measure of the psychic–corporeal relationship. It is this notion which always held together what we now think of as sciences and arts,[76] and ensured that the topics of the *quadrivium* always had a qualitative aesthetic dimension. To say that the essence of beauty is in number, as Augustine[77] and, later, Bonaventure and a host of medieval followers do, sounds to us like an attempt to reduce aesthetics to science and formal rules. However, this would be to neglect the fact that for the tradition, number had a qualitative dimension and a mysterious inexhaustible depth. It was in fact the very break up of this tradition which generated the duality of science and art, along with a series of other dualities in which the modern West remains trapped.

Active reception and the synthesis of desire and judgement

Augustine, as we have seen, reinvokes this Pythagorean tradition and adapts it to the outlook of his newly acquired Christian faith.[78] He regards both soul and body as numbers, and this ontology reveals a monism more fundamental than Augustinian dualism which commentators have more frequently insisted upon.[79] For Augustine, in addition to the unconscious regulation of all bodily movements by the soul, the knowing and desiring of finite things is a matter of specific musical proportions, and his treatment of musical sound in the *De Musica* is just one exemplification of this relation. His account of how we sense musical sound is a quite complex one, for, on the one hand, he rejects the Neo-Platonic view that the soul creates the body, since this is incompatible with the Christian view that all finite existences derive from a divine Creator, and yet, like the Neo-Platonists, he cannot accept that the soul as a more powerful number (a more intense harmony) can be causally influenced by the body.[80] In consequence, he will not allow, like Aristotle and later Aquinas, that the soul itself senses, since it is passively informed by corporeal stimuli. And yet his rejection of the Neo-Platonic position means that he must allow for some passivity in sensation. He incorporates this by stressing, first, that one's body passively receives sensations from other bodies,[81] and, second, that this event of reception *occasions* an active production by the soul, not of the physical sound itself, but of an internal image of that sound.[82] In this 'act' of occasioning, it is as if the sensation does pass into the soul, but is received in an entirely active manner because the soul transfigures the sensation into a comprehensible reality according to its recollection of eternal harmony – which, of course, includes all possible harmonies, corporeal and incorporeal. This, however, is not at all equivalent to a Kantian *a priori*, since there are no harmonic categories latent in the soul; on the contrary, the memory which the sensation stimulates is truly of divine transcendence. This is not, of course, for Augustine, based upon the pre-existence of the soul. Accordingly, he resolves the *aporia* of learning, namely, the question of how it is that the soul can search for, and later reactivate, harmonies which it does not at present know, by appeal to the role of desire. Indeed, for Augustine, desire always accompanies judgement, in such a way that even a realised judgement is *true* only in terms of its desiring anticipation of the relation of a present harmony to other future things with which it could come to be in harmony.[83] This co-belonging of desire and judgement is summed up for Augustine in the image of reason become the burning fire of charity.[84]

The hierarchy of numbers

According to this model of 'active reception', described above,[85] the numbers of sensation have priority, for Augustine, over the external sounding numbers.[86] After the numbers of sensation come the memorial numbers, which are in turn superior, because to sense any single harmony of two things one must already have brought together a merely remembered past sound with a sensed present sound. Above the memorial numbers come the numbers which judge spontaneously a sensory stimulus, and which allow the mind to create a sensory image on the occasion of a bodily stimulation.[87] However, above the initial number of judgement (*numeri sensuales*) comes a reflexive or recursive judgement (*numeri iudiciales*) which judges the first judgement, whether accepting, rejecting or modifying an initial enthusiasm or distaste.[88]

Numeri corporeales

This bare account of Augustine's classification, however, conceals certain nuances which are crucial for his musical psychology. First, although the sounding numbers (*numeri corporeales*) eventually drop out of consideration, Augustine never takes back his affirmation that one becomes aware of one's sense of harmonic proportion only from a particular instance of hearing an actual physical harmony.[89] So, once again, one can see that possession of a faculty of judgement does not in his case amount to a possession of *a priori* Kantian rules (if one is thinking of the first *Critique* and not the third).[90] Also, one can see how Augustine's Platonic theory of recollection actually fuses a 'memory' of the transcendent with a triggering-off of this memory by events in time which have empirically to be registered.[91]

Recursive judgement

The second nuance follows closely upon the first. It would be easy to imagine that Augustine's category of initial spontaneous judgement is freer and less ineffable than a possibly colder, rational or more codifiable, higher judgement. In fact, it is really not like this at all, because the recursive judgement is an open judgement, in principle never finished, and is therefore a non-codifiable judgement which always exceeds any given rules since these can always be subject to further judgement.[92] This higher judgement is an inherently incomplete judgement, but it is nonetheless a *true* judgement precisely because it is incomplete, since, as we have seen, nothing finite is truly equal to itself. Just as there is only a measure of objective equality insofar as finite things participate in divine unity, so also there is only a measure of subjective equality insofar as our judgement participates in the divine infinite judgement.[93] As we have seen, our lack of perfect judgement has to be supplemented by an exercise of true desire if there is to be any participation whatsoever in judgement. Thus we can see that the higher judgement is the very opposite of a *mathesis*, and Augustine frequently inveighs against a mechanical following of empty rules,[94] just as he celebrates rhythmic proportions which remain analogously the same in very different embodiments.[95] Moreover, he associates this empty rule-following with a judgement that does not refer itself to the divine infinite judgement, or does not refer the *usus* of finite things to eternal fruition: for if one is left merely with *usus*, one is left also with only a utilitarian calculation of the predictable effects of sounds. Without the higher judgement, spontaneous judgements would have to remain fixed and unquestionable, and it would become possible to have a strict science of musical harmony which one could deploy to produce predictable effects in the social sphere.[96] The two possible tendencies of judgement are contrasted by Augustine in terms of the opposite implications of the word *cura*. If we are merely *curious* about finite harmonies, then we will fall victim to the burdensome *care* of discovering and preserving them. If, on the other hand, one takes *care* to refer finite harmonies beyond themselves to eternity mediated by new relational arrivals in time, then one will discover that the yoke of this care is – after Christ's words cited by Augustine – easy, and its burden light.[97]

The measure of music

A third nuance must be mentioned. We have seen that, for Augustine, our judgement is inherently limited.[98] This circumstance should be connected with the non-dualism of his Pythagorean ontology, for according to this ontology, the contrast of objective unity with subjective judgement, so far invoked, must in fact be relativised. For the Antique and medieval outlook, there was no such thing as our post-Cartesian contrast between the objective fact measured and the subjective measurer. On the contrary, the heavenly bodies, for example, constituted at once the supreme harmony and the supreme *measure* of that harmony: they were their own best perfect measure.[99] Inversely, precisely to the degree that we are judges or measurers, we are measurers mainly of ourselves, 'ourselves' being identical with the proper proportions in which we stand to everything else. Or, to put this another way, we remain incorporated within the poem of the universe whose parts we seek to measure, and any true act of measuring can mean only our fulfilling our role within that poem. To measure music means no more than to sound our right note which no other can sound and which then forms part of the cosmic poem which is its own best measure.

Musical 'relativism'

This perspective, recalling Augustine's account of the originality of human art, allows him to attain to perspectives which to our ears sound 'post-Renaissance'. (The question of the degree to which such perspectives were in fact known in the Middle Ages should perhaps remain open.) Thus, Augustine can account for a certain relativity in aesthetic judgement, or the idea that there are certain things which one needs to be in the right position to appreciate, precisely because one is a constitutive part of that picture which one is appreciating. This perspective does not degenerate into relativism, because Augustine has faith that all these limited perspectives or instances are themselves beautifully integrated into the cosmic poem. This same perspectivalism is applied by Augustine to time as well as to space, and so to societies as well as to individuals, for he is able to recognise that judgement gives birth to contrasting customary norms which can themselves undergo change, and yet be integrated within an overall sense of rightly judged proportion.[100] For one can have a sense of different customs fitting different times and places. This socio-historical dimension is in accordance with Augustine's musical definition of salvation and one can relate it to remarks made elsewhere by Augustine, for example regarding the appropriateness of the Old Testament Law for a particular time and place in human history.

Reason versus passion

While, as we have seen, for Augustine and the tradition, music is the measure of the soul's relation to the body, in the post-Cartesian era the domain of music is split into two. For either, as in the case of Rameau's theory of music, it pertains to a physical principle which explains the passions as purely natural phenomena, or, as for Rousseau, music severs its link with measure of any kind and becomes a pure expression of subjective communion in successive impressions. A crucial consequence of this bifurcation of harmony and melody seems, in the cases of Rameau and Rousseau, to be a concomitant separation of reason and passion which, as we have seen above, were previously regarded as less obviously separable.

Musical 'work'

In recent twentieth-century musical theory, there is a debate between those who uphold a 'Platonic' theory of music, according to which music is an essentially mental phenomenon, for whom the 'real work' is something which exists outside its instantiation in performance, in parallel with the so-called Platonic view of mathematics according to which abstract numbers are realities, and others who take a nominalist approach. The former view was exemplified by Charles Ives, forerunner of musical modernism, who under the influence of American Trancendentalism saw performance as a lapse and at best a tiresome necessity: 'Why can't music go out in the same way it comes into a man', he wrote, 'without having to crawl over a fence of sounds, thoraxes, catguts, wire, wood and brass.'[101] By contrast, earlier composers – one might think of Bach – remained essentially craftsmen for whom composition and performance were mutually informing activities. In the case of the alternative consequence of the collapse of this integration of musical nominalism, a musical work is something continuously repeated as different, and has no essential identity whatsoever. This obviously tends towards a postmodern dissolution of the integrity of the 'work'.[102]

However, this alternative, like the Rameau–Rousseau debate, can be seen as the result of the breakdown of the Pythagorean, Platonic and Christian traditions of reflection upon music.[103] For so-called modern 'Platonism' is only a pseudo-Platonism infected by modern *a priori*-ism. According to a genuinely Platonic view, ideal music is not something possessed by the mind, but, on the contrary, arrives from without and is fully instantiated only in a transcendent source. Hence, while this view would allow that every composed work was in excess of its performed incarnations, nonetheless every new performance would constitute an indispensable means for recollecting aspects of that ideality of the original work which could not be known by us from the outset without its being instantiated in time. Hence, only the idea that there is an infinite eternal music holds in tension text and performance, and ensures that the ideality of a work is not something to do with the genius of the isolated individual composer (who, on the modern 'Platonic' view, constitutes an absolute origin), but with its participation in an unknown music, and thereby its co-ordination with all other true musical works, or human participations in eternal harmony.

The missing subject

Normally one sees modernity as the great age of the subject, and postmodernity as the time of the dissolution of the subject. However, we have just seen that there really is no characterised subject in modernity. For the Rameau-esque post-Cartesian view, the subject is just a passive mirror of a series of objective natural proportions which instil passions in us. (Ultimately, for Descartes, these passions are linked to pragmatic purposes of self-preservation and procreation.[104]) Conversely, for the Rousseauian full admission of emotions to primary subjectivity, emotions have become merely subjective and political, without reference to an objective nature. Therefore the integrity of passions, as genuinely conceived, is already threatened.

Music and the ontology of illusion

In contrast to the rationalist–Romantic oscillation described in the last section, Lacoue-Labarthe seems to be making an attempt to inscribe subjective indeterminacy and mimetic 'typing' into a fundamental ontology.[105] In a sense, he almost seeks, like Augustine, to link again psyche and cosmos, and yet, again, without transcendence, this becomes impossible. Instead, he merely brings the *modern* obliteration of the subject to fruition. Thus, a Rousseauian expression of emotion has collapsed into arbitrary preference which merely manifests an ineluctable rhythm which we cannot in any sense control.[106] Unconscious rhythmic processes are in command, and therefore the highest 'numbers' are no longer, as for Augustine, those of judgement, but rather, the sounding numbers (*numeri corporeales*) which we cannot in any way influence. Thus, for Lacoue-Labarthe, there is no 'active' reception of rhythm, but the subject is entirely at the mercy of an ineluctable process.[107] This is despite the fact that the reading of temporal flux in this anarchic way, rather than as participation in transcendence, is itself merely an act of subjective judgement. Lacoue-Labarthe conceals the moment of judgement in the affirmation that judgement has no purchase, no ontological reality beyond *illusion*.

At the mercy of rhythm

For Lacoue-Labarthe, our being passively at the mercy of rhythm means that we are also always passively entangled with the other. Since we *are* first through imitation of rhythm, our identity is first of all that of an other (as for Lacan). Therefore, since this 'other' is always past, 'we' are always already dead, always haunted by our own (lack of) identity. And this is a ghost with which we must always struggle. The self we have lost is always a self we must overcome, since we can establish our identity only by being different from the other who alone gives us identity. (This is the Girardian double-bind which Lacoue-Labarthe takes over.[108]) This means that the true situation of the self is that it has always lost itself in the mourned other, and yet this other never was one's self in the first place: what is mourned never *was*. Such anguish and agonism is, for Lacoue-Labarthe, precisely what constitutes the 'music' of our reality.[109]

Parodic Augustinianism

This outlook reads theologically like a nihilistic parody of the Augustinian view that a self involved in patterns of attempted domination, usurpation and rivalry, since it fails to envisage the possibility of analogical repetition (everything continuously in its proper place and time through a musical integration of flow and articulation, rationally ungraspable, and yet hearable as an echo of eternity), is indeed a self that has lost itself, but not a self that never was; rather, a true self whose possibility is still contained in God. Furthermore, besides the aspect of original sin in the loss of self, there is also, for Augustine, an ontological aspect germane to creation as such. Just as one cannot rationally grasp the echo of eternity in music, so also one cannot grasp the coherence of the self which has only a musical expression or 'measure'. This musical measure is indeed caught up in both melancholia and longing. But these things, for Augustine, are not to be immanently ontologised as final realities. Rather, they are signs of the rooting of times in eternity. Just because we cannot grasp our self does not mean that there *is* no self. Rather, it indicates that the self exceeds itself precisely because there is only self through the participation of self in transcendent unlimited subjectivity.

Political music

Individualism and relentless atonement

In all traditions, it seems, music, religion and politics are intimately linked. They all pertain to the most secret and ineffable emotional forces which bind us together. However, the Indian paradigm of music goes as far as possible in the direction of constituting the political through its deconstitution. This is because at the top of the social scale exists the king–guru who is the most powerful man by virtue of being the most free from corporeal and social ties. The very aim of the rise in the social, personal, biographical or musical scales is to rid oneself of relations and emerge supreme and purged from this ladder of ascent.[110] Thus, whereas in Greek culture the lone Pythagorean philosopher was a rebel, and Orphics comprised an exceptional 'cult', in India the isolated guru constituted the ultimate social aim. This is why Louis Dumont realised that individualism was born in the East, albeit in an other-worldly form. Such a political character of Indian music is all of a piece with its fusion with religious sacrifice. Music, on this view, is one mode of sacrificial offering which repeats and yet seeks to undo in reverse the original sacrificial constitution of the universe. For Hindu mythology, the universe came into being through the sacrificial sundering of an original primal man (*Purusa*) and this renders the whole of reality guilty. (Perhaps this is not so utterly unlike Heidegger's 'ontological guilt', attendant upon presence as such.) The point of our sacrifices is ceaselessly to atone for this guilt, and indeed, every expiration of breath can be integrated into this act of atonement. Through the musical flowing-out of breath, the self is gradually freed from its contamination by the guilt of appearance.[111]

Greece and the reserve of music

The Greek view of music and the social is radically otherwise. For Pythagoras and Plato, music is very close to law (*nomos*) and, indeed, for Plato, it is musical modes covering all matters of aesthetic style in the city which most require legislation, since this will produce the best characters and, from there on, more precise matters of law can be left to their equitable judgement.[112] The point of music, as of Greek religion, is not at all to escape from the human and the civic (not even for Socrates and Pythagoras, who were dissidents in the existing *polis*), but rather to grant to gods and to different types of human being what is properly due to them. Thus, the purpose of Greek sacrifice is not primarily or usually to atone, but rather to express a manifest order of respective proportions.[113] Whereas, for the Indian model, music and sacrifice flow away in offering without remainder, a 'remaining' portion of the Greek sacrificed animal, and of Greek music, persists to express the integrity of the city in harmonic proportions. This notion of a 'remainder' concords with the Western emphasis on harmony. So, just as we have seen that in relation to music there is neither *cosmos* nor psyche in the East, so now we see also that there is no *polis* either.

Keeping musical order

Through the Augustinian refraction, these three phenomena remain, although they are also challenged and reformed by Augustinian relationality which renders them part of one continuous reality. We have already begun to see this; now the analysis will be completed.

For Boethius, the Platonic tradition of regarding music as being of political significance is fully continued. This means that the rhetorical and instrumental aspects of music are just as crucial as the psychic aspect. Boethius discusses the way in which music wields a fundamental influence over a person's mood, character and behaviour.[114] This same outlook tended, in the Middle Ages and Renaissance, to accord music a medical use. By hearing particular kinds of harmony, the soul was able to mend distortions of the humours which, although of physical origin, disturb the balance of the soul. For the same tradition, disordered music reflects imbalances in the political, psychic and even cosmic orders, while, inversely, good music can help re-order the *polis*, the soul and even the *cosmos*. The latter constitutes an aspect of the magical use of music, most encouraged by the Hermetic tradition, but not necessarily at variance with an orthodox Christian outlook.[115]

Hindemith and interior versus exterior music

The twentieth-century composer Paul Hindemith, reacting against the attempt of the Nazis to censor music (an attempt which surely had little to do with a genuine, Platonic view of musical politics), sought to draw a fundamental contrast between the Boethian rhetorical view of music and the Augustinian view of true music as internal and spiritual. He described the Boethian view as *ethical* since it seeks to influence public ethos through external music, and the Augustinian view as *moral*, since it seeks to rise above external music and attain to psychic music.[116] However, this contrast is entirely erroneous. It ignores the way in which, as already described, a Platonic transcendent view of music holds the psychic and rhetorical aspects in balance. Historically, it also ignores the fact that Augustine and Boethius share a common Christianised inheritance. Boethius by no means omits an interior psychic aspect, while Augustine *is* interested in external, relational, aspects of music which involve the reciprocal effects of voice and musical instrument, each upon the other.

Distorted music

However, Augustine *does* contribute a modification of the Antique 'ethical' view of music. This is because he makes a 'democratic' distinction between the attempt to dominate others and genuine persuasion of others.[117] The domination of other people is an assertion of an absolute right of rule of one human soul over others. This rule, according to Augustine, is inherently unjust, because all human souls are on the same ontic level, and to assert psychic priority amounts to a reduction of the other person to a bodily instrument of one's soul.[118] For Augustine, the body is literally a musical instrument of the soul,[119] as such indispensable to the soul, and the very means by which the soul communicates itself to the *polis*, and so assumes ethical responsibilities. But the other person, however much one might make his body and voice part of a conducted choir, can never be reduced in his psychic aspect to a mere instrument. To do so would be to reduce the musical instrument to the merely instrumental, and such a move would mean that psychic numbers have been subordinated to bodily numbers, and the higher judgement to rule-bound spontaneous judgement. Domination of others through music can be achieved only through a distortion of musical harmonies in which psychic ends are manipulated towards false material goals of power for its own sake, knowledge for its own sake, and attainment of desire for its own sake, which is possessiveness.[120] Hence Augustine first of all democratises the notion of musical *ethos*,[121] and, second, insists that attempts to manipulate through propagandistic use of the arts inevitably involve use of perverse and distorted musical modes. There is no possibility of using good music to a bad end.[122]

263

The contagion of harmony

Inversely, good musical modes invoke, as part of their practice, a genuine persuasion of other people towards the good. This is because, for Augustine, the final human end of love of God includes love of one's neighbour, as he stresses in the *De Musica*.[123] It is impossible to be in psychic harmony with God without simultaneously trying to communicate this harmony as love to one's neighbour. This, for Augustine, is an inseparable aspect of music as offering, music as worship.

The agony of perfected music

Finally, Augustine provides a remarkable Christological integration of the theme of soul–body relation (*the* topos of music) with the question of the instrumental and political aspects of music. When discussing the seeming inappropriateness of the body influencing the soul, he allows, as we have seen, that this can occur by means of an 'active reception'. This is possible for Augustine because, although the beauty of the body is subordinate, nevertheless it has its own proper beauty which is qualitatively distinct, not merely a quantitatively lesser degree of psychic beauty.[124] Thus, it is possible for the soul to be jealous of corporeal beauty.[125] The body has a beauty of its own which it can communicate to the soul, and provides an irreplaceable assistance to the soul in reminding it of the plenitude of eternal beauty.[126] In consequence, Augustine is able to link this place for the body and for instrumental music to the event of the incarnation, and to the full manifestation of divine beauty in time in a human being possessing a body as well as a soul.[127] Christ can accomplish our salvation, can influence us, only through corporeal means. Moreover, Augustine argues that one effect of the fall is that the body often assumed a perverted command over the soul. Sin renders the soul passive, or apparently passive, setting up an ontological impossibility. Yet this circumstance prevents the soul from re-establishing the right order, since it is now weakened. Right order can only be re-established from the side of the body, and therefore, in a fallen world, corporeal and instrumental music acquires even more importance. Only God incarnate possesses the correct ordering of soul and body, and this can be mediated to us only by physical means. The restored order is therefore first seen, or glimpsed, in the external physical world. That which is beyond the world, the ultimate measure, nonetheless *contains* the world. As Christ's perfectly ordered body is inserted into a world of sin, this order is manifest as the suffering of Christ's body. This suffering is for us the first mode of access to a perfected music and beauty. Augustine says that 'neither its [the body's] wound nor its disease has deserved to be without the honour of some ornament'.[128] He then continues to the effect that 'the highest wisdom of God designed to assume this wound by means of a wonderful and ineffable sacrament when he took upon himself man without sin'.[129] For Augustine, therefore, the highest music in the fallen world, the redemptive music, is initially corporeal rather than psychic, although it is the *cure* of the soul. It is none other than the repeated sacrifice of Christ himself which is the music of the forever repeated Eucharist.

The passage through discordance

It follows, for Augustine, that even when the soul is suffering, since it is receiving something passively from the body (or at least appearing to do so, since actually what occurs is that on the occasion of a bodily suffering, the soul distorts its own harmony[130]), and so receiving a distorted music, nonetheless, by participation in Christ's sufferings, this discordance can be transfigured into a rightly ordered music. This redemptive process most of all fulfils Augustine's contention that nothing falls outside the harmony of the cosmic poem. Hence his Christian account of music introduces the new aesthetic idea that every apparent discord can, in the course of musical time, be granted its concordant place. Indeed, for Augustine, in a fallen world, true harmony can resound via this passage only through discordant noise which nonetheless ceases in time to be mere noise. The ontological dialectic of being and non-being in creation, reflected in music as the alternation of caesura and sounding note, is re-doubled by a salvific dialectic of discordance and concordance, which here constitutes the theme of sacrificial passion. Earlier we saw that for Augustine salvation means that everything is in its own proper time and place, that everything is separated by the appropriate intervals. Now we can add that in a post-fallen world, the proper time and place is always the place of the Cross, or rather, the temporal passage through the Cross.[131] In this sense *only* is music, for Augustine, a sacrifice, a mourning, and a Passion, not ontologically, but contingently and yet universally and inescapably, in a fallen order. This sacrifice and Passion is at once an undergoing of our sins and an offering to God and to others for their own healing. Later, it will be shown how this understanding of music as atoning is to be contrasted with the postmodern understanding of music as inherently sacrificial.

The commodification of music

We have seen that, in the case of Augustine, a balance is maintained between internal and performed music, just as earlier we saw that he maintained a balance between the fluctional and the articulated, and between the psychic and the cosmic. In the latter two instances, we saw how post-Cartesian philosophy dissolved this balance. In the case of the political dimension of music, a parallel breakdown occurs. First, the Rameau-inspired reduction of melody to obeisance before a primary natural harmony opens the way towards the idea of a manipulation of people's minds through their bodies, which is adverse to the traditional notion of a rhetorical effect of music upon the judgement of the soul. This can be seen to have encouraged the gradual commodification of music whereby it increasingly emanates from one centre, and is used to pacify, banalise, and compensate a mass audience.[132] Increasingly there has arisen a mass music in this idiom which is neither elite nor ethnic (or 'folk') in character.

Again, Rousseau provides an example of an opposite arm of bifurcation. Whereas for Rameau music is entirely naturalised, opening a way to an objectified political use, for Rousseau, music is, from the outset, political, and is natural only to a human social reality. This would seem to preclude the packaging and exploitation of music, but Rousseau is able to construe the political character of music in only formalistic terms. He reduces music to the event of association as such, without any hierarchical preference for certain modes over others. Music, therefore, seems to be a matter of allowing sympathy with the expression of other people's private emotions, or else with the expression of one particular ethos of one community. What is lacking here is the Augustinian notion that the subjectivity of measure is subordinate to the measured character of the measurer himself, his belonging within the scansions of the cosmic poem. For this allows that my recognition of the rhythm of the other (not just the *freedom* of the other, as for Hegel) is a necessary aspect of my own rhythm, in the same way that cultural expressions have validity only through the enterprise of harmonising one culture with another, one age with another, without obliterating their differences.

Music and sacrifice

The political function of music as holding people in thrall round one centre is fully acknowledged by postmodern theorists of music, especially Lacoue-Labarthe and Jacques Attali. They recognise also that this one centre is a sacrificial centre, as it was in different ways for ancient India, ancient Greece, St Augustine, and the Christian Middle Ages (when cosmic music had become also music of the Passion). So, once again it might seem that we have a postmodern retrieval of aspects of a premodern understanding of music. However, the postmodern sacrifice invoked is, if anything, more like the Indian sacrificial paradigm, but rendered more explicitly nihilistic. We have already seen how, for Lacoue-Labarthe, music is a tragically and yet necessarily substitutional reality. It is mourning for what has never been; it is the attempt of every note or character-type agonistically to oust its predecessor. What we hear in music, therefore, is always the discordant clash of incompatibles which are never to be subject to dialectical resolution. The only joy to be gleaned from this music must be the song of selfish triumph over one's dead rival, which is commensurate with an evasion of one's own deadness.[133] There is here no resurrection of the other,[134] and therefore no resurrection of the self either. Although Lacoue-Labarthe rejects René Girard's notion of an original murderous rivalry for which sacrifice, language and music are relatively less violent medicinal substitutes, this is only in order to advocate the view that such violent substitution for an imaginary naked original that never was has been the order of things from the beginning.[135] For Lacoue-Labarthe, all music is literally 'rough' music – that music which in European folk tradition was deployed to terrify and expel the unwanted scapegoat.

Primordial noise

The same perspective on music in all essential respects is articulated by Attali. What is crucial to his philosophy of the history of music, which he takes to be a philosophy of history as such, is the view that noise has ontological priority over music.[136] Thus, all music is but mitigated noise.[137] Such noise is seen as the precise point of intersection of real and symbolic violence, and, therefore, one might say, of redoubled violence. Noise is the most violent thing of all. Perhaps one could therefore argue for a structural similarity between such noise and the evil of phenomena in the Indian paradigm, which both music and sacrifice must atone for and ultimately expel. However, for Attali, no such ultimate expulsion is possible, and the only attainable Nirvana is a resignation to the flux of noise, and the chaos of music becomes merely private composition.[138] Attali takes this to be oppositional in relation to commodified identically repetitive music. But this is surely but its collusive reverse face, since it fails to re-establish a community of participation and still leaves the public space open to musical manipulation. And, indeed, it seems dishonest of Attali to proffer any positive musical politics since, if music is but mitigated noise, then, as he says, all music is, of its very essence, a domination, and there is no such thing as genuine persuasion. And the harmony of the cosmos is no more than a political ruse. Of course, it may often, or usually, have been such, but this should not hide from our view the truth that, if there is no cosmic harmony, then there is no ontological possibility of a time and space for social harmony. A radical politics has to have faith and hope that there is a concealed cosmic harmony, otherwise there is only postmodern despair.

Sacrifice and the closure of music

Since for Attali music is but mitigated noise, he argues that it has a function identical to that of Girard's sacrifice which substitutes for rivalrous violence.[139] Music is always a merely phenomenal and apparent harmony whose whole point is to exclude certain arbitrarily unwanted noises. This view, however, seems to assume the closure of the musical work which, as Attali points out, is true only of modern music. Every medieval composition was seen to run into every other, and to be open to future developments. The conception of music at this period was in fact strictly *liturgical*.

Participation and the possibility of harmony

Nonetheless, Attali shares with Augustine the view that none of our harmonies are perfect harmonies. But two things differentiate their outlooks. First, there is a generosity in Augustine's invocation of the plenitude of Being: that is to say, he recognises that a lower and limited harmony can still possess a certain inimitable, although lowly, perfection, like that of the body. The second difference concerns Augustine's interpretation of the fact that finite harmony is never perfect, but must always strive for perfection of equality. He does not read this as an attempt to suppress a preliminary chaos, which would render every harmony merely a lesser degree of chaos, but instead assumes that the imperfection of our harmonies is a sign that harmony is otherwise and elsewhere located: harmony is not our possession, but our borrowing from eternity. Thus, instead of mitigated noise, one has a sharing of rhythm to a degree. The mitigation of noise is a response only to the contingency of the interruption of harmony by sin. But because of the ontological priority of the participation model, noise itself can be perfectly integrated, through the innocent suffering of Christ and its imitation in our passionate music, into a harmony uncontaminated by violence, either real or symbolic, which is to say, discordant 'noise'.

Musical mathesis

Thus, it seems that the postmodern perspective on music is, after all, even more resolutely apolitical than the modern one, or rather, perhaps, realises an apoliticism intrinsic to musical enlightenment. It is impossible, given Lacoue-Labarthe and Attali's view of musical sacrifice, to have any hope for social harmony, since every harmony is merely an illusion – and expulsion of certain unwanted noises. To say, 'let all noises flourish in confusion', is only to invoke the mythical Girardian original scene. What would bind together such a society? It could only be certain formalised rules of a musical *mathesis*, implying a public musical puritanism beyond anything imagined by Plato. Thus, the only ethics which postmodernism can instil in the realm of 'music' would be a resigned acceptance of the impersonal flux, whose inevitable mediation via Apollonian appearances constituted, for Nietzsche, the endless sacrificial sundering of the Dionysian body of time. All that postmodernism does is repeat over and over the Nietzschian identification of tragedy with Dionysian music, where a lurid beauty (sublimity) is what reconciles us to suffering, death and loss. It is a new variant of an old Stoic impersonal and politically quietist theodicy.

Conclusion

This essay has been a brief appeal for a restoration of the integrity of the Western tradition concerning musical theory, which is an appeal for a restoration of the Western (Platonic–Christian) tradition as such. For against fashionable invocation of the non-Western, the pluralistic and the postmetaphysical, this essay has sought to show, especially in the last section, exactly why only this Western musical succession foreshadows a possible future political 'equality' or harmony. At the same time, it has been shown how this same tradition can heal the rift between body and soul, arts and sciences, etc., which are not a legacy of the tradition from its beginning, but only of its modern refraction. The non-dualism present in the notion of music as measure of the soul–body ratio has proven to be linked to a perspective for which reality itself is meaningful, and yet meaning is seen to be available only for a subjective judgement. For in music, uniquely, there is in a beautiful phrase at once an objectively expressible proportion, and subjective selection and appreciation of this proportion as beautiful. Meaning, therefore, is seen to be the *world's* meaning, and yet, at the same time, our *own* meaning.

Finally, we saw in the first section how music, for the traditional view, holds in balance time and space under transcendence. By contrast, after the rejection of transcendence, time and space become separate and are distorted as 'opposites' of one another. This process, which is characteristic of modernity, has simply been fully realised as nihilism in so-called postmodernity. It is therefore no accident that the very thing which postmodernism *most* denies is music, for its core belief is that flux and articulation are both necessary to each other and yet mutually cancelling. And yet in music we hear the flux only as articulated, and articulations only in the flux. It is impossible, rationally, to resolve the *aporias* of time. Neither a pure flow nor pure present moments make any coherent sense. And yet in music we *hear* this impossible reconciliation. To believe the evidence of our ears is therefore to deny nihilism. Moreover, it is to believe in transcendence. More, it is to believe in the healing of time, and, therefore, sacramentally to receive the incarnation of God in time, his Passion and resurrection. For theology, although it cannot provide a *logos* which once and for all resolves the *aporias* of time, can nonetheless develop another *logos* which indicates a positive reason why these *aporias* are irresolvable. That is to say, they are the mark of our created finitude. We are spared a denial of hearing harmony through our acknowledgement of the triune God. Furthermore, our hearing of the harmony despite and through undeniable worldly disharmonies can be taken as more than a mere mitigation of noise only if we take this harmony to be the echo of the re-beginning of human music in time by God himself.

Notes

1 The concept, not original with Augustine, was first put forward in the fourth century BC by the Pythagorean Archytas, and Plato adopted a similar formula in his education of the Philosopher–Guardian in the *Republic*. See Jamie James, *The Music of the Spheres: Music, Science and the Natural Order of the Universe* (London: Abacus, 1993), p. 72; Lydia Goehr, *The Imaginary Museum of Musical Works: An Essay in the Philosophy of Music* (Oxford: Clarendon Press, 1992), p. 130; Aristotle, *Metaphysics*, 985b23f, in Andrew Barker, *Greek Musical Writings*, Volume II, *Harmonic and Acoustic Theory* (Cambridge: Cambridge University Press, 1989), I. 5; Archytas, frag. 1 and frag. 2, in Barker, I. 19 and I. 20, respectively.

2 See Bonaventure's summary of Augustine's numerological ascent, *The Soul's Journey Into God*, tr. Ewert Cousins (London: S.P.C.K., 1978) Paragraph 10; see also Augustine, *De Musica Libri Sex* edited and translated into French by Guy Finaert and F.-J. Thonnard (Brussels: Desclée de Brouwer et Cie, 1947), VI. i. 1.

3 *Ista certe omnia quae carnalis sensus ministerio numeramus, et quaecumque in eis sunt, locales numeros qui videntur esse in aliquo statu, nisi praecedentibus intimis et in silentio temporalibus numeris qui sunt in motu, nec accipere illos possunt, nec habere* (*De Musica*, VI. xvii. 58).

4 Boethius, *Fundamentals of Music*, tr. Calvin M. Bower (New Haven: Yale University Press, 1989), I. 2.

5   See John Milbank, 'Sacred Triads: Augustine and the Indo-European Soul', *Modern Theology*, vol. 13 no. 4 (1997), pp. 451–474.

6   Lewis Rowell, 'The Idea of Music in India and the Ancient West', in Veikko Rantala *et al.* eds, *Essays on the Philosophy of Music* (Helsinki: The Philosophical Society of Finland, 1988), pp. 322–339; and Lewis Rowell, *Music and Musical Thought in Early India* (Chicago: University of Chicago Press, 1992).

7   Karl Potter (ed.), *Encyclopedia of Indian Philosophies* (Delhi: Motilal, 1981), Volume 3, pp. 553–556.

8   On the basic classification of Indian music as derived from a primarily vocal conception, see Sârngadeva, *Samgitaratnâkara*, Anandâsrama Sanskrit Series, (Poona, 1896), I. 3. 7. Although this text is a medieval metaphysical theory, it had roots in much earlier periods; see Arnold Bake, 'The Music of India', in Egon Wellesz, ed., *Ancient and Oriental Music* (Oxford: Oxford University Press, 1957, pp. 195–227), p. 197. According to the Indian metaphysical hierarchy of sound, instrumental noise is seen as a secondary manifestation of sound rather than sound per se; see Bake, p. 196.

9   'This prâna [silent life-breath], then, stirred by the fire of the body, goes gradually upwards and produces an extremely subtle sound in the navel, a subtle sound in the heart, a strong sound in the throat, a weak sound in the head, and in the mouth a sound with the qualities of art' (Sârngadeva, *Samgitaratnâkara*, I. 3. 3–5a).

10 Sârngadeva, *Samgitaratnâkara*, I. 2. 164b–165. This metaphysics of music presupposes a dialectic of the individual and the universal. For while, on the one hand, this model assumes a surrender of the individual to the universal, it remained for the individual alone to find the right way to realise this surrender. The means to this end was the human voice, or pure unmediated sound. See Bake, p. 198.

11 Boethius, *Fundamentals of Music*, I. 3; Rowell, 'The Idea of Music', pp. 332–333; *idem*, *Music and Musical Thought in Early India*, pp. 39–40. Concomitantly, a different approach to musical pitch arose. In contrast to the Eastern paradigm, according to which pitch was relative and had no connection with the names of the notes (see Bake, p. 211), the ancient Greeks had pitch pipes and could attain a pitch standard. Although there was, according to M. L. West, a degree of fluctuation, the notation system, with its array of keys and natural limitation of range, did presuppose a fixed standard of pitch. See M. L. West, *Ancient Greek Music* (Oxford: Clarendon Press, 1994), pp. 273–276; D. B. Monro, *The Modes of Ancient Greek Music* (Oxford: Clarendon Press, 1984), pp. 30–1; but see Barker, *Greek Musical Writings*, Volume II, pp. 16–17. On the centrality of the metaphor of plucking, see Archytas, frag. 1, in Barker, *Greek Musical Writings*, Volume II, I. 19; Plato, *Timaeus*, 67a-c; Aristotle, *De Anima*, 419b421a. The metaphor of plucking extended also to wind instruments: Ps.-Aristotelian *Problemata*, XI. 19, in Barker, *Greek Musical Writings*, Volume II, 4. 8.

12 M. L. West, pp. 191, 129, 208.

13 Giovanni Comotti, *Music in Greek and Roman Culture*, tr. Rosaria V. Munson (Baltimore, MD, and London: The Johns Hopkins University Press, 1989), p. 12; Curt Sachs, *A Short History of World Music* (London: Dennis Dobson Ltd, 1959), p. 27; Isobel Henderson, 'Ancient Greek Music', in Wellesc, *Ancient and Oriental Music*, p. 240.

14 Rowell cites Theon of Smyrna: 'The Pythagoreans, whom Plato follows in many respects, call music the harmonization of opposites, the unification of disparate things, and the conciliation of warring elements' ('The Idea of Music', p. 340, n.13).

15 Indeed, Philolaus stresses that it is the presence of a third principle, *harmonia*, which reconciled the dualities of the universe, frag. 10.; see also Porphyry, *Comm.*, 107.15ff; Archytas, frag. 2 in Barker, *Greek Musical Writings*, Volume II, I. 14, I. 8, I. 20, respectively. See also Plato, *Phaedo*, 86b; Aristotle, *De Anima*, 407b27; G. S. Kirk and J. E. Raven, *The Pre-Socratic Philosophers* (Cambridge: Cambridge University Press, 1975), pp. 237–239.

16 *De Musica*, VI. xi. 29.

17 The story of Pythagoras and the anvils suggests that concordant tones were being

produced in unison, as does Plato's account of the Sirens in the Myth of Er. See James, *The Music of the Spheres*, p. 79.

18 Rowell, 'The Idea of Music', pp. 329–339 and *passim*.

19 See Paul Henry Lang, *Music in Western Civilization* (New York: W. W. Norton & Co., 1941), p. 4,

20 Friedrich Nietzsche, *The Birth of Tragedy*, tr. Francis Golffing (N.Y.: Doubleday and Company Inc., 1956), pp. 1–146; Michael Allen Gillespie, *Nihilism Before Nietzsche* (Chicago: University of Chicago Press, 1996), pp. 205–209; Lang, *Music in Western Civilization*, p. 2; Philippe Lacoue-Labarthe, *Musica Ficta: Figures of Wagner* (Stanford: Stanford University Press, 1994), p. xvii.

21 Nino Perrotta, *Music and Culture in Italy from the Middle Ages to the Baroque* (Cambridge, MA: Harvard University Press, 1984), pp. 15–18.

22 Giulio Cottin, *Music of the Middle Ages* (Cambridge: Cambridge University Press, 1984), pp. 48–100; Reinhard Strohn, *The Rise of European Music, 1380–1500* (Cambridge: Cambridge University Press, 1993), pp. 321f.; Richard H. Hoppin, *Medieval Music* (New York: W. W. Norton and Co., 1978), pp. 215–241.

23 *Ibid.*, pp. 15–17, 369–370 n.14; William G. Waite, *The Rhythm of Twelfth-Century Polyphony: Its Theory and Practice* (New Haven, CT: Yale University Press, 1954), pp. 112–113; Craig Wright, *Music and Ceremony at Notre Dame of Paris 500–1550* (Cambridge: Cambridge University Press, 1989), pp. 281–288; Richard Crocker and David Hiley, eds, *The New Oxford History of Music* (Oxford: Oxford University Press, 1990), Volum II, p. 487,

24 Lang, *Music in Western Civilization*, pp. 139–141; on Galilei's opposition to polyphony, see James, *The Music of the Spheres*, pp. 95–100.

25 Frank L. Harrison, *Music in Medieval Britain* (London: Routledge & Kegan Paul, 1958), pp. 104–155; Hoppin, *Medieval Music*, pp. 87f.

26 Goehr, *The Imaginary Museum of Musical Works*, p. 132.

27 At VI. iv. 6 of *De Musica*, the Master argues that sounds which last longer are not to be compared in ratio with shorter sounds as eternity is compared with time. From this notion that longevity is no closer to eternity, we can infer that, for Augustine, eternity is qualitative, and that enforced persistence in time is an idolatrous pseudo-eternity. Indeed, throughout the *De Musica*, it is clear that the temporal is to be regarded as closer in likeness to eternity than the reified or the spatial. See, for example, VI. iv. 7, where the Master explains that the solid insensitivity of certain inert phenomena is not to be substituted or mistaken for the quality of peace, not least because, despite appearances, no finite thing is ever equal to itself. It seems that such stable substances as hair and nails can mislead the soul into such an idolatrous substitution. We later learn that it is the quality of open-endedness which most images eternity: *De Mus.*, VI. v. 15, VI. viii. 22, VI. xvii. 58.

28 Waite, *The Rhythms of Twelfth-Century Polyphony*, pp. 36–37.

29 *Ibid.*, pp. 36–39.

30 The ratios persist regardless of their actual longevity of duration: VI. ii. 3, VI. vii. 17–18, VI. xii. 35.

31 On this Pythagorean background, see Porphyry, *Comm.*, 30. 1–5; Philolaus, frag. 4; in Barker, *Greek Musical Writings*, Volume II, I.1, I.11, respectively.

32 *Ita coelestibus terrena subjecta, orbes temporum suorum numerosa successione quasi carmini universitatis associant* (*De Mus.*, VI. xi. 29). Cf. VI. vii. 19.

33 *Cur in silentiorum intervalis nulla fraude sensus offenditur, nisi quia eidem juri aequalitatis, etiamsi non sono, spatio tamen temporis quod debetur, exsolvitur?* (*De Mus.*, VI. x. 27).

34 . . . *et tamen in quantum imitantur, pulchra esse in suo genere et ordine suo, negare non possumus* (*De Mus.*, VI. x. 28). Cf. VI. iv. 7, VI. xiv. 46, VI. xvii. 56.

35 Emilie Zum Brunn, *St Augustine: Being and Nothingness* (New York: Paragon House Publishers, 1988), Ch. 3.

36 *De Mus.*, VI. xvii. 57.
37 *Ibid.*
38 *Unde, quaeso, ista, nisi ab illo summo atque aeterno principatu numerorum et similitudinis et aequalitatis et ordinis veniunt? Atqui naec si terrae ademeris, nihil erit. Quocirca omnipotens Deum terram fecit, et de nihilo terra facta est* (*De Mus.*, VI. xvii. 57). Cf. *De Libero Arbitrio*, II. xvii. 45–47.
39 While for Augustine the 'rest' constitutes rhythm, for Jacques Derrida and Philippe Lacoue-Labarthe, the 'hiatus' is primarily deconstitutive. See Derrida's Introduction, 'Desistance', to Lacoue-Labarthe's *Typography: Mimesis, Philosophy, Politics*, tr. Christopher Fynsk (Cambridge, MA: Harvard University Press, 1989), pp. 1–42; p. 35. It seems, therefore, that Derrida *et al.* have not offered an exhaustive phenomenology of the 'nothing'. Its presiding status could equally be used to prove the createdness of phenomenal reality.
40 See Catherine Pickstock, *After Writing: On the Liturgical Consummation of Philosophy* (Oxford: Blackwell Publishers, 1997), Ch. 2.
41 *De Mus.*, VI. viii. 21–22; VI. xvii. 58–59; see John Milbank, 'Sacred Triads'.
42 *De Mus.*, VI. xi. 29: the only true measure is in eternity. There is a dialectical irony here, for while Augustine stresses that enforced limitation is to be seen as inimical to any attempted 'imaging' of eternity, yet it is precisely our own remaining-within-limitation (spatial and temporal) which provides us with the only route by which to attain the infinite, albeit only partially. VI. xi. 30: *Quoniam si quis, verbi gratia, in amplissimarum pulcherrimarumque aedium uno aliquo angulo tanquam statua collocetur pulchritudinem illius fabricae sentire non poterit, cujus et ipse pars erit.*
43 VI. xi. 29.
44 VI. xvii. 56. See *De Beata Vita*, XXXIV, where Christ is described as the *summum modum.*
45 *Quamobrem quisquis fatetur nullam esse naturam, quae non ut sit quidquid est, appetat unitatem, suique similis in quantum potest essse conetur* . . . (VI. xvii. 56). See also VI. x. 26.
46 VI. xvii. 56.
47 VI. xi. 29, VI. xi. 30, VI. xiv. 46.
48 Every created thing which strives for the ultimate unity *atque ordinem proprium vel locis vel temporibus, vel in corpore quodam libramento salutem suam teneat* (VI. xvii. 56). This is a musical model of redemption. One's uniquely right position is nonetheless harmonious with the whole. Thus, redemption is at once aesthetic and ethical.
49 Downing A. Thomas, *Music and the Origins of Language: Theories from the French Enlightenment* (Cambridge University Press, 1995), pp. 82–142; Samuel Baud-Bovy, *Jean-Jacques Rousseau et la Musique* (Boudry-Neuchâtel: les Editions de la Baconnière, 1988), pp. 53–62, 77–80; Robert Wokler, 'The Controversy with Rameau and the *Essai sur l'origine des langues*', in *idem*, *Rousseau on Society, Politics, Music and Language: An Historical Interpretation of His Early Writings* (New York: Garland Publishing Inc., 1987), pp. 235–378.
50 *Traité de l'harmonie*, cited by Thomas, *Music and the Origins of Language*, p. 92.
51 *Ibid.*, p. 91
52 *Ibid.*, p. 93; Michael O'Dea, *Jean-Jacques Rousseau: Music, Illusion and Desire* (London: Macmillan, 1995), p. 45.
53 *Ibid.*, p. 91.
54 *Ibid.*, p. 137.
55 *Ibid.*, p. 139.
56 Arthur Schopenhauer, *The World as Will and Representation*, tr. E. F. J. Payne (New York: Dover Publications, Inc., 1958), Volume II, p. 448; Gillespie, *Nihilism Before Nietzsche*, pp. 190–199; Jean-Luc Nancy, *Les Muses* (Paris: Editions Galilée, 1994), p. 91 and *passim*; Malcolm Budd, 'The World as Embodied Music', *idem*, *Music and the Emotions: The Philosophical Theories* (London: Routledge & Kegan Paul, 1985), pp. 76–103; Ernst Bloch, 'The Philosophy of Music', in *idem*, *Essays on the Philosophy of Music*, tr. Peter

Palmer (Cambridge: Cambridge University Press, 1985), pp. 1–139, 127–128, 178–179. In his book, *Music and the Mind* (London: HarperCollins, 1992), pp. 128–149, Anthony Storr notes that Schopenhauer overlooks the fact that music is a language no less than poetry. However, Storr cites Tippett that music has to make use of artifice to express the flow of inner life, but that when this artifice is achieved, one no longer notices it. The inner life is ineluctably conveyed through it. Storr therefore seems to accept a notion of inner life as an essence removed from signs and so is perhaps in danger of the same kind of dualism.

57 *De Mus.*, VI. xi. 29.
58 Jacques Attali, *Noise: The Political Economy of Music*, tr. Brian Massumi (Minneapolis: University of Minnesota Press, 1985), Ch. 3.
59 Suzanne Langer uses a similar argument to criticise Henri Bergson's attempt to resist any symbolisation of duration, in *Feeling and Form: A Theory of Art Developed from Philosophy in a New Key* (London: Routledge & Kegan Paul, 1953), pp. 110–116.
60 *Critique of Pure Reason*, tr. Norman Kemp Smith (London: Macmillan, 1978), p. 213.
61 Lacoue-Labarthe, 'The Echo of the Subject', in *idem*, *Typography*, pp. 139–217, 149, 165–174, 195. 'We ("we") are rhythmed' (p. 202).
62 *Ibid.*, pp. 140–146.
63 *Ibid.*, pp. 196–203.
64 *Ibid.*, pp. 187–188.
65 Pickstock, *After Writing: On the Liturgical Consummation of Philosophy*, Ch. 2.
66 Augustine, *Confessions*, XI. 12–end.
67 'Rhythm, then, is heard. It is not seen – [it] is prior to the figure or to the visible schema whose appearance it conditions' (Lacoue-Labarthe, 'The Echo', p. 195). See also p. 145.
68 *Ibid.*, pp. 161, 173, 184, and *passim*.
69 In *Les Muses* Jean-Luc Nancy argues that all art is subordinate to the category of *techne* because for him there is no metaphysical transcendence, and therefore neither origin nor end. There are only means to endless ends, or proliferating technologies or arts. These arts correspond, according to Nancy, to infinite permutations of the senses, so that it seems that a culpably metaphysical subordination of art to a particular medium (such as writing) is displaced in favour of technology as such. Although such an account gestures towards a model of analogy and participation on the sensual level, and appears to move away from a Derridean metaphysic, it could be argued that Nancy substitutes writing for writing after all. By stressing that there are no ends, that everything is *techne*, Nancy smuggles in a disguised metaphysical origin by claiming *a priori* that art is a technique which cannot but produce new sensations. In contrast to the tradition, for which the supremacy of the poetic muse ensures that the act of poetic creation is never fully in command of itself and that there are ends beyond means, Nancy suggests that one can determine in advance what art will do. Such an assertion of limits is reducible to a transcendentalism or dissembling *mathesis* or metaphysical exaltation of writing.
70 Lacoue-Labarthe, *Musica Ficta* (*passim*).
71 *Ibid.*, pp. 174–179.
72 *Ibid.*, pp. 193–195. This represents, perhaps, a parodic immanentisation of the 'unhearable' music of the spheres (see above).
73 Comotti, *Music in Greek and Roman Culture*, p. 3; Henderson, 'Ancient Greek Music', pp. 377–378; Lang, *Music in Western Civilization*, p. 7; Goehr, *The Imaginary Museum*, pp. 123–124; James McKinnon, 'Early Western Civilization', in *idem* (ed.), *Antiquity in the Middle Ages: From Ancient Greece to the Fifteenth Century* (London: Macmillan, 1990), pp. 1–44; p. 3; H. M. Schueller, *The Idea of Music: An Introduction to Musical Aesthetics in Antiquity and the Middle Ages* (Michigan: Kalamazoo, 1988), p. 1.
74 Lacoue-Labarthe, *Musica Ficta*, pp. 140.

75 Bannerjea, *Philosophy of Gorakhnath*, pp. 1–22, 33–37, 62–74; Bake, 'The Music of India', p. 198.

76 *De Mus.*, VI. xii. 24.

77 *De Mus.*, VI. iv. 7, VI. v. 8.

78 See Robert I. O'Connell SJ, *Art and the Christian Intelligence in St Augustine* (Oxford: Basil Blackwell, 1978), pp. 10–27.

79 In his text, *In psalmum* cl, 8 (*Patrologia Latina*, p. xxxvii), Augustine offers a three-fold classification of sound which emphasises a fundamental non-dualism in his under-standing of the relationship between the soul and the body: 'by voice, that is by the throat and wind pipe of a singing man without any sort of instrument, by breath, as with the tibia or anything of that kind; by striking, as with the cithara or anything of that sort. Thus no type is omitted here [in Ps 150]: for there is voice in the chorus, breath in the trumpet and striking in the cithara; just like mind, spirit and body, but through similarity, not actual properties.'

80 *De Mus.*, VI. iv. 7, VI. v. 8.

81 *De Mus.*, VI. v. 9.

82 *De Mus.*, VI. iv. 7.

83 (a) VI. xii. 34: We could not begin to activate our desire for perfect equality unless it were already known somewhere. Thus, desire is already a kind of knowledge – or, could one say, desire is the way things are? – desire is what is known? (b) While it might seem to us natural to link 'curiosity' with the discovery of truth and therefore with knowledge, for Augustine, it is precisely that which leads us away from the truth. He argues that *curiositas* is a quality concerned only with the discernment of proportion-ality for its own sake – i.e. not in relation to other things. It does not, therefore, lead to genuine knowledge. This implies a second *aporia*, which is that one can 'know' some-thing only in relation to everything else, which means that we must know the known in relation to the unknowable. This is because we only occupy a limited corner of the poem of the universe, as Augustine constantly reminds us. Thus the only hope for knowledge lies in desire (VI. xiii. 39).

84 *Hi enim non scintillantibus humanis ratiocinationibus, sed validissimo et flagrantissimo charitatis igne purgantur* (VI. xvii. 59). In this passage, Augustine contrasts the scintilla of human reason to the infinitely more valid and most flagrant 'fire of charity'. The metaphor of increasing intensities of light stresses that reason and love are not opposed (as they are for a post-Enlightenment view), and that love is an immeasurably more powerful enlightenment. Further, the metaphor implies that genuine knowledge and purifica-tion (or purging by flames) are commensurate. By progressing from light to fire, Augustine's metaphor accomplishes a subtle overtone. First, the progression tempo-ralises the visual. And, second, the flames of charity are the 'site' of a transition from the visible to the temporal and the audible, a transition which does not leave one stage in order to arrive at the next, but combines each stage in a synthesis.

85 *De Mus.*, VI. v. 9–10; see Milbank, 'Sacred Triads'.

86 *De Mus.*, VI. iv. 5.

87 *De Mus.*, VI. i. 1–VI. i. 5.

88 *De Mus.*, VI. ix. 23–24. This higher judgement (*diligentior judicatio*) judges the 'delight' of the first, spontaneous, judgement. It is a meta-judgement which Augustine sees as consisting in 'more powerful numbers which judge our initial judgement'. His ascrip-tion of both kinds of judgement, the affective and the reflective, to an ascending scale of numbers, suggests that there is something more fundamental than any oppo-sition between affections and reason included here. Further, the reflective 'delay' of the higher judgement suggests that the possibility of further alteration of judgement is never foreclosed, that 'reason' is recursive and closely linked with desire and hope. See Augustine's own summary of the scale of numbers at VI. x. 25.

89 *De Mus.*, VI. ii. 3.

90   *De Mus.*, VI. xii. 36.

91   See Jean-Louis Chrétien, *L'Inoubliable et l'Inespéré* (Paris: Desclée de Brouwer, 1991).

92   See note 70 above.

93   VI. xiii. 38. For Augustine, beauty itself is a relation between things seen and our seeing of them, in a synthesis of the objective and subjective. Thus, everything becomes relative, but without disintegrating into mere 'taste'. The Master explains to the Disciple that although there are harmonies which lie beyond our recognition, this does not mean that things are beautiful only for our own point of view. Rather, our 'point of view' is itself another aspect of the work of art which composes the universe.

94   *De Mus.*, VI. xi. 32, VI. xi. 36. VI. xiii. 39: the Master argues that one should not become fixed by the numbers of (spontaneous) judgement, which contain the *regulae* of an art, like the purely immanent music he imagines at VI. xiii. 40. At the end of his treatise, Augustine notes that the promises of reason and false judgement (*rationis et scientiae fallici*) are to be avoided because they lack the higher (recursive) judgement.

95   *De Mus.*, VI. vii. 17.

96   *De Mus.*, VI. xiii. 42. See the next section of this essay: Reason versus passion.

97   . . . *et ex his curiositas nascitur ipso curae nomine inimica securitati, et vanitatis impos veritatis* (*De Mus.*, VI. xiii. 39). See also VI. v. 14.

98   *De Mus.*, VI. vii. 19, VI. viii. 21.

99   VI. x. 25: *bona modulatio* is defined as (a) a certain *motu libero*, free movement; (b) a movement ordained to an end which requires the beauty of that end. Certain implications arise from this definition. (a) The 'end' is the beauty of the free movement itself, which means that the beauty is not 'beyond' the movement. (b) The act of measuring is not only beautiful, but free; it is not 'over against' that which is measured. It is more an ontological than an epistemological category. (c) Its freeness also suggests that there is no given or static measurement. The act of measuring is a creative gesture (related to the way in which Augustine discerns a culturally specific aspect to the intervals which, paradoxically, also exceed particular instantiations.) The aim of measurement is not domination of the measured, but the beauty of the movement, a dynamic teleological aesthetic which seeks 'incorporation within' rather than 'dominion over' the measured phenomena. See the discussion of the word 'modulatio' in Finaert and Thonnard (eds), *De Musica Libri Sex*, p. 417 note 1.

100 *De Mus.*, VI. ii. 3, VI. vii. 19–20.

101 Cited by Goehr, *The Imaginary Museum of Musical Works*, p. 229.

102 See Jan L. Broeckx, 'Works and Plays in Music: An Inquiry into the Ontology of Musical Products' in *idem, Contemporary Views on Musical Style and Aesthetics* (Antwerp: Metropolis, 1979), pp. 126–162, 128–130.

103 On seeing the musical score and its performed instantiation as together constituting the musical work, see Cynthia M. Grund, 'How Philosophical Characterizations of a Musical Work Lose Sight of the 'Music' and How it Might be Put Back', in *idem, Constitutive Counterfactuality: The Logic of Interpretation in Metaphor and Music* (Copenhagen: Askeladden, 1997), pp. 63–79.

104 See Descartes, *Meditations on First Philosophy*, in *The Philosophical Writings*, tr. John Cottingham *et al.* (Cambridge University Press, 1984) volume II.

105 Lacoue-Labarthe, 'The Echo of the Subject', pp. 196–203.

106 *Ibid.*, pp. 175–179. See also Derrida, 'Desistance', p. 2.

107 Derrida thus ingenuously invokes the category of the middle voice in his Introduction, p. 5.

108 'The Echo of the Subject', pp. 153–158, and *passim*. See also John Milbank, 'Stories of Sacrifice: From Wellhausen to Girard', *Theory, Culture and Society*, vol. 12 (1995), pp. 15–46.

109 Lacoue-Labarthe, 'The Echo of the Subject', pp. 174–179.

110 Bannerjea, *Philosophy of Gorakhnath*, pp. 224–50; Potter, *Encyclopedia of Indian Philosophies*,

pp. 218–219; Bake, 'The Music of India', p. 199; Louis Dumont, *Homo hierarchicus: Essai sur le Système des Castes* (Paris, 1966); Jean-Pierre Vernant, 'The Individual within the City-State' in *idem, Mortals and Immortals: Collected Essays* (NJ: Princeton University Press, 1991), pp. 318–334; John Milbank, 'The End of Dialogue' in Gavin D'Costa (ed), *Christian Uniqueness Reconsidered: The Myth of a Pluralistic Theology of Religions* (NY: Orbis Books, 1970), pp. 174–179; I. C. Sharma, *Ethical Philosophies of India* (London: G. Allen & Unwin, 1965); and *Presuppositions of India's Philosophies* (Westport, CT: Greenwood Press, 1963).

111 Rowell, 'Ideas of Music'; Milbank, 'Stories of Sacrifice'.

112 West, *Ancient Greek Music*, pp. 31, 105, 152.f; Monro, *The Modes*, pp. 1–2, 8, 12.f, 29, 62–65; Comotti, *Music*, pp. 14–15; Lang, *Music in Western Civilization*, pp. 12–16; Sachs, *A Short History of World Music*, p. 25; Charles Villiers Stanford and Cecil Forsyth, *A History of Music* (London: Macmillan and Co., Ltd, 1916), pp. 63–68.

113 Vernant, 'The Individual within the City–State'; Milbank, 'The End of Dialogue'.

114 Boethius, *Fundamentals of Music*, p. 10.

115 This falls within the scope of benign natural magic, whereas some Renaissance attempts to effect even the supra–mundane angelic level seem to relate to a post–Christian magical hubris which challenges the sovereignty of the divine Creator.

116 Paul Hindemith, *A Composer's World: Horizons and Limitations* (Cambridge, MA: Harvard University Press, 1952), pp. 5–7, 13–17.

117 *De Mus.*, VI. xiii. 41–VI. xiv. 46.

118 *De Mus.*, VI. xiii. 42.

119 . . . *cum igitur ipsum sentire movere sit corpus adversus illum motum qui in eo factus est* . . . (*De Mus.*, VI. v. 15); Clement of Alexandria in the late second century also likened the human body to a musical instrument. See James, *The Music of the Spheres*, p. 70.

120 *De Mus.*, VI. xiii. 42, VI. xiii. 41.

121 The good use of numbers involves directing the hierarchical control of one's body towards developing equal relations with other people (VI. xiv. 45).

122 The progressing numbers and reacting numbers, insofar as they are applied to other people, should be directed towards uplifting and developing them, rather than dominating them (VI. xiv. 45).

123 Loving one's neighbour is part of 'keeping musical order' (VI. xiv. 46).

124 *De Mus.*, VI. iv. 7.

125 *De Mus.*, VI. xi. 29.

126 *De Mus.*, VI. ii. 3.

127 *De Mus.*, VI. iv. 7.

128 . . . *quod tamen habet sui generis pulchritudinem, et eo ipso dignitatem animae satis commendat, cujus nec plaga, nec morbus sine honore alicujus decoris meruit esse* (VI. iv. 7).

129 *De Mus.*, VI. iv. 7.

130 *De Mus.*, VI. iv. 7, VI v. 9.

131 Augustine's suggestion that dissonance can be redeemed without being obliterated is to be contrasted to Nietzsche's position after his rejection of Schopenhauer and Wagner; see *The Will to Power*, tr. Walter Kaufman and R. J. Hollingdale (London: Weidenfeld & Nicolson, 1957), §§835, 837, 838, 839, 840. Although his later position assumed an account of music as necessitating (1) a rhythmic development of harmony from consonance to dissonance and back again, and (2) a rhythmical shaping or demarcating of temporal periods, his new melodic goal of the rhythmic determination of the flux presupposed the need to transform dissonance into consonance (without remainder), of contradiction into concordance (see Gillespie, *Nihilism Before Nietzsche*, pp. 235–237). This desire to occlude chaos by willing an unflawed artifice of tonality, exemplified by the music of Offenbach which Nietzsche favoured (*ibid.*, p. 237), seems to uphold a false opposition of the mimetic and the creative, of beauty and truth. Moreover, just as he seems to assume that true harmony contains no dissonance, so

also, in his claim that music can never be called 'melody' because it is never whole (*ibid.*, p. 239), he arbitrarily rejects the traditional understanding that melody is *continuous* with this unfinishedness insofar as music is to be seen as a constituent (and echo) of eternal harmony.

132 Attali, *Noise*, Ch. 3; Broeckx, 'Works and Plays in Music', pp. 159–161.

133 (a) 'This is why the music laments – music in general laments, be it "joyous", "light", "pleasant" (inverting the lamentation into an exaltation of my immortality . . .). What touches or moves me in music, then, is my own mourning' ('The Echo', pp. 192–193); (b) 'The death of the other (the hero, the rival) is always at bottom my own death', ('The Echo', p. 192).

134 Lacoue-Labarthe is able to construe resurrection only as one's own triumph over the rival, which is always perforce illusory: *ibid.*, p. 154.

135 *Ibid.*, p. 204.

136 Attali, *Noise*, p. 3 and *passim*.

137 *Ibid.*, pp. 20–25.

138 *Ibid.*, final chapter, 'Composition'. See also Douglas Collins, 'Ritual Sacrifice: the Political Economy of Music', in *Perspectives on Musical Aesthetics*, ed. John Rahn (NY: W.W. Norton & Co., 1994), pp. 9–20, especially p. 20.

139 Attali, *Noise*, p. 30.

INDEX

Abel 184
absolutism: Papal 14
abstract art 227, 230
active reception 255–6, 260
Adam 152, 154, 164, 166; sin 183–4; *see also* New Adam
Aelred of Rievaulx 130, 171
aesthetics 15–17, 201–20; *see also* beauty
agape 12, 148–9
Alan of Lille 196
Allen, R.E. 149
alterity 214–16
amicitia 11
analogy 144, 233; doctrine of 94
anaplerosis 82
anarchism 182; Christian 14; eucharistic 194–8
androgyny 153
angels 48–9
Anscombe, G.E.M. 77
Anselm, St 11–12, 127–42
anthropology: patristic 183; theological 192
antimodernity 207
apologies 40
aporia 112
appearance 224
apprehension 56
Aquinas, T.: being 8–9; *corpus Christi* 209; faith 55–8; idols 233; metaphysics 94; property 187; rationality 110; revelation 5–6, 38, 42–9, 51–2; soul 256; theology 30
Aristotle 19; being 100; friendship 129; metaphysics 43, 53; sex 152; soul 256; thinking 19

arithmetic 243
art 220, 226; abstract 227, 230; subjectivity 16; *see also* music
artificial 45
ascension 163, 175–7
assent 55
Athanasius 164
atheism 82, 103, 205
atonement 265
Attali, J. 244, 266–8
audibility 253
Augustine, St: body 164–5; city 185; creation 13; desire 109–26; free will 202; friendship 127, 131, 132; music 19, 243, 246–50, 263–5; numbers 255–7; theology 30; *totus Christus* 212
authority 44, 47
autobiography: musical 252–5
Ayres, L. 212

Babel 184
Bacon, F. 18, 25, 51, 127
Badt, K. 227
Bahr, H. 225
Balthasar, H.U. von: aesthetics 17–18, 205–9; atheism 15; Church 212; erotics 144–8; love 12; nature 30; revelation 205–9; simultaneity 138–9
Barth, K. 21–3, 91, 148–9, 158, 163
Bataille, G. 13, 143–4
Bauerschmidt, F. 15, 17, 201–20
Bayer, O. 29
Beattie, T. 158–9
beauty 15; masculinity 166; music 264–5; number 255; *see also* aesthetics
becoming-self 130

278